The HAUNTING PAST

Perspectives on Latin America and the Caribbean

THE CHAINS OF INTERDEPENDENCE
U.S. POLICY TOWARD CENTRAL AMERICA, 1945–1954
Michael L. Krenn

A HOLY ALLIANCE?
THE CHURCH AND THE LEFT
IN COSTA RICA, 1932–1948
Eugene D. Miller

QUISQUEYA LA BELLA
THE DOMINICAN REPUBLIC IN HISTORICAL AND
CULTURAL PERSPECTIVE
Alan Cambeira

BRAZILIAN LEGACIES
Robert M. Levine

THE HAUNTING PAST
POLITICS, ECONOMICS AND RACE IN CARIBBEAN LIFE
Alvin O. Thompson

The HAUNTING PAST

Politics, Economics and Race in Caribbean Life

Alvin O. Thompson

Routledge
Taylor & Francis Group
LONDON AND NEW YORK

First published 1997 by M.E. Sharpe

Published 2015 by Routledge
2 Park Square, Milton Park, Abingdon, Oxon OX14 4RN
711 Third Avenue, New York, NY 10017, USA

Routledge is an imprint of the Taylor & Francis Group, an informa business

Library of Congress Cataloging-in-Publication Data

Thompson, Alvin O.
The haunting past : politics, economics and race in
Caribbean life / Alvin O. Thompson.
p. cm. — (Perspectives on Latin America and the Caribbean)
Includes bibliographical references (p.) and index.
ISBN 0-7656-0012-9 (hardcover) — ISBN 0-7656-0013-7 (pbk.)
1. West Indies—Politics and government. 2. West Indies—Economic
conditions. 3. West Indies—Race relations. I. Title.
II. Series.
F1621.T5 1997
972.9—dc21 96-52984
CIP

ISBN 13: 9780765600134 (pbk)
ISBN 13: 9780765600127 (hbk)

to

HILDA

my loving wife

75° W
USA
Miami
THE BAHAMAS
N
20 N
MEXICO
CUBA
DOMINICAN
REPUBLIC
PUERTO
RICO
Virgin Is
GREATER
ANTILLES
HAITI
JAMAICA
Leeward Is
BELIZE
Windward Is
GUATEMALA
HONDURAS
CARIBBEAN SEA
LESSER
ANTILLES
BARBADOS
EL
SALVADOR
NICARAGUA
Aruba
Curacao
Bonaire
Tobago
10 N
TRINIDAD
COSTA
RICA
PANAMA
VENEZUELA
PACIFIC
OCEAN
GUYANA
SURINAM
COLOMBIA
0 Miles 500
0 Km 800

Contents

Acknowledgements

I wish to take this opportunity to acknowledge the assistance given to me by Dr Andrew Downes, Dr Michael Howard and Dr Neville Duncan of the University of the West Indies at Cave Hill campus. They read various chapters and made valuable suggestions, which have clearly helped to improve the text. I also owe a special debt of gratitude to my wife for her untiring devotion, understanding and encouragement throughout the arduous process of writing a text of this kind. To her I can only give in return my love.

Alvin O. Thompson
July 1996

Abbreviations and Acronyms

ACS	Association of Caribbean States
AFTA	American Free Trade Association
CARICOM	Caribbean Community
CBI	Caribbean Basin Initiative
CDB	Caribbean Development Bank
CIDA	Canadian International Development Agency
CTO	Caribbean Tourism Organisation
EPZ	Export Processing Zone
EU	European Union
GATT	General Agreement on Tariffs & Trade
GDP	Gross Domestic Product
GNP	Gross National Product
IMF	International Monetary Fund
NAFTA	North American Free Trade Association
OECD	Organisation for Economic Cooperation & Development
OECS	Organisation of Eastern Caribbean States
PAHO	Pan-American Health Organisation
TNC	Transnational Corporation
U.	University
US(A)	United States (of America)
WTO	World Trade Organisation

Tables

Preface

Islands, scars of the waters
Islands, evidence of the wounds
Islands, crumbs
Islands unformed.[1]

Aimé Césaire

Studying the Caribbean past

The study of the past is imperative for any society that hopes to make meaningful progress. As the noted sociologist, Emile Durkheim, observed, 'It is only in carefully studying the past that we will be able to predict the future and to understand the present.'[2] C. L. R. James likewise states: 'The past of mankind and the future of mankind are historically and logically linked.'[3]

Caribbean people are being constantly admonished today by certain groups within our society to forget the more untoward aspects of our past. The trouble with this approach is that, even if it were possible to do so, this would mean forgetting almost our entire past as Caribbean peoples. However, this option is not available to us in any realistic way. The impact of the past is so much with us that we are simply not allowed to forget it. As David Lowenthal rightly observes, '[I]n the Caribbean the past is a living presence.'[4] Vidiadhar Naipaul, reflecting on the situation in Jamaica around 1960, commented: 'The pressures in Jamaica were not simply the pressures of race or those of poverty. They were the accumulated pressures of the slave society, the colonial society, the under-developed, over-populated agricultural country.'[5]

But Naipaul also touches upon one of the most sensitive aspects of Caribbean life when he asserts: 'West Indians are frightened and ashamed of the past.'[6] This is no idle or careless statement; rather it is one that reflects an uncomfortable and uncompromising reality. Orlando Patterson, one of the region's most renowned sociologists, speaks about 'the haunting recollection of each passing moment' which many Caribbean peoples have to endure.[7] This statement is particularly well understood by the 'children of Sisyphus',[8] the posterity of those who suffered the prostitution of themselves under the *encomienda*, slavery and indentureship. As time progresses and our historians, economists, political scientists, sociologists and other researchers dig into our past we shall be faced with more haunting revelations. We have, for instance, only begun to sketch the dimensions of Caribbean slavery. Much more work needs to be done on the psychological and psychiatric effects of that institution on both blacks and whites. Some studies on these have already been done and their conclusions are, to say the least, disturbing.

Perhaps the best contemporary example of the haunting past is what one writer recently referred to as the 'curse of Columbus' or 'the Columbus jinx' in the mythology of the people of the Dominican Republic. Although most of the inhabitants clearly do not believe in the myth, it has gained new currency recently at the inauguration of a new Columbian memorial lighthouse. The death of President Balaguer's sister just before the inauguration, and only two weeks after touring the lighthouse, was perceived by some Dominicans as yet another evil omen associated with the structure.

Over a century elapsed between the conception and construction of the lighthouse and when construction finally started several workmen were killed and the homes of several poor persons were rased to the ground to make room for it. On the actual date of inauguration a plane crashed in the area, killing the pilot and injuring three Spanish tourists. This reminded many Dominicans of what had happened four decades before, when three of four planes which had embarked on a pan-American tour to raise money for the structure crashed on the first leg of the tour. President Balaguer himself became blind before the structure was completed, and could not even be present at its inauguration, since he had to attend his sister's funeral.[9] Although the legend of the curse itself has no intrinsic merit, for Columbus' arrival in the region should be symbolised by anything but a lighthouse; his advent, along with that of his 'doom-burdened caravels',[10] was a rather dark period in Caribbean history.

Focus of the study

In this study, an attempt has been made to focus attention on three important aspects of Caribbean life: politics, economics and race. The political and economic systems constituted the two most important variables in the social order,[11] while race was the defining factor in social relations. The economic system was the principal vehicle for the underdevelopment and pauperisation of the region. The political system was the coercive apparatus to ensure that each of the different subordinate groups was kept in its place and did not disrupt the economic system unduly. Racism was the ideological justification for oppression and exploitation. Together, these three variables constituted an unholy trinity in the exploitation and oppression of the vast majority of the region's population and were instrumental in shaping Caribbean history and contemporary life. It will be shown in this study that they created a structure of adverse internal and external relationships which we have been unable to surmount in our quest for a better quality of life.

Other factors, such as gender, family, class and religion, have also been important formative influences on the history and culture of the region. However, neither time nor space would permit an exploration of these in any detail, although they will be mentioned in passing. It is also recognised that even with the restricted themes that have been selected, much more might have been said and greater comparisons might have been made with other third-world countries. However, the study is already fairly long necessitating rigor in the selection of issues and information.

Much of what has been said reinforces views by earlier writers about the dependent nature of the Caribbean situation, historically and in the present day. This is manifested not only in the economic realm, but also in other areas, such as politics, military security, sports and aspects of the region's culture.[12] This is not to deny the creativity which has also been part of the Caribbean experience and the impact of Caribbean migrants on outside societies in a wide variety of fields. But, as Bonham Richardson points out, and as we shall discuss later in greater detail, 'Local success is often achieved by those emigrating to North America or Europe and then returning, rather than by those who stay behind.'[13]

The study is written primarily for Caribbean peoples at home and in the diaspora. There has been an attempt to deal with the issues in a way that makes them intelligible to a very wide readership. I hope that I have succeeded in raising the consciousness of our peoples to a new dimension and that another voice has been added to the advocates of regional integration.

Use of terminologies

There has been a conscious and deliberate attempt to use the terms 'third-world' and 'underdeveloped', in spite of suggestions from certain quarters that these terms should be abandoned when dealing with the contemporary experience of ex-colonial peoples. Instead, terms such as 'developing' and 'less developed' are encouraged because, according to the exponents of this view, these help to focus more effectively on 'the varied processes of change that are actually taking place'.[14] Even though the latter terms are used more, the former are still relevant because underdevelopment has been, and still is, in large measure an active process in the relations between the former colonial and imperial countries. These terms explain more fully than their suggested substitutes the impact of historical and contemporary forces on the development of the Caribbean region.

In regard to the use of the term 'race' social scientists are increasingly seeking to avoid its use, in preference to the more precise term 'ethnic'. Roland Dixon stated, 'By migration and conquest the original racial factors, whatever they were, have been so interwoven and blended that the vast majority of all living men must have a complex racial ancestry, and such a thing as a pure race can hardly be expected to live.'[15] Therefore when the term 'race' is used in this study we are using it because it is the one which has remained with Caribbean peoples and which is perhaps best understood by our main target readership.

About the endnotes

In order to save space there is a system of very brief endnotes, just sufficient to allow the reader to find the exact text in the general bibliography. The bibliography itself is divided into two sections: newspapers; and books and periodicals.

Notes

1. Césaire, *Return*, 119.
2. Cited in Karabel, Halsey 'Educational research', 72-73.
3. James, 'Toussaint L'Ouverture to Fidel Castro', 332.
4. Lowenthal, *West Indian Societies*, 68.
5. Naipaul, *Middle Passage*. 224.
6. Naipaul, *Middle Passage*, 183.
7. Patterson, *Absence of Ruins*, 160.
8. Patterson, *Children of Sisyphus*, 1964.
9. Jimenez, 2.
10. Squire, 42.
11. Smith, *Plural Society*, 16.
12. See, for example, Richardson's chapter entitled 'Economic Dependency', in *The Caribbean*, 106-31; Horowitz, ed., *Peoples and Cultures of the Caribbean*.
13. Richardson, *The Caribbean, 4*.
14. Coleman & Nixson, 51.
15. Cited in Williams, *Hebrewisms*, 145.

Introduction

CHAPTER 1

The physiognomy of Caribbean colonialism

I dark in light expos'd
To daily fraud, contempt, abuse and wrong,
Within doors or without, still as a fool.
In power of others, never in my own;
Scarce half I seem to live, dead more than half.
O dark, dark, dark, amid the blaze of noon,
Irrecoverably dark, total Eclipse
Without all hope of day![1]

John Milton

Caribbean geography and ethnicity

In this study the term Caribbean is used to refer to the long, narrow chain consisting of thousands of islands and spreading from the tip of the Florida peninsula to the northern coast of South America. It also includes the mainland territories of Belize, Guyana, French Guiana, Suriname and the island of Bermuda in the far north. While these latter territories might not be included in a narrow definition of the term, their shared experience and present relations with the Caribbean islands justify their inclusion in this study.

The island territories of the Caribbean archipelago have been historically divided into the Greater Antilles and the Lesser Antilles. The former has been used to identify mainly the four largest islands of the archipelago – Cuba,

Table 1.1 Caribbean countries: area and population, 1994

	Area (sq. km)	Population
Anguilla	96	7,500
Antigua/Barbuda	442	67,000
Aruba	193	70,145
Bahamas	13,939	272,000
Barbados	430	260,000
Belize	22,965	211,000
Bermuda	53	63,000
British Virgin Islands	153	16,444
Cayman Islands	259	27,200
Cuba	110,860	10,978,000
Dominica	749	72,000
Dominican Republic	48,072	7,622,000
French Guiana	91,000	118,000
Grenada	345	92,000
Guadeloupe	1,780	421,000
Guyana	214,969	826,000
Haiti	27,750	7,008,000
Jamaica	10,991	2,497,000
Martinique	1,100	383,000
Montserrat	102	11,900
Netherlands Antilles	800	198,000
Puerto Rico	8,959	3,651,000
St Kitts/Nevis	261	41,000
St Lucia	616	160,000
St Vincent/Grenadines	389	110,000
Suriname	163,265	407,000
Trinidad and Tobago	5,128	1,295,000
Turks & Caicos	430	14,000
US Virgin Islands	355	111,000
Total	726,451	37,010,189

Sources: World Bank, *Social Indicators of Development* (Baltimore: The Johns Hopkins Univ. Press, 1996); *Keesing's Record of World Events*, 41 (London: Longman, 1995).[2]

Jamaica, Haiti and Puerto Rico – and their appendages. The Lesser Antilles comprise the islands in the eastern/southern section. Some writers, however, prefer to employ four basic divisions: the Greater Antilles, the Bahamas archipelago, the Lesser Antilles and the islands just off the northern coast of South America. Most of these islands are the results of volcanic activity, but some of them are composed of coral limestone.

The climate of the region as a whole is considered to be 'tropical marine', but there are important variations within the archipelago. As R. Dutton *et al* point out, '[T]he varied location, topography and exposure of the Caribbean islands give rise to a multitude of climatic variations.'[3] Nevertheless, all the territories experience sunshine for most of the year and this factor, along with their fine beaches, has made them attractive to tourists, especially in the winter months in the north.

A number of the islands are uninhabitable, consisting of mere rocks, while the others are inhabited by cosmopolitan populations. For instance, the Bahamas group consists of more than 700 islands and cays, but only about 22 of them are inhabited. Most of the islands of the region which are inhabited are very small in geographical size when viewed from a global perspective.

Trinidad, one of the larger islands, was once categorised by the Trinidadian writer, Vidiadhar Naipaul, as being 'only a dot on a map'.[4] For Naipaul, this statement was much more than a geographical one. It was a contemptuous dismissal of Trinidadian society as an insignificant, irrelevant and backward society in today's world. Samuel Selvon, another Trinidadian writer, around the same time wrote a novel about the same society, entitled *An Island is a World.*[5] For him, Trinidadian society was a microcosm of the world, a kind of global village, in which all the hopes, fears, anxieties and antagonisms of human society were being acted out, and in which the human predicament in the universe could be observed daily. Both Naipaul and Selvon might well have extended their observations to each of the territories of the region, which in many respects are similar to Trinidad. In one form or another, these two contrasting views of Trinidadian (and Caribbean) society can be found in both the historical and the contemporary literature.

The fact is that the Caribbean islands, in spite of their smallness, are very complex entities, with heterogenous populations and diverse cultural patterns that add to the richness of the human experience. The region has witnessed the migration of a large number of ethnic groups who, through varying degrees of miscegenation and culture-contact, have made the study of Caribbean ethnography and race relations an exceedingly complex matter but have also considerably enriched the cultural history of the region.[6]

The Amerindians are the earliest known migrants, having arrived in the Americas from Asia perhaps more than 30,000 years BC.[7] No firm date has been established for their arrival in the island archipelago, but it is generally believed that they occupied several islands centuries before the arrival of Columbus. Some archaeologists believe that Puerto Rico was settled from as early as 5,000 BC.[8] The Amerindians were subdivided into a number of ethnic groups, the most well-known being the Ciboneys, Arawaks (Tainos) and Caribs (Kalinagos). The mainland territories with which this study is concerned also hosted such groups as Mayas, Miskitos, Waraus, Akawois and Manaus. The decimation which followed their contact with the Europeans led to them becoming almost extinct in all the island territories. Today their largest numbers are located in the mainland territories of Belize, Guyana, Suriname and French Guiana. In the islands small pockets of them exist in Trinidad, St Vincent, St Lucia and Dominica. In the last three of these they constitute mainly mixed Carib/African groups, sometimes referred to as black

Caribs. In the 1790s most of the black Caribs of St Vincent were conquered and banished to Belize, where many of them have been gradually absorbed into the wider Belizean population.[9] In Aruba, the Amerindian population became so intermixed with Spaniards that it is generally believed that most Arubans today are of Spanish/Amerindian ancestry.[10]

With the advent of the Europeans a new dimension was added to race relations in the region. The Europeans superimposed themselves on the Amerindians, forming an 'aristocracy of the skin', but also wielding considerable political and economic power. The Spanish, French, British and Dutch were the most dominant nationalities, but the region also attracted a number of Danes, Irish, Scots, Germans and Portuguese. Some Caribbean countries, such as St Eustatius and St Thomas, experienced the residence of a large number of European nationalities, comprising mainly merchants and businessmen, in these active *entrepôts*. Even in less bustling colonies, such as Suriname and Berbice, a host of European nationalities might be represented in the heterogeneous garrisons comprising individuals who were often little better than mercenaries.

Whites were everywhere in the region, but in few colonies did they ever constitute a numerical majority for any substantial period of time. They did so in the early British, French and Dutch colonies before the era of large-scale African imports from the second half of the seventeenth century. In the Spanish territories, where large-scale plantation development did not get under way before the nineteenth century, they constituted an absolute majority for a long time. This was the situation in Cuba until at least the mid-nineteenth century, and in Santo Domingo (Dominican Republic) and Puerto Rico into the present century. In fact, most of the inhabitants of Puerto Rico and the Dominican Republic still regard themselves as white. In reality, many of them, though ostensibly white, are in fact of mixed blood. While still passing as white in the Caribbean, they are relegated to the category of Hispanics when they migrate to the USA. The Spanish territories apart, Europeans are still numerically conspicuous in such territories as Bermuda, the Bahamas, Barbados, the French Antilles and Saba. On the other hand their numbers are quite insignificant in Belize, Guyana, Suriname, Dominica, St Vincent and the Grenadines, Anguilla, Désirade and Haiti. A number of white communities still attempt to practise endogamy.[11]

The Africans constituted by far the largest element in the population of the region from the eighteenth century. They came from a large number of ethnic groups or nationalities, but the majority, and certainly the most well-known, of them came from the areas of modern Ghana, Nigeria, Senegal, Dahomey and Angola. The Africans were introduced in significant numbers into nearly every Caribbean territory and are today the most visible group in the region as a whole. In some territories, such as Jamaica, Dominica, Carriacou, Anguilla, Barbuda and the Caicos Islands, they constitute a very large and sometimes almost an exclusive majority. Brought into the region mainly as slaves, they have had the longest and hardest struggle to uplift themselves. Several of them now occupy important niches in all the main walks of life. In the majority of territories they have become the inheritors of political power, but their economic standing is still rather weak. Intermarrying and intermixing to a greater or lesser extent with the other ethnic groups, they have produced offspring of all shades and colours. The substantial free coloured populations of the slavery period were largely the result of their sexual unions with Europeans.

In the nineteenth and early twentieth centuries a number of Asians, chiefly East Indians, Chinese and Javanese, were introduced as indentured or contract labourers. Together, the total introduced into the region numbered perhaps just under one million.[12] Several Chinese, in addition, migrated as entirely free persons, that is, not as contract labourers. Many Asians returned to their homeland, either immediately after the expiry of their contracts or after they had acquired some capital, but the majority of them remained in the region. At present East Indians constitute an absolute majority of the population in Guyana and significant minorities in Trinidad and Suriname. In other territories they represent much smaller percentages of the population, and in some instances are not a homogeneous or even a clearly identifiable group. In the three territories with large East Indian populations, there is competition and sometimes conflict between them and the Africans as each group strives for political, economic and social power within those societies. Nevertheless, except in Guyana during the 1960s, relations have not been marked by large-scale communal violence between these two groups.

Apart from Cuba, Chinese migration has always been small in numbers, constituting, for instance, only about 3 per cent of the total number of contract labourers introduced into Suriname between 1853 and 1939.[13] Only in Cuba was the situation significantly different, where the Chinese constituted the overwhelming majority of contract labourers imported in the nineteenth century. In the following century an even larger number arrived as free labourers and business persons. Even so, because of rabid racism against them most of them were not allowed to remain for long periods in the island. Duvon Corbitt gives what he considers as a conservative estimate of approximately 275,000 Chinese who entered the island between 1847 and 1924. Of these not more than 50,000 were in the island in the latter year.[14]

The Javanese or Indonesians were recruited almost exclusively for the plantations in Suriname, but a few of them also found their way to the Dutch Antillean territories. They continued to be imported as contract labourers until 1939, a little more than two decades after East Indian immigration into that country had ceased officially. About 32,000 of them were imported into Suriname, and 20-25 per cent of those who survived re-migrated to their homeland. They are generally regarded as the least assimilated of the migrants into the region. They arrived in the country after the demise of slavery and at a time when an increasing number of Indians were drifting away from the plantations to set up their own villages. In time they too established villages in quite distinct locations from the Africans and Indians. Following the achievement of independence by Indonesia, their homeland, in 1949, about half of them gave up their Dutch citizenship and many of them re-migrated.[15] The census of 1980 listed them as constituting 16.3 per cent of Suriname's population.[16] Their presence is still largely rural; few have entered the mainstream of political and social life in the country and their overall impact on Surinamese society is small.

The Syrian/Lebanese (Levantines) are another group of Asians who migrated, albeit voluntarily, to the region in the present century.[17] They can be found in most of the territories of the region, but their numbers are always small. As in West Africa and elsewhere, they were able to carve a niche for themselves in the business sector of the region, but not without a good deal of animosity from other groups. Africans and other oppressed groups tended to view them as being given credit and other facilities denied to longer established groups in the society. There is some measure of truth in this assertion, but equally important is the fact that the Syrian/Lebanese made use of the breaks that they were offered, and often worked their way upwards where no breaks were to be obtained. Because of their small numbers they never maintained as distinct a presence in the various communities as some of the larger groups, but they continued to maintain close family ties both in the region and with their homeland. One of them, Edward Seaga, became prime minister of Jamaica from 1980 to 1989.

We must also mention the Jews who, while small in numbers in most of the Caribbean countries, maintained a distinct presence because of their religion and the long history of European anti-Semitism.[18] For a long time they were banned from entering some Caribbean territories. The Spanish were perhaps the most intolerant towards the Jews, banishing them in the late fifteenth century from continental Spain, confiscating their property and forbidding their entry into Spanish American possessions. The British and French did allow them on sufferance into some of their Caribbean territories, such as St Kitts, Barbados, Jamaica and Martinique, but they experienced political, religious and social disabilities which were imposed on them. It was in the Dutch territories that they were most welcome, or the least discriminated against. They became a significant and wealthy minority in Curaçao, and to a lesser extent in St Eustatius, Aruba and Suriname. Their economic success became a source both of envy and influence. Gradually their presence became more acceptable and they moved into higher social circles. In 1684 Denmark even appointed a Jewish governor in St Thomas. By the nineteenth century the Jews had become well-ensconced in Caribbean society and most of the disabilities against them had been or were soon to be lifted. Today, they exist as important entities only in a few territories such as Jamaica and Curaçao. This is partly because many of them migrated to the USA and elsewhere, and partly because over time small groups became virtually assimilated into the white upper stratum of society.

Historically the different groups mentioned above have been juxtaposed against each other in various ways: generally in competitive roles and sometimes in conflicting and even violent ones. There were areas and periods of cooperation also, a feature which has become much more common in the post-independence period.

Common to all the groups is the colonial experience which affected each in profound ways, although even so there were wide differences between various groups. Some groups, as we have seen, were exploited to a greater degree and for a longer period than others. That exploitation affected all groups deeply. Even the whites who exploited the other groups were themselves often exploited by metropolitan interests in Europe and came to resent their position as second-class Europeans.

Colonial oppression and violence

Dealing with the colonial experience more generally, we may confidently assert that the history of the Caribbean is largely – indeed, almost exclusively – one of exploitation. We have contributed much to the development of the international economy through our agricultural and mineral resources, but only very little to our own economic development. Bonham Richardson speaks about 'the obvious and thoroughgoing domination of the Caribbean region for centuries by external powerholders'.[19] Kathy McAfee has made the point that since the Columbian invasion the Caribbean has not really belonged to Caribbean peoples, but rather to foreign exploiters.[20] Ian McDonald has also written: 'For the original inhabitants of the Caribbean and the Americas, and for the Africans forced from their homelands subsequently into slavery in their millions, what that landfall led to turned out to be hideous tragedy.'[21] The long period of colonialism and the short period since independence have not allowed us to transform our political, economic and social systems to our best advantage. Some territories are indeed still wearing the death shrouds of colonialism.

Colonialism was sometimes justified as manifest destiny, the natural overflow by a virile nation of its original boundaries. This is often defended by the colonisers, and sometimes by the colonised, as a major leap forward in the material, social, cultural and spiritual advancement of colonial peoples: the major, indeed the essential, element in their transition from 'anarchy' to 'order', from 'oppression' to 'liberation', from 'barbarism' to 'civilisation'. The exponents of this view hold that the imposition of colonial rule often became necessary to bring peace to 'tribal' communities locked in endemic warfare and death struggles. Colonial rule, they declare, delivered these communities from such genocidal activities (as did the slave trade). Colonial rule is also credited with bringing unprecedented material advancement to the colonised in the form of roads, railways, harbours, a wide range of technologies, new crops, new markets and finance capital. Further, colonial rule is said to have been responsible for the abolition of slavery, infanticide and cannibalism. It is also viewed as being responsible for the institution of a wide range of personal liberties, democratic institutions, European concepts of justice and fair play, education and medical services. Colonialism, in short, was humanitarianism at work, holistic medicine, the panacea for the major ills afflicting backward societies. It followed logically that colonialists were not villains or scoundrels, but humanitarians and gentlemen.[22]

For Sir Frederick Lugard, architect of the system of indirect rule in British tropical Africa, British rule was 'bringing to the dark places of the earth, the abode of barbarism and cruelty, the torch of culture and progress'.[23] Sir Alan Burns, former governor of Nigeria and Belize, and later British representative on the United Nations Trusteeship Council, 1947-56, is even more certain of the benefits conferred by modern European colonialism:

> We have put a stop to slavery and human sacrifice, we have checked the cruelty and corruption of indigenous rulers, we have stamped out certain diseases and reduced the incidence of others, we have brought a measure of education to people who were generally illiterate. We have developed backward countries by the construction of roads and railways, we have opened up mines and improved on the primitive agriculture of the past. We have allowed trade to develop under the protection of a firm administration . . . . If British merchants and mining magnates have been enriched by the development of the colonies . . . so, above all, have been the inhabitants of the territories themselves.[24]

Thus the European apologists argued, and apparently convinced themselves, that colonialism constituted overall a positive benefit to the colonised. More than this, they argued that the acquisition of colonies was often an altruistic act carried out at great material and social sacrifice to the colonisers. It was part of the white man's burden to civilise the rest of the world. The Europeans thus created large empires and set themselves up as the great umpires. Burns was also convinced that anti-colonialism against the British was 'based on emotion rather than on reason'.[25]

The Comte de Gobineau, regarded as the founder of the school of Nordic racial supremacy around the mid-nineteenth century, was convinced that Europeans had the right to rule all the non-European peoples of the world and that they needed to rule Africans, in particular, under a 'strict despotism'.[26] Some years earlier the British statesman, Thomas B. Macaulay, had declared concerning the East Indians, 'There never, perhaps, existed a people so thoroughly fitted by nature and by habit for a foreign yoke.'[27] Other European racists, notably the Germans Heinrich von Treitsche (1834-1896) and General Friedrich von Bernhardi (1849-1930), believed that it was the mission of the whites to rule the rest of the world.[28]

It would be naïve to dismiss all the material and social achievements of the colonisers as being either negative or inconsequential. In material terms roads, railways, harbours and telegraphic services constituted clear improvements in the communications network of colonial territories. Similarly, certain aspects of Western education and certain exotic crops expanded the range of material and social services available in some colonies. Nevertheless, an increasingly large body of third-world, and even first-world, scholars are arguing that the balance sheet of colonialism shows a series of gains for the coloniser at the expense of the colonised. They are convinced that the developments mentioned above served in the main to underdevelop the colonial areas; or, to put it another way, that colonialism placed the colonised areas in an increasingly adverse economic relationship to the European/North American countries.

Some apologists for colonialism have countered the argument about the largely negative impact of colonialism by asserting that third-world underdevelopment was largely, if not completely, a function of the political, social and economic forces at work in the pre-colonial period. This has been asserted vociferously in the cases of certain Asian and African countries.[29] In the case of the Caribbean, however, where the indigenous populations and their political, economic and social systems were almost completely annihilated and replaced by European ones in the early years of the colonial period, this explanation is quite untenable. Colonialism, which has occupied almost the entire 500 years of the region's recorded history, is clearly the force behind the underdevelopment of the region.

Burns identifies three basic forms of modern colonialism: first, 'conventional colonialism', that is, the acquisition of overseas territories; secondly, economic control of politically independent countries; and thirdly, the establishment of overseas military and naval bases.[30] The Caribbean has been, and still is, the victim of all three forms.

Colonialism, by its very nature, is based upon parasitic and oppressive relationships. While it may, and often does, produce great material rewards for the coloniser, it is based upon bankrupt ethics. This was best exemplified in regard to the slave trade and slavery, a lucrative business, but one in which morality was low and mortality high. As Gibbon Wakefield pointed out in 1849, the reasons for slavery were 'not moral, but economical circumstances; they relate[d] not to vice and virtue, but to production'.[31]

Jan Carew considers the horse and rider as the most appropriate image to describe the relations between the coloniser and the colonised .[32] August Bebel put it this way before the German Reichstag in 1899: 'Whenever we turn to the history of colonialism, during the last three centuries, we always encounter deeds of violence and oppression against colonial peoples, abuses that not uncommonly end with their complete extermination. The impelling motive is always gold, gold and more gold.'[33]

Bebel's views about colonialism and the extermination of people are especially significant for the Caribbean. Almost the entire history of the region for the last 500 years has been one of colonial domination and mass destruction. To understand colonialism is to understand Caribbean history, and to understand Caribbean history is to understand colonialism. The region has been the most thoroughly colonised area in the world.

Bebel rightly suggests that oppression is an important and inevitable feature of colonialism. Other writers strongly endorse this viewpoint. Colonialism, by its very nature, also breeds tensions and conflicts between the coloniser and the colonised, whose interests are not only incompatible but diametrically opposed. Colonial rule is achieved and maintained through the dominance of an expatriate elite whose main goal is to obtain wealth as quickly as possible and at the expense of the colonised. It provides an opportunity for the human materialistic instinct to have full sway. In Paulo Freire's view, the essential element in oppression is domination. The oppressors seek to dominate everything around them: earth, property, production, the creations of men, men themselves: 'everything is reduced to the status of objects at . . . [their] disposal'.[34] Freire elaborates on this aspect of domination:

> In their unrestrained eagerness to possess, the oppressors develop the conviction that it is possible for them to transform everything into objects of their purchasing power; hence their strictly materialistic concept of existence. Money is the measure of all things, and profit the primary goal. For the oppressors, what is worthwhile is to have more – always more – even at the cost of the oppressed having less or

having nothing. For them, *to be is to have* and to be of the 'having' class.[35]

Thus the oppressors, in their urge to dominate, reduce both objects and people to 'things', recreating them according to the oppressors' will and pleasure.

Albert Memmi focuses upon another aspect of oppression: its capacity to dehumanise both the oppressed and the oppressor. In his own words: '[O]ppression is the greatest calamity of humanity. It diverts and pollutes the best energies of man – of oppressed and oppressor alike. For if colonization destroys the colonised, it also rots the coloniser.'[36] Aimé Césaire affirms that 'the coloniser . . . in order to ease his conscience gets into the habit of seeing the other man as *an animal*, accustoms himself to treating him as an animal, and tends objectively to transform *himself* into an animal'. He calls this the 'boomerang effect of colonisation'.[37]

While predator and prey might live side-by-side, at any time the former might suddenly turn around and gobble up the latter. Freire sees this as the result of the oppressors' 'necrophilic view' of the world, which 'kills life'.[38] This is an important component of the attempt to delineate the pathology of colonialism. Apart from the extermination of whole populations is the sadistic treatment of individuals. Bartolomé de las Casas offers gruesome details on this score in his recital of the brutal treatment of the Amerindians at the hands of the Spanish, where heads, arms and legs were amputated by the blow of the sword, people were roasted on grids and dogs were unleashed on people to disembowel them. R. A. J. van Lier points out, that slavery gave 'psychopathic types a good chance to follow their worst inclinations and even invited psychopathic behaviour by creating an extreme situation of dominance and submission'.[39] For the oppressed, the psychological effects are often witnessed in the high incidence of depression, drunkenness, low self-esteem, uncertainty in action, suicide and dependency. Erich Fromm thinks that deep emotional dependence can lead the oppressed to 'necrophilic behaviour', such as the destruction of themselves or their fellow sufferers.[40] The oppressors, of course, fervently declare that they are humanising the society and offering the oppressed a better quality of life.

Western colonialism, especially in the Caribbean, is often viewed as a specially brutal form of oppression, a kind of slavery, so that even those who are not legally enslaved are still perceived as being under a form of slavery. It follows, then, that those legally enslaved are doubly oppressed. Given the gender bias in colonial, as in most other countries, women have suffered under a third tier of oppression. Such oppression eventually leads to physical, social and psychological death. This is clearly demonstrated in Orlando Patterson's work, *Slavery and Social Death*.[41]

The haunting past makes its loudest echo in respect of this yoke. Many Caribbean writers, and even persons on talk shows and in the streets, compare the present-day situation with slavery. The plight of the Haitian workers is a case in point, particularly those who work (voluntarily or involuntarily) in the labour camps in the neighbouring Dominican Republic on the modern sugar plantations. The association of sugar with modern slavery is in this instance actual.[42] In other instances it is a mental association, for example, in the cases of Barbados and Guyana, where the local people often refuse to work on the sugar estates because of their past association with slavery.

Clive Thomas deals with the issue more broadly, writing about the 'slave' status of the region's modern proletariat.[43] David Lowenthal refers to a survey conducted in 1969 in St Vincent by a University of the West Indies (UWI) development mission, which concluded that most of the people were 'living in a way which, in terms of material and environmental conditions, could scarcely be removed from . . . slavery'. The situation in Dominica in 1967 was similar.[44] Nigel Boland distinguishes between emancipation from slavery as an 'event' and as a 'human social condition'.[45] We may add a third category: slavery as a mental condition. The posterity of the slaves are still seeking to rediscover and reassert their lost humanity. The grim reality is that in most Caribbean territories the vast majority are still living in the shadow of slavery. This point is forcefully made by Naipaul:

> So many things in these West Indian territories . . . speak of slavery. There is slavery in the vegetation. In the sugarcane brought by Columbus . . . . In the breadfruit, cheap slave food . . . in the saltfish still beloved by the islanders. Slavery in the absence of family life, in the laughter in the cinema at films of German concentration camps, in the fondness of terms for racial abuse, in the physical brutality of strong to weak . . . .[46]

Colonialism is usually accompanied by physical violence, and always by psychological violence. The Senegalese poet David Diop shows us the face of misery brought about by colonialism. Let us listen to him:

> Suffer, poor Negro! . . .
> The whip crackles
> Crackles on your sweaty and bloody back.
>
> . . . .
>
> Suffer, poor Negro!
> Your children are hungry
> Hungry and your house is empty
> Empty of your wife who sleeps

Sleeps on your master's bed.
Suffer, poor Negro!
Negro, black as misery![47]

Here Diop depicts deprivation and destitution in their physical, mental and emotional aspects; his is also a picture of violence – to himself, his wife and his children, at the physical, economic, sexual and psychological levels. It is a picture of total domination under colonialism. The picture is stark, but it is not uncommon in the experience of the colonised. Any serious study of the history of the Caribbean will soon reveal the depth and breadth of the violence which has engulfed the region.

Violence is the red thread, so to speak, that runs throughout the region. That colour is not simply symbolic; sometimes it was literal, through the large amount of blood that was shed wantonly in the quest for profit, power and pleasure. John Stedman wrote in 1796 that Suriname was 'reeking and dyed with the blood of African negroes'.[48] Rev. James Phillippo wrote in 1843 that the whole history of colonialism in the Caribbean was 'only a succession of wars, usurpations, crimes, misery, and vice . . . all is one revolting scene of infamy, bloodshed, and unmitigated woe, of insecure peace and open disturbance, of the abuse of power, and of the reaction of misery against oppression'.[49] Aimé Césaire writes in a more poetic strain of lagoons of blood and death, instead of water-lilies: 'How much blood in my memory, how many lagoons! . . . . My memory is circled with blood. My remembrance is girdled with corpses.'[50]

It is the practice and institutionalisation of violence at all levels that constitute the most fundamental characteristics of colonialism. This pervasive violence, both covert and overt, touches all aspects of colonial life, political, economic, social and psychological. State violence is usually perceived by the oppressors as a legitimate tool, in order to keep the criminal elements in check and maintain peace and goodwill towards men. The colonisers have sometimes even sought to justify such violence on the basis of the inherent criminality of the colonised. While there has been some debate among European writers (Nikolaas Tinbergen, Konrad Lorenz, Sigmund Freud, etc.) about hereditary tendencies leading towards criminality and violence in certain individuals, they do not view such tendencies as widespread or generalised throughout whole populations. Moreover, there is a much larger body of scholars who completely reject the view that such tendencies are hereditary.

It is interesting that it was the Europeans who sent their criminal types abroad to colonise the Americas, Australia, New Zealand, Mozambique and other places. For some years Devil's Island, just off Cayenne, was used as a French penal colony. But there is no evidence that the Caribbean territories were colonised on a large scale by the criminal types from any of the migrant areas. Colonialism, however, did criminalise large numbers of oppressed persons for actions which in free societies would have been regarded as legitimate pursuits, and in fact all the colonised were viewed as potential or actual criminals, especially during the period of slavery. The oppressors therefore sought to legitimise their use of state violence to keep the oppressed in their place.

Sidney Hook declares: 'The use of physical coercion by duly constituted government, either as a method of defense or as a means of consolidating its rule, collecting taxes and the like, raises no particular problem of social ethics – once the sovereignty of the government is accepted – but only a question of expediency.' For Hook, violence only raises 'really troublesome issues' when it is used by 'subordinate groups' to redefine the *status quo*.[51] He does not address the relevant issue of what constitutes a legitimate government, whose sovereignty is accepted. Is the government of the colonisers, for instance, legitimate? Nor does he address the question of the morality of the excess of force, or the use of terror as an instrument of control, widely employed by colonial and other governments. He does, however, note: 'Wide-scale use of violence results in a brutalization of those who employ it.'[52] It is precisely this failure by many writers on the subject of violence, especially in the colonial context, to recognise its role in establishing and maintaining so-called legitimate but nevertheless oppressive regimes that has caused more radical writers like Frantz Fanon to be highly critical of them.

Apart from the physical violence which accompanies colonialism and which it breeds, there is the cultural and psychological violence it unleashes. Colonialism inevitably entails some form of cultural invasion. The invaders penetrate the cultural context of the invaded group and impose their own world view on the latter.[53] The result is that the invaded lose a sense of cultural continuity, which in turn curbs their self-expression and/or directs it in ways more suitable to the interests of the invaders. Thus, Bulhan (paraphrasing Fanon), writes, 'Colonialism is . . . neither a harmonizing force nor a phenomenon allowing the simple grafting of its elements into what already existed. Once the native submits he ceases to exist as an independent, self-defining entity. He becomes defined and then defines himself in relation to his oppressor.'[54]

The particular definition given to the oppressed by the oppressors depends upon the objective that the latter have in mind. At the lowest level the oppressed are defined as objects, things, forms of property. At the highest level they are defined as inferior beings, who simply ape their oppressors. This is where myths and stereotypes about the oppressed become so important in destroying their old perceptions of themselves and redefining them in the image of the oppressors. A Manichaen dichotomy is established between the two groups: the oppressors are gods, the oppressed are devils; the oppressors are good, the oppressed are evil; the oppressors are civilised, the oppressed are savage; the oppressors are humane, the oppressed are cruel; the oppressors are beautiful, the oppressed are ugly; the oppressors are wise, the oppressed are stupid; the oppressors are ingenious, the oppressed are ingenuous; the oppressors are all things, the oppressed are nothing. The oppressors also seek to define the oppressed in their own language. Soon the oppressed learn to mouth the shibboleths of their oppressors, often forgetting or despising their own language. Once this happens there is every chance of oppression and domination becoming entrenched in the lives of these individuals. At the group level, the oppressors are at pains to point out that the oppressed either have no history, or such a mean and barbaric history that it is not worth being studied by civilised peoples.

The German philosopher, Georg W. F. Hegel, expressed the views that the new world had no real history and that the Amerindians built no durable civilisations, since these vanished shortly after they came into contact with European civilisations. Africans south of the Sahara ('Africa proper', according to him) was 'no historical part of the World', since it had 'no movement or development to exhibit . . . . What we properly understand by Africa, is Unhistorical, Undeveloped Spirit, still involved in the conditions of mere nature.' While he believed that history began in China, and also that India later became part of the historical process, for him Chinese and Indian civilisations were essentially static rather than dynamic (in them 'the fixedness of a character . . . recurs perpetually'), so that 'China and India lie, as it were, still outside the World's History'. For Hegel, 'In the Frigid and in the Torrid zone the locality of World-historical peoples cannot be found.' The old world, or more precisely Europe, was 'the scene of the World's History'.[55]

In the nineteenth century also the famous British utilitarian philosopher, James Mill, expressed the view that there were only two civilisations in history – those of ancient Greece and modern Europe.[56] John Stuart Mill, his son, contributed the view that 'The greater part of the world has, properly speaking, no history.'[57] Much more recently (1963), the British historian, Hugh Trevor-Roper, contemptuously dismissed the idea that places like Africa could have had any history apart from the European activities in that continent. According to him, apart from such activities, 'the rest is darkness . . . and darkness is not the subject of history'. It would therefore be a waste of time to 'amuse ourselves with the unrewarding gyrations of barbarous tribes in picturesque but irrelevant corners of the globe'.[58] In 1938 Reginald Coupland, a British historian, had said much the same thing about the East Africans who lived beyond the European settlements on the coast: 'Not many miles back from their settlements and ports and market-places a curtain falls, shrouding the vast interior of the continent in impenetrable darkness.'[59]

This view of non-European peoples, or at least some of them, as being outside the realms of real history, was strengthened by the European division of human endeavour and activity into pre-history and history. Although the merit of such a division is dubious, it is generally employed to distinguish between the reconstruction of history largely from unwritten and written records respectively. It is often used in the colonial context to differentiate between the pre-European and the European periods (the non-historical and the historical periods). For instance, John Squire, in a poem that otherwise captures the essence of the first encounter between Amerindians and Europeans, seems subconsciously to repeat the myth about the static nature of the indigenous society:

> There was an Indian, who had known no change;
> Who strayed content along a sunlit beach
> Gathering shells.[60]

Thus over the centuries that the Amerindians had been in the region they had not witnessed any significant historical changes in their societies – they had been content to stray along sunlight beaches, gathering shells, until the Europeans came; and then change began.

Burns wrote in 1954 in his *History of the British West Indies* that the history of the region 'is mainly the story of the white conquerors and settlers, as the much larger Negro population, during the centuries of slavery, had little to do, save indirectly with the shaping of events'.[61] Burns thus dismissed explicitly the slavery period, and implicitly the pre-European and the post-emancipation periods, of Caribbean history as having no historical significance outside of European colonialism.

For these, writers the history of the colonies was viewed as being really the extension of European history overseas, that is, European imperial history. France asserted that the colonies were really La France d'Outre-Mer (overseas France). It followed, therefore, that the history of the French colonies would really be the history of overseas France. The British, on the other hand, saw their empire as the creation of Greater Britain, though one in which there were greater and lesser beings: the British bulldogs on the one hand, and the colonial underdogs on the other. The activities of the colonised were either irrelevant or only peripheral to the historical process, depending on their impact on the colonisers. Coupland makes this point strikingly in the case of the East Africans: 'On nearly all, though not quite all, its pages the history of East Africa is only the history of its invaders .... In the foreground, too, on the historical stage itself, the East Africans are always the great majority, dumb actors for the most part, doing nothing that seems important . . . and yet quite indispensable.'[62]

Though backward and benighted, the colonised had to learn the history of their colonisers, French, Dutch, British, Spanish, etc. The natives must be made to understand that Europe stood like a colossus at the centre of the world.

While the colonised were robbed of their historical legacy and placed on the periphery of European history, they were expected to be grateful that they were dragged into history by the Europeans, even if it was in this incidental way. Coupland goes a step further and proudly affirms that after about only 50 years of European rule in East Africa, it was so transformed politically, economically and socially that its inhabitants were 'now at last in a position to begin to make East African history themselves'.[63]

This great historical myth about the absence of history unsettled very many of the colonised, for essentially not to have a history is not to exist. Thus particularly harsh attacks noted above on Africa as a continent without a history must be understood. The great civilisations of Meroë, Axum, Mali, Songhai and Zimbabwe are dismissed as barbaric and not worthy of intellectual pursuit, and Egyptian civilisation is either declared Semitic or white Hamitic. The dismissal of Africans as a people without a history served admirably the function, from the European standpoint, of justifying their enslavement and treating them as brute beasts in the Americas, as we shall show more fully when dealing with Edward Long's stereotypes of them in Chapter 7.

The elimination of the natives from the historical process has had a profound influence upon their psyches and upon their perception of themselves. Naipaul, who has sought and apparently found pleasure in exile in Europe, dismissed Trinidadian society in 1960 as one with an 'absence of history',[64] a term he might well have applied to the Caribbean as a whole. He does depict the region as having a history, but to him this history is 'squalid',[65] which perhaps amounts to essentially the same thing. The Guyanese poet, A. J. Seymour, in an attempt to counter this negativity, has sought to focus attention upon people's history. In his poem, 'Tomorrow Belongs to the People', he declares:

> The people is a lumbering giant
> That holds history in his hand.
>
> ....
>
> History is theirs,
> Because history doesn't belong
> To the kings, and the governors and the legislature

History basically
Is the work men do with their hands
When they battle with the earth
And grow food and dig materials
For other people's profits and other people's skill . . . .[66]

Without belittling Seymour's feelings, we must point out that today the dominant themes and dates in our history are still largely those that relate to European activities in the region.

There are other myths which are used to make the oppressed contented with their lot. The oppressors strive to impress upon the oppressed that the social order in which they are now living is the natural order, and even the divine order, of society. Religion is sometimes used to reinforce this myth. Christianity came to the Caribbean in the baggage of the Europeans and with a distinctive European personality. It was used to bolster the systems of oppression. Its egalitarian doctrines were suppressed and its exhortations to obedience and contentment were stressed. Count Nikolaus von Zinzendorf, founder and head of the Moravians in Europe, on a visit to some slaves in the Danish Virgin Islands (later US Virgin Islands) in 1739, enjoined them to be contented with their lot because God punished their ancestors for their sins by making them slaves and Christianity would only liberate them from their wicked ways, not from their masters.[67] In South Africa under the apartheid regime blacks were ritualistically taught in school to be contented with a diet of mealies (maize), which was deemed to be the best food for them.[68]

Myths served yet another function – acting as a palliative to the consciences of the oppressors. Thus among the myths which they developed were that slaves enjoyed crop time; it was impossible to overwork a slave; whites became more tired from sitting in a boat for a day than the blacks who rowed it all day long; blacks worked best when it was hottest. The mythology associated with European colonialism is widespread and it is important to recognise that many of the myths informed the subconscious of both the oppressors and the oppressed and helped to define the boundaries between the two, thus reinforcing the process of domination.

The oppressed respond in three basic ways to their situation. Firstly, some submit to the process of oppression and are content to be under the rule of the oppressors. These usually do not recognise or understand fully the nature of their oppression. They have the lowest self-images, and accept the view of the oppressors that they are inferior beings. They are convinced that the oppressors are right, just and humane. They are thus content to eat mealies while the oppressors eat steak. They live without hope and die without dignity.

The second category comprises those who want to become part of the system of oppression. This category is very broad. At the base are those who seek recruitment into the ranks of the oppressors to help in maintaining the system of oppression at the most elemental levels of terror and violence. They are armed with uniforms, batons and guns, their symbols of loyalty, and these give them the feeling that they are sharing power *with* the oppressors. They have a misplaced sense of duty, often suffer from delusions of grandeur, and develop false notions of their own importance. At the slightest provocation they unleash brutalities on the ordinary civilians. This not only serves to keep the 'natives' quiet, but demonstrates their loyalty to the oppressors. To be loyal is to be good, and to be good is to be loyal. These, however, do not seek power in their own right or for themselves and so they present no threat to the oppressors. Nevertheless, they are watched closely for any signs of disloyalty, which might bring down the full wrath of the oppressors upon them.

Higher up, but still in the second category, are those who partially accept the definition of the oppressors, but feel that by emulating them they could join the fellowship of the oppressors. They are usually drawn from the educated middle class and the local business community. These do not really wish to dismantle the structure of oppression, but rather to become part of the ruling class. The oppressors are always willing to allow a few of these aspirants to be associated with their administration. This serves to give the impression that the system is not as rigidly coercive as it really is. It also serves to deflect some of the hostility from the expatriates to the locals. The expatriates, of course, always reserve the right to assimilate or to eliminate those who pose any threat to their authority. This is always a dirty job, and is thus often seen as a last option once colonial rule has been firmly established for some time. The ideal is to rule with as little overt violence as possible, since this helps to create a better environment for economic and social exploitation. However, there are always some within this group of locals who have greater ambitions than to share power with the expatriates. They conceive of a new social order in which the expatriate group is expelled and the local one takes over the reins of power. For them the *summum bonum* is to take over the apparatus of oppression virtually intact. This, they declare, is the achievement of independence. They emerge from chrysalises into ugly butterflies, having suffered a distorted metamorphosis. Though often politically impotent and bereft of ideas, independence gives many of them the opportunity they crave to exercise their sorry talents. This is why in many of the so-called independent states the structure of oppression has not changed, it has only changed hands.

The third category comprises those who see the oppressors for what they really are, parasites on the body politic that need to be removed. These constitute the prime resisters, the revolutionaries. Curiously enough, some of these have been trained in the European system, that is, in the educational, administrative and military institutions of the oppressors. This training sharpens their intellect and gives them a fuller appreciation of the draconian nature of colonial rule. While they belong to the middle class by virtue of training, their sympathies lie with the lower classes, those who are under the most abject forms of oppression and domination. They begin to form people's organisations and whip up grassroots support for the cause of national liberation. They raise the level of revolutionary consciousness of the oppressed and sometimes resort to counter-violence.

Fanon sanctions the use of counter-violence by the oppressed against their oppressors. For him such violence, although not structured in the same way as that of the oppressors, is not chaotic or nihilistic in its perception and use. It is constructive, with very specific ends in view: the first and main one being the elimination of the oppressive government. Fanon believes that counter-violence helps to create a sense of unity among the oppressed. It liberates them not only from the tyranny of the minority, but from their own inferiority complexes. It is a panegyric to their fallen comrades; it is a new symphony of life; it is cathartic; it humanises the oppressed.[69] They can now feel the pulse of life throbbing through every vein and every muscle. Jean-Paul Sartre sees this kind of violence as creating the 'self', establishing the worth of the 'self'.[70] Freire stresses the humanising power of such violence:

> Whereas the violence of the oppressors prevents the oppressed from being fully human, the response of the latter to this violence is grounded in the desire to pursue the right to be human. As the oppressors dehumanize others and violate their rights, they themselves also become dehumanized. As the oppressed, fighting to be human, take away the oppressors' power to dominate and suppress, they restore to the oppressors the humanity they had lost in the exercise of oppression.[71]

There can be no doubt that everywhere the removal of the oppressors, forcibly or otherwise, brings with it a moment of triumph, eddies of feeling, sometimes a spontaneous burst of euphoria, even if this is often followed by the troubled sequences of creating a new and just society in the post-colonial period. There is always the danger that when the liberators finally expel the expatriates and come to taste power, they may become corrupt. Power has a curious way of corrupting people, even some who before seemed incorruptible. Thus many liberators of yesterday may become the oppressors of today. This is well-illustrated in the Caribbean in Haiti, where the first flush of liberation from slavery and colonial rule brought on a glow of ecstasy, which soon gave way to the continuing contradictions of colour, class, creed and greed, and the struggle for economic independence. The result has been a series of dictatorial regimes, introducing new forces and forms of oppression and forcing the people to seek a new revolution.

The transition from liberators to oppressors has only partly to do with the exercise of power. It is also a function of the socialisation of the would-be liberators in a culture of violence and oppression, so that they often subconsciously imbibe the mentality of the oppressors. This emphasises both the nature and the strength of the dependency complex which colonialism bequeaths to the post-colonial society.

Dominique O. Mannoni concluded that this dependency among the Malagasy was an inherent (perhaps even hereditary) trait, predating the arrival of the Europeans. He saw them as children who never grew up and who had no desire to grow up. French colonialism, according to him, proved to be the panacea for this problem: a curious but happy conjunction of one set of peoples with an urge to dominate, and another with a complementary urge to be dominated.[72] Fanon, however, in a detailed and eloquent rebuttal of Mannoni, demolished his colonialist view of Malagasy society, which, of course, had wider implications for colonial societies in general. He made it clear that the dependency perceived by Mannoni was a function of colonialism rather than a pre-colonial feature of Malagasy society.[73] But Fanon is nevertheless aware that the dependency complex in which Malagasy, Caribbean, and other third-world countries are bound is like a three-ply cord which cannot easily be broken.

The situation is exacerbated by disunity within both the colonial and the post-colonial states. Disunity is a prominent feature of colonialism and is indeed an important weapon in the arsenal of the oppressors. Indeed, the theory of divide and rule is held in great merit in the history of Western colonialism. Any move that might help to keep the oppressed disunited was deemed fair game: ethnicity, colour, class, religion, even geography.

Caribbean disunity

Caribbean disunity will be discussed more fully in subsequent chapters. However, it is important to note here that the geographical factors and the struggle for empire among the European nations helped to foster disunity, and this is seen most clearly in the political balkanisation of the region. Even islands which are in very close proximity to each other were often held by different European powers, thus breaking up the communication links established in pre-European times. For instance, in the double island chain of the Leeward Islands (part of the Lesser Antilles), the links were forged in the following way by the various imperial powers (based upon the most recent identity with an imperial power): Anguilla (British), Saint Martin/Sint Maarten (French and Dutch), St Barthélemy (French), Saba (Dutch), St Eustatius (Dutch), St Kitts (British), Nevis (British), Antigua (British), Montserrat (British), Guadeloupe (French), Marie-Galante (French) and Dominica (British).[74] Some islands were even split into two by rival imperial powers. For instance, Haiti or Hispaniola was divided into Saint Domingue (French) and Santo Domingo (Spanish); another small island was divided into Saint Martin (French) and Sint Maarten (Dutch). St Kitts was divided in the seventeenth and early eighteenth centuries between the French and the British.

Changing political and economic circumstances and somewhat improved communications within the region (but sometimes via the USA) have resulted in a much larger number of Caribbean peoples travelling to the various islands. Most of these visits are brief and are often hindered by immigration laws which make it easier for Europeans and North Americans than for Caribbean nationals to enter the territories. Caribbean peoples generally know far more about events and activities in the metropolitan countries than they do about those in the various territories of the region. Richardson declares that insularity is 'the Caribbean's geographical hallmark'.[75] However, Caribbean insularity is much more than a geographical hallmark: it is an historical experience and an emotional and psychological condition.

Politically the manifestation of insularity continues to be a very disturbing reality of Caribbean life. If the abortive British West Indies Federation tells us about anything, it is the strength of insular pride. Few of us want to yield an inch of ground or a blade of grass to achieve wider political unity. Indeed, it seems that with the attainment of formal political independence this sense of insularity has increased appreciably. Believing that we have won our independence, we find it hard to concede a measure of it for the wider regional good. We fail to appreciate that our chances of achieving and maintaining real independence (difficult as that is) become appreciably greater through a shared experience of interdependence among the various territories which comprise the region. But formal political independence has instead led us into a false perception of our own importance within the regional community, so that some of the multi-island states are even seeking to fragment further, as each island charts its own course in the troubled waters of the region and the globe. Ironically, while holding on to this tenuous political independence in relation to each other, we are daily losing it to outside forces, especially to the behemoth to the north. The region's sad epigraph may well be: 'To each his own, and the devil take the hindmost.'

Recognising the political fragmentation of the region and the persistent threat to its sovereignty, some writers have focused on the ideological aspects of Caribbean nationhood. For example, Susan Craig dedicates her two-volume (edited) sociological work, on the *Contemporary Caribbean,* to the 'Caribbean Nation'. C. L. R. James envisages the formation of a new Caribbean 'nation', encompassing all the former colonial entities and all the linguistic groups in the region. Craig notes further what she perceives as the 'wholeness' of the Caribbean experience.[76] No doubt this wholeness refers to the many similarities in the colonial history of the individual territories, as Rex Nettleford, for example, has stressed, including 'resistance to slavery, colonialism and economic exploitation as well as . . . the aftermath of that experience indicated in racism'.[77]

At the economic level perhaps the basic conditioning factor is an inheritance of mutually competitive economies, in which each of the territories strives, more often individually than jointly, for the crumbs which fall from the tables of our erstwhile colonial masters and our present-day exploiters. It should not be forgotten that it was only in the nineteenth century that the colonies were allowed to trade with foreign countries. In fact, for a long time they were not even permitted to trade with each other, even when they belonged to the same colonial power. The fact that most of them produced basically the same staples for export served to strengthen the bonds with the imperial powers, rather than with each other.

Thus, our yesterdays have not helped us to forge any significant degree of economic unity, as evidenced in the individual approaches of Caribbean Community (CARICOM) countries to entry into and/or relations with the North American Free Trade Association (NAFTA). This disunity continues in spite of the dangers looming on the economic horizon. The region is being squeezed by international market forces such as the generally depreciating terms of trade for third-world commodity products, the establishment of large trading blocs such as the European Union (EU) and NAFTA, and the attempts to dismantle fiscal and other protective barriers against outside competition through the General Agreement on Tariffs and Trade (GATT). Nearly every Caribbean economy is currently in a precarious situation and some are in a parlous one, for example, Haiti, Guyana, Jamaica, the Dominican Republic and Cuba. Of course, this economic predicament is not due entirely to external forces but, as we have stated above, they constitute the basic conditioning factors historically.

Socially, the inequalities in the region which give rise to the feeling that 'massa day ain't done' or 'emancipation still coming' are based upon many factors, not least among which are race/ethnicity and colour. The vast majority of the labouring poor have been and still are black. In some countries they are almost exclusively so. Europeans, Syrians and Chinese are rarely seen doing menial jobs, especially outside the home. They are found only rarely among the unemployed, regardless of their educational attainments. Thus unemployment, both as a cause and an effect of social inequalities, is best mirrored in the ethnic differences. The persistence of race and colour prejudices and discrimination, although in much more covert forms than before, tells us that this aspect of our past is still very much alive, with all its hurtful consequences.

Scientific racism, or what is often referred to as Social Darwinism, became a prominent aspect of European intellectual thought concerning 'subject peoples', especially after the publication of Charles Darwin's *Origin of Species* in 1859, about six years after Gobineau had written his *Essai sur l'inégalité des races humaines*. Darwin's work was used by racists to emphasise the supreme position of the white Nordic 'race' and the inferior position of other groups, especially the Africans, in the 'great chain of being'. H. Stewart Chamberlain's *The Foundations of the Nineteenth Century* (1899) became a seminal work in the quest to establish the intellectual basis for white supremacy, and was widely acclaimed in the USA and European countries. White racism was to reach its extreme form in Nazism under Adolf Hitler, expressed in his practice of genocidal racism.

Racism, dominant in European thought and actions for centuries, was given a fillip in the period of the new imperialism, in the late nineteenth century, with the conquest of Africa and the overrunning of most of Asia, including parts of China and Japan. Arguably, the first half of the present century witnessed a much more widespread and vitriolic white racism than previously. This was witnessed in views about the 'yellow peril' resulting from Chinese and Japanese migration to Europe and the USA, the holocausts which engulfed some 6 million Jews and thousands of Africans, the lynching of blacks by the Ku Klux Klan in America, and the establishment of the apartheid regime of the white settlers (Boers/Afrikaners), also directed against blacks, in South Africa. Overt racism was a feature of European relations with other peoples up to the very recent past.

It was common for Europeans to talk about 'white blood',[78] presumably as distinct from 'black', 'yellow' or 'coloured' blood. Recognising that biologically all blood is red, some Europeans felt that racial mixing could lead to blood contamination of the white race, and that this could lead to race degeneration. The white racist supremacists showed much concern with maintaining the purity of blood.

European and American writers also used to stress what they perceived as the barely human characteristics of some of the colonised peoples. For instance, several questioned whether these people could properly be classified as human beings, and, if so, whether they were not really a different species from the descendants of Adam. Were they not closer to apes than to men (men-like apes or, at best, ape-like men)?

Racism has created a lot of tension and bitterness in human societies, much of which still remains especially where there are more than one large racial or ethnic group. The reasons for racial and ethnic conflict are complex. As David Lowenthal points out, concerning the Caribbean, '[T]here are few aspects of West Indian life that race and colour do not significantly touch.'[79]

Race and colour prejudice is therefore much more than a relic of the past; it is the intrusion and persistence of the past into the present. Mutually reinforcing cleavages of race and colour have left us with bitter memories and antagonistic relationships. These do not usually burst into open conflicts, but they often manifest themselves in sharp verbal exchanges, suspicious attitudes, feelings of resentment, and inferiority and superiority complexes. Arguably the race and colour problem is the most bitter and divisive legacy which we have inherited from our colonial past. In this sense the past definitely runs deep. The issue is more than skin deep; it often runs in the blood.

Many Caribbean nationals are haunted by this past, not least among which are some of those who hold on to social and economic power and are afraid that racial strife will prove to be their undoing. These seek to hide the issue under a bushel rather than let it come out into the open, be discussed and dealt with sensibly.

This should not be taken to suggest that race and ethnicity are the only reasons for the social and economic inequalities existing in the region. Other factors include the structure of the economies, property and especially land ownership, fiscal policies, access to credit and loans, and the wider political environment. Any strategy for the rational development of the region must offer equal access by all ethnic groups to the region's resources and equal opportunities for personal and group advancement.

Caribbean societies have inherited a legacy not only of disunity but also of dependency. To some extent this was the result of the high value placed upon imports as opposed to local produce. This is perhaps best exemplified in the dependency on sugar cane, itself an imported crop, as the historical basis of the Caribbean economy. The ex-Cuban slave, Esteban Montejo, speaks about 'The sugar cane madness.'[80] Eric Williams muses that something so sweet should have occasioned such crime and bloodshed. Naipaul calls it 'a brutal plant', 'an ugly crop' with 'an ugly history'; for him cane is bitter.[81] Of course, the region has historically been dependent on imports, not only of sugar, but also of other commercial crops, peoples, cultures, diseases, technologies and ideologies, from Asia, Africa and Europe. This has continued over the years with an increasingly strong emphasis on imports from North America in technology, technical expertise, food, fashion and entertainment. This has helped to dull our spirit of creativity and inventiveness.[82] It has also led to dependency and has been a major disincentive to regional integration.

It is most of all the creative and inventive impulse within an individual or a society which liberates it from dependency. When that spirit is dulled or dormant the individual or society becomes simply an imitator, producing poor carbon copies of other peoples' creations. Caribbean scientists, artists and writers all recognise this fact; and this is why there is such widespread concern in the region today with the issue of cultural authenticity. But the search for such authenticity is bedevilled by the fear that we will never achieve it, and that we will always be regarded as pale imitators of Asians, Africans and Europeans. Many of our artists and writers are enchained by the recognition that our own people often reject our efforts as being inferior until they receive the signet of approval and the accompanying insignia from Europe or America, in the form of a major award such as a Nobel prize.[83] This applies not only to creative works, but also to university degrees, senior promotions and Commission reports. Thus we bring in experts and pay them large sums of money to do what our local experts can often do better because they know the local situations. Many of these foreign experts simply tell us what we know already. In this stifled atmosphere people tend to become satisfied with mediocrity and not to strive for excellence. They become highly critical of the few who attempt to do so.

Perceptions of the region

Over the broad historical period foreigners and sometimes locals have voiced their various perceptions of the region, most of which have been pejorative. One of the earliest perceptions was that the area was a zone of exploitation, a place where one could become rich quickly or, as the Europeans used to say, where one could make a killing. Sometimes this was literally so, because a large number of people were killed in the attempt to make a killing. This was the dominant view of the region until the eighteenth century. We may note, for instance, the numerous attempts made by Europeans to find El Dorado, the mythical city of gold. When the search for that city waned it was replaced by searches to find other mineral treasures in Guyana, Hispaniola (Haiti and the Dominican Republic), Cuba and the mainland territories of Mexico and Peru. Linked with this was the search for agricultural wealth through the identification of suitable tropical staples and the exploitation of the fertile soils. This will be appreciated better when it is understood that the Caribbean colonies were created with one end in view: to produce commodities for export, to the benefit of Europe. The Caribbean migrants came, voluntarily or involuntarily, exclusively to effect the economic exploitation of the region. Thus the societies which emerged were quite different from those where people have settled on the land for generations, and where economic activities are intended to create the conditions for improving the quality of the material and social life of the inhabitants. The philosophical basis of Caribbean migration was also quite different from that which led to European migration to such places as Australia, New Zealand, North America and southern Africa, which were generally perceived of as colonies of settlement (although even in these cases there was large-scale exploitation of the indigenous populations). The perception of the Caribbean colonies as territories of exploitation profoundly influenced the entire character of Caribbean society. It was a case of materialism and avarice at their worst.

Secondly, and linked with the above, was the view that the region's indigenous populations were simply fit to be servant peoples. Servitude, as we have already stated, became one of the hallmarks of political, economic and social relations which developed in the region through the institutions of oppression and exploitation. The region has been seen over the years, in a more complete sense than elsewhere, as a catchment area of servant peoples. Arguably this perception has not disappeared completely from the minds of foreign investors and others. In practice there is often a thin line today between service and servitude, especially in the tourist and offshore sectors of the region's economy. Some foreigners still expect our peoples literally to bend backwards in order to serve them.

Thirdly, the region was considered for a long time as a death trap. This can be seen notably in the records of the early seventeenth century, when the mortality rate among European adventurers and colonists was quite high, perhaps not as high as in West Africa, but nevertheless alarmingly high. Richard Dunn called the region a 'demographic disaster area', and added: 'Everyone seemed caught up in a race between quick wealth and quick death.'[84] This was due to the prevalence of a number of diseases, mostly introduced from Europe, including measles, cholera, scarlet fever, diphtheria, mumps, whooping cough, pleurisy, bubonic plague, typhoid, gonorrhea, tuberculosis, malaria and yellow fever (the last two probably introduced from Africa).[85] Malaria, in particular, wiped out thousands of Amerindians. Until recently the Europeans did not accept that they were the human vectors of most of the dreaded diseases which plagued the region, that they were not only macro-parasites but that they were the agents of certain micro-parasites.[86]

Guyana, Suriname, Jamaica and Trinidad acquired especially fearsome reputations as an adverse disease environment well into the nineteenth century. Barbados, St Eustatius and a few other islands had a better reputation for salubrity. Gradually, as effective control was established over the most dreaded diseases such as malaria and yellow fever, the islands acquired a more wholesome reputation. Nevertheless, as late as the 1930s a large number of diseases, including hookworm, tuberculosis and malaria, made heavy wastage of human life, especially among the infant population.[87]

The concept of the region being a death trap also had a lot to do with natural disasters such as hurricanes and volcanoes,[88] and human disasters resulting from European warfare and slave insurrections. By the eighteenth century slave insurrections had become endemic in the region, and so whites who had made a killing preferred not to stay around and risk being killed themselves. They re-migrated to Europe, and as a result the region suffered from the adverse effects of a marked occurrence of absentee landlordism.

Fourthly, the region was perceived as a culturally backward society, a perception that still lingers on in some circles. This perception was worse in relation to the Protestant communities (the Dutch and British) than the Catholic (the Spanish and French). The Spanish and French built several magnificent and durable structures; most of them were forts and churches, and many of them still exist today in Cuba, Puerto Rico, Guadeloupe, St Lucia and elsewhere. The Dutch and the British also built stone structures, but these were usually of much less magnificence and durability than those in the Catholic countries. In the case of the Dutch in Guyana, they did not build a single enduring structure; not a single church, fort or mansion seems to have survived their presence there; nearly all their structures were built of wood rather than stone, which quickly eroded because of climatic conditions and neglect. Even in those colonies where the Europeans built sizeable stone structures, they paid only limited attention to the development of social and cultural institutions.

The church was the chief social institution in all the colonies, but while most colonists observed the rituals associated with Christianity (for instance, baptism communion, and burial of the dead), few bothered to pay more than lip service to the tenets of their religion in respect of holy living and treating their neighbours as themselves. The church apart, few other social institutions were prominent in the region before that time. For instance, there were few schools in the region before the nineteenth century. Those who wished to have a sound education had to go to Europe or North America to pursue it. Some planters were well-educated and had small private libraries, but as a whole they were not particularly interested in literary pursuits. In any case, the Caribbean never developed a reputation for literary or scientific enquiry during this period, nor for the display of a high level of culture. Contrariwise, it developed a reputation as a place where the coarse and the vulgar resided, an area of cultural darkness.

Fifthly, the region has come to be seen in more recent times as a poverty-stricken area, largely denuded of natural resources. This was the perception from the early nineteenth century, with one or two notable exceptions, such as Cuba and perhaps Guyana, in both of which the sugar culture was developing at a rapid pace. Africa and Asia were being viewed increasingly as areas to which the Europeans should look for the agricultural and mineral products which they needed, so that from the nineteenth century the Caribbean territories became considered as part of the white man's burden, or the burden of empire. Indeed, the region is still largely perceived by both locals and foreigners as being incapable of standing on its own financially, and requiring the constant injection of finance capital in the form of loans and grants-in-aid. Haiti is looked upon as the fatal example in this respect, although Guyana and the Dominican Republic may rival it for its unenviable position.

At the same time, there is ambivalence about the region as a financial desert. The growth of the tourism industry demonstrates that there is still a lot of money to be made by those who know how to exploit the region and its resources. The use of various islands also as tax havens, casino resorts and places for drug-trafficking, money-laundering and other shady activities is causing the region to acquire a new reputation in international financial circles.

Outsiders' perceptions of the region over a period of time seem to have been largely negative. Even where they were positive (that, for example, the soils were fertile), they were largely in terms of the region's potential as an area of exploitation.

The long period of oppression through the *encomienda*, slavery, indentureship and other forms of exploitation has left the region with a confusion about it's history, heroes, legacy, culture and identity. The word 'confusion' seems to crop up frequently in discussions about Caribbean identity. Rex Nettleford declares that the ethnic and cultural variety existing within the region is often seen as confusion: 'Variety . . . at worst spells confusion, periodically inviting self-doubt and equivocation.'[89] On racism, Lowenthal notes the 'confusion' existing in the region about whether it is still of any significance generally or even in a given territory.[90] The Trinidadian, Elliot Bastien states: 'To discuss racism in a West Indian context is to become hopelessly confused.'[91] On national identity the Trinidadian novelist Samuel Selvon writes about his home country: 'When I look at the scene here I find it all confusing;' and again, 'I do not know if I am East Indian, Trinidadian, or West Indian.'[92] Another Trinidadian, the Mighty Explainer, says in the calypso *Mr African* that 'the African man has his confused mind'.[93] On the regional identity, Black Stalin, another calypsonian from the same country, declared in *The Caribbean Man* that the British West Indies Federation ended in 'confusion'.[94]

Several writers have recently articulated their perception of the Caribbean peoples in terms of their regional identity. Clive Thomas points to their poverty and powerlessness; Samuel Selvon refers to them as 'a crippled and voiceless community'; Vidiadhar Naipaul sees them as 'mimic men', a 'people who are unsure of themselves', but with an 'abundance of talent'; Philip Mason calls them historically 'the most colonial of all colonial societies', where the search for roots is 'stronger than anywhere else in the world'; Tom Barry (*et al.*) views them as 'a hodgepodge of nationalities, languages, and cultures'.[95] In spite of these categorisations, many writers still realise that there is a good deal of similarity and even commonality among the various territories. Alec Waugh refers to them as 'a family of islands'. Mason likewise asserts: 'Though each of the island societies is unique, there is a strong resemblance between them. Indeed, progressively closer study of them seems first to underline their differences and later to reassert their underlying resemblance.' Barry (*et al.*) in spite of the characterisation noted above, assert that sugar, slavery and common economic difficulties have given the region 'a single identity'.[96]

There has been a good deal of debate about the overall impact of Europe on the Caribbean and no doubt the debate will continue for a long time. Some stress what they perceive as the positive impact of Europe on the region, including the transformation from undeveloped to developing territories, the introduction of more advanced political, economic and social systems, and the general humanisation of the environment. Indeed, there is a growing field of scholars who focus attention upon the positive achievements of Caribbean peoples, perceiving a high level of creativity in the region from the days of slavery onwards, in such aspects as the reinterpretation of African religions for survival and even revolutionary purposes; indigenous versions of African folklore; the rich variety of local dialects and languages; and international recognition in literature by such writers as Jacques Stéphen Alexis (Haiti), Alejo Carpentier (Cuba), Edouard Glissant (Martinique), Luis Rafael Sánchez (Puerto Rico), Simone Schwartz-Bart (Guadeloupe), Vidiadhar Naipaul (Trinidad), Edward Kamau Brathwaite (Barbados), Sir Arthur Lewis (St Lucia), and Derek Walcott (St Lucia). The last two of these are Nobel laureates.

In sport several writers point to the record-breaking achievements of the West Indies cricket team(s); the most outstanding international record on a per head basis in the area of track and field by Jamaica; and an outstanding record by Cuba in many sporting disciplines; and the internationalisation of Caribbean music, best represented by the reggae strains and its chief icon, Bob Marley. The positive thinkers also view the region as one of the most stable political areas in the world, and assert that present ethnic relations are on the whole devoid of overt conflict.

Others argue that while one may laud some of these achievements, most of them are recent, and that the most significant historical and contemporary aspects of the Caribbean reality are poverty, servitude, consumerism, authoritarianism, racism and violence. It is in this context that one must understand Naipaul's assertion that 'West Indians are frightened and ashamed of the past'.[97] Césaire appears to hold the same view, as exemplified by his description of Fort-de-France, Martinique, in the 1950s: 'At the end of the dawn, this inert city, with its lepers, consumption, famines, fears, hidden in ravines, fears perched in trees, fears sunk in the soil, fears drifting in the sky, accumulations of fears with their fumeroles of anguish.'[98]

Some writers see the European impact as a 'de-civilising' and even 'demonising' influence, a view forcefully put forward by Jan Carew,[99] who points out that Shakespeare's Caliban is 'the demonised version of the Carib that Columbus' febrile imagination had invented'.[100] Naipaul sees the impact of Europe on the region as creating a ghastly – perhaps even ghostly – situation, 'where civilisation turned satanic, perverting those it attracted'. He refers to the territories as 'the islands of this satanic sea'. Yet curiously enough, and apparently without being conscious of it, he mentions the Isles of the Saints (Iles des Saintes) in the very next sentence.[101] It is this Manichaen dualism and incongruity of 'satan' and 'saints' that makes the region at once both repelling and alluring. Here a San Salvador, there a Devil's Island. The wheat and the tares must grow together . . . .[102]

Notes

1. The Poetical Works of John Milton, II, 66-67.
2. The population figures are based mainly on the latest estimates available to the World Bank. In the case of a few countries where figures are given by the World Bank we have used *Keesing's Record.* The World Bank data on geographical size appear to have been rounded off to the nearest full number.
3. Dutton *et al.*, 62.
4. Naipaul, *Middle Passage*, 42.
5. Selvon, *Island*.
6. For a more detailed study of the different racial/ethnic groups in the region see Lowenthal, *West Indian Societies,* 76-212. For works on migration see Rosemary Brana-Shute, *Bibliography.* For the Commonwealth Caribbean in the post-emancipation period, see Thompson, 'Historical Writing'.
7. For two detailed studies on the Amerindians see Denevan Steward, ed., *Handbook.* See general bibliography for further works.
8. Sherlock, 5.
9. For studies on the black Caribs, see Taylor, 'Island Caribs of Dominica'; Taylor, *Black Carib of British Honduras*. See also general bibliography.
10. Koot, 139.
11. Lowenthal, *West Indian Societies*, 133-34. The discussion here relates to creole whites and to whites normally resident in the region.
12. We do not have any available estimates of the Chinese imported into the region. However, according to one source those who migrated involuntarily or voluntarily to Cuba numbered around 300,000 (Corbitt, *Chinese in Cuba,* 1). The number of East Indian migrants is

generally accepted as being around 500,000 (see Augier *et al.*, 209). Javanese migrants into Suriname are usually put at around 32,000 (Lowenthal, *West Indian Societies*, 190).

13. Hira, 190.
14. Corbitt, *Chinese in Cuba*, 103, 105, 117. See general bibliography for other works.
15. Lowenthal, *West Indian Societies*, 190. See also general bibliography.
16. *South America, Central America and Caribbean (1993)*, 570.
17. Very few works are available on the Syrians or Lebanese. These include Nicholls, 'No Hawkers', 415-31; Ammar, 'They Came From the Middle East"; *Papers Relating to the Foreign Relations of the United States* (Washington, DC: US Govt Printing Office), 1903:598-600; 1905:393-404, 532-42; 1906:897-901; 1912:523-41, 575-85; 1913:576, 580-81, 584-89 (deals with US Syrians trading with Haiti). See also general bibliography.
18. Lowenthal, *West Indian Societies*, 194-95. See also general bibliography.
19. Richardson, *The Caribbean*, 3.
20. McAfee, 11.
21. McDonald, 6.
22. See John Gunther, *Inside Africa*, cited in Burns, *Defence of Colonies*, 25.
23. Lugard, 618; see also 613.
24. Burns, *Defence of Colonies*, 23-24; see also 25-41. For a discussion of this aspect in the context of British rule in India, see Bearce, 40-41.
25. Burns, *Defence of Colonies*, 5.
26. De Gobineau, 238.
27. Macaulay, 329.
28. Poliakov, 301.
29. See Bauer, *Dissent*, 147-63; Bauer, *Equality*, 66-85.
30. Burns, *Defence of Colonies*, 16. Burns accused the USA of practising all three forms of colonialism, but the accusation might be applied to other developed countries.
31. Wakefield, *A View of the Art of Colonization*, 323, cited in Williams, *Capitalism*, 6.
32. Carew, 27.
33. Cited by Stoecker & Sebald, 60.
34. Freire, 34.
35. Freire, 34-35.
36. Memmi, xviii.
37. Césaire, *Discourse*, 20.
38. Freire, 36.
39. Introduction to Stedman, *Narrative*, viii.
40. Erich Fromm, *The Heart of Man* (1966), cited in Freire, 40.
41. Patterson, *Slavery and Social Death*.
42. See Lundahl, 128-32; Wingfield, 98-100; Corten, 349-66; Lemoine, *Bitter Sugar*.
43. Thomas, *Poor*, 369.
44. Cited in Lowenthal, *West Indian Societies*, 69.
45. Boland, 'Systems of Domination', 107.
46. Naipaul, *Middle Passage*, 182-83.
47. Diop, from Léopold Senghor's *Anthologie*, 175-76 (translation author's).
48. Cited in Naipaul, *Middle Passage*, 183.
49. Rev. James Phillippo, *Jamaica: Its Past and Present State*, 19, cited in Ragatz, ix.
50. Césaire, *Return*, 73-75.
51. Hook, 264.
52. Hook, 267.
53. On this aspect, see Freire, 121.
54. Bulhan, 93-94.
55. Hegel, 80-87, 99, 116.
56. Bearce, 71.
57. Mill, 136.

58. Trevor-Roper, 871.
59. Coupland, *East Africa,* 14.
60. Squire, 42.
61. Burns, *British West Indies*, 5.
62. Coupland, 14.
63. Coupland, *East Africa*, 13-14.
64. Naipaul, *Middle Passage*, 54.
65. Naipaul, *Middle Passage*, 67.
66. Seymour, 53-54.
67. Cited in Hutton, 44-45.
68. Freida Troup gives the following example of such brainwashing: 'What is it you live on/ Kaffir in the Kraal?/ Mealies, missis, mealies/ And they make us strong and tall./ What is it you grind boy,/ For horses and for kine?/ Cobs and mealies, missis,/ And they make them fat and fine.' (*South Africa*, 325-26).
69. Fanon, *Wretched*. On Fanon's philosophy, see also Bulhan, 117; May, 192-93.
70. Cited in May, 187-88.
71. Freire, 32.
72. Mannoni, 58-62.
73. Fanon, *Black Skin,* 83-108.
74. Many of the small islands which are dependencies of the main ones have been omitted.
75. Richardson, *The Caribbean*, 14.
76. Craig, ed., *Contemporary Caribbean*, I, vii, xx, 1, 3.
77. Nettleford, 6.
78. Burns, *Colour Prejudice*, 19; Bacchus, 72.
79. Lowenthal, *West Indian Societies*, 1.
80. Montejo, 86.
81. Williams, Capitalism, 27; Naipaul, *Middle Passage*, 62, 119.
82. Walter Rodney makes a similar point in relation to Africa (*Europe,* 114-15).
83. On this point, see Naipaul, *Middle Passage*, 41-42.
84. Dunn, 333-34. On the health situation in the British Caribbean around the end of the nineteenth century, see Rupert Boyce, *Health Progress in the West Indies*.
85. *The Christopher Columbus Encyclopedia*, I, 227.
86. Some excellent studies have appeared recently on the subject of the incidence of disease in the region during the period up to the nineteenth century. These have shown clearly that the Caribbean was perceived for a long time as an adverse disease environment. See, for instance, Sheridan, *Doctors and Slaves*; Higman, *Slave Populations of the British Caribbean*; Crosby, *Columbian Exchange*.
87. Williams, *Columbus to Castro*, 451-55.
88. According to Dutton *et al.*, the Lesser Antilles contain 30 active or potentially active volcanoes, the most active of which in historical times has been La Soufrière in St Vincent. On May 7, 1902 it erupted, killing 1,565 people. The next day Mt Pelée in Martinique also erupted, killing 30,000 people (Dutton *et al.*, 32-33).
89. Nettleford, 3.
90. Lowenthal, *West Indian Societies*, 22.
91. Bastien, 38-39.
92. Selvon, 'Three Into One Can't Go', 23.
93. Cited by Deosarran, 107.
94. Cited by Deosarran, 112.
95. Thomas, *Poor*; Selvon, 'Three Into One Can't Go', 23; Naipaul, *Mimic Men*; *ibid.*, *Middle Passage*, 47, 231; Mason, Foreword to Lowenthal's *West Indian Societies*, ix; Barry *et al.*, 1.
96. Barry *et al.*, 2; Mason, in Lowenthal's *West Indian Societies*, vii; Waugh, *A Family of Islands*.
97. Naipaul, *Middle Passage*, 183.
98. Césaire, *Return*, 15-17.

99. Carew, 6, 26, 28.
100. Carew, 6.
101. Naipaul, *Middle Passage*, 204.
102. *Holy Bible*, Matthew 24:29-30.

Politics

CHAPTER 2

The undemocratic and fragmented tradition

Unless those who govern can be freely criticized by their subjects, and unless there is competition for popular favour between groups genuinely independent of one another, government can never be truly responsible to the people and therefore democratic.[1]

John Plamenatz

The four most prominent aspects of the oppressive political system which Caribbean peoples have inherited are: first, the absence of an indigenous political tradition; second, the absence of a democratic tradition; third, the presence of a tradition of political fragmentation; and fourth, the presence of a tradition of political violence. These are caused by factors including the extermination of the indigenous population, the government of the various countries by oligarchic and autocratic regimes, numerous wars conducted in the quest for empire and internal military expeditions to keep the oppressed majority in their place.

Absence of an indigenous political tradition

Columbus seems to have realised that the basis of political and social interaction among the Amerindians, or at least among the Arawaks, was mutualism and communalism rather than self-aggrandisement and violence. Bartolomé de Las Casas' view of the Arawaks as the most gentle and peaceful people on earth was first voiced by Columbus.[2] But whatever merits the indigenous political systems might have had, the Europeans considered them primitive. They proved incapable of withstanding the deliberate assault of the newcomers, who often exterminated the chiefs and herded the people into the *encomiendas*.

On the mainland and in the few island habitats where the Amerindians continue to exist, their numbers and political and social systems are so fragmented and attenuated that they can hardly be described as indigenous. The office of chieftain, in particular, went through extensive modifications under the impact of the various Europeans – Spanish, Portuguese, Dutch, French and British. Where that office is retained today it bears little or no resemblance to what obtained at the time of the European arrival.[3] Moreover, the Amerindians as a group are not in the mainstream of the political life of any Caribbean territory, and this means that their present political institutions, where they exist, tend to be treated as relics of a bygone era. At best, their political systems and traditions have influenced present political systems and ideas in the region only in the most marginal way. The absence of an indigenous political base has wide implications for the structures and functions of the political systems of the region.

These systems are direct transplants from Europe, brought by the Europeans, with all their traditions and assumptions about gender, class, race and the divine right to rule. Their models of government have over time been inscribed on Caribbean minds, hearts and psyches as though they are holy writ. For instance, it is difficult for most of us, in the Commonwealth Caribbean, to think of workable alternative systems of government outside the 'Westminster model'. Even those of us who manage to break out of this mould generally end up with a Eurocentric alternative model, usually (until recently) the Marxist/Leninist or the social democratic model. However, this captive mentality is not confined to politics; it pervades our entire life, and sometimes it seems to be the very life-force of our existence.

Colonisation was not accompanied by transplantation to the Caribbean of the political systems of Africa or India, whence the largest numbers of the region's peoples originated – apart, of course, from Europeans who also had a significant demographic presence. Also the Chinese, who though not in large numbers in most Caribbean countries, came in significant numbers to Cuba and some Latin American mainland territories. Apart from the Europeans, the other migrants were unable to transplant their political systems, although some of these were very ancient, going back to the pre-Christian era, having developed and matured long before Western European political systems did. A study of these systems will show that, contrary to popular belief, they were complex, intricate and elaborate.

For example, the Yoruba political system in the early eighteenth century had a threefold distribution of state power (the Alafin, the Oyo Misi and the Ogboni), and the rules and regulations to limit the exercise of arbitrary power by any individual or group were as sophisticated as any other constitution or political system in the world at that time. Unfortunately, its constitution did not guarantee its political integrity absolutely, for in the second half of the century various individuals were able to amend and manipulate the constitution to their own personal ends. The point here is that the political world of what is today Nigeria, Ghana, Benin (and other communities) from which the vast majority of immigrants were drawn as servile labourers[4] was organised through complex constitutions and systems of checks and balances not inferior in any way to what existed in Europe at the time.

However, these political systems were not deliberately transplanted to the Americas, because the Europeans did not perceive the immigrants as being fit to engage in any sort of political activities. In Europe itself the masses of the people were perceived at that time as apolitical, so that it was inconceivable that Africans brought to the Americas as slaves would have been deemed as having any political will. Thus whatever aspects of African political culture were brought to the region were coincidental, in so far as among those who came in the baggage of the slave trade were some members of the African nobility, warriors, a few priests and some who belonged to segmented political societies (in Igboland, for example) which practised a system of village democracies. These often became political thorns in the sides of the master class through the initiation of and participation in slave unrest. The only examples of the transplantation of the political systems of the oppressed were the maroon communities which developed in some Caribbean societies, notably in Suriname, Cuba, Jamaica, Santo Domingo and Haiti, and mainland territories such as Colombia, Ecuador and Brazil.

Absence of a democratic tradition

Colonialism and political domination

The political history of the region is also devoid of a democratic political tradition. People today, politicians and others, speak about our democratic tradition or our democratic inheritance. The fact, however, is that colonialism by its very nature leaves little or no scope for the development of democratic institutions or traditions, since it is essentially the imposition of an alien political authority upon oppressed peoples. This kind of government is undemocratic in the most fundamental way, in that it does not derive its right to govern from the consent of the governed. As Plamenatz observes, 'Alien rule and democracy are clearly incompatible', and 'foreign rule, in the very nature of the case, is undemocratic; the foreigner imposes or has imposed his rule by force'.[5] The instruments or institutions of government imposed by that alien authority must also be undemocratic, although over time they may acquire the status of legitimacy both locally and internationally. Thus Britain, France, Spain, Denmark, the Netherlands and the USA obtained international recognition of the legitimacy of their rule over territories which they had acquired in the Caribbean and elsewhere, usually through the exercise of force. At the domestic level, however, their institutions remained undemocratic. Although the colonial master might associate members of the local elite in various aspects of the local government, this was far from the institution of a democratic system, since that elite either directly or indirectly derived its right to participate in the government from the will of the colonial master rather than from that of the people. Therefore, such activities did not constitute the establishment of a democratic system or the beginnings of a democratic tradition.

In the specific context of the Caribbean, colonialism established a relationship between the metropolitan (core) area and the colonial (periphery) area in which all the important political (and other) decisions were made in the former rather than the latter area. This system continued intact in most of the territories of the region until after the Second World War. Those territories that managed to escape from the system before then only managed to do so through the achievement of their independence by violence.

In order to govern the territories which they conquer, imperial governments have to establish some form of ongoing political authority there. The nature and scope of this government usually depend upon the political philosophy of the imperial government, the sizes of the local and the new immigrant population (that is, the settler population from the conquering community), the sophistication of the indigenous political systems, the strength of the resistance to colonial rule, the size of the colonial territory, the degree of modernisation of the communications network and the economic gains perceived by the conquerors. Where colonial conquest is expected to be accompanied by massive exploitation of the economic resources of the conquered territories and the expatriation of profits, the political and associated military apparatuses of colonialism usually seek to ensure that the expatriate elite are firmly in control of the local government.

In some parts of India and West Africa where there were many highly developed political systems, problems of communication, a small cadre of expatriate officials and a natural environment considered hostile to Europeans' health, the local elite became more closely associated with the expatriate officials in the government of the territories than elsewhere. In East Africa, South Africa, Australia, New Zealand and North America, which saw the migration of large European resident populations and the alienation of large tracts of land to them in a short space of time, the local indigenous elite either played no part or only a very minor one in the government of the colonial territory until nationalist activities forced the imperialists to modify the system.

In the Caribbean for most of the colonial period the white settler population and certain specially dispatched expatriate officials ran the local governments exclusively, although the accompanying conditions were not always the same as in the colonial territories already described. Only in few Caribbean territories were large white populations resident for any significant length of time. There was a dominant white population in Barbados for about 50 years after its settlement by Englishmen around 1627; after that it was overtaken by the new immigrant African population. In Cuba the white population constituted an absolute numerical majority up to around the mid-nineteenth century, and much later in Santo Domingo (later Dominican Republic) and Puerto Rico. In all the other large plantation colonies the white population was surpassed in number much earlier by the black (and coloured) one.

The draconian economic system unleashed on the colonies determined that the tightest form of political and military control was absolutely necessary, which meant in effect white control. Except when the exigencies of foreign invasion or the activities of the maroons dictated it, the Europeans did not want to associate the Africans with the maintenance of the political and social control of the colonies. Whenever the whites did have to associate them in that way, they remained in mortal dread of insurrection by the very blacks whom they had armed. While in the vast majority of cases their fears proved to be unfounded, on a few occasions the blacks did turn their guns against their oppressors, notably in St Domingue in the 1790s.[6]

Although white power ruled the colonies for a long time, the majority of the whites did not exercise political power in the colonial government in any of them until the nineteenth century. On the plantation, where a system of autarky prevailed for most of the slavery period, the political control of the master was very real and almost absolute. Outside the plantation, however, only a small group of whites exercised conscious political power. The worst in this respect were the Spanish and French colonies, which were governed by decrees emanating from the imperial governments in Europe. These colonies did not usually have legislative assemblies and reflected the pattern of government in the imperial countries. The government in Castile (Spain) was not being conducted on the elective principle, while in France the Estates General had not sat since 1614. It was unlikely, therefore, that government in the Spanish and French colonies would be conducted other than on the same autocratic principles in operation in Europe.

In both sets of colonies the administration was run largely by expatriate officials. In the Spanish colonies, with a much larger land area to administer in the Americas than the French, the variety of offices and number of officials were much larger. In the Caribbean itself administrative areas known as presidencies and captaincies-general were created at various points in time, under the control of a senior expatriate official. He was assisted by an *audiencia*, which was both a court of law and an advisory council, also made up mostly of expatriate officials. At the lower level, the system allowed for the establishment of municipalities run by *cabildos* or local councils. At the outset such councils were elective, but they ceased to be so in most instances long before 1700. Seats on the council were then acquired through appointment by the local governors and later on they were sold by the Crown for life. Still later, they became hereditary offices on payment of transfer fees. The whole system of government in the Spanish colonies came to be the prerogative of a small oligarchy, which used its power and influence to further its narrow self-interests.[7]

Spain's intransigence towards the granting of political concessions to its Caribbean colonies of Cuba and Puerto Rico hardened in the nineteenth century, especially after its mainland colonies had forcibly seized independence. Usually, the captain-general governed with a strong arm and used repression as a means of containing liberal sentiments.[8] This happened notably during the captaincy-general of Miguel de Tacón in Cuba, in 1834-38. The imperial government was itself caught between liberal and conservative forces at home, and concessions granted to the colonies tended to reflect the strength of the liberal vote in the Cortes or Spanish parliament. The failure to carry out promised liberal reforms in Cuba led to the Cuban War of Independence in 1895-98. The Americans entered Cuba in 1898 with the declared intention of delivering it from the tyranny of Spanish rule. However, when the war was over neither the Cubans nor the Puerto Ricans (who had been finally granted some measure of autonomy by the Spanish government in 1897) enjoyed the independence for which they had hoped.

The principle of government without representative institutions prevailed in the French as in the Spanish territories, with minor concessions from time to time, until the nineteenth century. The two senior officials were the governor and the *intendant*. The former was often a person of noble birth and of some military experience. His chief tasks were concerned with the defence of the colony and the enforcement of the commercial regulations laid down by the imperial government. The *intendant* was concerned with the other aspects of the colonial administration, a task in which he was sometimes assisted by a council. He had mainly administrative and judicial powers, hearing appeals from the courts of first instance. The colonial councils were usually composed of senior expatriate officials and a few colonists appointed by the governor. Elective assemblies were not usually allowed in the colonies. In rare instances relating to the imposition of special taxes the Crown might listen to the views of representative assemblies specially summoned for such a purpose, but did not bind itself either to summon such assemblies or to submit to their views. The vast majority of whites in the French colonies therefore did not have much say in the colonial government, which they themselves viewed as autocratic. It was only in 1787, and then for a rather brief period, that they were allowed elective assemblies based upon contemporary models in France.

During the early days of the French Revolution the resident whites in St Domingue joined in the cry for *la liberté*, which to them simply meant at the outset freedom to run the colony without interference from the metropolis. In 1794 the French colonies were constitutionally assimilated to metropolitan France (that is, they were deemed to be integral parts of the metropolitan country). They were given the right to send a few representatives to the French National Assembly, whose laws were to be applicable in the former colonies. They also received the right to have elective assemblies on the departmental model as in France. This system was abolished by Napoleon shortly after his accession to power and the colonies were once again governed by decrees from France.

During the nineteenth century French policy fluctuated between assimilation and treating the colonies as distinct entities. Colonial assemblies (colonial councils and general councils, as they were called at various times) were established and abolished at the caprice of the French government. The franchise was gradually extended to all free adult males. In 1848, the newly liberated adult male slaves were given the right to vote, but this was soon revoked and they had to wait some 30 years before the franchise was restored to them. In the 1850s the colonies were allowed a great measure of legislative autonomy and a certain degree of fiscal autonomy. In the 1870s they were considered to be fully incorporated colonies and were given *communes de plein exercice*. They thus enjoyed a degree of autonomy almost equal to what existed in the *communes* in metropolitan France. Universal suffrage to the adult male population was restored, municipal councils were established, and they were allowed to send a small number of deputies to the French National Assembly in Paris.[9] This body, as before, legislated for the colonies on important issues, but the token representation in the National Assembly did not allow them any meaningful participation in the politics of the metropolis.

In 1946 their status was changed from colonies to departments, which meant that legally they were on the same footing as departments (or provinces) of metropolitan France. Each department was allowed to elect a general council, but with a prefect appointed by the French government heading the administration. Since 1974 a regional council has been created for each of the three departments (Martinique, Guadeloupe and French Guiana), with responsibility for economic and social planning.[10] However, many persons in and outside these territories see this status as at best an ambivalent one, in which the territories are neither colonies nor independent entities.

In the Dutch territories the system was somewhat different. Gradually, from the late seventeenth century the colonies were allowed to establish local councils, comprising a few high government officials and influential colonists, to assist the commander or governor in administering the colonies' affairs. Sometimes the appointment to the council was by election by the more influential members of the free population; sometimes the appointment was through a system of selection by the commander, on the nomination of a select group of officials; while in other instances election was through the West India Company (WIC), a chartered company, with little or no consultation with the local colonial elite. The Netherlands Antilles, for instance, did not have an elected assembly until the franchise law of 1937, giving the vote to a mere (estimated) 6 per cent of the island's male population.[11] Suriname, which enjoyed some electoral representation at an earlier period, had an electorate comprising only about 2 per cent of the population between 1901 and 1936.[12]

There were thus several variations in the Dutch system from colony to colony, and even within a given colony over a period of time. The courts (or councils) of policy, as they were called, were at the outset expected to have only advisory functions, but they gradually arrogated to themselves legislative ones. They wielded the greatest power in the colonies of Essequibo/Demerara and Berbice at the end of the eighteenth century. In addition, in their role of courts of criminal justice, they exercised the main judicial functions within the colonies.[13]

The laws made in the Dutch colonies were subject to ratification, modification or annulment by the WIC, and/or by the States General (the Netherlands government). These metropolitan bodies also had power to initiate laws for the government of the colonies, in which case the latter had no constitutional option but to implement them. The Dutch system, however, allowed for a much greater measure of recognisable authority for the local colonial governments than the early Spanish or French ones.

The British system went the furthest before the nineteenth century in granting concessions to the white colonists; after that date it became increasingly restrictive until the end of the Second World War. From around the mid-seventeenth century the imperial government recognised the right of the colonies to have their own legislatures, to pass laws specifically relating to their colony. Such laws were to reflect the spirit of English. The imperial power reserved the right to ratify, reject and/or suggest modifications to all laws passed in the colonies. Laws passed in the colonies might go into immediate effect while awaiting imperial assent, but the governor could exercise a discretionary or temporary veto power, holding any law in abeyance until the imperial will was known. The imperial government, on its part, gave up the authority to make laws governing the colonies except for matters of an external nature.[14]

This system of government gave the colonists latitude to make whatever laws they considered necessary for the proper running of the colony. The overriding power of the metropolitan government was exercised from time-to -time, but on the whole was very light on the colonies before the era of slave emancipation when metropolitan and colonial legislatures were often locked in battle over the passage of certain laws. The latter generally showed themselves extremely reluctant to ameliorate the conditions of the slaves to the satisfaction of the imperial authorities.[15]

Before the nineteenth century the franchise was exercised by a narrow white elite who had to qualify for the same on the basis of income or property. There was therefore no question of giving the franchise to whites on the basis of colour or ancestry. This ensured that the locus of local power remained in the hands of the white upper class, who were also in the main the large merchants and plantation owners. This oligarchic control of power was resented by the poor whites and the other groups in the society; but that oligarchy itself chafed under metropolitan control, either when any particular piece of legislation was disallowed or when their external (usually trade) relations were restricted by the overarching authority and interests of the imperial power.

In the nineteenth century the British government sought to restrict the powers exercised by the local power-brokers. This was partly the result of the difficulties they were experiencing in getting them to pass ameliorative legislation on behalf of the slaves. Thus the colonies of St Lucia and Trinidad, acquired by conquest in the nineteenth century and which had not known legislative institutions similar to those in existence in the older British colonies, were governed under what became known as the Crown colony system of government, by which the Crown governed through appointed representatives to the colonial legislature and ultimately through decrees emanating from Europe. It was in these colonies that they were able to make the first meaningful strides in passing the new slave laws.

In the post-emancipation period, when a growing number of non-whites were qualifying for the franchise and election to the old legislative assemblies, the numerically declining white elite began to fear that the local legislatures would be taken over by the 'black masses'. The Morant Bay Uprising in Jamaica in 1865 proved to be the catalyst that finally convinced the colonial elite that they should hand over political power to the imperial government. This they did, with the exceptions of Barbados, Bahamas, Bermuda and Guyana, before the end of the century. The imperial government took over the reins of power and governed with the help of the local elite, sometimes with a few locally elected persons, until after the Second World War.

The Crown colony form of government was not different from the old colonial system; under both, the masses of the people were denied any direct participation in the political process. As late as 1938, for instance, only 7 per cent of the adult population of Trinidad and Tobago had the right to vote.[16] In the 1870s in Barbados only one in every 124 persons (1,300 out of a population of 162,000) had the right to the franchise, and as late as 1945 no more than one in 20 adults were eligible.[17] As Lowenthal rightly asserts, up to that time the exercise of the ballot was perceived as a privilege rather than a right.[18]

In the British and Dutch Caribbean (which together constituted by far the largest number of territories, though not the largest populations, in the region) the whites remained in control of the colonial legislatures until after the Second World War. As time went by the franchise was widened and access to the legislative chambers made available to a limited number of non-whites, but the system still remained very restrictive until after the Second World War. In 1954 the Netherlands government created the tripartite kingdom of the Netherlands–Suriname, the Netherlands Antilles and the Netherlands itself. The colonies were now given control over most of their internal affairs; the Government of the Kingdom, located in the Netherlands, reserved responsibility in such areas as defence, foreign affairs, legal security, and kept the power to override legislative and administrative measures. The Government of the Kingdom comprised the entire Netherlands government and representatives of the Suriname and Antillean governments. Each of these last two had only one vote, so that the imperial government continued to exercise definitive control over the vital sectors of the political life of the colonies.[19]

In 1975 Suriname became independent, and since 1981 the Netherlands government has conceded in principle the right of each of the six Antillean territories to self-determination. In 1986 Aruba achieved separation from the Dutch Antillean Federation (*status aparte*) and a quasi-independent status politically (but not economically) from the metropolitan power. The other territories of the Netherlands Antilles (the Antilles of the Five – Bonaire, Curaçao, St Maarten, St Eustatius and Saba) are recognised as belonging to an autonomous federation of the Kingdom of the Netherlands. Aruba was due to receive full independence in 1996 as a result of opting out of the federation, but it opted instead for special status with the Netherlands government.[20] At present the Netherlands government is still ultimately responsible for the external relations of the Antilles, including defence.[21]

In the British colonies the changes were more gradual and piecemeal from one territory to another, but by the 1970s most of them had not only received adult suffrage and internal self-government, but even independence. The territories still not independent (by choice?) are Anguilla, Bermuda, the British Virgin Islands, the Turks and Caicos Islands, the Cayman Islands and Montserrat.

Of the Francophone territories, Haiti achieved its independence in 1804 in one of the most violent confrontations in the new world between the colonisers and the colonised. The French overseas departments of Martinique, Guadeloupe and French Guiana have remained within the French fold, that is, they are considered to be integral parts politically of continental France, with no separate representation in international fora. Theoretically, persons born in these territories can hold the highest office in metropolitan France. In spite of a certain measure of autonomy being accorded these territories, especially from the 1960s, critics say that for all practical purposes they are completely assimilated to metropolitan France. In 1981 René Achéen and Francis Rifaux expressed the view: 'When we consider the ultra-centralist tendencies of French administration, it is correct to insist on the 'total', 'perfect' character of this assimilation and integration.'[22] Naipaul commented: 'Assimilation is in a way to accept a permanent inferiority.'[23] Having visited Martinique in 1959, he asserted: 'Martinique is France, and more than in appearance, that France has here succeeded, as she has perhaps nowhere else, in her *"mission civilisatrice"*, there can be no doubt.'[24] This has not changed appreciably since that date.

Of the Spanish territories, the Dominican Republic and Cuba became independent, the former in 1844, the latter in 1898, both as a result of armed uprising.[25] Puerto Rico, the other former Spanish territory, became a victim of US imperialism after the Cuban War of Independence, in which the USA participated on the side of the Cubans.[26] The Puerto Ricans also wanted their independence, but the USA would have none of it. Instead, they forced the Spanish to cede the island to them, and thus the Puerto Ricans simply exchanged one taskmaster for another. Since then Puerto Rico has gone through various phases of autonomy *vis-à-vis* the USA. Its present status is that of a self-governing Commonwealth or free associate state in relation to the USA, but according to Gautier-Mayoral it is 'a territory granted barely 15% of all powers of government'. She points out:

> [T]he Commonwealth Constitution is rather poor, since it leaves not only the usual foreign relations and defense in the hands of the

> metropolitan power, but also customs, military draft, citizenship, regulation of immigration and aliens, post office, control of internal and external communications, presence of military bases in Puerto Rico, obligatory use of US freighters for shipping, minimum wages, and so on, in the hands of Congress.[27]

The US government has made a few concessions by allowing the island a limited amount of free trade with some countries and participation as a separate entity in international cultural and sporting events. Some regard the status of the island as being just one step short of independence while permitting certain economic benefits. Others see it as the perpetuation of a colonial relationship between the two countries, which the governing elite in neither of them is anxious to sever.[28]

The US Virgin Islands which were formerly the Danish Virgin Islands, were purchased by the USA from Denmark in 1917 in order to enhance US strategic interests in the region. The USA hold on this area seems, if anything, to be firmer than in Puerto Rico and there is little challenge to its authority in the islands. In 1993 only 27.4 per cent of the electorate turned out to vote on the issue of the territory's political status as regards the USA. Nevertheless, 90 per cent of those who voted were either in favour of maintaining the present status or seeking an enhanced status, but not independence.[29]

Protests against existing political status have manifested themselves in several of the non-independent territories. In the French zone, in particular, groups of communists, socialists and other radicals have been conducting for some time what they regard as national liberation activities. However, the separatist factions in these departments have not been able to command substantial number of supporters. In 1983 the Martinique Independence Movement, the most vocal of the pro-independence groups in that island, gained less than 3 per cent of the votes for the regional council. In 1990 the pro-independents gained 22 per cent of the votes to this Council, but still fared badly when compared with other major political parties.[30]

In Puerto Rico the independence movement has been even weaker. Two small pro-independence groups exist and have been accused of employing violence sporadically to achieve their objectives. The more well-known of the two, the Puerto Rican Popular Army, claimed responsibility for several attacks on US and Puerto Rican military targets, until its strength was attenuated by Federal Bureau of Investigation (FBI) raids.[31]

In the Dutch and British territories which are not independent the conflicts do not usually break out into violent confrontations between the colonisers and the colonised. In fact, the conflicts are more often between different islands or different parties within the same political framework. Thus it is quite common to find conflicts resulting from the juggling for the little political space that has been granted by the imperial power, notably in the islands of the Netherlands Antilles.[32] There is also considerable friction at the level of the party, each competing against the other, sometimes merging, sometimes subdividing and sometimes disappearing altogether, all in quick (dis)order. But this 'make and break' phenomenon is not unique to the territories which are under imperial control; it is equally common in the independent countries.

At the same time it should be pointed out that the vast majority of independent Caribbean countries have seen changes of government through the electoral process. While at times elections are accompanied by much turbulence and accusations of electoral fraud, by and large the results reflect the workings of a democratic electoral process. Outsiders view the Caribbean as a whole as a stable democratic area, in which, with a few notable exceptions, basic human rights to free speech, the formation of political organisations, membership in trade unions, and the like, are not only enshrined in the constitutions, but actually honoured, in spite of the obvious weaknesses in the inherited parliamentary models.

Weaknesses in the inherited parliamentary models

Critics of the inherited parliamentary models consider that democracy is much more than the free exercise of the franchise or relinquishing power when defeated at the polls.[33] They view the Western models as having only the façade without the substance of democracy. They argue, that universal adult suffrage and the multiparty system may mean that the party with the best demagogues or the most attractive manifesto wins the election but fails to implement – or even to attempt to implement – the programmes outlined in the manifesto.[34] They say that voting by constituency, which is the dominant electoral system in the region,[35] often means that a party can obtain a substantial majority of seats in parliament, but a minority of the votes cast. This is more likely to be so when several parties contest the elections. Very often also the system offers limited and not very attractive choices between contesting political parties.

Others complain that the European models with their provision for an official opposition, and with a person who is usually paid a special salary and given special allowances as leader of the opposition, have built into them the seeds of parliamentary conflict; the opposition feel that it is their duty to oppose the government. Sir James Tudor, late Government Minister of Barbados, expressed the view that there were some persons outside parliament who were attempting to 'usurp the proper role of the parliamentary opposition, whose duty it certainly is to harass and torment the government of the day'.[36] Thus the role of opposition parties may be reduced to opposing even measures that are clearly for the good of the nation as a whole. It is rare in the operation of the European parliamentary models as practised in the Caribbean for government and opposition to agree on any proposed piece of legislation. These parliamentary models are therefore seen by their critics as being based on the conflict theory of politics, that is, that 'politics is a process of conflict between groups'.[37] But there are those who feel strongly that a dynamic official opposition helps to ensure that the democratic system functions reasonably well, by keeping the government (or party) in power on its toes, and keeping before the public eye issues which might otherwise pass unnoticed.

Another criticism levelled against the inherited models is that they are particularly unsuited to certain multi-ethnic communities, especially where ethnicity is a prominent aspect of life. There is always the danger that majority rule may lead to the entrenchment of the majority ethnic group, as happened in Sri Lanka and is a distinct possibility in Guyana, Suriname and Trinidad and Tobago. There are also those who rue the fact that the existing constitutions do not make provision for recalling governments that have become unpopular before their terms of office have expired.

Clearly, the inherited models have their supporters, their critics and even their enemies. The reality is that the democracy practised in the region makes little or no provision for the involvement of the people, apart from the periodic casting of votes. This often leads to sectional and even individual interests being promoted by the government in power at the expense of those of the wider population. This runs directly counter to the democratic ideal, which is concerned with general rather than sectional interests. As Barry points out, 'The prevailing problem in traditional democratic theory is that of reconciling the aim of "government of the people" with the obvious fact that government itself is a minority activity.'[38]

The perpetuation of these undemocratic practices is facilitated by various factors. The fact that we are barely a generation away from political independence means that the founding fathers of independence and/or their immediate families are often still in the forefront of politics. A grateful populace still sees them as saints or national icons, carved as it were in stone and enshrined in glory in the national memory. Any word or action against them may be viewed as sacrilege.

Since independence new leaders have emerged, but often with ideas of government similar to those of their erstwhile masters. As is common, especially in third-world countries, many Caribbean politicians have come to view politics as an end in itself rather than as a means towards achieving the larger goal of the economic and social transformation of their countries, for the betterment of the people as a whole. They see politics as a lifetime career or profession and an opportunity to enhance their personal power over individuals, improve their self-image and increase their material wealth. Some indeed have grown from rags to riches as professional politicians and professional rascals. They have a lot of charisma, but little character. They may even see the country over which they rule as their personal fiefdom, and develop new political dynasties, thus lengthening the rule of their family or their party.

The recent institution of universal adult suffrage and of popular participation in politics has made it possible for unscrupulous political leaders to manipulate voters' lists, ballot boxes and constituency boundaries in order to continue their rule. They also manipulate such important institutions as the mass media (the press, the radio and television in particular), the army, police and judiciary. These politicians also exercise control by instilling fear into the minds of their opponents by dismissing them from government jobs, refusing government scholarships or educational grants to them or their children, and unleashing physical violence against them.

The most brutal recent instance in the Commonwealth Caribbean of a government destroying the political opposition is the assassination of the Guyanese historian and politician Walter Rodney by the Burnham regime in 1980. The Bouterse military regime in Suriname also eliminated some 15 political and trade union opponents in 1982 on the pretext that they were attempting to escape from lawful custody. In Jamaica political violence by supporters of both of the major parties has accounted for hundreds being killed, including more than 800 in the violence immediately preceding parliamentary elections in 1980. Unless those who hold the reins of government can be freely criticised and unless the system allows for free and open elections to power by the people, a truly democratic system has no chance of emerging.[39]

With few exceptions, Caribbean countries have not developed the range and sophistication of political, economic and social organisations which would help to ensure the maintenance of the democratic process. As Plamenatz points out, 'For democracy to be real there must be in the community, not only at least two independent parties, but a great variety of other organisations speaking for all sections of the people. There must be at every level of society experienced negotiators and organizers who can bring effective pressure to bear on government.'[40] In western Europe, for instance, there are a large number of competing non-parliamentary groups articulating their views on what is happening in and out of parliament. They act as political pressure groups and include such organisations as trade unions, social clubs, business and professional associations, colleges and universities, and the news media.

These different organisations are involved in a wide range of activities, including political education, mobilisation, discussion, investigation, offering alternative solutions, and protest. They thus provide further checks and balances, outside the defined constitutional arrangements, against the exercise of arbitrary power. Because most of them are not linked to any particular political party they are able to articulate their views with some objectivity. They therefore help to shape people's ideas on politics and on the government in power. They serve to ensure that the government has at least some accountability to the people for its actions. This is an important aspect of any democratic system.

In the Caribbean, partly because of the short period since independence and partly because of the dominance of the major political and social institutions at the time of independence, there has been little scope for the emergence of the plethora of non-parliamentary institutions which exist in older democracies. Even when they do exist in the Caribbean, their political role is weak, and they sometimes become the creatures of the dominant political parties. This is especially true of the principal trade unions, out of which the major political parties historically emerged. These unions support the government when their own party is in power and oppose it when their party is in opposition.

The most autocratic regimes are often the ones that proclaim loudest their commitment to democracy. Violence against individuals or groups is explained as acts being conducted in the name and on behalf of the people, in order to preserve their democratic rights. The postponement of elections, the militarisation of the country, the suppression of the press and innumerable other undemocratic acts are declared to be in the interest of preserving the people's rights. Even when it is palpable that some regimes have lost popular support, the incumbents may refuse to step down; or, as in military regimes, they continue to interfere in politics even when civilian governments have been ostensibly restored to power. Two outstanding recent examples are the Bouterse regime in Suriname in 1987 and the military-backed regime in Haiti following the overthrow of Jean-Bertrand Aristide in 1991.

It is perhaps only through a long and painful process that we shall achieve political systems or models that are peculiarly adapted to our historical, ethnic and cultural circumstances. The absence of an indigenous political tradition is a great lacuna. It must be reiterated that while the existence of European political institutions in the region are centuries old, democratic institutions are much more recent. Over the years political traditions have been built up in the region, but we are now trying to initiate a democratic tradition. For instance, Bermuda and Barbados boast of having the second and third oldest parliaments respectively (established in 1620 and 1627) in the British Commonwealth. What this demonstrates, however, is that they have long parliamentary traditions, but not democratic ones, since those parliaments were controlled until the post war era by a narrow oligarchy.

Post-independence dictatorial regimes

The undemocratic extreme is reached in dictatorial regimes. The Caribbean has had a long history of such rule, as we have seen earlier. However, attention will be focused here on those that have emerged since political independence. Haiti provides the longest and most fatal example, with terror and violence as the handmaidens of authoritarianism. Looking at the present century, seven different presidents ruled the country between 1908 and 1915, followed by the dictatorship of the Americans from 1915 to 1934. The most notorious example of a Haitian dictator is François 'Papa Doc' Duvalier, who ruled the country with an iron-fisted administration from 1957 until his death in 1971. To some Haitians he was a kind of villainous hero, especially at the outset of his rule, since he maintained black political dominance over the mulattos and was viewed as the epitome of *noirisme* (a kind of Haitian version of *négritude*). He was succeeded by his son, Jean-Claude Duvalier, who ruled only slightly less brutally until popular uprisings forced him to flee the country in 1986. Since then Haiti has experienced a new wave of political turmoil, with a number of people raised to the office of president in short succession, and with the army continuing to play a decisive role in politics.

The first truly democratically elected president was Jean-Bertrand Aristide, who assumed office in 1990. However, it is thought that the character of this priest without vestments was fatally flawed and that he too had a bent towards autocratic rule. A coalition of military and civilian dictators overthrew him and ruled from September 1991 to October 1994, when he was returned in the baggage of the USA and its supposed allies,[41] the CARICOM countries, to serve out the rest of his elected term of office. The present government under René Préval, who was elected to office in December 1995, is striving to show some sensitivity to the interests of the Haitian people and the views of the international community. The inhabitants of this sad country have experienced bitter days and now hope fervently for better ones.

The neighbouring Dominican Republic has been equally unfortunate since independence. The country has had a history from Spanish times to the present littered with corruption. It has been the victim of a number of coups and attempted coups and has experienced the rule of a number of dictators. It is said that between 1844 and 1930 it had 50 presidents, 30 revolutions and 22 constitutions.[44] (It also suffered American occupation between 1916 and 1924). It has had some of the worst dictators in the region, including the unholy trinity of Pedro Santana, Buenaventura Báez and Ulises Heureaux between 1844 and 1899, and Rafael Trujillo from 1930 to 1961. It has experienced twists and turns and a brief dalliance with democracy from 1978 to 1986. But, as in the case of Haiti, its politics continue to be rocked by intrigues, scandals, fraudulent elections, military interventions, civilian protests and demonstrations, and the loss of human life.

Cuba, though perhaps not in the same mould as the other two, has also witnessed the subversion of the rights of the people by dictatorial regimes, not least among which were those of Gerardo Machado (1925-33), and Fulgencio Batista (1952-58). Earlier, as military strong-man (1933-40), Batista made and unmade seven presidents. Franklin Knight sums up the corruption of the presidents during this period:

> All used public office to serve private ends and showed scant respect for human rights. Machado and Batista were the most notorious, employing military force, selective assassinations, and constitutional manipulations to gain and keep office. Political corruption extended to the lowest ranks of government. One-fifth of the candidates in the 1922 elections had criminal records, and a frequent occupation of the legislatures was the passage of amnesty bills exonerating members of the government from past criminal actions.[43]

Many of the dictators have used their political position to accumulate massive fortunes. After the demise of the Trujillo family, for instance, the government of Juan Bosch planned to settle 70,000 peasant families on 1 million acres of former Trujillo property.[44] Ramon Grau San Martín, president of Cuba 1944-48, was arraigned on a charge of misappropriating $174 million from the public funds. In July 1950 a group of people entered the Havana court house and seized the documents which the government was using to establish its case against him.[45]

Liberal or democratic constitutions, such as those in Cuba in 1940, the Dominican Republic in 1963 and Haiti in 1991, have been short-lived. Writers argue that not only are these three territories devoid of a tradition of democratic government, but that they also lack a tradition of constitutional government.[46]

The recently independent countries have inherited a framework within which they can build democratic traditions. All the independence constitutions since the Second World War have explicitly recognised fundamental human rights, including universal adult suffrage, the election of governments which reflect the will of the majority, and the separation of the legislative, executive and judicial organs of state. However, this is juxtaposed against a long history of undemocratic government during the colonial era.

No constitution can, of course, act as the watchdog of people's rights. Constitutions are man-made and can be manipulated by people to suit their private and sometimes undemocratic ends. Ultimately, therefore, it is the citizens themselves who have to act as the watchdogs of their own rights. In the newly independent territories, threats to the inherited system have come from both military and civilian sources, but happily only in few instances. There were, for example, the machinations of the Gairy regime in Grenada, which was forcibly replaced by a new government born of a coup in 1979 and a further one in 1983 before some semblance of stability was restored. There was also the Burnham regime in Guyana which employed undemocratic methods from the 1960s to the 1980s in order to retain political control and enhance its power in the government and the country at large. In Suriname there were several military breaches of the parliamentary system by the Bouterse regime in the 1980s, punctuated by at least three abortive coups by military factions to remove him and significant guerrilla action (by as many as five groups) in the interior provinces. Dominica witnessed an abortive attempt at the armed overthrow of the government of Eugenia Charles by a group led by Patrick John, a former prime minister. In Trinidad and Tobago the army mutinied in 1970 and raised unrealised fears that it would attempt to overthrow the government. Twenty years later a radical Muslim group, the Jamaat-al-Muslimeen, made an unsuccessful grab for power.

Even when there is no military coup there is often a kind of political coup, in which the ruling party takes over the apparatus of the state and governs with an iron hand. In such instances the party and the state become closely intertwined. This sometimes reaches extreme forms in the doctrine of party paramountcy, by which is meant that the party supersedes the parliament in determining state policy. The most extreme form of the government-party relationship is one in which the party is deemed to be the government and *vice versa*. This results in the governmental apparatus being absorbed or integrated into that of the party. Elections are abolished or the constitution is bent out of shape to make it impossible for the ruling party to be defeated at elections, state funds are employed for party purposes, and so on. The Caribbean has had its share of such models of government under communist and so-called democratic regimes in Cuba, Haiti, the Dominican Republic, Grenada and Guyana.

Communist and socialist models

The failure of Western democratic models to meet the aspirations of the masses resulted sometimes in the emergence of Marxist/Leninist and other socialist models as alternative systems of government. These models, with their strong emphasis on political, economic and social egalitarianism, have historically appealed to a wide cross-section of deprived peoples, although recent events in eastern Europe in particular have forced socialist ideologues to beat a hasty retreat.

Communist and socialist models are generally viewed as antithetical to Western democratic ones. However, both in Europe and the Caribbean attempts were made to reconcile them, and even to graft the one on to the other. In the Caribbean attempts were made by parliamentary and non-parliamentary groups to do so, for example in Jamaica, Guyana, the French Antilles and the Dominican Republic. Among the many communist and socialist groups which emerged in the region are: the Communist Party of Cuba; in Haiti the Haitian Communist Party and the Popular Socialist Party; the Communist Party of Martinique and the Socialist Federation of Martinique; in Guyana the People's Progressive Party and the Working People's Alliance; the New Jewel Movement and the Maurice Bishop Patriotic Front in Grenada; in the Dominican Republic the Fourteenth of June Movement, the Dominican Communist Party, the Dominican Popular Movement, the Dominican Revolutionary Party and the Revolutionary Nationalist Party; the Progressive Union of Workers and Peasants in Suriname; and the Workers' Party of Jamaica and People's National Party in Jamaica. Some of these joined the Socialist International and established close ties with the Soviet Union.

All Caribbean territories since the end of the Second World War have been host to socialist formations, but some of these have been quite insignificant in the struggle for social and economic reform and can hardly even be called political pressure groups. A few, however, have been in the forefront of politics at the local and even regional level. By far the most important are the communist groups in Cuba, culminating in the formation of the Communist Party of Cuba in 1965. This party is the sole legal one in that island; in fact, there is little or no difference between the party and the government. The country is governed by a socialist constitution, using that of the former Soviet Union as its model, but modifying it in important respects. Elections have been organised since 1976 within the framework of the Communist Party of Cuba, that being the only group allowed to field candidates.

In the elections held in February 1993 the government allowed the electorate for the first time since the communist take-over to elect candidates directly to the National Assembly. Only one candidate was put forward for each seat, the electorate being allowed to cast a positive or negative vote. Any candidate with less than 50 per cent of the votes cast was to be replaced by another one. The elections were projected by *Prensa Latina* as having all the virtues of democracy without its vices.[47] In the early days of the revolution Castro had promised to restore the democratic constitution of 1940, but so far he has not lived up to his promise.

Apart from international concern at the failure of the present regime to hold multiparty elections, there are repeated allegations of human rights violations, including freedom of speech, freedom of the press and freedom to form political parties. The detention and imprisonment of political dissidents and human rights activists, in particular, have caused the UN Human Rights Commission to request permission to send a team to Cuba. Cuba has refused such requests, claiming that the allegations are part of US propaganda against the country.[48] Nevertheless, there is much disquiet in international corridors at the human rights record of the present regime, and this has adversely affected its relations with a number of Caribbean and other countries.

Fidel Castro is struggling to preserve the Communist model in face of its demise in the former Soviet Union and other parts of eastern Europe and its considerable weakening in China. He is also battling, as he has been since the early 1960s, against the subversion of his regime by the USA, which wishes to see the Western democratic model restored. In fact, the USA is preparing for the day when Castro will leave power, to ensure that the Cuban exiles in Miami and elsewhere may return home rejoicing, bringing in the sheaves of American-style democracy.

Castroism and communism (or, more accurately, Castro's brand of communism) became institutionalised in the Cuban government as a result of an armed revolution in that country in 1959. As noted above, a coup d'état brought Maurice Bishop to power in Grenada in 1979, but the situation there was quite different from Cuba. The corruption of the Gairy regime in Grenada never reached the depths of the regimes of Batista and his predecessors in Cuba. Grenada also never developed socialist formations comparable with those in Cuba, either in the pre- or post-revolutionary phase of the struggle. In fact, some critics see the regime under Bishop as one involved in a dalliance rather than a marriage with communism, more or less in the genre of the first Michael Manley, and the Forbes Burnham regimes. In Grenada, however, what distinguished it from these regimes was its forcible entry into power.

Moreover, its failure to hold elections during its four-year term of office, and especially in its early years when it seemed to have the goodwill of most of the Caribbean leaders, must have contributed to its demise. Among the reasons given for its failure to do so was its fear of counter-revolutionary forces destroying the 'people's revolution' through manipulation of the ballot. Thus the security of the revolution, here as in other third-world countries, was to be ensured by the bullet rather than the ballot. Ironically, it was the bullet that brought about the destruction of the revolution. The prime minister, Maurice Bishop, and several of his top brass were executed in 1983 by the more left-wing faction in his government and the army. A US invasion shortly afterwards brought an end to this experiment with Marxist ideology and the eventual restoration of a civilian government under a democratic constitution.[49]

Communist ideas and groups, of course, existed in the region long before the accession to power of Castro and Bishop in 1959 and 1979 respectively. In fact, within a few years of the Bolshevik Revolution in Russia in 1917 there were communist groups in the French territories of Martinique and Guadeloupe. In the 1930s and 1940s there were also vibrant Communist and socialist groups in Cuba, participating in politics both inside and outside the governmental structure and at the trade union level. Small Communist groups also existed, but fitfully, in the Dominican Republic from the 1940s, being as often persecuted as tolerated by the dictatorial regimes in power. Guyana was the first country in the region to elect a Marxist/Leninist regime under the leadership of Dr Cheddi Jagan in 1953. It did not last long, partly because Guyana was still a colony and partly because neither the UK nor the American government wanted to see a Marxist regime in power. The government was therefore dissolved by the UK government, and subsequent attempts by Jagan to establish a communist regime failed.

In Martinique, Guadeloupe and French Guiana socialist and communist groups have traditionally commanded a large percentage of the votes since the Second World War. Socialism in the French colonies developed under the wing of the various socialist parties in France. For instance, the Socialist Federation of Martinique in the 1980s was affiliated to the metropolitan-based French Socialist Party.[50] Since the Second World War France has had strong socialist groups which have played major roles in French government and politics. Socialist groups have captured power there from time to time in free elections.[51] Similarly, in the French Caribbean colonies, communist and socialist parties have either dominated or been a significant force in the elections to the regional councils and the general councils in recent years.

There is, of course, a significant difference between the three French Caribbean colonies, on the one hand, and Cuba, Guyana and Grenada on the other. The last three countries are independent, the first three are not. The former are therefore sheltered from the hostilities they might otherwise have encountered at the regional and international levels by virtue of their opting for a socialist political model. Equally important is the fact that because of their status as departments of metropolitan France the major laws governing them are made in the metropolis, so that they have little scope to effect and institutionalise socialist forms within the government that are not acceptable to the metropolis. The brand of socialism most favoured by the French is ideologically, structurally and functionally quite different from Marxism/Leninism, and Western democracies seem to have little trouble maintaining fraternal relations with French socialist governments.

Within the Caribbean ideological differences proved to be a major stumbling block in developing relations among the various countries.

Although the official position of CARICOM was to ignore such differences, in practice the situation was quite different. The Bishop regime ran foul of a number of its CARICOM partners both at CARICOM meetings and elsewhere, and there was no love lost between it and that of Tom Adams of Barbados or Eugenia Charles of Dominica.

The situation in Cuba is worse. It publicly repudiated its early policy of giving succour to freedom fighters in Latin America and the Caribbean, and the 'big four' of the Commonwealth Caribbean – Guyana, Barbados, Jamaica and Trinidad – once again accepted it into the comity of Caribbean nations in 1972. However, it is still out in the cold in its relations with several other Caribbean countries. Some of them would, no doubt, readily restore it to full fellowship, but are intimidated from doing so by the American eagle. In fact, many are convinced that the only reason for the stance of some Caribbean countries against Cuba is the increased pressure brought to bear by the US government under the presidents George Bush and Bill Clinton to topple the present Cuban regime. In 1993, at a meeting of CARICOM heads of government in Dominica, it was agreed to establish a CARICOM-Cuban Joint Commission.[52] So far, this has remained a paper initiative.

Apart from Cuba, the Caribbean is unlikely to have to deal in the near future with any Marxist/Leninist regime, or even any left-of-centre socialist regime. Communism/socialism had been on a gradual retreat even before the demise of the Soviet Union and the other eastern European communist states, which acted as a precipitant, so that many leftists in the region no longer fly their ideological banners publicly. Some socialist groups, such as the Workers Party of Jamaica and its counterpart in Barbados, are either defunct or moribund. This is not to suggest that the Western democratic models will receive a new lease of life in the region. The impatience of groups that are fed up with the functioning – or rather malfunctioning – of the inherited Western models may lead to further unconstitutional interventions in the political process to achieve governmental change, such as has recently happened in Trinidad with the Jamaat-al-Muslimeen. We may be no closer to developing a democratic tradition than when political independence was first achieved.

Tradition of political fragmentation

Another far-reaching effect of European colonial rule is the excessive political fragmentation of the region. The present situation is the unfortunate result of an ill-conceived colonial system of administration, in which in the early days little or no attempt was made to govern the territories as a single entity. By the time the colonial governments got around to attempting to do so, insular feelings were already strong and any move towards union was viewed with suspicion and sometimes open hostility.

The Caribbean thus remains the most balkanised place on earth. This small region has no less than six different European and American political traditions (French, UK, Danish, Spanish, Dutch and US). There are also a large number of small, independent states, each of which shows a high level of parochialism and considers nationals of other Caribbean territories as foreigners.

The region, never strong on the concept of political unity, has seen further impediments strewn in the way in the last thirty years. Political independence has simply served to reinforce the parochial, now called national, spirit. The small states in the region are particularly wary that they may be swallowed up geographically and demographically by the large ones. This fear has to be addressed seriously and sympathetically, if progress is going to be made on any sort of political union.

At present three contradictory impulses exist concerning such a union. The first is the desire to perpetuate some form of European or American political sovereignty. Some view the statuses of the present British colonies (Bermuda, the British Virgin Islands, the Caymans, the Turks and Caicos, Anguilla and Montserrat), and of Puerto Rico, the US Virgin Islands, the Netherlands Antilles and the French Antilles as the persistence of colonialism, or 'deferred independence'. Others see a confusion of identity, a reluctance to break the umbilical cords which tie these territories to the so-called mother countries. These territories have also been called subsidised or welfare colonies. It would seem, indeed, that in the majority of cases the choice not to opt for political independence is in reality dominated by hard, cold economic facts, based upon a perception of what independence would entail, rather than an emotional or sentimental attachment to the imperial power.

Bermuda is, of course, in a strong economic position to claim independence: it enjoys one of the highest incomes per head in the world and low unemployment. Nevertheless, Bermudians have persistently voted to retain the political links with the imperial power, fearing that political independence would open the floodgates of extremist political ideology. Bermudians also fear that political independence may lead to a decline in tourism and in foreign investment. Independence might also mean an end to certain preferential financial benefits it enjoys in the financial markets in the UK and because of its status as an Overseas Territory in association with the European Union. Similar, though perhaps more muted, concerns probably lie at the heart of the weak calls for political independence from, for example, the Turks and Caicos Islands and the Cayman Islands. However, the Bahamas, a country in which the same fears were voiced prior to independence, has not experienced such a situation.

In Curaçao economic considerations also explain why 73 per cent of those voting in 1993 elected to retain the present status of that island *vis-à-vis* the Netherlands government. This was not surprising since the Netherlands' annual aid to the Dutch Antillean Federation (which includes Curaçao) stood at that date at US$160 million.[53] In Puerto Rico, 29 per cent of the disposable income derives from metropolitan financial transfers.[54] In the French colonies financial transfers from the metropolis are estimated at 75 per cent of total income. In French Guiana, in addition, the European Space Agency at Kourou is expected to spend US$4.5 billion by 2000, and less than 5 per cent of the inhabitants are interested in independence.[55] Neville Duncan has written about the economies of the French territories: 'The French government has created conditions which would make it absolutely foolish, in material terms, for Martinique, Guadeloupe and French Guyana to want to be independent states.'[56] This kind of dependency was highlighted in the statement in 1976 of a member of the local Martinican business community (peeved over what he considered to be the failure of the metropolitan government to ensure that the interests of the Départements d'Outre-Mer were not overlooked in negotiations with the African, Caribbean and Pacific countries): 'There is only one thing more foolish than depending on the French administration, this would be to depend on an autonomous West Indian administration.'[57]

Giraud argues that the French colonies moved over time 'from dependency to dependency' (that is, one situation of dependency to another), and that they 'have always been in a situation of total dependency on the [metropolitan] mainland'. He also asserts that '[French] Antillean political life today is structured along the same power lines as in France, reproducing exactly mainland political cleavages'; the Antillean parties are mostly 'mere regional structures or even smaller branches of French parties'; that they do not perceive a political future outside the French framework, and that this is true even of the 'autonomists'. Giraud sees the link with France generally as resulting in 'a many-faceted metropolitanization of Guadeloupe and Martinique – absolute economic dependency, total mimetic education, deep acculturation, in short, self-dispossession'.[58]

These observations raise the wider issue of the capacity of mini-states to exist as viable, independent political (and economic) entities in today's world. C. L. R. James, in one of his most cynical comments, declared them to be historical absurdities, and any analysis of their future as separate entities 'immorality or sadism'.[59] Similarly, Lowenthal points to Anguilla, which by a plebiscite in 1967 opted to secede from union with St Kitts and Nevis. He describes the island's natural resources as composed of 'saltpans and a sandy soil'.[60]

There are those who believe that such small states will either have to gravitate towards a larger land mass and political and economic system, or be gobbled up by a more powerful state. The exponents of both views have some peg on which to hang their hats. There are several examples of territories seeking to be annexed to others. In 1821 Santo Domingo (Dominican Republic) sought to become part of the newly independent territory of Gran Colombia, and in 1870 President Buenaventura Báez sought annexation of the now independent Dominican Republic to the USA. Between the 1840s and the 1860s some Cuban planters expressed the wish that their island should become a US state. Much more recently, Puerto Ricans have sought full integration as a state into the US polity. Canada has also been regarded as the apple of the eye by some Caribbean territories which have wanted to sever ties with their imperial overlord. Thus in 1884 Jamaica, Barbados and the Leeward Islands called for annexation to that country as did the Turks and Caicos Islands as recently as 1974. In no instance, however, was such a petition granted. Canada was certainly reluctant to bear the UK's burden of empire. The USA, while casting avid eyes on Cuba and the Dominican Republic, hesitated because of internal and external opposition. However, in the present century the USA virtually reduced Cuba to an American colony, formally colonised Puerto Rico, and invaded and occupied the Dominican Republic on more than one occasion.

The second contradictory impulse is the further balkanisation of the region. Christian Girault observes that 'in the Caribbean archipelago the elements of diversity tend to overshadow the trends towards unity.'[61] There is much truth in this observation. The relationship between St Kitts and Nevis is an unhappy one, and at the time of writing the latter is in the process of formally separating from the twin-island federation. Until recently also, Tobago was threatening to opt out of the unitary state with Trinidad and to seek its own fortunes as a mini-state. Barbuda is unhappy with its relationship with its larger and less underdeveloped partner, Antigua, from whom it sought unsuccessfully to separate at the time of independence in 1981. Bequia experiences an uneasy relationship with St Vincent. The smaller and less developed Bahamian islands look with envy on the material development of Providence and Grand Bahama. The different levels of dependency can perhaps best be illustrated by noting that Petite Martinique is a kind of dependency of Carriacou, which in itself is a dependency of Grenada, which before independence was a dependency of the UK.[62]

The problem is not confined to the Commonwealth Caribbean. Curaçao and St Maarten in the Netherlands Antilles smart under what they consider to be the heavy financial burden they have to bear to supplement the meagre earnings of the other members of the group, although they themselves are net recipients of aid from the continental Netherlands. A fraternal (as distinct from forced) political union among them in the foreseeable future therefore seems bleak. The Netherlands government's concession of the right of each of the six Antillean territories to pursue its own political destiny thus raises the possibility of even further balkanisation of the region. In the French zone, an independent union among the various territories encounters basically the same kinds of problems as in the UK and Dutch zones. The dependencies of Guadeloupe (Marie-Galante, La Désirade, St Barthélemy, Iles des Saintes and St Martin) are not enchanted with their satellite relationship with that department. In the Spanish zone, which consists of three of the largest territories (including Puerto Rico), political union, or even some form of political cooperation, is entirely out of the question.

Several solutions have been attempted to address the grievances articulated by the satellite communities. One is to detach them from the main territories, thus reinforcing the fissiparous tendencies. This was the decision taken for the Turks and Caicos Islands, the Cayman Islands and Belize in the case of Jamaica and Anguilla in the case of St Kitts and Nevis. It was also the solution agreed on for Aruba, which now enjoys a separate status within the Tripartite Kingdom of the Netherlands. The second solution is to grant the territories greater autonomy while maintaining the basic structural relationships. This solution has been attempted with only limited success for Nevis and Tobago. The third solution is to spend more money on development, which was attempted for the Bahamian islands and also for Tobago. It is possible, however, that greater political fragmentation will be the result of such expressions of discontent, although it is doubtful whether this will help to resolve the economic and social problems which gave rise to grievances in the first place.

The third contradictory impulse is the attempt to form some kind of political union, or at least to achieve closer political cooperation. Historically, the most successful attempt at closer political association was the Leeward Islands Federation, comprising the various British Leeward Islands colonies, from 1871 to 1956. Its longevity had nothing to do with its efficiency or popularity, for it was a frequent whipping horse of Caribbean politicians. It was a weak federation, foisted on the colonies by the UK government which wanted to rationalise its policies and integrate its administrative services in the region. Caribbean politicians often complained that it was cumbersome, lacking in power to achieve any significant economic changes in the region, politically backward since it was based upon a Crown colony system of government and wasteful of taxpayers' money. Nevertheless, the UK government kept it intact, with minor modifications periodically, until its dissolution in 1956 to make room for the larger British West Indian Federation.[63]

When the latter finally spluttered into action in 1958 it proved to be a feeble creature. C. L. R. James referred to it as a 'ramshackle collection of individual structures which were joined together and labelled "Federation"'.[64] It was more or less still-born and experienced a short and traumatic life before its death in 1962. Immediately before and during its existence all the basic fears and anxieties that have historically divided the Anglophone Caribbean were etched out in vivid relief. Major difficulties surfaced over such issues as the federal capital, freedom of movement of the federal population within the area, territorial representation within the federal government, responsibility for various services such as education, agriculture, loans and taxation, the general scope of federal legislation and the exercise of residual powers. In the end, a weak federation emerged, with residual powers in the hands of the unit territories, and with the federal government denied the power of taxation for five years. The problem of movement of the federal population was not satisfactorily resolved. Certain territories, because of economic, ideological, ethnic and other reasons, refused to join the federation: Guyana, Belize, the British Virgin Islands, the Bahamas, Bermuda, the Turks and Caicos Islands and the Cayman Islands.

No sooner was the federation inaugurated than it was overtaken by economic and political vicissitudes and a good deal of personality conflict and ill-will. In 1962 Jamaica laid the axe to the root of the tree by declaring her secession from the federation. Trinidad's retort that one from ten leaves nought sounded the death knoll for the hapless experiment. A few romantic federalists, instead of allowing it to expire quietly, tried to pick up the pieces in a federation of the 'Little Eight' and then the 'Little Seven', but soon discovered that the writing was on the wall and that, like Humpty Dumpty, they could not be put together again. Thus federation became an inevitable casualty to the insularity that has dominated the region since the beginning of colonialism.

In spite of the sad history of the various federal experiments in the Commonwealth Caribbean, some of the region's nationalists are still convinced that this must be the ultimate, if not the proximate, goal of CARICOM's efforts at integration. Arthur Lewis was sure that a federal structure was essential to the preservation and promotion of the rights and interests of the region's peoples: 'The fundamental reason for federating these islands is that it is then only that good government can be assured to their peoples.'[65] Clive Thomas considers that some form of unity is necessary to any meaningful efforts to eliminate regional poverty: 'The resolute and relentless pursuit of the interests of the poor and powerless requires an equally resolute and relentless pursuit of regional unity. Indeed, in a real sense, neither is achiev- able by itself.'[66] These sentiments, however, are difficult to translate into anything concrete, since each small unit is bent upon asserting a stubborn independence. The approach to unity is encumbered by a minefield of constraints.

The recent West Indian Commission set up by CARICOM under the chairmanship of Sir Shridath Ramphal, conscious of these constraints, has not set political federation as one of the goals of the Community.[67] Many Caribbean politicians would view proposals for a new Commonwealth Caribbean federation as nothing more than political graffiti. For instance, Edward Seaga, former prime minister and leader of the opposition in Jamaica, made it clear recently that his party had no interest in participating in a new federation.[68] James Mitchell, prime minister of St Vincent and the Grenadines, made his government's position equally clear in July 1994, when he stated: 'Political union is dead, and I do not even see any flowers at the graveside.'[69] Nevertheless, a few politicians are trying to create limited unions. Patrick Manning, ex-prime minister of Trinidad and Tobago, not so long ago sought to create a political union involving his country, Guyana and Barbados. We may likewise note the recent feeble efforts of the OECS Windward group (Dominica, St Lucia, St Vincent and the Grenadines and Grenada) to achieve some form of political union. These initiatives have so far proved to be nothing more than timid steps in the right direction. In fact, the prime minister of Grenada declared in 1994 that he had placed the matter on an indefinite hold, while seeking to strengthen other forms of integration.[70]

Political union or even functional cooperation among the other language groups in the region seems to be no less fraught with difficulties. The two most hopeful areas are the Netherlands Antilles and the French territories. Each of these is still bound to the imperial power and, in spite of the doubts which we have expressed above, it may just be possible to hold them together in a post-colonial era. The Spanish territories are the worst off, due to their widely differing political paths since the demise of Spanish rule.

Attempts are currently being made to give flesh to the Association of Caribbean States (ACS), an organisation established on July 24, 1994 by more than 20 Caribbean and Latin American Heads of state and government in Cartagena (Colombia). The ACS has the potential to incorporate 37 states, with a combined population of 202 million, a gross domestic product of US$508 billion and merchandise trade of US$180 million.[71] It is seen mainly as an economic bloc, but is also a forum for broad consultation and cooperation among its member countries on regional and international issues. Michael Manley, former prime minister of Jamaica, apparently sees it as an important stage in the establishment of a political forum and even a political power bloc.[72] Time will reveal the extent to which his faith in the new regional grouping was well-founded.

The larger issue of a political union embracing Latin America and the Caribbean, or even the Caribbean alone, requires a supreme optimist to envisage. But the Haitian, Anténor Firmin, in his *Lettres de Saint Thomas*

(1910), called for a federation of the entire region.[73] C. L. R. James was another Pan-Caribbean visionary, who wrote about a Caribbean 'nation' which would comprise all the territories and language groups in the region. He was so convinced of the righteousness of his cause that he was prepared to establish 'the new order . . . if even violence is needed' to do so.[74] Wickham, in more opaque language, endorses James' view, and suggests that only violence will effect unity within the region. In his own words: '. . . the most antagon- istic factor is the hostility of a state of separateness and fragmentation to the emergence of the essential human ingredient of union: the leadership of a strong, even cruel, and visionary, even obsessed, personality, blessed with the unquenchable fire of a conviction of his or her own destiny – an Alexander, a Napoleon, a Kublai Khan.'[75] Cynics might be tempted to view the idea of a political virtuoso forging unity on the anvil of violence, or even persuasion, as nothing more than a whispering hope or the reveries of a Utopian.

Notes

1. Plamenatz, 18, 66.
2. Extract from Journal of Columbus, Dec. 24, 1492, cited in Knight, *Genesis*, 15-16.
3. For works on the Amerindian political systems see: Thompson, *Colonialism*, 7-9, 191-208; Steward, ed., *Handbook of South American Indians*, IV; Denevan.
4. See Law, 61-77; Forde & Kaberry.
5. Plamenatz, 1, 92.
6. For works on the revolution in St Domingue, see James, *Black Jacobins*; Geggus, 402-18; Ott, *Haitian Revolution*.
7. See Fieldhouse, *Colonial Empires*; Lockhart & Schwartz, *Early Latin America*; Gibson, *Spain in America*.
8. Vergne, 187, 192.
9. At present French Guiana sends two deputies to Paris, and Martinique and Guadeloupe four each (*South America, Central America and the Caribbean (1993)*, 315, 322, 406; *Keesing's Record*, 40 (1994), R42-43.
10. See Fieldhouse, *Colonial Empires*, 34-47, 303-24; Miles, 35-41; Lasserre & Mabileau, 82-102; Murch; *South America, Central America and the Caribbean (1993)*, 315, 322, 406; *Keesing's Record*, 40 (1994), R42-43.
11. Verton, 66.
12. Hira, 197.
13. Goslinga, 80-81, 102-08, 139, 270-87, 293-301.
14. Spurdle; Wrong.
15. See Burn, *Emancipation and Apprenticeship*; Mathieson; Coupland, *British Anti-Slavery Movement*; Green.
16. Lowenthal, *West Indian Societies*, 63.
17. Craton, 'Continuity and Change', 201.
18. Lowenthal, *West Indian Societies*, 63.
19. Gowricharn, 288.
20. *Keesing's Record*, 40 (1994), R48.
21. Verton, 'Politics and Government in Curaçao', 67-68; Croes & Alam, 87-89; *The Europa World Year Book (1991)*, II, 1939, 1944, 2476; *South America, Central America and the Caribbean (1993)*, 450.

22. Achéen & Rifaux, 193.
23. Naipaul, *Middle Passage*, 165.
24. Naipaul, *Middle Passage*, 196.
25. In 1822, the Dominican Republic was invaded and incorporated into independent Haiti, and it was only in 1844, after several conflicts between the two, that it was able to free itself finally of Haitian rule. In 1861 one of its presidents, Pedro Santana, arranged for it to become a colony of Spain once again, but this act proved unpopular among the Dominican peoples. The Spanish government finally pulled out of the country in 1865 (Bell, 25-52).
26. The conflict between the Spanish and the Americans is sometimes referred to as The Spanish-American War.
27. Gautier-Mayoral, 163, 167.
28. *Keesing's Record*, 40 (1994), R58. For a recent discussion on the constitutional relationship between the USA and Puerto Rico see Silvestrini, 147-67.
29. *The Europa World Year Book (1991)*, II, 2978; *Keesing's Record*, 40 (1994), R59.
30. *South America, Central America and the Caribbean (1993)*, 406; *The Europa World Year Book (1991)*, I,1078-82.
31. *South America, Central America and the Caribbean (1993)*, 548; *The Europa World Year Book (1991), II*, 2957.
32. Croes & Alam, 87-89; Klomp, 104.
33. See Duncan, 'Political Violence', 72-74.
34. Fidel Castro referred to the multiparty system as 'imperialism's' great instrument to keep societies fragmented" (Cited by Bengelsdorf, 193-94).
35. The system of proportional representation is in operation in a few territories, for instance, in Guyana. It is also employed in the French colonies to elect representatives to the National Assembly in Paris, but not to local councils.
36. *Daily Nation* (Barbadian newspaper), Sept. 24, 1992:6.
37. Barry, 252.
38. Barry, 264.
39. Plamenatz, 66.
40. Plamenatz, 66.
41. The latest US involvement in Haiti will be discussed more fully in the following chapter.
42. Wiarda, 33.
43. Knight, *Genesis*, 258.
44. Wiarda, 208.
45. Stokes, *Violence*,173.
46. This view was expressed by Sumner Welles concerning the Dominican Republic (see *Naboth"s Vineyard*, 903).
47. 'Castro's Confident', 10A.
48. *Daily Nation*, Mar. 29, 1993:6.
49. For works on the Grenada revolution see Bishop, *In Nobody's Backyard*; Heine, *A Revolution Aborted*; Emmanuel, Brathwaite & Barriteau, *Political Change*. See Chapter 3 for a more detailed discussion of the US intervention in the country.
50. For further details on this aspect, see Miles,45-55.
51. For instance, the presidency was held by the socialists for 14 years, until 1995 when they were defeated by the conservatives under Jacques Chirac ('Chirac Wins French Polls',10A).
52. 'Caricom Response Vital',6.
53. *Keesing's Record*, 40 (1994), R48.
54. Gautier-Mayoral, 174.
55. *South America, Central America and the Caribbean (1993)*, 315; Gautier-Mayoral, 174. On French economic subsidies to the Antilles see Giraud, 235-36, 241).
56. Duncan, 'Tendency to Dependency?' 8A.
57. Cited by Achéen & Rifaux, 208.
58. Giraud, 235, 241, 242.

59. James, 'Birth of a Nation', 6.
60. Lowenthal, *West Indian Societies*, 10-11.
61. Girault, 187.
62. Clarke, 'Sovereignty',34.
63. For works on the federation and the federal idea see Lowenthal, ed., *West Indies Federation*; Wallace; Salmon. See also general bibliography.
64. James, 'Birth of a Nation', 10.
65. Lewis, *The Agony of the Eight*, 20.
66. Thomas, *Poor*, 367.
67. Singh, 'Key to Caricom Success Given', 15.
68. *Barbados Sunday Advocate* (newspaper), Feb. 1, 1992:11.
69. Cited in Singh, 'Contrasting Views on Regional Unity', 14.
70. 'Grenada Backtracks on Political Union', 10.
71. Gill.
72. Niles & Boyce, 'Trinidad Vies for ACS', 13; 'Forum for Consultation', 19B; 'Manley Hails Ramphal and ACS', 15A.
73. Plummer, *Haiti and the Great Powers*, 76.
74. James, 'Birth of a Nation', 10.
75. Wickham, 6A.

CHAPTER 3

The politics of violence

Colonialism denies human rights to human beings whom it has subdued by violence, and keeps them by force in a state of misery and ignorance.[1]

Jean-Paul Sartre

Although the Caribbean has a short history of democracy, it has a long one of political violence, an important characteristic of which is that much of it originated with the invading imperialist hordes who established themselves as the new lords of the region. As Stoecker observes, colonialism, based as it is on conquest and the forcible dispossession of the local inhabitants by foreign forces, 'inevitably engenders brutality and inhumanity toward the conquered'.[2]

Structural context of internal political violence

The culture of oppression, violence and injustice which marked the history of the region under colonialism was expressed through institutions, foremost among which were the colonial governments, which did not play *laissez-faire* roles in the economic and social life of the colonies. The politico-military apparatus of the state which should have been employed to protect the rights and freedoms of the people was turned instead largely against them. Colonial governments were generally more concerned with upholding and promoting the interests of a narrow oligarchy, which controlled economic and social power. The governments ensured that the inequalities existing in the society were embodied in the colonial laws and buttressed by written sanctions and military force. They, in tandem with the judiciaries (which sometimes comprised some of the same officials), ensured that there was nothing like impartial justice meted out to all persons, regardless of race, class, colour or gender. They also ensured, for a long time, that the poor were exploited by the rich, the slaves by their masters, the blacks and coloureds by the whites, and the women by the men.

Edmund Burke, the great British statesman of the late eighteenth century, understood that a just political order was one which helped to free people, not to oppress them.[3] This is why he fought against British tyranny in India. Others, such as Abbé Raynal and Hillard d'Auberteuil, recognised the iniquities of the system of government in the Caribbean, but no European champion of the oppressed went beyond attempting to get rid of the worst features of labour oppression.

Rodney outlines three main functions of the colonial government: first, to protect national interests against competition from foreign capitalists; second, to arbitrate in matters involving its own capitalists; and third, to guarantee the best conditions for the exploitation of the local inhabitants. This last function he considers to be the most crucial.[4] At least up to the end of the Second World War imperial governments considered it axiomatic that colonies existed for the benefit of the imperial power, or so-called mother country. The colonial governments were therefore expected to spare no effort to ensure that the imperial state benefited to the fullest from its association with the colonies, although in practice this did not always happen.

The minimum function of the colonial government was the preservation of law and order. Much of this was concerned with ensuring that the subordinate groups were kept in their place. The slightest infraction of the law often brought down disproportionately harsh sentences. Correspondingly, much lighter sentences were imposed upon members of the upper class for similar infractions, and sometimes they were allowed to go scot free. Thus crime and punishment often had more to do with the social standing of a person than with the inherent nature of the act itself.

The colonial government was also expected to employ its power to tax and to grant tax exemptions to make sure that the subordinate groups paid more than their fair share of taxes. Especially in the post-emancipation period, the system of indirect taxation (particularly on essential goods for the poor) placed an onerous burden on the lower classes, a situation which was aggravated because such colonial revenues were used to subsidise planter activities, the most notorious examples being state subsidies to immigration. Colonial governments used their authority and power to hinder the lower classes from pursuing certain economic activities (such as the cultivation of certain crops) which were regarded as threatening the economic well-being of the plantocracy.

The governments therefore played both a direct and an indirect (but no less coercive) role in oppressing the lower classes. Colonial governments were not interested in such matters as creating and maintaining equal economic, social and other opportunities for all groups within the colonial state, but rather in the promotion of the interests of a narrow, expatriate clique.

Although naked exploitation was the motive force behind colonialism, from time to time imperial governments sought to give the impression that they had the interests of the 'natives' equally at heart, and even on occasion that these interests were paramount. Such sentiments, for instance, were voiced by Queen Isabella in respect of the Amerindians; they were also voiced by the British in the nineteenth century concerning their Caribbean territories and India, and in the twentieth century in regard to Kenya. In spite of this, continued colonial oppression led to massive revolt in each instance.

The history of the region is chequered with frequent Amerindian revolts against the Spanish, and equally frequent revolts of oppressed people against the British in the Caribbean between 1865 and the 1930s. The large-scale Indian uprising (the 'Indian Mutiny') of 1857 and the Kikuyu (Mau-Mau) uprisings of the 1950s speak to the failure of European notions of paramountcy and trusteeship in relation to oppressed peoples. The Europeans (the British) felt betrayed: they were overwhelmed by the ingratitude and wickedness of the 'natives'. Bearce points out that in India, 'They were horrified that a people they believed were barbarous and backward could challenge or injure a civilised people.' Burns wrote that the Kikuyu were 'Mau Mau murderers', and that their actions constituted a 'reversion to barbarism', and a display of 'primitive and blind fury'.[3] It seems to be extremely difficult for oppressors to understand the reactions of the oppressed, especially when the former view themselves as the civilisers of the 'barbarians'.

In the Caribbean, the face of European oppression was witnessed most clearly in the systems of the *encomienda*, slavery and indentureship, which related mainly to the Amerindian, African and Asian populations respectively. Most Amerindians and Africans, and a significant number of Asians, were unwillingly and even violently removed from their homelands or places of residence and transferred to European plantations or mining enterprises. This happened also, although to a much lesser extent, to European indentured labourers brought to the region.

Violence against Amerindians

European violence against the Amerindians started outside the context of the *encomienda*, which was the institutional framework within which they were oppressed. It is interesting, and more than symbolic, that a fort was the first building which the Europeans sought to erect in the Americas (specifically, in Hispaniola). It signalled clearly the aggressive military and political intentions of the newcomers against their peaceful Amerindian hosts. The building of forts, or some kind of fortification, was usually one of the first activities which the Europeans undertook, once they had determined on establishing a permanent presence in a given territory. This was true of the Americas, as it was of Africa and Asia. Usually, too, it was not incipient hostility of the indigenous peoples to the newcomers that led the latter to adopt this course of action; rather it was the European desire to impose their authority on them, if necessary by violence. This was strikingly illustrated in the case of the Amerindians of Hispaniola, whom Columbus considered at the outset to be peaceful and friendly. The journal of Columbus, on December 26, 1492, includes the following passage:

> I have given orders for a tower and a fort, both well built, and a large cellar, not because I believe that such defences will be necessary. I believe that with the force I have with me I could subjugate the whole island . . . . Still, it is advisable to build this tower, being so far away from your Highnesses. The people may thus know the skill of the subjects of your Highnesses, and what they can do; and will obey them with love and fear.[6]

Within Hispaniola (or Santo Domingo) which the Spanish made their headquarters in the region, the drama soon unfolded with the complete routing of the Amerindians in 1495 in the battle of Vega Real. The Spanish used horses, which were a novelty to the Amerindians, to break their ranks and then let slip the dogs of war. These bloodhounds ripped many of the inhabitants apart, and the swordsmen completed the havoc begun by the dogs.[7] This was the first but not the last time that bloodhounds would be employed in attempts to subdue the colonial population. These animals were used extensively in the Spanish Caribbean, especially in Cuba, to ferret out maroons.[8] In the 1790s they were imported into Jamaica to assist in putting down a maroon uprising. They were also introduced by the French into Haiti in the last phase of the struggle for independence to assist in bringing that colony to heel.[9] It is said that they were trained specifically to attack black persons.

The frightening weapons from the newcomers' arsenal of destruction resulted in the complete rout of the Amerindians in Hispaniola. The Spanish then subjected them to tribute in the form of cotton and gold, took away large portions of their land, and eventually herded them into labour groups under the *encomienda* system, referred to by Las Casas as 'that gigantically tyrannical system'.[10] In some instances the Spanish 'gods' made fun with Amerindian lives, attempting to see who could cut off an Amerindian head with a single blow of the sword, which is reminiscent of some lines from Shakespeare (extrapolated from a different context):

> As flies to wanton boys are we to the gods, –
> They kill us for their sport.[11]

As the population in Hispaniola was ravaged the Spanish raided the neighbouring islands of the Bahamas and the mainland territories of South America for fresh workers, introducing these as slaves under very exacting conditions. What was writ large in Hispaniola also unfolded on a smaller scale in such places as Cuba, Jamaica and Puerto Rico as time went by. By the mid-sixteenth century the Amerindian population of the various territories, reckoned variously at between 500,000 and 2 million people at the time of the Spanish arrival, hardly numbered 50,000. The Spanish gradually moved their centre of empire to the mainland, to continue the exploitation of the land and the indigenous inhabitants more effectively.

Within the Southern Caribbean, or the Lesser Antilles, which had been neglected by the Spanish, the drama unfolded more slowly but no less inexorably, with the gradual wiping out of the local inhabitants in most of the territories by the French, English and Dutch. Amerindian resistance to the European invasion was often stout and determined, but they lacked an equivalent culture of violence and the degree of military sophistication of the Europeans to win in the long run. The last determined resistance was made by the black Caribs (a miscegenated African/Amerindian group) of St Vincent in the 1790s, but the British eventually overcame them and shipped the vanquished to the more remote settlement of Honduras.[12] With the eradication of the Amerindians the Europeans could now consider themselves the legitimate inheritors of their lands. As Mintz says, 'The European colonist had transformed himself into host, simply through having eliminated his native predecessors.'[13]

Violence against Africans

The slaughter of the Amerindians was but a preview of what awaited the Africans. An equally brutal treatment, and a more sustained one, was to be their lot. The mortality rate of the African slaves on the plantations was extremely high. There is still much debate concerning the average life-span of slaves on Caribbean plantations. Roberto Simenson estimated that the average period of servitude of Brazilian slaves was seven years. Goslinga put the period at eight years for those in Berbice in the eighteenth century. Helly estimated the period at ten years for those in Cuba around the mid-nineteenth century. Roberts states that the average life-span of slaves on Guyanese plantations in the early nineteenth century was less than 23 years.[14]

The extreme brutality of the slave system was underscored by the fact that, with the exceptions of Barbados and Curaçao,[15] slave populations did not reproduce themselves naturally in the Caribbean, that is, by an excess of births over deaths; this is remarkable because, except in the most extreme circumstances, human populations naturally reproduce themselves. In China, India, and Africa, in spite of diseases, famines, floods, cyclones and other natural disasters, the populations continue to increase. This was also the case in the early post-slavery period in the Caribbean, when the black population began to reproduce itself for the first time. Seen in this light, slavery was nothing less than a genocidal institution.

Slaves were overworked, underfed and badly clothed and housed. It was quite common for a slave to be listed as 'aged' or 'invalided' on the plantation records by the age of 50 years, although this did not necessarily exempt him or her from some sort of estate work. While the hostile disease environment exacted its toll on the bodies of the slaves, already mangled by lack of proper care, the situation was often exacerbated by a number of physical brutalities meted out to them by their masters or overlords.

Slaves were frequently whipped, and were given several hundred lashes with horse-whips or similar instruments. They were also hanged on meat hooks, burnt slowly at the stake, raped, placed in stocks, worked on tread mills, forced to wear iron collars with protruding spikes around their necks and branded; they had their Achilles tendons severed, arms amputated, teeth ripped out, flesh torn away with red-hot tongs, backs cut with saws, fresh fæces placed in their mouths, hot wax poured upon them, and so on.[16] Naipaul declares of Stedman's account of planters' atrocities towards their slaves in Suriname: 'Stedman's story is terrifying and in its nauseous catalogue of atrocities resembles accounts of German concentration camps during the last war . . . . The Suriname he describes is like one vast concentration camp, with the difference that visitors were welcome to look around and make notes and sketches.'[17]

The brutalities meted out to the slaves were all part of the politics of control of the slave community, for the colonial laws generally gave the masters considerable political and social control over the slaves. As R. van Lier says of Suriname in the eighteenth century, 'Because of the fact that the state granted planters full disciplinary authority over their slaves – the so-called domestic jurisdiction – the plantation assumed to some extent the character of a public institution. As a result planters became as it were agents of the state, wielding authority over a large subjugated labour mass.'[18] In 1770 the Director-General, Storm van's Gravesande, pointed out that the master in Demerara and Essequibo was virtually exempt from the jurisdiction of the court as long as the slave emerged from the stocks alive.[19]

The political system not only gave the masters considerable latitude over the slaves, but until the last days of slavery denied the latter access to the courts to seek redress for wrongs committed against them either by their master or by a third party. The master might sue in court on behalf of his slave, but only in the context of his proprietary rights over that individual. The Dutch and English laws did not generally recognise the slave as a person according to law (except when he/she committed an offence); the French and Spanish laws did so but in practice the politico-judicial system allowed the masters to treat their slaves as though they lacked human attributes.[20]

Slave unrest

Slaves naturally sought to free themselves from the harsh regime of slavery. Marronage and armed revolt were the favoured methods of doing so, though these were not always possible, especially in small, island communities. All the large territories contained significant maroon communities. The most well-known were those of Pinar del Río and Las Villas in Cuba, the Blue Mountains and the Cockpit Country in Jamaica, Le Maniel in St Domingue, and the Boni, Saramaka and Djuka in Suriname.[21] It is not convenient here to detail the various maroon wars, such as those in the cockpit country of Jamaica, the Pinar del Río swamplands of Cuba, and the hinterland of the Guianas. On many occasions European expeditions blundering their way through unfamiliar terrain were cut to pieces.

The whites saw maroon activities as the savage expression of a barbarian horde. This was certainly so of those maroons whom the Dutch referred to as 'bush negroes'. The association of the term 'bush' with these Africans was much more than a botanical expression. In the eyes of the planter class the forest in all its wild magnificence was reduced to the 'bush', which became associated with everything that was dark, sinister, even unholy. Bushmen, as in South Africa, were deemed to be wild men.

In the Caribbean the bush was contrasted with the plantation: the one primeval, the other cultivated; the one the work of nature in its uncultured state, the other the creation of civilised men. Those who chose to be denizens of the former were therefore perceived as opting out of civilisation and into barbarism. For the whites, therefore, the bush became the symbol, perhaps even the embodiment, of primitive evil and anarchy, in contrast to the plantation which they perceived as the symbol of order. But they also perceived the bush as the nemesis of the plantation, not only because of its tendency to creep up on the latter and even to engulf it when the land was neglected for long periods, but also because maroons issued forth periodically from the bush to harass the plantations. Thus the whites employed numerous pejorative terms to categorise the maroons or bush negroes: beasts, snakes, gangrene, vermin, pernicious scum, chronic plague, hydra, etc.[22] In contrast the blacks thought that maroon activities were the clearest political expression of the fact that they were men of like passion to the whites.

Maroons who were apprehended by expeditions sent to ferret them out usually received the worst treatment, for they had dared to defy the system and to set up communities of their own. They had tasted the sweet air of freedom and therefore could not be put with the rest of the slaves to contaminate them, at least not if they had been living in maroon communities for more than six months. Almost invariably the leaders of such communities were put to death after undergoing various forms of torture, while their followers might be worked in the colony's chain gang for life or transported to some remote part of the region, such as Honduras.

Some writers argue that slave unrest and uprisings in the Caribbean in the nineteenth century played an important role in hastening the demise of the slave system.[23] Events in the last years of slavery in such territories as Haiti, Barbados, Demerara, Jamaica, French Guiana, Martinique, Suriname, St Eustatius, St Maarten and Cuba would certainly give strong support to this viewpoint. There can be little doubt that slavery and the unrest which it engendered created almost permanent warfare in the region, punctuated by temporary and uncertain truces. Revolts underlined the fragility of the relations between the oppressors and the oppressed.

Oppressed groups did not confine their protests to the slavery period. They engaged in numerous small-scale protests and also many large-scale ones aimed at redressing political, economic and social grievances against the ruling classes. Space prevents us from dealing with these protests in detail. However, the frequent riots and revolts in Haiti during the nineteenth and twentieth centuries must be mentioned, notably the armed *piquets* and *cacos* in the north and south; the latter became deeply involved in politics, particularly during the period between 1907 and 1915. There were also a large number of peasant revolts in the late nineteenth and early twentieth centuries in Cuba, as well as internal revolts against the despotism of the ruling class up to the fall of the Batista regime in 1959. The Morant Bay uprising in Jamaica in 1865, the Martinique revolt of 1870, and the revolts in the British Caribbean in the 1930s should also be mentioned briefly.[24] Many of these protests involved not only blacks, but coloureds, whites and Indians.

Asians

By the time that Asian indentured servants were being brought into the region, around the mid-nineteenth century, the most draconian aspects of labour control had been eliminated due to the pressure of the imperial governments on the local elites to get rid of the most atrocious pieces of legislation. Still,

Asians and especially East Indians suffered greatly. Because the system of indentureship tied the Indians to specific plantations for a certain period of time, usually 5-10 years, they had little opportunity to escape from brutal masters. It was quite common for masters and their subordinate staff to overwork and underpay their indentured servants, molest their wives and whip them or have them incarcerated when they complained. According to Eric Williams, 'The Indian immigrants lived in the shadow of the jail.'[25] Again, the political directorate operated in concert with the plantation owners to ensure that the maximum amount of work was squeezed out of the Indians. It was only gradually after 1871, as a result of the report of a commission of inquiry into the treatment of Indians in Guyana, that the conditions of the Indian indentureds were ameliorated.

Like all other oppressed groups the Indians had no guaranteed access to the colonial legislatures or the colonial courts to seek redress for their wrongs, and much of the violence meted out to them went unpunished. Indians, like every other oppressed group in the society, protested by both non-violent and violent means. In both Guyana and Trinidad they rioted on several occasions, especially between 1870 and 1918,[26] against the particular conditions which they faced.

White violence against Whites

This is not to suggest that white violence was directed exclusively against other racial groups within colonial society. Sometimes that violence was directed inward against other whites, usually lower-class. This was notably the case during the days of white indentureship in the English and French islands, when lower-class whites, criminals, political prisoners and others were shipped out by fair and foul means to the Caribbean. Hilary Beckles has shown that in several instances in Barbados the treatment meted out to these whites was hardly different from that meted out to the black slaves, and that sometimes the two groups joined together to withstand their mutual oppressors.[27] However, the phenomenon of white indentureship in the region was of short duration, giving way by the end of the seventeenth century to a full-blown system of African slavery.

Everywhere in the Caribbean oppressed groups have resisted the oppression and institutionalised violence of the ruling elites periodically. This was seen in the upheavals of the free colonists throughout most of the region against tyrannical government by expatriate officials or their local representatives. The conflicts of interest, both local and expatriate, in St Domingue which saw uprisings in 1670, 1723, 1769 and 1789, have been analysed by Gordon Lewis.[28]

The situation in Cuba in the nineteenth century was even more explosive. The colonists fought hard and long to secure some measure of autonomy from the imperial government, which went through periodic bouts of liberalism and conservatism, giving the colonists slightly more liberal constitutions and revoking them shortly after. Especially from 1868, Cuban nationalists at home and abroad started a long struggle for independence, which culminated in 1898 in ousting the Spanish permanently, with US assistance. Nevertheless, Cuban independence was not assured, for (as we shall show in greater detail later) the USA sought to replace Spain as the arbiter of Cuban destiny.[29]

In the Dutch territories also, the free colonists were engaged in petty disputes with the expatriate officials continually throughout the eighteenth century. Only occasionally did this break out into open conflict, such as in Suriname in the 1740s and 1750s, and in Demerara in 1795. In the British colonies similar feuding between colonists and expatriate officials, and more occasionally between rich and poor whites, characterised the political and social landscape of the islands.

Externally-generated violence

Quite apart from the internal violence which wrought havoc in the Caribbean countries, there was the frequent incidence of external or imported violence. This had mainly to do with European warfare, often beginning in Europe itself and spilling over into the Caribbean. As Goslinga put it, the Caribbean became 'a scene of never-ending rivalry'.[30] This caused Williams to refer to it as the 'cockpit of Europe'.[31] From the sixteenth right up to the twentieth century the region was caught up in the vortex of European warfare and the struggle for empire, which resulted in destruction, dispossession and domination. By roughly the mid-sixteenth century so important was the region, and by extension the Spanish American mainland, as a theatre of warfare that there developed a tacit understanding among the various European contenders for power in the new world that even when there was peace in Europe the area beyond the prime meridian would be considered a zone of war. Hence the popular slogan, 'No peace beyond the line.'[32]

The sixteenth and early seventeenth centuries saw a spate of European activities aimed at despoiling Spain of the treasures which it had acquired in the new world, destroying its forts and other established positions there and weakening it overall, so that the other European powers could have what they considered to be their rightful places in the Caribbean sun. This was the period of the dare-devil activities of corsairs, privateers and sea-rovers, such as François Le Clerc and Sir Francis Drake, who attacked and sacked settlements, including Nombre de Dios, Cartagena and Panama. The wanton destruction was well-rewarded by their governments at home, as part of the national plan to defeat Spain.[33]

In the seventeenth century the periodic activities of men like John Hawkins and Francis Drake gave way to the more permanent and widespread activities of men who made isolated areas in the Caribbean their habitats. Tortuga and the more remote areas in Hispaniola and Jamaica were ideally situated dens of these sea-rovers, as the Dutch called them. Filibusterers, corsairs or buccaneers – different terms applied to them by Europeans – their occupation remained the same: brigandage. As in the earlier period, men such as Henry Morgan and Jean-Baptiste du Casse have been memorialised in the annals of English and French seafaring in the Caribbean.

In wartime in particular, they were given commissions by European governments to engage the enemy. In reality, they owed allegiance to no nation, but were a law unto themselves. They stole, killed and destroyed. Alexander Exquemelin, a buccaneer, freely admitted that they were a brutal, selfish and lawless breed. Most of their attacks were conducted against Spanish shipping and settlements, since these were the most lucrative prizes. Together with the activities of the regular navies of the European rivals of Spain, they helped to force the latter into acknowledging the right of other European countries to own colonies in the new world.

By the early seventeenth century corsairing and buccaneering were considered to be secondary naval or military activities as warfare became focused on engaging the enemy through regular ships of war and men trained specifically. This was the rationale behind the formation of the Dutch West India Company in 1621. It was a joint-stock company in which the state held the largest share and agreed to contribute a certain number of ships and men in the event of war with the enemy. The ships of the West India Company became the training ground for the Dutch navy and produced some admirals regarded by the Dutch as among the most brilliant officers in their naval history. Among these were Piet Heyn, Joost van de Trappen, Maarten Thijssen and Michiel Adriaanszoon de Ruyter.

By the late seventeenth century the activities of the buccaneers were fading into history and legend. Their acts were eventually proscribed and those who engaged in them were deemed pirates, subject to the death penalty if apprehended and convicted. Some of them drifted into more sedentary pursuits. Henry Morgan became governor of Jamaica and received a knighthood as the capstone for his contribution to the enhancement of English imperial interests.[34]

The eighteenth century was marked by the struggle to achieve supremacy in the Caribbean. Part of the strategy was to acquire enemy colonies if possible and to destroy them when acquisition was difficult or impossible. Thus the wars of this century were extremely destructive, as more and better-equipped naval vessels were dispatched to the Caribbean front. Many colonies were sacked, some of them several times. Colonies changed hands fairly frequently during periods of warfare,[35] being either retained by the victorious power after the war or exchanged for territorial or trading concessions elsewhere.[36]

At the height of the conflict in the eighteenth century St Lucia changed hands seven times within about half a century. In the late eighteenth century the Dutch Guiana territories were also shuttled from one imperial power to another. For instance, between 1780 and 1803 the colonies of Essequibo/ Demerara and Berbice experienced this cycle of control: Dutch-British-French-Dutch-British-Dutch-British. St Eustatius went through a similar cycle between 1780 and 1816: Dutch-British-French-Dutch-French-British-Dutch. This imperial shuttle upset the balance of life in the colonies and reflected the political, economic and social uncertainties which generally afflicted the colonies in the struggle for precedence among the imperial powers. The inhabitants were never consulted when decisions were made at the conference tables to cede them to alien powers, whether in wartime or peacetime. Their fate was determined at the whim and caprice of the colonisers.

The destruction to property, equipment and slaves resulting from European warfare in the eighteenth century was massive. It is said that in 1781, during the War of American Independence (1776-83), the British looted and damaged St Eustatius, from which it never recovered. One observer described it in 1775 as 'a place of vast traffic from every quarter of the globe'.[37] Up to two years before it was sacked, it could boast of being the chief emporium in the region, with an estimated 3,500 ships doing business there.[38] The major wars of this century span quite a number of years: the War of the Spanish Succession (1702-13), the War of Jenkins' Ear(1739-48), phasing into the War of the Austrian Succession (1744-48), the Seven Years' War (1756-63), the War of American Independence (1776-83) and the French revolutionary and Napoleonic wars (1793-1802 and 1803-15). A century of little warfare followed, apart from Spanish conflicts with the nationalists in Cuba, but it was resumed, of course, during the First and Second World Wars. In the latter the British agreed to a 99-year lease of land to the USA to set up air bases in Guyana, Trinidad, St Lucia, Jamaica, Antigua, Bermuda and the Bahamas.[39]

US imperialism

The US presence in the region has been accompanied by growing involvement in the day-to-day life of the countries and use of covert and overt forces to promote its interests. Activities began on a peaceful note, when the various American colonies in the seventeenth and eighteenth centuries traded with both British and foreign colonies in a wide range of commodities. The first major US politico-military involvement took place during their war of independence. When the USA achieved independence and began to grow rapidly as an economic, naval and military power, it began to flex its muscles. It first asserted, by force of arms against the British in 1812-14, its right to carry on trade as a neutral (non-combatant) power during the Napoleonic wars with the enemies of Britain. Shortly afterwards, it promulgated the Monroe Doctrine (1823), upholding the right of the Spanish American colonies to revolt for their independence and asserting that any attempt on the part of any power to bring them back under the bondage of colonialism would be regarded as an unfriendly act towards the United States.

Curiously enough, while posing as the champion of the oppressed at this time, the USA refused to give political and diplomatic recognition to newly independent Haiti, in contrast to its strident attitude over the independence of the Latin American countries. Haiti showed solidarity with the aims and objectives of the Latin American countries that were seeking to cast off the imperial yoke. It gave asylum to Francisco Miranda in 1805 and Simón Bolívar in 1815 and 1816. Both of these revolutionaries received material assistance from Haiti in men, money and munitions. In spite of this, for several years the country remained friendless among the new Latin American republics, which were unwilling to incur the wrath of the USA by befriending it. Thus an invitation extended to Haiti by Panama to attend the Panama Congress (the first inter-American one) in 1826 was withdrawn under pressure from the USA. In 1822 the Haitian government made a written request to the US government to have the country recognised by the USA as an independent nation, but was rebuffed.

France gave a qualified recognition of the independence of Haiti in 1825 and outright recognition in 1838, and the UK gave partial recognition in the following year, but the USA did not recognise it until 1862.[40] For some years, therefore, Haiti lay outside the scope of the Monroe Doctrine. True, an increasing but still rather limited trade was carried on between the two countries during this period of diplomatic hiatus. Clearly, it was not the French failure until 1825 to recognise the independence of its former colony, nor the threat to use force to bring it back into the imperial fold, that accounted for the US attitude towards Haiti. The answer seems to lie in US racist attitudes towards the newly emergent black republic.

In spite of these double standards, the USA continued to pose as the champion of the oppressed. It gave shelter to a number of Cuban nationalists operating from there in the nineteenth century. Gradually, however, it became clear that the USA was casting avid eyes on the Cuban prize, and indeed by the mid-nineteenth century some Southerners were arguing that the US territorial engrossment of Cuba was part of its manifest destiny.[41] By 1898, therefore, when the USA entered the independence struggle on the side of the Cubans, it was fairly clear although it was disavowed at the time, that its intention was to make Cuba either its colony or its political satellite. This latter objective was revealed in 1902 when the USA forced the Cubans to insert the Platt Amendment into their constitution, giving the Americans 'the right to intervene' in Cuban life 'for the preservation of Cuban independence.'[42] The amendment also gave the USA the right to lease coaling stations, such as Guantánamo Bay, which they later acquired. These provisions and the other clauses of the amendment constituted a humiliating derogation of the sovereignty of the Cuban people over their own country. By that time, US capital investment in the island constituted the largest single source of foreign investment, estimated in 1895 by Richard Olney, US Secretary of State, at $50 million.[43] US investment was to grow by leaps and bounds in the next 20 years.

Around this time in 1898, the USA acquired Puerto Rico as a colony from Spain, thus aborting its efforts to become independent. Nationalist attempts in the next few decades to eliminate or modify US rule in the island were met with the heavy hand of the new imperialists. As in other parts of the region, the Americans moved quickly after their occupation to set up military bases in the neighbouring islands of Vieques and Culebra.[44]

This scenario was part of a wider one in which the USA was seeking to become the premier foreign power in the region. In fact, the USA came increasingly to view the Caribbean Sea as an American lake or basin, and the various territories as lying on her soft underbelly. Admiral Alfred Mahan (renowned for his monumental work on naval history) said that the Caribbean should become an American Mediterranean. After the opening of the Panama Canal in 1914, the USA began to feel that the entire Caribbean region was of 'fundamental strategic importance to it'.[45] The USA was bent not only upon promoting its strategic and economic interests in the region, but upon doing so by force if necessary. The words of President Theodore Roosevelt in 1904 that the USA reserved the right to 'exercise . . . an international police power' in Caribbean and Latin American territories to prevent 'chronic wrong doing'[46] amply expressed the USA's philosophical and interventionist stance. It is in this context, therefore, that we must view the several interventions of the USA in Cuba in the present century, including the overt ones in 1906-08, 1912 and 1916, and the more covert ones in 1921, 1933 and 1961 (the 'Bay of Pigs' expedition) to secure governments acceptable to it.

Three of the most recent acts of hostility against Cuba – the first covert and the two others overt – may be mentioned here briefly. The first was the invasion of the island in 1991 by a small group of guerrillas operating from their base in the USA. They were allegedly part of a larger group calling itself 'Commando L' and dedicated to the overthrow of the Castro regime. Three of the invaders were apprehended, tried and convicted by the Cuban court as terrorists. In spite of appeals for clemency from private and public institutions in Europe, their leader, Eduardo Díaz Betancourt, was executed. As a result there was a hue and cry from Castro's enemies in the USA and the European Union cancelled a technical mission which it was about to send to Cuba.[47]

The second and third acts of hostility by the USA, were the so-called Cuban Democracy Act (or the Torricelli Act), and the Cuban Liberty and Democratic Solidarity Act (the Helms-Burton Act) which became law in 1992 and 1996 respectively. The Torricelli law prohibits US subsidiary companies abroad from conducting business with Cuba and bars ships trading with Cuba from entering US ports for six months.

The Helms-Burton Act, among other features, seeks to deny aid to countries dealing with Cuba, requires foreign companies to declare any property they possess in Cuba that had been confiscated from its American owners by the Castro government, allows Americans to sue such companies in US courts for compensation for such property, prohibits companies trading with Cuba carrying on economic relations with the USA, bars entry to persons dealing in US confiscated property, and provides a policy framework for the US government to assist an elected Cuban government. It was signed by the US president, Bill Clinton, in March 1996, and is to come into effect on August 1, 1996. The president's reluctance to sign it gave way after the downing of two small civilian planes in February by the Cuban authorities. The latter alleged that the planes were flown by 'Brothers to the Rescue,' a Cuban-American organisation believed to have links with the US Central Intelligence Agency, and had been violating Cuban airspace and had refused to quit the area when asked by the Cuban authorities to do so.

The Helms-Burton law has been condemned by many major economic and political groups of states, such as the UN General Assembly, the Organization of American States, the European Union, Mexico and Canada (the two partners of the USA in NAFTA) and CARICOM. It is clearly a breach of international law, because it seeks to extend US domestic law beyond its own boundaries. It seeks to tell another country with whom it can trade and the conditions under which it can do so. As the European Union has stated, it is a serious violation of the principles of the GATT and the World Trade Organization.[48]

In the case of the Dominican Republic, the USA intervened covertly in 1905 and more openly in 1916, remaining in control until 1924; another intervention followed in 1965. US influence has been deeply felt in its politics throughout the present century. Howard Wiarda, whose sympathies clearly lay with the USA, said in 1969: 'Although the word 'satellite' has emotional connotations which may properly be avoided, US involvement in the Dominican Republic in recent years has been so extensive that the question may be raised of just how extensive Dominican sovereignty over its own affairs is.'[49] The situation remains the same up to the present; but it is not only the US government but also numerous US transnational corporations that influence the politics of the country also.

Haiti became the victim of armed US aggression in the present century, preceded by about 50 years of political and diplomatic intrigue. In the latter part of the nineteenth century the USA thought more than once of annexing the country (along with the Dominican Republic), especially to acquire the excellent harbour of Môle St Nicolas. Between 1857 and 1900 the US navy intervened around 20 times on behalf of US business interests in the country.[50] The Americans finally invaded the country in 1915 and remained there until 1934. The excuses given were the standard ones, such as the breakdown of law and order and the threat to American lives and property.[51] But the major reason for their invasion was to further their own economic and political interests.

In a specious attempt to legitimise the invasion and its control over the Haitian administration, the USA in 1917 tried to get the incumbent Haitian legislature to promulgate a new, US-drafted constitution. This the legislature refused to do and so it was banished to the political wilderness for 12 years. Meanwhile, a plebiscite, comprising less then 5 per cent of the electorate, 'approved' the new constitution.[52] The USA also restored the hated *corvée* (forced labour) for public works during its period of occupation and there was a period of US-inspired racism in hotels, restaurants and public places. Senior Haitian officials were among those treated as second-class citizens in the land of their birth.

Many nationalists in Haiti and the Dominican Republic viewed the invasion of their countries as a form of recolonisation and some of them put up stout resistance, resulting in considerable spilling of blood and loss of life as the invaders sought to impose their will on a reluctant populace. The Americans referred to the Dominican guerrillas as 'bandits', refusing to confer on them the more dignified and accurate title of freedom fighters. The resistance in Haiti was led by Charlemagne Peralte, at the head of his *caco* guerrillas. The Americans, however, employing coordinated ground and air assaults, put down the resistance with frightening brutality. Bellegarde-Smith estimates that as many as 50,000 Haitians were killed during the US operations.[53]

The most recent US intervention in Haiti was in 1994 to restore to power the president, Jean-Bertrand Aristide, who had been ousted by a military coup in 1991. On this occasion the USA was more cautious about intervening, because some US politicians feared that their country might become embroiled in a domestic conflict which would force members of the military to remain in Haiti for an indefinite period and were convinced that the best solution was to let the Haitians solve the problem by themselves. Rumour also surfaced in the USA that Aristide himself had a bent towards authoritarianism, was not politically astute, and might even be mentally and emotionally unstable.

At the same time, the US government was faced with the pressing problem of the thousands of Haitian boat-people, who were leaving their country in unseaworthy vessels in desperate efforts to escape the political and economic crisis which had swept over the country. Many of these lost their lives in their attempts to reach the American shore, while others were picked up at sea and held in makeshift camps in Florida, Guantánamo and elsewhere. The US government failed to accord them the status granted to Cuban refugees, and was harshly criticised for this blatantly discriminatory policy, which was perceived as being motivated not simply by political but also by racist ideology. Aristide's involuntary exile in the USA itself did not help matters, still less so when he began urging the US government to restore him to power. In the end, the USA agreed to do so, on the understanding that he would not seek a new term of office once his first term had run its course.

The USA's decision to intervene militarily was endorsed by the UN Security Council and CARICOM. As it turned out, the threat of force was enough to get the illegal regime out of power and into exile, through a negotiated arrangement with the USA. Many Haitian patriots, especially those who had suffered at the hands of the military regime, resented this and denounced the USA for negotiating rather than putting the perpetrators on trial. Thus there were mixed feelings about the US presence in Haiti, on the restoration of Aristide to power in late 1994.

The US played power-broker, not only in ousting the military regime, but also in restructuring the Haitian army, constabulary and even the civilian government. Aristide found that many of the US policies and actions conflicted with his own, causing ill-will. The situation was exacerbated by Emmanuel Constant's confession in December 1995 that he had been a paid agent of the US Central Intelligence Agency between 1991 and 1994. Constant had been head of the extreme right wing of the Front for the Advancement and Progress of Haiti (FRAPH), a paramilitary organisation known to have tortured and murdered thousands of Aristide's supporters during his exile.[54] An uneasy relationship existed between the US military in Haiti and the newly restored government. The situation has been relieved somewhat by the USA's decision to turn over the responsibility of peace-keeping to the UN and the election of René Préval as Aristide's replacement.

In the southern Caribbean, the USA were overtly involved in its politics in 1983 when it intervened in Grenada militarily, to put an end to Bernard Coard's regime, which had executed Maurice Bishop and his chief supporters. It was alleged that Coard's group, which had emerged from a split in the command structure of the Bishop government, represented the more extreme communist elements in the country and that Coard was their ideological leader.

The important point is that the rupture and executions gave the US government the opportunity to intervene and put down the leftist regime, which they had clearly wanted to do for some time. However, it must be noted that the USA obtained the support of the governor-general of Grenada, Tom Adams, the prime minister of Barbados, and some other Caribbean political leaders. But the intervention was also remarkable for the fact that it was the first time that the USA intervened militarily in a former British colony (part of what is known as the Commonwealth Caribbean), an area which the British still regard as part of their sphere of influence. The intervention also served to divide CARICOM, since some of the leaders condemned it, others condoned it, and still others supported it. To many Caribbeans it justified their fears that the USA will flex its muscles in any part of the region when it perceives a threat to its ideological interests.

US military involvement in the region from the late nineteenth century can better be appreciated by emphasising that what was happening in the Caribbean was part of a much wider activity, in which the USA was striving to gain control of territories in Central America and the Pacific, in order to enhance it's global economic and strategic interests. Thus at the end of the last century the US achieved territorial control over such Pacific territories as the Hawaiian islands, the Philippines and Guam. In the early twentieth century the USA assisted Panama to break away from Colombia, following which it secured permission from the newly created republic to cut the Panama Canal and govern Panama virtually as it's own territory. A 17-km corridor along the canal was ceded to it 'in perpetuity', excluding the government of Panama. The USA also became militarily involved in the politics of Nicaragua, El Salvador, Costa Rica and other Latin American countries. Since the Second World War the USA has been unquestionably the major foreign power in Latin American and Caribbean affairs. The so-called independence of the Caribbean territories has simply given the USA greater latitude for its covert and overt operations, destabilising and subverting governments it deems inimical to its interests.

An excuse commonly employed by the US government for military invasion of third-world countries is the threat they pose to their more peaceful neighbours and, in the case of the Caribbean, to hemispheric security. These were two of the reasons they gave for their invasion of Grenada in 1983 (under the guise of an invitation from the island's governor-general). Grenada was declared to be the launching pad for covert Communist military activities in Latin America and the Caribbean (similar charges were laid against Cuba and Nicaragua). The USA alleged that these countries possessed armies and weapons which were both too numerous and too sophisticated for their defensive needs. In spite of this, the USA was able to invade and defeat the Grenadian national army with ease, thus proving how vulnerable Grenada was to alien invasion, even with its allegedly sophisticated weaponry.

Even if it were true that in some places before to the US intervention the countries' political oligarchies were suppressing the rights and freedoms of the mass of the people, this could hardly justify the USA's unilateral decision to intervene. Plamenatz makes the point: 'The lover of freedom, however strong his love, will seldom allow that free countries can rightfully intervene in the affairs of countries that are not free in order to compel them to freedom.'[55] The wisdom of this observation is seen in the failure of US intervention so far to ensure democratic freedoms to the citizens of Haiti, the Dominican Republic and Cuba.

The fact is that the so-called 'great democracy' has attempted on several occasions to further the cause of democracy in the Caribbean, Latin America and elsewhere by undemocratic means. The effect of its actions has been to strengthen the region's autocratic and despotic traditions. Instead of fostering the rule of law, as the Americans claimed, they fostered the rule of government by naked force, for example, in the forcible insistence that Cuba include the Platt amendment in its constitution, and their unpopular and undemocratic rule in the Dominican Republic, Haiti and Nicaragua (mainland). Even in Puerto Rico and the Danish Virgin Islands (later US Virgin Islands), where they acquired *de jure* control, they did so by purchasing them from their former colonial masters without consulting the local inhabitants. It was not surprising, therefore, that the Puerto Ricans viewed the US actions as a stab in the back. For several decades, like the inhabitants of those territories that the USA invaded and occupied, they viewed US rule as a foreign dictatorship. The situation was exacerbated by the fact that the US military and/or marine governed the Dominican Republic, Haiti and the Virgin Islands until 1931.

Ironically, local paramilitary forces trained by the USA during the time of their occupation of the Dominican Republic and Haiti, learning from the example of US rule, placed and/or maintained dictators in power, such as Trujillo, the ruler of the Dominican Republic from 1930 to 1961 and one of the worst dictators that the region has known. Similar paramilitaries intervened in the making and unmaking of the dictators in Haiti between 1946 and 1957 (Dumarsais Estimé, Paul Magloire and Daniel Fignolé), before Duvalier acceded to power in 1957.

The USA supported dictators in Caribbean and Latin American countries when it was in its best interest to do so. In Cuba, for example, it supported the dictatorships of Mario Garcia Manacal, Gerardo Machado and Fulgencio Batista. In the Dominican Republic it supported the Trujillo regime until its last days. It intervened to stop the supporters of Juan Bosch from regaining power from the military regime that had usurped it, convinced that his return would lead to a Communist regime.[56] Elsewhere in Latin America, as in Chile, it supported the regime of the dictator Augusto Pinochet Ugarte who had forcibly ousted and killed the democratically elected socialist leader Salvador Allende. All these regimes which the USA supported were notorious for their human rights abuses, including the torture and assassination of political opponents. The USA also used its power and influence in the region to breach local laws and constitutions in order to purchase large tracts of landed property in such places as Puerto Rico and Haiti, to secure Guantánamo Bay as a coaling station in Cuba and to get sovereignty over the Panama Canal area.

It is clear that the various phases of the USA's policy in the Caribbean and Latin America – the Monroe Doctrine of James Monroe, the 'big stick' policy of Theodore Roosevelt, the 'dollar diplomacy' of William Taft, the 'good neighbour' policy of Franklin D. Roosevelt, the 'Alliance for Progress' of John F. Kennedy, the 'Caribbean Basin Initiative' of Ronald Reagan, the 'Enterprise for the Americas Initiative' of George Bush and the 'Partnership for Prosperity' of Bill Clinton – were aspects of the process of US domination of the region. The USA uses aid and special concessions to Caribbean and Latin American countries as forms of political leverage, to foist itself on the recipients of the benefits.[57] This can be seen in its policy of exclusion of Cuba (and for some time Grenada) from certain regional fora, for instance the Conference of the Americas in Miami in 1994. The USA also uses aid and trade policies to influence the votes of the recipient countries in international fora such as the UN.

Today, since the collapse of the Soviet Union, America bestrides the world like a colossus. This narrows the scope for independent political action by the Caribbean territories – or at least action which the Americans consider to be against their national interests. The ultimate objective of the USA is to eliminate all European political control and influence in the region, leaving it as the sole power-broker. Viewed in these terms, US willingness to see the achievement of independence by the territories still under some form of European control must be seen as more than an anti-imperialist stance. Rather it must be regarded as an essential stage in US hegemonic control over the entire region. More disturbing still is the view put forward by Gorostiaga: 'The underlying assumption of US policy towards the region appears to be that its own geopolitical interests are incompatible with the emergence of genuinely independent nation states.'[58] There is indeed cause to wonder whether the independence of the Caribbean territories is more chimerical than real.

Meaning of violence for Caribbean development

Throughout its history the Caribbean has been the scene of external and internal violence. Other countries and societies have experienced violence, and no country has been fortunate enough to escape it. However, the Caribbean, with its short recorded history, has had much more than its fair share. Violence became almost endemic, especially between the sixteenth and the nineteenth centuries. But it is not simply the scale of that violence that is significant; more noteworthy is the socio-political context in which much of it has been perpetrated. Violence has been used to wipe out whole populations (Amerindians) deemed inferior to the Europeans, and to suppress millions of others (Africans) on the basis of their supposed racial and human inferiority. Various territories of the region and sometimes even sections of an island that were in peaceful dialogue with each other were caught up in the maelstrom of violent confrontations because their rival imperial powers were at war with each other.

European warfare spilled over into the region as part of the larger struggle for empire, and the inhabitants often understood little and cared less about its causes. The region was engulfed in warfare in the eighteenth century over such issues as the succession to the Spanish and the Austrian thrones. However, the worst case of Caribbean involvement in matters that were of little importance to them directly were the First and Second World Wars. Many Caribbean nationals gave their lives not for the global freedom of humanity, as many supposed, but for European continental and imperial causes.

Those who contest this statement should note the clarification which Sir Winston Churchill, the British prime minister, gave to the significance of the Atlantic Charter, which he signed with the US president, Franklin D. Roosevelt, on August 16, 1941. Churchill made it clear that the clause in the charter which affirmed 'the right of all peoples to choose the form of government under which they will live' and which expressed the wish 'to see sovereign rights and self-government restored to those who have been forcibly deprived of them',[59] was not applicable to the colonies. He declared that he had not become prime minister of Britain 'to preside over the liquidation of the British Empire;' the clause was intended to refer to those eastern European countries which had recently been deprived of their sovereignty.[60]

Similarly, Charles de Gaulle, head of the Free French government in exile in Britain, while receiving his greatest overseas support from the African countries, did not promise anything substantial by way of independence or even self-government when he met leaders (none of whom was born in Africa, and only one of whom was black) at the Brazzaville Conference in the French Congo in 1944. Under his direction the conference agreed that it was 'impossible to entertain any ideas of autonomy, any possibility of evolution outside the French empire; an ultimate self-governing constitution for the colonies, even at a distant date, is to be rejected.'[61] After the war he showed that he was no more prepared than Churchill to offer the colonies any great freedoms as a result of the sacrifices which they had made for the war effort. The 1946 French constitution, which included sections relating to the colonies, was a minor step forward on the route to political freedom.[62] Caribbean and other third-world peoples were (or were at least perceived by the main leaders of France and Britain to be) fighting for the freedom of European peoples rather than their own.

Violence in the region has led to much economic wastage. Historically, trade and war in those parts of the world where the European powers were contending for supremacy were seen as a hand-in-glove activity. This, however, only made sense when the victorious power gobbled up (or sought to gobble up) the lion's share of the trade. For the Caribbean, however, it meant considerable destruction of its economic assets. The region is no doubt much the poorer as a result.

Violence has also resulted in political, economic and social discontinuities. The changing of colonies from the control of one European power to another, sometimes frequently, as a result of the exigencies of war, led to sudden breaks in political rule and the disruption of political processes. Sometimes it led to the superimposition of new European political, economic and judicial systems over the existing ones. This happened in Guyana where the British colonial institutions replaced the Dutch ones in a rather cumbersome way. The same happened when British rule was superimposed on Spanish rule in Trinidad and French rule in St Lucia. It was equally true of US rule which displaced Spanish rule in Puerto Rico and Danish rule in the Virgin Islands.

These territories underwent painful adjustments to the rule of peoples of an alien language, culture and political and historical traditions. Economic relationships with the former imperial power often had to be unscrambled, new currencies introduced, and new land and commercial laws promulgated, usually in the interest of the new colonisers. Many inhabitants who had become rich under the old regime lost their wealth and social positions under the new; and often a new landed and mercantile elite emerged from among the new imperialists. For the poor, of course, it simply meant one exploiter replacing another. In some places, such as in Puerto Rico, it also meant a more rigorous regime of labour exploitation.

One of the dangers of large-scale and persistent violence is the psychological effect that it has on people, who came to view violence as the normal solution to their problems. Thus incidents of parental brutality towards children in the early and even later post-emancipation periods may be explained, at least in part, by the influence of the slavery period.[63] There can be little doubt that the tradition of government in the interest of a narrow clique and of the institutionalisation of political and social violence, particularly against the poor, is causing an increasing number of the urban and rural proletariat and their allied intelligentsia to resort to another tradition: physically violent confrontations to express their discontent with the political directorate.

Those who adopt a violent response are labelled as anarchists of one kind or another. As Duncan observes: 'In this perspective, people become 'criminals', 'preachers of violence', 'outcasts', 'terrorists', 'mad people', 'drug addicts and pushers', 'wildcat strikers', 'guerrillas', and 'rebels'. They are so categorized in order to be dealt with using exceptional measures.'[64]

Such measures usually involve overt violence, one result of which is the increasing militarisation of the region for internal as much as for external security. But as Duncan again points out, 'A predominantly law-and-order response may only settle for a while but not resolve the underlying causes of conflict that lead to violence.'[65] In the early nineteenth century the Haitian, Baron De vastey (son of a French father and a Haitian mother), justified the appeal to arms by Haitians to achieve their independence on nationalist grounds and also on the extreme brutality of the French regime.[66]

Since the 1848 publication of the *Communist Manifesto*, classical Marxists have adopted the view that the capitalist, bourgeois regimes will not relinquish power willingly and will therefore have to be overthrown by force. However, modern Marxists point out that the violence of the oppressed proletariat would be essentially re-active rather than pro-active violence, that is, that the proletariat would react to institutional and other forms of violence, rather than initiate it.

Such violence is seen as part of a struggle to achieve basic freedoms and human rights, and is contrasted with the violence of the oppressors and exploiters. Fanon argued that violence often becomes necessary to remove undemocratic and unpopular regimes,[67] and Walter Rodney, somewhat influenced by Fanon, came to the same conclusion.[68] Further afield, but deeply influencing the thinking of Caribbean radicals, was the experience of the African National Congress (ANC) of South Africa. After 49 years of officially pursuing a non-violent policy towards the white racist regime, the leaders decided in 1961 that they had to resort to violence to achieve their objectives. That policy of armed dialogue, in addition to international pressures, played a major role in dismantling the racist regime.

Not all advocates of radical change view violence as a solution to the problem of entrenched undemocratic regimes. The tactic of civil disobedience, as practised by Mahatma Gandhi in India and Martin Luther King, Jr in the USA, has its adherents, but the strength of its appeal remains a matter of speculation.

A further effect of violence has been the waste and cheapening of human life. Goslinga's statement that the inhabitants of Suriname in the eighteenth century were 'surrounded by death all the time',[69] is true of many other societies for a much longer period. In the nineteenth century the Cuban ex-slave, Juan Francisco Manzano, wrote in a parody of the white plantocracy in Cuba that 'life is cheap'.[70] That view of the cheapness of life, especially if it is not white, has not passed away with the passing of time. Still today we are brainwashed into accepting the death of Native Americans and Native Australians in clashes with white Americans or Australians with little concern. However, when a white person dies at the hands of one of the indigenous peoples we feel a sense of loss, because our sensibilities have been cultured that way. The reaction is instinctive, even when our rational faculties would dictate otherwise. The fact is that some of us see the deaths of Native Americans, Native Australians, Vietnamese, Indians, Africans and Iraqis on any scale simply as statistics, and not even vital statistics. But when white Europeans, Americans or Australians die we count them in human terms. Shakespeare wrote in *Julius Caesar*:

> When beggars die there are no comets seen;
> The heavens themselves blaze forth the death of princes.[71]

In the Caribbean many beggars have died, and many will continue to die if we do not do something about it. We have to change the image of the beggar to that of the prince, where the life of each human being will have some meaning and death will be seen as a tragic loss. The words of the poet John Donne seem particularly apt: 'No man is an Iland, entire of it selfe; every man is a peice of the Continent, a part of the maine . . . any mans death diminishes me because I am involved in Mankinde; And therefore never send to know for whom the bell tolls; It tolls for thee.'[72]

Notes

1. Introduction to Memmi, xxiv.
2. Stoecker, 125.
3. Bearce, 19.
4. Rodney, *Europe*, 179.
5. Bearce, 233-35; Burns, *Defence of Colonies*, 34, 37-38, 51.
6. Cited in Williams, *Documents*, I, 50.

7. Williams, *Documents*, I, 88-89.
8. See Philalethes, 60-63.
9. Beard, 265; Lowenthal, *West Indian Societies*, 53; Williams, *Documents*, I, 88-89; Price, *Maroon Societies*, 60-63; Campbell, *Maroons of Jamaica*, 2, 216, 229-30. See 229 of the last-mentioned work for examples of the ferocity of the Cuban bloodhounds dispatched to Jamaica in 1795.
10. Cited in Williams, *Documents*, I, 97.
11. *King Lear*, Act IV, Sc.I.
12. See Gullick.
13. Mintz, 'The Caribbean as a Socio-Cultural Area', 23.
14. Bastide,34; Goslinga, 463; Helly, 89; Roberts, 238-43. Herbert Klein criticises the widely-held view in nineteenth-century literature on Latin America that the average working life of an African slave 'entering adulthood' was only seven years. Nevertheless, in the same paragraph he gives the average life-span of 'native-born Latin American slaves' as 'the low 20s'. Assuming that their period of adulthood began at 15 years, this would make their average adult working life roughly seven years. Klein evidently believed that locally born slaves had a higher life expectancy than African-born ones (see Klein, 159). For a detailed analysis of slave mortality in the British Caribbean in the nineteenth century, see Higman, *Slave Populations*, 314-48.
15. Beckles, *Natural Rebels*, 20; Hoetink, 'Suriname and Curaçao', 67.
16. See Thompson, *Colonialism*, 116-18; Hall, *In Miserable Slavery*, 46, 60, 72-73.
17. Naipaul, *Middle Passage*, 184.
18. Van Lier, 23.
19. Harris & de Villiers, II, 638.
20. For discussion of Caribbean slave laws see Goveia; Hall, *Social Control*; Hall, 'Slave Laws', 174-86; Knight, *Slave Society in Cuba*; Debien, *Les Esclaves*.
21. The most wide-ranging work on maroon communities is *Maroon Societies*, edited by Richard Price. It contains specific chapters on Suriname, French Guiana, Jamaica, Cuba, St Domingue, Mexico, Brazil, Colombia and the USA, besides general chapters on maroon communities. For other works on the subject see Bastide; Campbell, *Maroons of Jamaica*; Fouchard; De Groot, *Djuka Society*; Debien, 'Le Marronage', 3-44; De Groot, 'The Boni Maroon War', 30-48; Kopytoff, 'The Maroons of Jamaica'.
22. Price, *To Slay the Hydra*.
23. See, for instance, Hart, *Slaves Who Abolished Slavery*; Craton, *Testing the Chains*, 241-321; Hall, *Slave Society*, 213-27; Beckles, *Black Rebellion*, 86-87.
24. For more detailed information on revolts and protests in the post-emancipation period see Paquin; Nicholls, *Dessalines to Duvalier*; Pérez, *Lords of the Mountain*; Heuman; Boland, *On the March*.
25. Williams, *History Trinidad and Tobago*, 107.
26. See Haraksingh, 'Control and Resistance', 61-77; Ramnarine, 'East Indian Disturbances', 119-141; Singh.
27. Beckles, *White Servitude*, 98-114; see also Watts, 201.
28. Lewis, *Main Currents*, 248; see also Frostin.
29. For works on the Cuban political situation in the nineteenth century see Thomas, *Cuba*; Foner, *History of Cuba*; Pérez, *Cuba Between Empires*.
30. Goslinga, 96.
31. Williams, *Columbus to Castro*, 69.
32. According to the Bridenbaughs, the term 'beyond the line' meant "the boundless area west of the longitude of the outmost of the Azores and south of the Tropic of Cancer" (Bridenbaugh & Bridenbaugh, 3).
33. Sauer, *Early Spanish Main*; Andrews; Boxer.
34. See Esquemelin (Exquemelin); Haring; Allen, *Admiral Sir Henry Morgan*; Marx.
35. Barbados is said to have been the only Caribbean colony never to have changed hands from

the time of its foundation until the day it achieved its independence.
36. For a detailed study, and one of the best, on the interrelationship of war and trade in the middle years of the eighteenth century, see Pares, *War and Trade.*
37. Cited in Knight, *Genesis*, 117.
38. Claypole & Robottom, 56; Hoetink, 'The Dutch Caribbean', 103. For a brief history of the island during this period see Attema, 33-48.
39. The most comprehensive work on the impact of the war on the Caribbean is Baptiste's. Other important works include: Post, *Strike the Iron*; Langenberg, 80-92; Smith, 'Battle of the Caribbean', 976-82; Smith, 'Martinique in World War II', 169-74; Greenburg, 70-83; Joseph, 23-67.
40. Bellegarde-Smith, 49-52; Ott, 192.
41. Foner, *History of Cuba*, II, 11, 31.
42. For a detailed discussion on the Platt Amendment see Foner, *Spanish-Cuban-American War*, II, 599-632; see also Pérez, *Cuba Between Empires*, 315-27. The full text of the Amendment is given in Pérez, 323-24.
43. Foner, *History of Cuba*, II, 297.
44. Silvestrini, 148, 154.
45. Wiarda, 925.
46. Cited in Langley, 29.
47. *Daily Nation*, Jan. 10, 1992: 13; Jan. 24, 1992:12.
48. *San Francisco Chronicle News Service*, Mar. 15, 1996.
49. Wiarda, 213.
50. Schmidt, 31.
51. See Plummer, *Haiti and the Great Powers*, 229.
52. Plummer, *Haiti and the United States*, 102.
53. Bellegarde-Smith, 80.
54. *Keesing's Record*, 41 (1995), 40860.
55. Plamenatz, 23.
56. Gleijeses, *Dominican Crisis.*
57. McAfee, 39.
58. Gorostiaga, 17.
59. Cited in Louis, 123-24.
60. See Crowder, *Second World War*, 22; Aluko, 622.
61. Cited in Suret-Canale, 487.
62. Crowder, *Second World War*, 41-42; Morgenthau & Behrman, 616-19; Crowder & O'Brien, 664-71.
63. Naipaul, *Middle Passage*, 183. The phenomenon of the psychosis of violence is discussed by Fanon in some detail, in the case of Algerians and Europeans who experienced the Algerian War of Liberation, 1954-62 (see *Wretched of the Earth*, 200-50).
64. Duncan, 'Political Violence', 55.
65. Duncan, 'Political Violence', 72.
66. Lewis, *Main Currents*, 254-55.
67. Fanon, *Wretched of the Earth*, 27-84.
68. Rodney, *Walter Rodney Speaks*, 44-45.
69. Goslinga, 374.
70. Manzano, *Poems by a Slave in the Island of Cuba Recently Liberated*, cited in Foner, *History of Cuba*, I, 195.
71. *Julius Caesar*, Act II, Sc.II.
72. Donne, *Devotions*, cited in Oxford *Dictionary of Quotations*, 253.

Economics

CHAPTER 4

The resource dimension

[A]n old poverty rotting under the sun, silently; an old silence covering the tepid pustules, the frightful inanity of our raison d'être.[1]

Aime Césaire

Introduction

According to a recent World Health Organisation report, poverty is the greatest single cause of death, disease and suffering. More than one-fifth of the estimated 5.6 billion people in the world live in extreme poverty, almost one-third of the world's children are undernourished, and about half of the world's population have no access to necessary drugs.[2] Coleman and Nixson showed that rural poverty was a growing phenomenon in Latin America (including the Caribbean), Asia and Africa, linked with high levels of unemployment and underemployment.[3] This situation particularly affects women and youths. The rich are becoming richer and the poor poorer in a number of countries.

International financial institutions rank the Caribbean in an intermediate place between the industrialised countries and the other developing countries.[4] In terms of the quality of life Barbados, the Bahamas, the Netherlands Antilles, the Turks and Caicos, the Caymans and Bermuda fit much more neatly into this category than the rest of the region does.

Table 4.1 Caribbean Countries According to Estimated Income, 1994 (GNP per head)[5]

Low[a]	**Lower-middle**[b]	**Upper-middle**[c]	**High**[d]
Guyana	Belize	Antigua/Barbuda	Aruba
Haiti	Cuba	Barbados	Bahamas
	Dominica	French Guiana	Bermuda
	Dom. Republic	Guadeloupe	Cayman Is.
	Grenada	Martinique	US Virgin Is.
	Jamaica	Puerto Rico	Netherlands Ant.
	St Vincent and the Grenadines	St Kitts and Nevis	
	Suriname	St Lucia	
		T'dad and Tobago	

[a] US$725 or less. [b] US$726-$2,895. [c] US$2,896-$8,955. [d] US$8,956 or more.
Source: World Bank, *Social Indicators of Development, 1996*, 394-95.

Although a few Caribbean countries have experienced consistently high growth rates in the last 20-30 years, the vast majority have had to struggle for most of the period from 1980 when they began to experience severe recession. This situation has been exacerbated by continuous growth in the region's population. In some places it has doubled every 20 years since the present century,[6] and would have been higher had it not been for the outlet provided by emigration. Fertility rates in the region have dropped since the Second World War, but so have mortality rates (with the notable exceptions of the Dominican Republic and Haiti).[7] Population growth is therefore still unacceptably high in terms of the performance of the region's economies.

Great disparities exist within the Caribbean in respect of levels of income, natural resource endowment and access to health and educational facilities. Statistics such as GNP, GDP, numbers of radios and televisions, volumes of production of raw materials and manufactured goods may push a country into the high-income or middle-income bracket. However, these statistics often obscure or overlook the human side of development, such as the social distribution of goods and services, and the improvement in the quality of life of the population as a whole. In several parts of the region there is evidence of widespread poverty in the midst of pockets of affluence. Clive Thomas refers to the mass of Caribbean people as 'the poor and the powerless'.[8] What awaits a large number of them is an uncertain life and a certain death.

In 1990 the unemployment rate in Guadeloupe was estimated at 31 per cent, and in 1993 in Martinique and Barbados at 21.6 and 25 per cent respectively, figures which have not improved appreciably since then. In 1989 about 60 per cent of Puerto Ricans were said to be at or below the poverty line.[9] Comparable levels of unemployment and poverty have also been recorded for Haiti, the Dominican Republic and Guyana. In 1990 the World Bank reported the level of poverty in Haiti at 70 per cent in the cities and 80 per cent in the rural areas.[10] UN statistics for 1990-95 show infant mortality in Haiti at 86.2 per cent per 1,000 live births (one of the highest in the world), while in the Dominican Republic it stood fairly high at 42 per cent, and in Guyana at 48 per cent.[11] In April 1994 Sir Neville Nicholls, president of the Caribbean Development Bank (CDB), stated that recent surveys showed that the incidence of poverty in Guyana was 43 per cent, in Jamaica 33 per cent and St Lucia 23 per cent. The average for CARICOM as a whole was some 33 per cent.[12]

In 1991 USAID underlined its budget request for the region by noting: 'Widespread malnutrition, illiteracy, deficient educational and training opportunities, poor health conditions, and inadequate housing threaten to erode the foundations of the region's fragile democratic institutions and limit prospects for economic growth over the long term.'[13] The growing poverty and its implications for the health of Caribbean peoples were also underlined in a statement in April 1994 by Dr Franklin White, Director of the Caribbean Epidemiology Centre, to the Associated Press. He said that creeping poverty was causing a number of fatal diseases, including malaria, typhoid, cholera and tuberculosis, to revisit the region after an absence of many years; the situation was directly associated with a decline in levels of sanitation, a deterioration in the quality of water for drinking and other health purposes, and also a deterioration in the infrastructure of health facilities. He declared that the present incidence of tuberculosis, almost completely expelled from the region in the 1970s, could be used as a barometer of the declining health situation; the incidence of this disease in the late 1970s and 1980s was significantly lower than the world average of 10 per 100,000. However, in the last three or four years it had grown higher than the world average. He also pointed out that malaria was experiencing a new lease of life in Suriname, Guyana, Belize and Venezuela.[14]

In 1994 the leaders of CARICOM called for the establishment of a 'new global humanitarian order' to respond to the widening gap between rich and poor countries. They noted that unless urgent steps were taken to redress the situation of growing poverty, the result would be feelings of frustration and hopelessness among the poor, posing threats to democratic governments and international peace and security.[15]

It is quite possible that many Caribbean countries will revert to the conditions of poverty and squalor which resulted in the riots of the 1930s in the Commonwealth Caribbean. In fact, it is arguable that in some countries, such as Guyana, Jamaica, Haiti, the Dominican Republic and Cuba, conditions prevailing in large sections of those countries are already reminiscent of those existing in the 1930s. Haiti's annual GNP declined from an already low estimate of US$300 per head in 1985 to US$220 in 1994.[16] Cuba's financial situation is at present so critical that the government cannot afford to buy badly needed medicine. In August 1995 Uruguay agreed to send Cuba more than 1 million packages of medicine. This, however, was not a philanthropic act. The date for safe usage of the medicine had expired and Uruguay was about to dump it. It is said that the Cuban trade company, Medi-Cuba, requested that the medicine be sent. A Cuban official explained, 'Although we produce a large amount of medicine in Cuba, we lack certain medications due to a shortage of primary products which are very expensive.'[17] It is perhaps apposite to recall here the words of Louis Jean-Jacques Acaau, the leader of the peasant revolt in Haiti in the 1840s: 'The population of the countryside . . . is murmuring in its poverty.'[18]

The raw realism of Caribbean life is that the economies are small, fragile, open ones, characterised by great external exploitation. This has been one of the sad legacies of colonialism. Like third-world countries generally, the Caribbean displays its international relations in clear characteristics: a high ratio of international trade to national product; a high level of commodity (primary) production relative to total national production; high concentration on few commodities; high concentration of exports to developed countries; high imports of food, manufactured goods, technology and managerial skills; high levels of external borrowing and debt financing; and a high level of expatriate ownership and control of the means of production, distribution and exchange. The disjunction existing in Caribbean economies manifests itself, for example, in great disparities in urban and rural development and uneven spatial distribution of goods and services.[19] We must never lose sight of the fact that the most important single factor is the structural dependence which characterises the economic (and other) relationships between the region and the developed countries, due to specific historical factors. Clive Thomas defines structural dependence as 'the extent to which the economic structure of . . . economies depends on foreign trade, payments, capital, technology, and decision-making to generate domestic economic processes'.[20]

Resource endowment theory

Various theories have been advanced to explain the present poverty and underdevelopment in the Caribbean countries. The most popular one is that the region as a whole and the individual countries in particular, with few exceptions, suffer from limited resource endowment. This theory is usually related to: potentially marketable natural resources; geographical size; and population density.

Potentially marketable resources

Some writers treat the concept of potentially marketable resources, as related to discussions about a country's capacity for development, in a static rather than a dynamic way. In reality it is part of an historical process, in which the market value of natural resources may appreciate or depreciate according to the historical forces operating upon it. For instance, poor management of the ecosystem may severely deplete a country's marketable resources and therefore its capacity for future growth. Ecosystems may be destroyed by natural or man-made factors. A particular attribute that may have had little or no economic value at a given point in time may become of great economic importance. Much depends upon the demand for a particular good or service and the cost of production. This is true, for example, of the economic utilisation of the sea and sand in the Caribbean (and other countries), which before the Second World War were of little economic value. Also a country's resource endowment can be enhanced by international factor movements, such as capital, technology and skills, which, as in some third-world countries, complement abundant factors such as labour.

The prevailing view is that most Caribbean countries have a highly skewed natural resource endowment and that the region as a whole is restricted in its capacity for economic diversity. The main problem with this argument is that, when compared with several European countries, the region can scarcely be said to be inferior to them in natural resources. Russia, Germany and France apart, the other European countries seem to be far poorer in natural resources than their levels of development would suggest. In fact, Russia, which is one of the richest European countries in terms of natural resources, is one of the poorest in terms of income per head. Japan was also able to achieve a high growth rate without a wide range of natural resources. The fact is that all of the highly developed European countries and the fast-developing Asian ones depend heavily on the import of certain raw materials from the under-developed countries in Asia, Africa, Latin America and the Caribbean to produce processed goods for their domestic and export markets.

Through a system of unequal exchange and assigning specific production roles to various third-world countries – a system deliberately developed during the colonial era – the Europeans of the North Atlantic countries, in particular, were able to achieve a decisive advantage over the rest of the world in the manufacture and distribution of goods. Thus, for example, the Caribbean was assigned the role of producing mainly sugar, Brazil coffee, Ghana cocoa, Uganda cotton, Senegal peanuts and Vietnam rice. Many third-world economies that at one stage had cultivated a wide range of crops have become monocultural in response to the massive reorientation of their economies during the colonial period. By contrast, none of the European countries practises monoculture, being fully aware of the hazards of doing so.

The North Atlantic European countries depend upon the third-world countries not only for much of their agricultural commodities, but also for a great deal of their mineral needs, such as petroleum, bauxite, copper, tin, manganese, nickel, gold and diamonds. These are important natural resources for which the third-world receives very little in comparison with the huge profits derived by the developed countries. The latter refine and resell the raw materials or utilise them to manufacture a large variety of products. The high value-added prices for manufactured products, when set against the low prices for primary commodities and the general depreciating terms of trade between developed and underdeveloped countries, account in great measure for the declining economic levels in a large number of countries belonging to the latter group. The developed countries are particularly strong in the area of skills production. This gives them a comparative advantage over third-world countries in such matters as management, banking and scientific and technological development.

It has been argued that some European countries, for example, Denmark and Switzerland, did not have strong colonial links but nevertheless enjoy very high levels of GNP per head. Their development is therefore seen as simply the result of economic policies which reflect a rational approach to the development of small states. It must be conceded that the possession of colonies does not in itself guarantee riches to the imperial power. We also agree that countries without colonies, or a significant 'colonial tradition', can experience high levels of development. Much depends upon specific factors. However, as Walter Rodney has argued, in the context of Europe in the last two centuries, colonialism had such a pervasive effect that even those countries with few or no colonies benefited substantially. This was effected through the increasing integration of their economies – as seen in regard to trade, manufacture, investments, technological transfers, etc. – which was part of the spin-off of colonialism. Thus, according to Rodney, 'lack of colonies on the part of any capitalist nation was not a barrier to enjoying the fruits of exploiting the colonial and semi-colonial world'.[21]

The activities of such transnational corporations (TNCs) as Unilever, Lloyds and Barclays Bank substantiate this viewpoint. To quote Rodney again: 'The composition of Unilever should serve as a warning that colonialism was not simply a matter of ties between a given colony and its mother country, but between colonies on the one hand and metropoles on the other . . . . The rewards spread through the capitalist system in such a way that even those capitalist countries who were not colonial powers were also beneficiaries of the spoils.'[22]

Rodney specifically names Switzerland as among those countries which benefited from Unilever's undertakings and he notes that Swiss and Danish capital was widely employed in financial activities in colonial Africa.[23] Using Africa as his example, he observes that unlike the political partition, the economic partition knew no visible boundaries: 'It consisted of the proportions in which capitalist powers divided up among themselves the monetary and non-monetary gains from colonial Africa.'[24]

Denmark has few natural resources. Its main mineral resources are natural gas and sand, the latter not much exploited so far. Industry, including manufacturing, is by far its major revenue earner. In spite of its natural resource deficiency, it has important industries in the areas of food processing, steel and metals, chemicals and pharmaceutics, printing and publishing, machinery and electronic goods. Service industries also constitute an important sector of its economy. In 1994 it had an estimated GNP per head of US$28,110, one of the highest in Europe.[25]

Switzerland is not a major agricultural producer, although, like most European countries, it does provide a range of agricultural commodities, including sugar beet, potatoes, wheat and dairy products. Nor is the country rich in mineral wealth, for 'it is not richly endowed with mineral deposits, and only rock salt and building materials are mined'. Yet the country has a strong industrial sector, the most important branches of which are precision engineering (especially clocks and watches), heavy engineering, machine building, textiles, chocolates, chemicals and pharmaceuticals. It has been able to harness hydroelectric power and has also developed nuclear power for industrial uses. Together these provide most of its electricity output.

Switzerland is also an important centre of international finance, the Zurich stock exchange being one of the largest in Europe. Insurance and tourism are also important components of its service industries. Its proximity to other large centres of production, such as Germany and France, has no doubt also been an important factor in its development. Its concentration on developing its human resource potential and its heavy focus on certain highly specialised industries have given it an important niche market continentally and globally. Foreign direct investment and its neutrality in world affairs have enhanced its economic position within the global community. In 1994 its GNP per head was estimated at US$37,180, the second highest in the world for that year, after Luxembourg.[26]

Although these two countries are not endowed with rich natural resources, they nevertheless have strong economies, based upon manufacturing and service industries. One of the crucial variables is the application of scientific and technological skills to agricultural and industrial development. The capacity of Switzerland, for instance, to harness the power of water and of the atom has considerably enhanced its production capacity, and made the country much less dependent on imported sources of energy. Similarly, the business and management skills of these two countries have enhanced their attractiveness as service centres. They are representative of several other European countries and prove that limited natural resources are not a barrier to development.

Several Caribbean countries possess the natural resources needed to produce hydroelectric and geothermal energy. The waterfalls of Guyana, Suriname and French Guiana and the volcanic mountains of the Windward Islands are important potential sources of such energy, yet the region continues to be afflicted by a heavy foreign currency drain in order to import fossil fuel. Many rural households are still without electricity and there are frequent power cuts in Cuba, Haiti, the Dominican Republic and Guyana. The contrast between the European and Caribbean countries cited here underlines the fact that no meaningful discussion of comparative levels of development can take place outside the wider historical context in which the respective societies are placed.

Geographical size

Geographical size, does not *ipso facto* equate with economic size. For instance, Canada is larger in geographical size, but much smaller in economic size, than the USA. In fact, it is considered a small economy. Clive Thomas says that size in itself is just one, and not the most important, variable in underdevelopment and structural dependence:

> Smallness is not interpreted here as an attribute of material reality capable by itself of creating social forms. On the contrary, it is interpreted simply as constituting, in a certain sense, an additional dimension to underdevelopment, while underdevelopment itself can in turn only be explained in terms of historical dialectics. Thus size is not simply and crudely a constraint imposed by nature on social development.[27]

He also says that *'the universal perception of size'* has had a fatal deterministic impact upon the capacity of small third-world countries to '*master and to bring their environment into the service of society*'.[28]

William Demas, however, argues that the size of a given territory is the most important determining factor in its development. Small countries are confined to the development of small economies which cannot achieve self-sustained economic growth. Factors which limit small economies include too large populations in relation to natural resources, and too small populations in relation to economies of scale and economic diversification;

extreme difficulty, if not inability, to establish a capital and goods sector; forced specialisation in a small range of commodities; and heavy dependence on foreign markets and other external aids to development, especially foreign exchange which constitutes a permanent aspect of the national economy. Demas does recognise that other factors such as management, technology, political and social philosophy, and the impact of external forces – historical and contemporary – are also important variables in national economic development.[29] Nevertheless, he still appears to believe that small size creates almost insoluble problems to development.

Table 4.2 Area, population and GNP of selected small countries, 1994

Country	Area (sq. km)	Population ('000)	GNP (US$) (per head)
Belgium	30,519	10,116	22,920
Bermuda	53	63	27,720
Denmark	43,075	5,205	28,110
Hong Kong	1,071	6,061	21,650
Luxembourg	2,586	404	39,850
Netherlands	33,937	15,3812	1,970
Singapore	623	2,930	23,360
Switzerland	41,293	6,994	37,180

Source: World Bank, *Social Indicators of Development, 1996.*

The Caribbean consists mainly of a number of small units. Among the smallest of the autonomous ones are Montserrat, Bermuda and Aruba. Even the largest island countries, such as Cuba, the Dominican Republic, Haiti, the Bahamas and Jamaica, are quite small in comparison with most other independent geopolitical entities around the world. Three of the four largest countries – Guyana, Suriname and French Guiana – lie on the Central or South American mainland (see Table 4.1). Making comparisons with the more advanced European countries, the Netherlands and Belgium are a little larger than Haiti and Denmark and Switzerland are smaller than the Dominican Republic. Other advanced European countries which are much smaller geographically than the larger Caribbean islands include San Marino (60.5 sq. km), Monaco (1.95 sq. km) and Luxembourg (2,586 sq. km).[30] Within the broader Caribbean area, Bermuda with a geographical size of only 53 sq. km is among those countries in the highest income bracket. In 1988, it was ranked by the World Bank as having the second highest GNP per head in the world (US$24,370).[31] It is important to note here that geographically small communities have often remained economically small ones because of the structure of the relationships which they have developed with foreign countries. They have generally been locked historically into a staple-producer relationship which has generated chronic dependency. This is an important reason why the Caribbean situation is so different from Switzerland, Luxembourg and Denmark, which are also small geographic entities.

These observations tell us that size, while important to a point, is not the determining factor in the quality of life it is possible to attain. We should also note that while the Caribbean, even as a combined unit, is still small in the economic sense, it is roughly twice the geographical size of Germany and Japan, three times that of the UK, and one-and-a-third times that of France.

Population size and density

Related to the issue of geographical size is the view that the region is 'overpopulated' and that this puts unbearable pressure upon its resources. The whole issue of overpopulation, of course, relates to a large extent to the perception of the role of people in the developmental process. As Lappe and Collins state:

> We are made to think of people as an economic liability when, in reality, all the wealth of any country begins with people – *with human labor*. The economic success of a nation does not depend so much on rich natural resources as on how effectively its people can be motivated and their labor utilized. People appear as a liability *only* in a certain type of economic system: one in which economic success is not measured by the well-being of all the people; one in which production is increasingly monopolized by a few; and one in which technology is used to exclude people from the production process so as to maximize the profit the landlord makes on each worker. People are not born marginal.[32]

There are no agreed criteria by which to measure overpopulation, but one yardstick often applied is the ratio of persons to total land space,[33] or population density. Judged by this criterion, the region is one of the more densely populated parts of the earth; but even so there is a wide differential in the population densities of the various countries. In 1994, for instance, Bermuda at one extreme had an estimated density of 1,188.67 per sq. km, while at the other, French Guiana had a density of 1.47 per sq. km.

The data in Table 4.4 show that population densities in some Caribbean countries are not out of line with those of some of the world's most advanced countries, including Luxembourg and Switzerland which, according to World Bank estimates, had the first and second highest GNP per head in the world in 1994. Hong Kong and Singapore, also, small countries with population densities roughly 4.76 and 3.95 times that of Bermuda, have nevertheless managed to achieve GNP per head sizes comparable with those of some of the

Table 4.3 Comparison of combined population of Caribbean with selected countries, 1994.

	Population, ('000)	%
Caribbean	37,010	100.0
Canada	29,248	79.0
Belgium	10,116	27.3
Denmark	5,205	14.1
France	57,928	156.5
Germany	81,516	220.3
Netherlands	15,381	41.6
Singapore	2,930	7.9
Switzerland	6,994	18.9
US	260,650	704.3

Source: Compiled from World Bank, *Social Indicators of Development*, 1996.

Table 4.4 Estimated population sizes, densities and GNPs of selected Caribbean and other countries, 1994.

	Density (per sq. km)	GNP (US$) (per head)
Caribbean countries		
Bahamas	19.51	11,790
Barbados	604.65	6,530
Belize	9.19	2,550
Bermuda	1,188.67	27,720
Dominican Republic	158.55	1,320
Grenada	266.67	2,620
Guyana	3.84	530
Haiti	252.54	220
St Kitts and Nevis	157.08	4,760
St Lucia	259.74	3,450
Suriname	2.49	870
Other countries		
Canada	2.93	19,570
Denmark	120.84	28,110
Hong Kong	5,659.20	21,650
Iceland	3.78	24,590
Japan	330.75	34,630
Luxembourg	156.23	39,850
Netherlands	453.22	21,970
Singapore	4,703.05	23,360
Switzerland	169.37	37,180
United Kingdom	239.22	18,410

Source: Compiled fromWorld Bank, *Social Indicators of Development*, 1996.

most advanced European countries. Singapore continues to experience strong economic growth, spearheaded by manufacturing and financial services. In 1993 it was the world's third largest oil refining centre, after Rotterdam and

Houston, and one of the world's three main oil trading centres, along with London and New York.[34]

Taiwan, also, with a population density of about 578 per sq. km 1984 (higher than many Caribbean countries), continues to experience high economic growth rates in real terms, at almost 7 per cent average per year over the last few years.[35] It has experienced continued trade surpluses since the mid-1970s, and also surpluses on its current-account balance. It places strong emphasis on technological sophistication, access to capital markets, air and sea communications, reducing land and labour costs, economic deregulation and opening its markets to international economic forces.[36] The observations above underline the point that no discussion of overpopulation would be complete without some consideration of other factors affecting a country's capacity to ensure a certain standard of living for its citizens.

Historically, communities have relieved their population densities through emigration, more intensive or extensive exploitation of their productive resources, export expansion and scientific and technological innovations. According to some 'challenge-and-response' theorists, migration on a large scale is usually a last resort when all other attempts to alleviate the situation fail. This certainly appears to be the case in respect of the Caribbean. Emigration has been the main vent for the so-called surplus population of the region. Because of the failure to solve many of the pressing economic and social problems and the greater opportunities in metropolitan countries, there has been large-scale migration to North America and Europe. Geographically speaking, however, such countries as Belize, Guyana, French Guiana, Suriname and Cuba have the capacity to absorb the surplus population from the more densely populated areas of the region. The problem is not one of space, but rather the economic and social costs of this absorption.

Human resources

No discussion of a region's resource endowment is complete, or even meaningful, without attention being paid to the human resources. Basil Springer refers to Mr Khoo, a businessman from Singapore, who stated that his country considers the human capital as its most precious resource and that it has built its modern economy upon that principle. Mr Khoo said: 'As a nation we should try to develop our potential to the full, using our resources to the maximum advantage. This means developing our people as our most precious resources – to the fullest. We can afford to invest heavily in our people . . . .' The West Indian Commission Report of 1992 stresses that 'Economic development is first and foremost about people and the quality of their lives.'[38] The report emphasises: 'The search for self-sustained growth is a quest for resources with which to enhance the lifestyles of all Caribbean peoples'; and that 'the deficiencies which most threaten our West Indian future are the deficiencies which pervade educational systems in the region at the present time'.[39]

The enhancement of human capital through training makes the critical difference in national output as measured, for instance, in increases in land use and physical reproducible capital. Human capital is by far the greatest form of wealth in any country. As Lester Thurow says, education for development has three major potential economic benefits. Firstly, by changing a person from a low-productivity to a high-productivity individual it can make both a quantitative and a qualitative change in his economic output and, by extension, in the national economic output (that is, it increases the productivity of the country's physical capital). Secondly, it can lead to changes in the income distribution between rich and poor and thus lessen the incidence of poverty in a country. Thirdly, it can lead to social mobility, thus breaking down the rigidity of class systems.[40]

Unfortunately, the Caribbean, like most other third-world countries, has historically placed little emphasis upon the development of its human capital, in contrast to the large sums spent on the development of physical capital such as buildings and equipment. Moreover, when money has been spent on its human resource it has not always placed the emphasis in the right place. The wastage of its human resource was horrendous under slavery, a result of race, gender and class factors. As the Cuban ex-slave Juan Francisco Manzano wrote, in the words of the planter class of his time:

> We purchase slaves to cultivate our plains,
> We don't want saints or scholars to cut canes;
> We buy a Negro for his flesh and bone,
> He must have muscle – brains, he need have none.[41]

It was this kind of brainless approach to human resource development which kept the vast majority of the populations of the various colonies on the margin of social, political and economic development for a very long time.

When the first feeble efforts were made to educate the blacks in the nineteenth century, especially in the early post-emancipation period, it was with the intention of keeping them as a docile and dependent labouring population. Only gradually and uncertainly did the colonies find their way establishing an organised system of education, from primary to tertiary level. Even so, for a long time differential access to education, based upon persistent race, class and gender discrimination, remained a hallmark of the system, and arguably still exists in some countries today.

The low priority placed on human resource development was also seen in the failure of the colonies to develop educational institutions of any note even for the white master class. This was because it was possible for completely illiterate persons to acquire economic, social and even political power through the ownership of large plantations. The low social status of the vast majority of people who came to the colonies, especially to the French, British and Dutch zones, meant that for a long period there would be no strong demand for educational institutions. In most instances where a sound education was deemed desirable for young boys of planter and mercantile families, they were sent to Europe. More occasionally young girls were sent to finishing schools abroad to teach them the refinements of polite society.

These factors help to explain the late development of education in the colonies. It is estimated that 55-80 per cent of Haitians over 15 years are illiterate. In Puerto Rico, which was colonised by the Spanish from the early sixteenth century, it was only from around the mid-seventeenth century that elementary education was introduced on a systematic basic, and then only for a small group.[42] At the time of the US takeover the illiteracy rate is thought to have been about 80 per cent.[43] In Cuba, where some secondary and tertiary institutions existed from the mid-sixteenth century, instruction was carried on by the religious orders which emphasised a religious and classical education. At the time of the revolution in 1959 Cuba had one of the highest illiteracy rates in the region. In 1538 the first university in the new world was established in Santo Domingo (Dominican Republic), with a similar emphasis on religion and the classics. Secondary and tertiary educational institutions were introduced much earlier in the Spanish colonies than in others, but the emphasis was always on making cultured 'gentlemen' of the recipients of such education. The situation in the French, British and Dutch countries was, if anything, worse than in the Spanish ones.

Early Caribbean education did not address issues such as the application of science and technology to problems of development. This was seen in the technological backwardness of the sugar economy (with the notable exception of Cuba) and the wider regional economy up to the early nineteenth century. Up to that time in most colonies the hoe and the machete remained the basic tools for the cultivation of sugar, based on cheap labour input. Windmills and horse-drawn mills remained in operation during the pre-emancipation period, and steam mills were only introduced after.

The limited use of fertilisers, the late application of steam to sugar processing and the late development of centrifugals, clarifiers and vacuum pans were all symptoms of the technological backwardness of the industry at that period. All the technologies were imported from Europe.

In dealing with the issue of technological transfer we must acknowledge that when the first Europeans arrived in the region they brought with them the most advanced technologies available in Europe at that time. It was, in fact, their technological superiority over the indigenous inhabitants, particularly in weaponry, that ensured their conquest of the new world. Weaponry apart, they introduced a wide range of iron tools which constituted a substantial advance over the wooden and stone implements which the indigenous peoples employed. The new tools allowed for greater efficiency in such applications as felling trees, building boats, cultivating the soil, hunting, fishing and building houses. European technology and organisational skills revolutionised agriculture in the region. Unfortunately, for most of the island peoples and a large number of the mainland ones the coming of the white man brought also a new and unprecedented regime of coercion, so that it was largely the Europeans who benefited from the new technologies introduced. These technologies were not applied to the general development of the various communities within the region, but to a select few.

It is important now for the region to develop its own capacity to set up technological industries to produce machinery, tools and other equipment, since at present very little of the technology utilised is manufactured locally and the technological heart of the region resides in the metropolitan countries. Vital foreign exchange is spent in order to import machinery and spare parts, and also to import foreign technicians to set up, service and repair the machines. With the rapid obsolescence of machinery in today's world, it becomes increasingly necessary to import fresh stock in short spaces of time. There is a need to develop technology that is appropriate and most economical to the region. Experiments with the use of solar energy, wave energy and biogas, for example, need encouragement and funding from governments and private businesses, so that the appropriate technologies can be developed.

At present the region is served by a wide range of secondary and tertiary educational institutions. The best of these can hold their own against similar institutions anywhere in the world. Among these are the universities of Santo Domingo (Dominican Republic), Havana, Oriente, Las Villas (Cuba), Puerto Rico and the West Indies (Jamaica, Trinidad and Barbados). In addition there are an increasing number of technological colleges and institutes, most of which have been founded since the Second World War. But there are not enough of them and there is a critical shortage in some important branches of learning. We need far more research institutions in every branch of learning that is relevant to our development. We also need more libraries, books, magazines, publishing houses and bookstores carrying academic materials. We need to create a much better atmosphere, fostering scientific enquiry and academic and intellectual discussion and exchanges.

The travel and residence of skilled persons within the region should be facilitated. Because of the population size and the level of economic development of most Caribbean countries it is impossible for a single territory to support the research and professional interests of skilled persons, such as architects, agronomists, physicists, biologists, engineers, medical practitioners, actuaries and business and management personnel. It is only by creating wider opportunities for employing and paying them attractive salaries that we can hope to retain their services. Our failure to do so has encouraged the brain-drain to more developed countries. Initiative has been taken recently by some CARICOM members to facilitate travel, residence and work within the treaty area by graduates of the University of the West Indies.

At the elementary and secondary levels there are still many woeful deficiencies, such as school overcrowding, a shortage of teachers, poorly constructed and maintained buildings, inadequate library facilities, including out-of-date books, and high rates of absenteeism (or drop-outs). There is therefore still a considerable wastage of the human resource potential, beginning from the lowest rungs of the educational ladder. High levels of illiteracy in such countries as the Dominican Republic and Haiti point to the necessity of a more concerted attack on this problem. Ginzberg, in his work *Human Resources: the Wealth of a Nation*, argues that illiteracy not only poses a threat to a nation's security and economic progress, but also to an individual's capacity to take proper care of his/her family and to make the most beneficial choices in life.[44]

The problem is that these needs, although pressing, come at a time when most Caribbean countries are seeking not simply to trim but to slash their national budgets, often the result of IMF and other austerity programmes into which the governments have entered with lending agencies abroad. But cutting back on the educational budgets is, at best, short-sighted; there is simply no hope for the development of the region until the human resource factor takes the primary place in development planning. The question should not be whether we can afford to invest in the development of our human potential, but rather whether we can afford not to do so. All economies should, and small fragile ones must, develop their human resources to the full if they hope to improve the quality of life for their people significantly in the long term. Céspedes asserts that a sound education is 'an indispensable tool for the full realization of the national potential for economic, social, and cultural development'.[45]

Caribbean agriculture

Ian McDonald reminds us that the Americas have been a major contributor to the cornucopia of Europe and the wider world. Four of the seven global major crops – white potatoes, sweet potatoes, maize (corn), and cassava (manioc) –

originated in the Americas (the other three staples being wheat, barley and rice). He also notes that foods such as sunflower nuts and peanuts are among a long list of other exotic foods from the Americas which have 'transformed Europe and all the world since then'.[46]

At the time of the Columbian invasion agriculture constituted the mainstay of the Caribbean economy. It remained this way for the next 450 years. Today the situation is modified, since manufacturing and service industries play significant roles in certain territories. Agriculture, however, still remains very important to the economies of Haiti, the Dominican Republic, Guyana, Cuba and Belize, but it contributes little to the GDP of Antigua, Bahamas, Barbados, Montserrat and Trinidad.[47] Ramsaran identifies three basic reasons for this change. Firstly, Caribbean peoples and governments have come to conceptualise development in terms of manufacturing industries. Secondly, agriculture is increasingly associated with backwardness and underdevelopment. Thirdly, Caribbean governments have not implemented adequate measures to protect and advance agriculture. These factors have a bad effect not only on regional agricultural exports, but also on the production of food for local consumption.[48]

Some economists argue that perhaps the most serious problem facing the region's agriculture is that poor soil types and soil erosion have made it uncompetitive in the global market. Thomas identifies natural and manmade factors which adversely affect the region's agriculture. These include: undifferentiated climatic conditions and soil resources; erosion caused by natural and human agencies; the extensive alienation of agricultural land for non-agricultural purposes; problems with water availability, leading to inundation or drought; the ravages of pests and diseases resulting in a high percentage of crop damage or loss; and the great cost of agricultural production on a comparative world basis.[49]

This gives a bleak picture of the prospects for viable agricultural activities in the region. Nevertheless, it is clear from Thomas that he is sure that the problems besetting the region's agriculture are caused far more by historical than by deterministic factors. Among these are overriding emphases on exports, expropriation and expatriation of surplus, little emphasis on developing a viable peasantry, capitalist land tenure systems, monoculture, and regional political and economic fragmentation. In fact, he is firm that given the necessary structural adjustments agriculture can become a thriving economic activity again.[50]

In spite of these circumstances, the region has much to offer. It remains a significant producer of sugar – Cuba is still the world's largest producer. It produces crops for exports such as coffee (Jamaica Blue Mountain coffee being among the best in the world), cocoa and tobacco (Cuba being noteworthy for the high quality of its cigars). The usual comment made in this context concerns the expense of regional production of these commodities, caused largely by high wages, soil depletion, plant obsolescence and imported materials. This indicates the need to continue to make efforts to rationalise and to introduce new scientific and technological inputs into both production and processing.

Manufacturing must be seen as an important complement to agriculture, in which the raw materials are processed in the country producing them, or at any rate in the region. The sugar cane, in particular, has a number of potential usages, apart from the manufacture of sugar, molasses and rum. Among these are the manufacture of bagasse, bagasse charcoal, bagasse concrete, briquettes, methane, methanol, ethyl alcohol, acetic acid, butonol-acetone, lactic acid, citric acid, glycerol, dextran, monosodium glutamate, lysine, xanthan gum, aconitic acid, itaconic acid, pulp and paper, paper board, box board, corrugated board, fibre board, particle board, furfural, alpha-cellulose, xylitol, plastics, filter mud (as fertiliser and animal feed), soil conditioner, mulch, poultry litter and cane wax.[51] In theory, therefore, there is considerable scope for the utilisation of the sugar cane outside its traditional usages, but weak economic relationships, tradition and limited scientific and technological expertise have prevented fuller use being made of this commodity. Some of the possibilities listed above might turn out to be impracticable, even when the necessary feasibility and scientific studies are carried out. But the production of some of these commodities might prove viable in the domestic and regional markets, if not in the international ones. Cuba is one of the few countries in the region that have made consistent attempts at cane-based industries, such as plastics, fuel, detergents and chemicals.[52] Economic circumstances, however, have limited the success of these efforts.

Greater emphasis also needs to be placed on non-sugar agriculture, especially because of the growing tourism sector and the increasing import food bills. Apart from the crops mentioned above, the region produces in varying quantities many agricultural products, some for the overseas market and others for the regional and domestic markets. These include: corn, cabbage, lettuce, calalu, cassava, rice, nutmeg, coconuts, bananas, beans, legumes, white potatoes, sweet potatoes, carrots, oranges, grape fruits, pineapples, pawpaws (papayas), tomatoes and mangoes. The list of regional products is, of course, much longer than the above, but those items mentioned are intended simply to give an indication of the range of food products that the region is able to provide for its domestic needs as well as sometimes for export.

The region is rich in marine products, and most of the territories are able to meet local demand for fresh marine food and sometimes to export the excess. In addition, a few territories, usually those on the mainland such as Guyana,

Suriname and Belize, possess the natural resources to engage in dairy farming on a large scale, although poor transportation facilities and restricted access to markets have been two of the main hindrances to meaningful exploitation. Some island territories, including Jamaica, Cuba, Haiti, the Dominican Republic and Barbados, also engage in dairy farming and the raising of other livestock.

Large imports of food

In spite of the potential to feed itself, for a long time the region has been a major importer of food, sometimes importing in processed form food that it had earlier sold abroad in its raw state. Thus large quantities of corn flakes, bran flakes, canned fruit, raw and processed livestock and dairy products, marine food and vegetables are imported annually. It is estimated that most Caribbean countries import at least 50 per cent of the food they consume, and that Antigua/Barbuda, Puerto Rico, Barbados, Bermuda, the Bahamas and Trinidad and Tobago import about 80 per cent. The Bahamian food import bill in 1991 was estimated at US$280 million.[53] Barry *et al.* estimates that in the early 1980s the region spent some US$800 million on food imports from the USA alone, and that this figure was roughly one-half of its current-accounts deficit.[54] The annual food bill is at present well over US$1 billion.

The failure of the region to provide for its own food needs has historically manifested itself in a number of ways, such as chronic food shortages (resulting in hoarding), malnutrition, starvation, expensive food imports causing heavy drain on foreign exchange, exploitation of the rich by the poor and economic dependency.

Heavy imports of food began in the early days of the sugar revolution and large-scale plantation slavery in the mid-seventeenth century. The resultant vulnerability of the region was aggravated by periodic shortages, even in times of peace. This situation was exacerbated in times of European warfare in the region when food supplies could not easily reach the colonies. The most well-known case was during the American War of Independence and its immediate aftermath when numerous slaves died from starvation, including an estimated 15,000 in Jamaica between 1780 and 1787.[55] Following the independence of the former American colonies, those British Caribbean countries which had been heavily dependent on them for much of their food were faced with greater food shortages and for several years increasing food import bills.[56]

Malnutrition due to food insecurity was very evident in the 1930s. Coupled with such diseases as tuberculosis, yellow fever, malaria and dental caries, and other social factors such as inadequate housing and poor sanitation facilities, it played a significant part in the overall poor health of the population.[57] Nutritional deficiencies result in high infant mortality, stunted physical growth, mental retardation, and lethargy.

Lappe and Collins point out: 'The security of any people has historically rested in meeting its own basic food needs. Thus every country should mobilize its own food resources to meet its own needs first. Only then can trade serve to expand choices rather than to deprive people of the benefits from the resources that are rightfully theirs.'[58] In addition, 'Food producing resources are misused when they are diverted, as they increasingly are, away from meeting basic food needs and toward the satisfaction of those already fed.'[59] The Caribbean has been particularly guilty of this failing.

In general, governments, corporations and the propertied elite have concentrated on the production of cash crops for export rather on the production of food for domestic consumption, due to the structural preference to concentrate on export commodities and the perceived need to earn foreign exchange. Thus, in some instances food needed for domestic use has actually been diverted to overseas markets. This has been so recently in Guyana, in respect of rice and sugar, Barbados in regard to sugar and the Dominican Republic and Haiti in respect of beef. Similarly in the Sahelian area of West Africa during the drought of 1970-74 billions of dollars of food was being exported while people were dying of starvation. The result is competition between local and overseas consumers for food that should rightfully be available first to the community that produces it, and dramatically underlines Thomas' view of the 'dynamic divergence between domestic resources and domestic demand'.[60] It demonstrates forcefully our distorted view of our priorities as a basically agricultural community.

The tradition of importing food dies hard. Most of the staples and many of the other foods that we grow today were first imported into the region during the colonial period. These include crops such as sugar cane, coffee, rice, coconut, banana, breadfruit, yam, ackee, Guinea corn, mango and okra. Imported animals include the cow, pig, sheep, goat and chicken. Among the foods of indigenous origin are the white potato (now imported from Europe), sweet potato, tomato, cassava, maize, pawpaw (papaya), peppers, pineapple, avocado, beans, cocoa, various kinds of nuts, iguana and various seafoods. The importance of exotic foods to our daily diet is symptomatic of the penchant we have for importing a variety of processed foods from abroad.

Plantation agriculture

Since the Columbian invasion the Caribbean has always favoured plantation agriculture over peasant agriculture. The arrival of the Spanish led to large-scale alienation of land and established an entirely different relationship between land and labour, the two most important factors of production. The European concept of individual land tenure was new and altogether strange to the indigenous peoples. The Europeans saw land almost exclusively as an economic asset and an important aspect of the market economy. Land had commercial value and so could be bought, sold, leased both to locals and foreigners, or otherwise utilised as individuals saw fit, even if such use was inimical to the interests of the community as a whole. Thus prime farming land might be put to use for cattle-ranching (or, more recently, for the erection of hotels and golf courses).

By contrast, in traditional Amerindian societies, as in some African and Asian ones, land had economic and social, but not commercial, value. The people did not own the land; rather it was the land that owned the people. Mother Earth spawned them and to Mother Earth they would return, so that whether in life or death the silver cord that bound the two together would not be broken.[61] Thus the land had a mystical aspect in death as in life. For the living the land gave permanence, stability and meaning to the material universe. The blessings of the gods and ancestors were expressed in its fruitfulness. In response gratitude was expressed in the elaborate rituals surrounding planting and reaping. The land existed to meet the needs of the entire society, not just a small elite at the expense of the wider community of souls. As a unit of social value, it helped to keep the community together in a stable and coherent social relationship.

The Europeans, by introducing individual ownership and commercial speculation in land, helped to break up the coherence of the indigenous groups. Within a short space of time numerous groups who had lived on and worked the land to earn a living became dispossessed communities. This dispossession made the indigenous peoples, in effect, pariahs in the land of their birth (as was to be the pattern several centuries later in South Africa). It reduced them to nothing more than a servile labour force working for and at the pleasure of their new masters. This ownership of the land, accompanied by ownership of their persons, was the foundation on which the Europeans sought to build the superstructure of the colonial empires.

This pattern of exploitation of the labouring poor was, of course, a prominent feature in the history of state development and class formation. In Europe during the Middle Ages the barons brutally exploited the *villeins* or serfs who constituted a sort of peasantry at that time. The Russian lords did the same to the *muhzik*, the Egyptian lords to the *fellahin* and the Indian lords to the *raiyats*. Often this exploitation of the peasantry and the complete dispossession of their land rights constituted an important factor in large-scale structural developments in the fields of science and technology, such as the building of extensive waterways, roads, palaces and pyramids, which led to the structural transformation of societies in western Europe, China, India, Egypt and elsewhere.

In the Caribbean this pattern was also evident, though on a greatly reduced scale, because of the emphasis on the expatriation of profits to Europe. We must therefore look there to find structural changes that might have occurred in the Caribbean had the surplus capital remained here for development. The major inputs were the creation of the infrastructure necessary for the development of plantation agriculture and the actual cultivation of plantation crops. The pattern of exploitation began with the dispossession of the right of the indigenous peoples to occupy and utilise the land for their benefit.

Plantation agriculture is still the most important component of the region's agricultural system, which Beckford sees as one of the prime reasons for the persistent poverty.[62] For instance, today an estimated 66 per cent of the arable land in Guadeloupe, 70 per cent in Martinique, and 77 per cent in Barbados are devoted to plantation production for export. Overall, it is estimated that more than 50 per cent of the productive land in the region is given over to agriculture (including dairy farming) for export. The plantations still occupy the best land and are usually controlled by an elite which has the readiest access to capital, cheap labour and markets. This elite is closely associated with the mercantile elite, local and foreign, which controls the distribution and exchange sectors of the economy. Plantation agriculture does earn foreign exchange, but much of it is spent on importing equipment, fertilisers and other inputs into production, paying debts to foreign creditors and fees to commission agents, and importing luxury goods. It is widely believed that a significant amount of foreign exchange is spirited away by the business community and deposited in foreign banks.

At the same time, plantation agriculture is closely associated historically in the Caribbean, Latin America and other third-world countries with a strong orientation towards monoculture with all its hazards. Monocultural economies generally fail to stagger crop production throughout the year, resulting in high levels of seasonal unemployment and underemployment. Such economies are also particularly vulnerable to the vagaries of crop diseases, drought, flood and fluctuations in the global market, such as those which affected staple production in all third-world countries in the 1970s and 1980s. Many plantation owners also control large tracts of arable land which are not brought under cultivation; they are left fallow or given over to grazing a few cattle, as for example in Haiti, the Dominican Republic and Colombia.

While plantation cultivation, especially in the case of sugar plantations, remains the dominant agricultural activity in the region, it is not an attractive sector of the economy for the labour market. The social context of the cultivation of sugar up to and including modern times, as in the Dominican

Republic, means that many continue to associate it with slavery (see Chapter 1). Here, it is apposite to cite Orlando Patterson's pointed remarks on the reason why Caribbean peoples of African descent still shy away from working on the sugar plantations.

> Do we ask the Jew to live and work in the concentration camps of Germany? Do we ask a recently released prisoner who has been unjustly imprisoned for the better part of his life to continue living in his cell? Do we expect him to like it? Is it not natural for him to loathe it and despise it? Why then, is it that when the ex-slaves and their descendants express an abhorrence for the sugar estate we do not accept the obvious explanation?[63]

Although agriculture generally is not very attractive to Caribbean peoples, many more than at present would be prepared to work their own lands rather than cultivate the plantations.

Peasant agriculture

Food is all around the Caribbean, yet the food of the Caribbean is hunger. No doubt with a view to redressing this situation Nicholls called recently for 'fuller participation in opportunities for productive use of available resources by facilitating self-organisation, empowerment and ownership or control over resources to the poor'. He also pointed to the need for new 'production patterns to achieve more balanced and broadly based economic incentives for both labour and capital and rural and urban development'.[64]

One of the groups theoretically well-placed to redress the situation is the peasantry. In peasant economies arable land is generally utilised more efficiently than in plantation economies, in terms of cost per unit of output.[65] Historically, peasant societies have placed primary emphasis on the production of food for domestic consumption, and only secondarily on cash crops for export. This was the experience, for instance, of peasant societies in Asia and Africa in the period before the Europeans came and engineered the reorientation of their economies to the production and export of cash crops.

Peasant farming constituted the main agricultural system at the time of the Columbian invasion of the Caribbean. A vibrant peasantry existed in many parts of the region, including Hispaniola, Cuba, Jamaica and Puerto Rico, which, however, was substantially destroyed by European demands for labour for mining, the regimentation of the indigenous peoples under the *encomienda* system and the wanton disregard with which cattle were allowed to graze on the Amerindian provision fields.

During slavery a proto-peasantry emerged, in most instances utilising land unfit for cash crops. In such places as Jamaica, Grenada and St Vincent mountainous areas were used, while in Barbados it was 'rab' (marginally arable) land.[66] Proto-peasants played a strong role in supplementing the meagre rations which slaves received from their masters. In addition to these black groups there were white peasants in such countries as Puerto Rico, Cuba, Santo Domingo (the Dominican Republic) and Barbados.

The post-emancipation period is generally regarded as the time when the peasantry emerged as a significant group. Even so, there were important differences in the sizes and viability of these groups in the various countries and even within a given territory. Especially in the smaller countries, the peasantry struggled simply to emerge as an identifiable group because of the limited land space available to them. This was true, for instance, of St Kitts, Antigua and Barbados.

In Haiti, where the post-emancipation period started the earliest, peasant groups began to emerge as Africans occupied estates of white and coloured planters who had been displaced during the struggle for independence. Others retreated to the mountains and began to cultivate the soil there. Government policy under various rulers such as Henri Christophe, Alexandre Pétion and Jean Pierre Boyer shifted between dividing up the plantations into peasant and small farming communities and retaining the plantation system intact. But the emphasis of successive governments on plantation rather than peasant culture meant that insufficient attention was paid to the development of a viable peasantry.[67]

Elsewhere in the region, peasant communities developed as ex-slaves squatted on state lands or abandoned estates, or made sacrifices to purchase land. In Guyana in the 1840s they often pooled their resources to purchase encumbered estates or large lots. In 1842 there were over 4,000 freehold properties and by 1852 the number had risen to 11,152.[68] In Jamaica Baptist missionaries often bought encumbered estates and resold them in smaller lots to their parishioners. Eisner estimates that there were about 200 free villages in 1842, comprising about 100,000 acres in all. By 1902 there were 133,169 freehold properties of under 50 acres each (that is, owned by peasants and small farmers).[69]

The development of the peasantry in the French islands in the post-emancipation period can also be gauged from the number of smallholders. Wyndham estimates that in 1855 the number of such persons amounted to 2,713 in Guadeloupe and 2,521 in Martinique; by the 1890s the number in each instance had increased to about 9,000.[70]

Peasants in post-emancipation society, while cultivating some of the old cash crops (sugar, coffee, cocoa and tobacco) and new ones (pimento, nutmeg, arrowroot, ginger and banana), were chiefly responsible for the cultivation of food crops directed mainly at the internal market in the early days. These included coconut, pineapple, citrus, ground provisions and rice. Some of them were also involved in dairy farming on a small scale. Their activities considerably elaborated the internal marketing economy of the region and constituted the first major effort at import substitution. They created new sources of income, raised their standard of living above that of the slavery period, and contributed to the overall expansion of the colonial economies. Eric Williams notes the significant increase in the French Caribbean just one year after emancipation in the import of flour, cheese, salted meat, soap, oils, textiles, shoes, hats, wine and a variety of other commodities.[71]

In a few places, such as Haiti, Jamaica, St Vincent and Grenada, sugar production suffered a drastic decline in the post-emancipation period. In Jamaica, average sugar exports between 1828 and 1835 amounted to 90,000 hogsheads; in 1859 it was only 28,000 hogsheads. The industry did not return to health during the rest of the century. Ground provisions and bananas, peasant productions, made up for a significant part of revenue lost as a result of the decline in sugar production.[72] In St Vincent arrowroot exports partially filled the gap, rising from 60,000 lb on the eve of emancipation to 1,352,250 lb in 1857.[73] Generally, however, sugar remained the dominant export crop in the region and the volume expanded significantly in Cuba, Guyana, Trinidad and Suriname, so that peasant cultivation was not necessarily taking place at the expense of sugar culture. Nevertheless, the activities of the peasants usually ran counter to official government policy which sought to retain them as a labour force dependent exclusively on the plantations. Thus they suffered, and continue to suffer, from governmental failure to make a full commitment to the necessary structural adjustments to the economic landscape in order to make them a sustained and dynamic force in the region. Certainly they have never been offered the attention and financial assistance comparable with what has always been offered to the plantation sector (and more recently the industrial one).

In the early post-emancipation period in the British and French Caribbean various measures were adopted by the colonial governments and the allied plantocracy of the day to hamper the peasants' progress. In the first place, where compensation money was paid to bring an end to slavery (in the British, French, Spanish and Dutch countries) it was given to the oppressors rather than the oppressed, the perpetrators rather than the victims of slavery. The freed persons thus had to rely entirely on their own initiatives to gain money in order to purchase land. The problem of land acquisition and development remained for a long time the most crucial aspect in terms of the rise of a peasantry, for without these there could be no peasantry. Thus, whether it was in Jamaica, Antigua, Martinique, Cuba, or any other Caribbean country, the peasantry usually faced an uphill struggle to acquire land and install the most basic infrastructure for cultivation, except in those instances where they acquired former plantations. Nevertheless, the peasants survived owing to their own willpower to break away from utter dependence upon autocratic regimes for their livelihood. But they exist today as a group on the economic fringes of society.

Peasant agriculture in the region has historically suffered from such factors as uneconomic land sizes, the poor (often marginal) quality of agricultural land, inadequate irrigation and transportation facilities, limited scientific and technological inputs, insufficient emphasis on the utilisation of livestock as a complement to agriculture, plant and insect pests, shortage of capital and credit, lack of government subsidies to encourage production by way of duty-free equipment and guaranteed prices, marketing problems leading to spoilage of crops in the fields or in the storage areas, predial larceny and poor management. Many of these still affect agriculture generally in the region, but they are much worse for the peasantry.

In Guyana (between 1954 and 1964) and Cuba (in the 1960s) the national governments were involved in massive land settlement schemes on behalf of the peasantry. These schemes involved governmental assistance with the clearing of the land and provision of roads, water and sometimes electricity. The Cuban experiment has been much more successful than the one in Guyana. Today the Cuban peasants contribute to a much larger portion of the domestic economy than before, and the incidence of malnutrition has dropped remarkably.[74] However, the plantation sector remains the chief agricultural one both in Cuba and Guyana, and peasant production still suffers from many ills.

Structural adjustment programmes have worsened the problems facing the peasants. Government subsidies for seeds, fertilisers, equipment, marketing, etc., have been removed. Increases in production costs have also arisen because of currency devaluations. The result is that the peasants find it much more difficult to purchase vitally needed inputs for their farming activities, and when they manage to do so they are often forced to demand higher prices than formerly for their crops in order to break even. As prices for local foods escalate, many consumers find it cheaper to purchase food imported from the USA and other developed countries.

Another 'evil under the sun' is that, in spite of peasant farmers' associations and cooperatives, peasants are often forced to sell their produce to subsidiaries of overseas conglomerates or government marketing boards at less than the production cost; not only is any surplus extracted in this way, but also some of their original investment capital. Sometimes this means that their net income is less than if they had sold their labour to a larger producer. The whole vicious cycle has led to the pauperisation of the peasants, the abandonment of the land,

and the supplementing of earnings by working part-time on plantations during the crop season and elsewhere during the out-of-crop season.

Cecilia Karch writes of the peasants in Barbados as 'living virtually on the edge of starvation'. René Achéen and Francis Rifaux refer to those in Martinique and Guadeloupe as living 'in extreme misery', with a standard of living that 'barely keeps them alive'.[75] Jamaica, Puerto Rico, the Dominican Republic and Haiti provide some of the most striking examples of the destitution of the peasantry, but we shall only detail the last of these: the worst-case scenario.

Haitian peasants are barely wresting a living from the land, and tottering on the edge of survival. The fertile valleys are monopolised by the big business concerns which concentrate on the production of sugar, coffee and cattle for export, leaving the semi-arid and marginally arable hillsides to the peasants. These areas are quite unsuitable for intensive farming. When the natural vegetation is removed for fuel and other purposes the land becomes denuded; bleaching, landslides and soil erosion take place, resulting in increasingly poor crop yields. Lundahl informs us that the average Haitian peasant has access to only two tools, a hoe and/or a machete, and that the lack of credit is 'a major cause of the almost total degree of technological stagnation within Haitian agriculture'.[76]

The Haitian peasants have been kept in a backward and illiterate state. They have rarely had the sympathy of the state authorities in their quest for economic and social improvement. Their antagonists have been the main vested-interest groups: government, army, big business and even the clergy. Insouciance and outright hostility have been demonstrated by these groups. Paquin asserts that nowadays their most ruthless and immediate tormentor is the Chef de Section or Rural Police Officer. He wields considerable authority, even exercising a kind of judicial power over life and property. The peasants see themselves as helpless. According to him, 'The Haitian peasants live in the dark ages. Their huts are without electricity and running water. Hygiene facilities are practically non-existent . . . .'[77]

They seldom eat meat, and when they do it is dried meat. For many of them their meat is their tears. With poverty stalking the land and misery growing ever more profound and widespread, their conditions forcibly replicate those of the slavery period. For them, the legal institutions of slavery have been abolished, but the practices persist.

The failure of food production in Haiti to meet ordinary domestic needs has forced it to be a recipient of food aid from the USA, like its neighbour, the Dominican Republic. This is both tragic and ironic, since when the Spanish arrived in the island (which they named Hispaniola), that is today divided into these two independent countries, they admired the land and peoples for their productive capacity. Perhaps with some exaggeration, the Spanish considered it the richest land in the world, where every plant would grow. Columbus thought that it was 'wonderful to see those valleys and rivers of sweet water and the cultivated fields'. He was also impressed with the well-fed and robust appearance of the inhabitants, whom he declared to be 'stout and lusty'.[78] However, the Spanish, French and US arrivals in the island changed that picture drastically, as the plantation system took root and developed.

The history of the peasantry over the last century and a-half is one in which hope promised much but reality produced little. The shadow proved to be larger than the substance. It is therefore not surprising that many peasants today, economically marginalised have a long, dismal view of the future.

The region is theoretically capable of providing for its own nutritional needs. However, this can only be effected through a radical programme of agrarian reform, including a new approach to land distribution and utilisation, as part of a wider programme to develop an internally-propelled and regionally-oriented economy.

Other resources

Apart from its agricultural resources, the region is endowed with extensive forest resources, some minerals, fine beaches, a sunny climate and a favourable international strategic location. The main forest resources are in the mainland countries of Guyana, French Guiana, Suriname, Belize and to a lesser extent Cuba. Yet here again we continue to import a large quantity of our lumber and other forest products from abroad, chiefly from North America, which we have done since the seventeenth century. For centuries colonial officials, land speculators and merchants have commented on the little use made of the forestry resources on the one hand, and the indiscriminate spoilation of them on the other (principally in the islands). The larger countries contain not only extensive areas capable of being exploited for lumber, but other resources such as resins, fibres, herbs and medicinal plants. In the Guianas the indigenous peoples were accustomed to utilising the ita palm for food, shelter, fibre and other products. In spite of the many uses to which it was capable of being adapted, the European colonists never bothered to develop its potential or even to use it on any regular basis.

Minerals in commercially exploitable quantities in the region include bauxite in Jamaica, Guyana and Suriname; gold in Suriname and Guyana; nickel in Haiti and Cuba; ferro-nickel in the Dominican Republic; and petroleum and natural gas in Trinidad and small amounts in Barbados. There are other minerals, which are only mined to a small extent at present, some of which in the future might prove to be commercially viable. These include manganese, diamonds, phosphate, salt and kaolin.

The region is one of the largest importers of crude oil for refinement and transshipment. In the 1970s it refined more than 2 million barrels of oil per day. Since the 1980s there has been a downturn in the operations of its refineries, partly because the US federal authorities allowed the construction of large offshore terminals on the US Gulf of Mexico and the eastern coasts, and partly because OPEC quotas reduced Venezuela's crude petroleum production. This led to a closure of the Lago plant on Aruba in 1985. In 1990 an agreement reached with Exxon allowed for the Lago Oil and Transport Co, its subsidiary, to reopen the plant partially. Part of the 4.2 million barrel storage facility was subsequently leased to Saudi Arabia. The Shell refinery on Curaçao was purchased by the Antilles government in 1985 and then leased to a Venezuelan company.[79]

Trinidad saw a reduction in its petroleum production from 230,000 barrels per day (bpd) in 1978 to 150,000 bpd between 1988 and 1990. Refining increased in the early 1990s as a result of an agreement reached with Venezuela to process its crude petroleum. In 1992 its refining output was 112,252 bpd. The island has substantial natural gas facilities, which are currently being exploited on a larger scale than before to make up for some of the revenue lost due to the decline in the petroleum industry.[80]

US and European facilities associated with the oil industry (exploration, production, refining and transshipment) existed in the 1980s in at least 13 Caribbean countries: the Netherlands Antilles, the Bahamas, Trinidad, the US Virgin Islands, Antigua, Barbados, Cuba, the Dominican Republic, Jamaica, Martinique, Puerto Rico, St Kitts and Nevis, and St Lucia. Among the major oil companies operating in the region were Shell, Standard Oil, Amerada Hess Oil, Mobil Oil, Exxon, Texaco and Gulf Oil. Quite apart from the production and refinement of oil, the strategic importance of the region to the US oil industry is underlined by the fact that over 50 per cent of its oil imports passes through the Caribbean Sea.

The Caribbean is also a significant producer of bauxite, although production levels have declined drastically since the 1980s due to management and marketing problems and foreign competition. It is estimated that in 1970 the five bauxite-producing countries in the region (Guyana, Jamaica, Haiti, Suriname and the Dominican Republic) together produced about 48 per cent of the world's output of bauxite, but that by 1982 production had dropped to about 18 per cent.[81] Guyana boasts of having calcined bauxite, the highest grade of bauxite, which gives it special importance as a bauxite-producing country. However, in the 1970s it lost its virtual monopoly of the market for this grade of bauxite when China gained a significant market share. Its share of the market dropped from 75 per cent in 1975 to 45 per cent in 1984 and 30 per cent in 1989. The situation worsened for Guyana when Brazil entered the market for high-grade bauxite.

Jamaica, which produces a lower grade of bauxite, also saw its revenue from the industry decline during the 1980s. This was due to the vagaries of the world market and also to the ravages wrought by Hurricane Gilbert. The revenue in 1991 was US$656 million, which in 1993 was reduced to US$531 million. Alumina exports stagnated between 1981 and 1985 at 1.6 million metric tons, and then steadily increased to 3 million metric tons by 1992.[83] The Dominican Republic and Suriname did not have much luck with bauxite during this period; the small operation in Haiti closed altogether in 1983 when the US-owned Reynolds Co pulled out of the island because of uneconomic operations.

Obviously, the region has lost ground in regard to its percentile control of the world market for bauxite and its related products. Nevertheless, the value of the industry to developed countries for aircraft and military equipment makes these resources of strategic importance to them and, in the hemispheric context, particularly to the USA. It must be noted that although the known mineral resources of the region are limited in variety and small in volume, they constitute significant money-earning potential for small countries with modest populations. For instance, in the early 1990s earnings from the bauxite industry accounted for 40 per cent of the revenue of the Suriname government, while alumina alone accounted in 1991 for 71 per cent of total exports.[84]

Our other important natural resources are our harbours, beaches, sand, sea, coral reefs, variety of fauna and flora and topographical features all of which play, important roles in making the region an important tourism destination. The tourism industry is the world's fastest growing industry, and in the Caribbean it is a multibillion dollar industry annually.

Strategic location

Any discussion of a country's or region's resource endowment must take into account its geographic location in respect of its neighbours and the international commercial and strategic network. Location can have both a positive and a negative effect. A country or a region that is poor in soil or mineral resources may nevertheless acquire an important position in the global economy because of its strategic location. This is true, for instance, of Gibraltar, Mauritius, the Suez Canal and the Cape of Good Hope in the context of European maritime rivalry in the Mediterranean Sea and the Indian Ocean. The fact that the Caribbean lies astride the main sea lanes between the American continents and Europe has given it a strategic importance starting with the early days of Spanish colonisation.

The Caribbean became a major cog in the Spanish defence of its riches and possessions in the new world from the sixteenth century, with Havana as the central point of its defence system. It was one of the major points of rendezvous for the Spanish treasure ships sailing to Europe. It possessed a large fort and facilities for the repair of large ships. Havana and other harbours in the Caribbean lost their strategic position for a time with the decline in European warfare in the region in the nineteenth century, but regained it in the present century, and especially since the Second World War, with the growing importance of the Caribbean Sea to US shipping and security interests. Its proximity to the USA has not only enhanced its strategic importance in the global network of trade, but has made it a vital part of America's programme of economic expansion and domination.

The Caribbean as a strategic economic zone was enhanced by the cutting of the Panama Canal and the fact that a number of the islands lie in a strategic position *vis-à-vis* it (see Chapter 3). Today, two-thirds of US oil imports, over half of its strategic minerals, and over half of its foreign trade pass through the Caribbean, Panama and the Gulf of Mexico.[85] Thus any threat to the security of the area is perceived as a threat to the economic interests of the USA. This situation is not new. In the late nineteenth and early twentieth centuries the USA experienced feelings of unease at the growth of German economic interests in Haiti, and eventually used force to push out the Germans and ensconce itself in that country.

The Caribbean has always attracted big business to its shores, a fact which gives the lie to a view of its economic insignificance. However, its major problem has always been how to translate its strategic advantages into hard cash while at the same time maintaining its territorial and political sovereignty and improving the welfare of its citizens. If experience teaches us any lessons it is that the countries in the region are witnessing a forced compromise of their sovereignty without any significant economic benefits.

Notes

1. Césaire, *Return*, 11.
2. Cited in 'UN: Poverty, a Leading Killer', 10.
3. Coleman & Nixson, 35.
4. Ramsaran, *Commonwealth Caribbean*, xv.
5. The territories omitted are not mentioned in the World Bank classification, nor are GNP figures available for them.
6. Clarke, 'Sovereignty', 35.
7. Clarke, 'Sovereignty', 35.
8. Thomas, *Poor*.
9. *South America, Central America and the Caribbean (1995)*, 334, 442; Knight, *Genesis*, 164; *Keesing's Record*, 40 (1994), R34.

10. Cited in McAfee, 17.
11. *Statistical Yearbook for Latin America and the Caribbean*, 53.
12. 'Call for War on Poverty in the Region', 12.
13. Cited in McAfee, 23.
14. 'Deadly Diseases Returning to Region', 12A.
15. 'CARICOM Calls for New Order', 10.
16. World Bank, *Social Indicators of Development, 1996.*
17. 'Cuba Gets "Gift" of Expired Medicine', 16C.
18. Cited in Nicholls, *Haiti in Caribbean Context*, 92-95.
19. See Thomas, *Dependence*, 59.
20. Thomas, *Dependence*, 30.
21. Rodney, *Europe*, 96-97.
22. Rodney, *Europe*, 209.
23. Rodney, *Europe*, 209.
24. Rodney, Europe, 209. This observation applies equally to the Caribbean during the period of the slave trade and slavery. Brandenburg (part of modern Germany), for instance, benefited from slave dealing, even at a time when it had no new world colonies. Goods to be used in the acquisition of slaves from Africa, bound for the Caribbean, were manufactured in various European countries not actually possessing colonies.
25. *The Europa World Year Book (1991)*, I, 876; World Bank, *World Tables 1995, Keesing's Record* 42, (1994), 105.
26. *The Europa World Year Book* (*1991*), II, 2514-15; World Bank, *World Tables 1995, Keesing's Record,* 42, (1994), 125.
27. Thomas, *Dependence*, 30.
28. Thomas, *Dependence*, 52. Italics in quotation itself.
29. Demas, *Economics of Development*. For a review article on this work see Best, 'Survival and Size', 29-34.
30. *Keesing's Record*, 40 (1994).
31. *The Europa World Year Book*, (*1991*), II, 2839.
32. Lappe & Collins, 29.
33. Overpopulation theories differ in regard to whether one should take into account total land space, arable land, irrigable land, swampland, deserts, wasteland, and other land (suitable, for example, only for erecting buildings). Traditional African societies had no concept of wasteland, since to Africans all land was useful. Modern ecological studies are showing increasingly the importance of swamplands and wastelands in the total ecological profile of human societies. The fact is, too, that in modern societies lands that were once considered to be useless are becoming increasingly useful as technology is applied to bringing them into productive processes. An outstanding example is Israeli application of trickle irrigation to areas in the Neger desert.
34. *Keesing's Record*, 40 (1994), R83-84.
35. In 1994 its growth rate at 1991 prices was 6.5 per cent (Taiwan Statistical Data Bank (1995), 1, 8, 9).
36. *Keesing's Record*, 40 (1994), R85-86.
37. Cited in Springer, 'People – Most Precious Resource,' 8.
38. *Time for Action*, 98.
39. *Time for Action*, 74, 98.
40. Thurow, 332-33.
41. *Poems by a Slave in the Island of Cuba Recently Liberated*, cited in Foner, *History of Cuba*, I, 195.
42. Costas, 31.
43. Bou, 8.
44. Ginzberg, 54-56.
45. Céspedes, 53.

46. 'Quincentenary', 6.
47. Thomas, *Poor*, 133-34.
48. Ramsaran, *Commonwealth Caribbean*, 44.
49. Thomas, *Poor*, 116-20.
50. Thomas, *Poor*, 352-70.
51. Paturau. See Thomas' work which discusses the limited use made of the sugar cane in Guyana to manufacture by-products (*Plantations*, 55).
52. Barry *et al.*, 38.
53. *South America, Central America and the Caribbean* (1993), 86.
54. Barry *et al.*, 30.
55. Williams, *Columbus to Castro*, 226.
56. See Williams, *Columbus to Castro*, 226-27 for prices of food imported into the British Caribbean immediately after the war.
57. Williams, *Columbus to Castro*, 452.
58. Lappe & Collins, 8.
59. Lappe & Collins, 15.
60. Thomas, *Dependence*, 60.
61. The ancient Israelite seemed to understand this when he wrote, 'Dust thou art and unto dust shalt thou return' (*Holy Bible*, Gen. 3:19).
62. Beckford.
63. Patterson, 'Social Aspects of the Sugar Industry', 66.
64. 'Call for War on Poverty in the Region', 12.
65. Lappe & Collins, 184.
66. Mintz & Hall, 3-26.
67. See Nicholls, *Haiti in Caribbean Context*, 92-95; Williams, *Columbus to Castro*, 333; LaCerte, 42-47.
68. Williams, *Columbus to Castro*, 337; Farley, 100-02.
69. Eisner, 210-11, 220.
70. Wyndham, 97, 100.
71. Williams, *Columbus to Castro*, 335-36, 339.
72. Eisner, 9, 53, 80; Williams, *Columbus to Castro*, 339.
73. Williams, *Columbus to Castro*, 339.
74. See Griffin, 135.
75. Karch, 220; Achéen & Rifaux, 199; see also Burac, 383-403.
76. Lundahl, 25, 37.
77. Paquin, 239.
78. Journal of Columbus, Dec. 16, 1492, cited in Williams, *Documents*, I, 19-20.
79. *South America, Central America and the Caribbean*, (*1995*), 466.
80. *South America, Central America and the Caribbean*, (*1995*), 601.
81. Thomas, *Poor*, 105.
82. *South America, Central America and the Caribbean*, (*1995*), 365.
83. *South America, Central America and the Caribbean*, (*1995*), 408.
84. *South America, Central America and the Caribbean*, (1995), 589.
85. Thomas, *Poor*, 337.

CHAPTER 5

Distorted development path I

The ultimate purpose of development is to expand the capabilities of people, to increase their ability to lead long and healthy lives, to enable them to cultivate their talents and interests, and to afford them an opportunity to live in dignity and with self-respect.[1]

Keith Griffin & Azizur Khan

Introduction

Our discussion of resource endowment entails a consideration of the vital issue of the control and management of resources. Since the Columbian invasion of the Caribbean the ownership and management of the region's main productive resources, and of the means of distribution and exchange have been largely in expatriate hands. The vast majority of owners have refused to live in the region for any length of time, so that there has always been a great deal of absentee ownership. In Suriname in 1813, 297 of the 319 plantations were owned by absentees,[2] which was quite typical of most territories in the pre- emancipation period. The situation has not changed appreciably, although the industrial and financial sectors have largely replaced the plantations as the dominant economic concerns.

This expatriate and absentee dominance has had widespread and largely negative consequences for the development and utilisation of the region's assets. The level of commitment to regional development and more equitable income distribution could rarely match that of local business persons. What Ragatz said about the plantocratic and mercantile elite in slavery days still holds true today: 'No considerable body of persons inspired by motives higher than the desire to extract the greatest possible amount of wealth from them in the shortest possible time ever reached the smiling shores of the Caribbean colonies.'[3]

The colonisers, of course, and modern exploiters always insist that they are developing the resources for the benefit of the 'natives' and the rest of the world, a view forcefully expressed in 1922 by Sir Frederick Lugard, British High Commissioner in Nigeria, in his philosophy of the 'dual mandate'.[4] In practice, however, that mandate was usually implemented in a very partial way, with the expatriates largely benefiting from the major economic enterprises. The local economies became increasingly distorted and oriented towards the satisfaction of a narrow expatriate elite and their equally narrow local allies. The result was often growth in terms of money values and volume of production without a parallel development in the quality of the lives of the mass of the people.

This was noticeable in the Caribbean from the slavery period when the region was transformed from a subsistence economy to a cash crop (export) one. Pares, Ragatz and Williams have detailed the huge profits made from plantation enterprise by a small corps of merchants and plantation owners, at the expense of the masses.[5] While GDP rose appreciably, the lot of the worker became worse. This situation has persisted for much of the post-slavery period. For instance, conditions in the British Caribbean, Puerto Rico and the Dominican Republic in the 1930s, measured by such indices as wages, nutrition, health facilities, housing and general living conditions, were quite reminiscent of the immediate post-slavery period a century earlier.[6] For a number of people in the region their material circumstances have still not improved appreciably. Coleman and Nixson remind us that it is possible to have 'economic growth with negative development in that, although average incomes may have risen, the economic lot of the mass of the population would have deteriorated and negative or no progress would have been made in transforming personal attitudes and institutions in the manner required by modernization ideals'.[7] There are factors that may account for this, including repressive political systems (see Chapter 2), inequalities in income distribution and unequal access to education, primary healthcare, financial credit and technology.

Such has been the experience of Caribbean peoples for much of the period since the Columbian adventure. The deprivation and disequilibrium in the region's economies are prime manifestations of the distorted development path that it has taken. What we see is not an absence of development, but rather the presence of a specific kind of development, a dependent rather than autonomous one.

Dependent versus autonomous development

We use the terms 'dependent' and 'autonomous' with caution since we realise that all countries are to a greater or lesser extent dependent upon others, both directly and indirectly, to assist them in their economic development. However, sometimes the relationships between two countries develop in such a way that one becomes in a subtle (or open) way the exploiter and the other the exploited. When this happens it can be said that the latter has lost its economic (and often its political) autonomy. Four main characteristics of autonomous development are freedom from unwanted interference, freedom of trade, the accumulation and utilisation of domestic savings, and strong indigenous management. The Caribbean has been found wanting in all four of these.

Since the Columbian invasion external interference in the region's economy has been very great. Production has not been integrated vertically, but has been truncated at the level of raw materials. For a long time production not only took place under the shadow of imperialism, but involved, among other factors, the dominance of an expatriate elite, dictating (as we have seen above) both the nature and the pace of that development. André Gunder Frank's view is that Latin American dependency is due to internal and external factors in roughly equal proportions.[8] In the case of the Caribbean, however, while it is also obvious that these two factors are clearly present, we think that external factors weigh more heavily as an explanation of the historical reasons for dependency. The external constraints imposed by the imperial powers in such crucial areas as manufacturing, banking facilities, trade and communications created the basic conditions for dependency. Some local capitalists latched on to the expatriate ones in the exploitation of the region, but the former have always remained subordinate to the latter.

This interference in the region's economy, which is still typical, (although in more subtle forms),[9] contrasts sharply with what happens in western Europe, the USA and Canada. Even in the cases of Russia and other eastern European countries where the West is pumping billions of dollars into their economies, the level of interference is not nearly comparable with that in most Caribbean, Latin American, African and Asian countries. The USA, in particular, has been pressuring Japan to remove import restrictions and to open up its economy more fully to the global (really US) market forces. However, by and large, Japan has been able to resist.

A second way in which autonomous development expresses itself is through the ability to trade with friendly countries without undue and unfair pressure being exerted by a third party to hinder that trade. Dos Santos expresses the view that the only solution for a dependent country which wishes to assert its autonomy is to change its internal structure. He is, however, fully aware of the dangers of attempting to break out of the dependency relationship. As he states, it is 'a course which necessarily leads to confrontation with the existing international structure'.[10] This has certainly been the Caribbean experience. For instance, the pressures brought to bear by the USA to hinder foreign and even regional trade amongst such countries as Cuba, Grenada and Jamaica (and Nicaragua) at various periods since the Second World War, demonstrate clearly the difficulties of breaking away from the stranglehold of the metropolitan countries.

The USA has proscribed trade and all fraternal relations between itself and Cuba, and has used its influence to secure its isolation for a long time from almost all other Latin American and Caribbean countries. It has also made sure that Cuba is denied access to such lending institutions as the World Bank and the IMF. The decision of CARICOM countries in 1993 to establish a CARICOM-Cuba Joint Commission has not been well-received by the US administration, although it has exerted no overt pressure on CARICOM countries to rescind it.[11] The main reason for the USA's attitude towards Cuba is that, like other Caribbean and Latin American countries, it has attempted to pursue a path of autonomous development.

A third way in which autonomous development can be viewed is by looking at the capacity of a country to generate domestic savings, which places it in a sound position to ensure high levels of capital flows to local enterprises, rather than having to approach foreign capital markets. This helps to keep its foreign debt in check and creates a more stable economic environment, with positive implications for the rate of inflation and the capacity to generate domestic employment.

Failure to generate sufficient domestic savings almost inevitably leads countries to seek access to international capital markets. But for poor countries this often means having to implement draconian measures of structural adjustment, which render them more vulnerable than before to international market forces. European countries are usually able to access international money markets without too much interference in their domestic affairs, but not third-world countries.

A country's access to capital to execute its economic programme (for example, to purchase or develop technology and skills) is indispensable to a strategy of development; and it is here most of all that the region has always been found lacking, even during the halcyon days of sugar. Many planters found it difficult to raise the necessary capital locally or abroad for their pioneering plantation ventures, and many of those who were able to do so had to pay usurious rates. Some were forced to mortgage their Caribbean possessions to the money lenders in Europe. More important in the long run was the fact that because plantation profits were expatriated to Europe, little capital remained in the region for local investment. For example, no banking facilities were established until the nineteenth century, since all important banking and commercial transactions were carried out by the European commercial houses and banks, through a system of bills of exchange, that is, promissory notes drawn on commercial houses or banks in Europe. This involuntary flight of capital from the region at a critical stage in its development crippled it and reduced it to dependency on Europe for its capital needs, while at the same time enhancing capital formation in Europe.

We cannot emphasise this too strongly. In spite of the degradation of slavery, indentureship and other forms of labour oppression, if the profits from the various economic enterprises in the Caribbean had been allowed to remain for reinvestment locally, the region would have been much further along the path of infrastructural development, technological change and overall material progress (with positive social and political benefits) than it is. Indeed, the gravamen of the charge against colonialism is that, with few exceptions, it robbed the colonies of opportunities for capital accumulation and local investment, while at the same time increasing capital availability and enhancing the development of the so-called mother countries. This was like robbing the infant to feed the mother! The infant, robbed, never came to adulthood in the true sense of the word, but remained a feeble, underdeveloped and dependent creature.

The situation in the Caribbean and other third-world countries is in striking contrast to the white settlement colonies in North America, New Zealand and Australia. The colonial power divested them of little or no capital and allowed them a greater measure of economic, political and social freedoms than most other colonies. This was a prime factor in their more rapid material advancement than the colonies of exploitation in Latin America, Asia, Africa and the Caribbean.

The lack of investment capital remains a major problem in all Caribbean countries and for most pioneering undertakings. Indeed, almost all large-scale undertakings, especially heavy industries such as bauxite mining/smelting, and oil drilling/refining, are financed through foreign borrowing and foreign investment. This has also meant the indigenous development of only low-level technology and the import of high-level technology, which constitute a further burden on the region's foreign reserves. By constantly expatriating the region's economic surplus to Europe and North America the imperialist countries have extracted the means of self-sustaining growth. This has been an important factor in the incapacity to keep up with the pace of development in the metropolitan countries.

Modern revisionists and apologists for colonialism try to tell us that the colonies contributed little to the development of the metropolitan economies. In the specific context of the contribution of the British Caribbean colonies, they have attacked Eric Williams' masterpiece, *Capitalism and Slavery*, as distorted economic history.[12] Nevertheless, that work stands like a cube, ever on its base no matter how it is turned. But we do not have to rely on Williams alone. Contemporary British economists and historians were well aware of the value of the slave colonies to the imperial power and some wondered what the British economy would have been like without these colonies. It was only in the last days of slavery that the value of the colonies to the imperial power was seriously questioned. Ragatz reminds us that in the rosy days of slavery 'as wealthy as a West Indian' was proverbial in Britain.[13] While, therefore, exact estimates of the contribution of the colonies to the imperial economy are not possible, it seems sounder to rely on the contemporary sources than on present-day revisionists.

A fourth way in which autonomous development manifests itself is in the availability of qualified and competent indigenous management at the highest levels of the economy and administration, without which all planning and execution of economic (and related social and political) programmes are severely handicapped. Indigenous managers are likely to be more sympathetic to the needs of the society, and more committed to finding solutions and accepting lower remuneration packages than foreign managers.

At the same time we are only too aware that poor countries find it difficult to train and to retain indigenous top-level management. More attractive salaries, conditions of work, prospects for promotion, and social ambience have led to the massive brain-drain from third-world to developed countries, forcing the latter to do without or to import such management at very high cost. The problem (as we have stated in Chapter 1) is compounded by the fact that the dependency in which the Caribbean has been placed for centuries, in regard to management as in most other areas, has caused us to view overseas managers as foreign experts, even when more qualified locals are available.

At no time since the European arrival in the region has the process of development followed a normal path to three successive lines of economic development: the internal market economy, then the regional market and finally the international market. With greater sophistication the lines of development become increasingly integrated, so they operate harmoniously to produce the greatest good. In the Caribbean, however, since the onset of colonialism the overriding emphasis has been on the development of links with the international market economy, although this was restricted because the colonies were only allowed to trade with foreign territories through the medium of the imperialist state. The result has been the distortion and underdevelopment of both the internal and the regional market economies.

The internal market

Distortion and underdevelopment are shown in several ways in respect of the first line of rational development, that of the internal market economy. We shall highlight three here: a rudimentary communications system, the neglect of certain areas of a country, and the failure to integrate the various sectors of the economy.

No country can hope to achieve economic development without a proper communications network. A modern transportation system is vital to the modernisation and integration of the economy of each individual country and the region as a whole. The movement of goods and services and the linking of rural and urban communities can only be achieved through improving the transport network. As Ekundare has stated, '[S]ince production is not complete until the product has been effectively marketed to consumers, the amount of transport available and its overall efficiency limits the volume of economic activity and thus the economic growth of a country.'[14]

It is difficult to speak even today of a network of roads or other forms of transport in most Caribbean countries. The land communication usually consists of a few trunk roads scattered here and there, with some connecting (secondary) ones. It is a system of basic penetration. Except for the very small island territories such as Bermuda, Aruba, Curaçao and Barbados, the infrastructure of communication – roads, railways, airstrips, telecommunications, etc., remains weak. In some countries, such as Dominica, the Dominican Republic, Haiti, Belize, Suriname and Guyana, the only communication links between certain areas are those which nature has provided (rivers) or miserable dirt-track roads, which are impassable by vehicular traffic in wet weather. It was only in those sections of the country with which the colonial power was principally concerned, usually the plantation segment, that any attempt was made to provide trunk roads and railways to expatriate the primary products. Until this day the producers for the domestic market generally have to put up with poor facilities.

Puerto Rico's network of trunk roads has been expanded under US sovereignty and today all its major cities and towns are linked by motorways. However, the situation in many of the rural areas is still appalling. Over the last three decades Cuba has made a strenuous attempt to overcome the communications problem, through the elaboration of a wide network of trunk roads. Still, in 1989 the country was estimated as having only 14,480 km of paved roads, and some 33,440 km of unpaved ones (1985), most of which could only be used by motor vehicles during the dry season. There were also 14,519 km of railways in 1990, connecting most of the main towns, but only 4,881 km were being used for passenger service.[15] In 1990 the Dominican Republic possessed only 17,227 km of paved roads, but there exists a motorway from Santo Domingo to Port-au-Prince, the capitals of the Dominican Republic and Haiti respectively. The railways totalled only 1,600 km and were used mainly to service the sugar industry.[16] In the 1960s the Guyana government began an ambitious attempt to cut a trunk road some 400 km from north to south, but this project came to naught through the inability of the government to sustain the financial costs and, according to some, through management inefficiencies.

The second way in which colonialism distorted the internal marketing system was by the neglect of certain parts of the country, usually those outside the plantation sector and more recently the industrial sector. This led to very uneven development between the plantation sector and the other sectors. Today with the coming of foreign-oriented industrialism and the growth of urban communities, it is distorting even further the development of town and country. This is particularly true of the larger countries. The rational integration of town and country, and of various sections of the country, into the internal marketing economy, is indispensable to sustainable national development. This has been understood and practised by the economically advanced countries in Europe and America, and also by Japan.

The third area of distortion (which follows logically from above) is the development of only very limited backward and forward linkages of various sectors of the economy. Thus plantation production was largely dissociated from the domestic economic sector. The emphasis on export production meant that the product elaboration of a given commodity would take place at the metropolitan rather than the colonial end. Specific metropolitan legislation ensured that the colonies did not process the raw materials that they produced. To have allowed this would have been to defeat the very purpose for maintaining colonies.

It was only gradually, after the Second World War, that the colonies moved towards some measure of industrialisation. At the outset the focus was on industrialisation with a view to import substitution rather than export. A fillip had actually been given to such undertakings by the disruption of much non-military manufacturing in Europe because of the war and by the inability or unwillingness of European shipping to run the enemy gauntlet. By the end of the war, therefore, a number of nascent light manufacturing activities were in operation in the Caribbean region. European governments, never pleased with the efforts of third-world countries to develop an indigenous industrial base, attempted after the war to discourage these activities. They nevertheless stopped short of actually prohibiting them. This was due partly to the strong nationalist sentiments in favour of these industries and partly to the fact that Europe was moving increasingly into heavy industry, with which the region could not hope to compete in the near future. Moreover, it soon became evident that the path to import substitution through industrialisation was strewn with impediments.

One of these was that the Caribbean territories had to import much of the raw materials needed for their manufacturing plants. These materials, as Cuba soon found out, were often more expensive than the manufactured goods purchased from abroad; so that in some cases governments or private entrepreneurs were paying more for imported raw materials than for the imported manufactured goods made out of the same kind of materials. Also linked with the above was the high cost of equipment and spare parts which had to be imported. There was likewise the problem (mentioned above) of limited markets for the finished products. Thus, while the postwar era did see a burst of economic activity by way of import substitution, many of these industries soon went out of existence.

The regional market

The second line of rational development is the strengthening of trade and economic cooperation with other regional economies. This too was understood by Europe, which put strong emphasis throughout the colonial period on regional economic cooperation in Europe itself and in more recent times on regional economic integration in the European Union (EU). All the countries of the EU have stronger economic ties with each other than they do with outsiders. In 1994 65.8 per cent of Denmark's imports and 58.7 per cent of its exports related to trade with the EU, while the figures for Germany were 55.8 per cent and 57.8 per cent respectively.[17] According to the *Monthly Bulletin of Statistics*, in 1994 and 1995 trade among the EU countries amounted to well over half of their total trade.[18]

While the economy of Europe was becoming integrated, even in the midst of war among its various countries, those of the third-world countries in the Caribbean and elsewhere were fragmenting. Through neglect, marginalisation or massive exploitation, colonialism exacerbated and in some instances grossly distorted the levels of development between different states or communities.

In the Caribbean for some three centuries no regional trade was officially permitted, not even for goods which the metropolitan power could not produce, since colonial trade was in theory, and to a large extent in practice, restricted to a bilateral relationship between the so-called mother country and the colony (the core/periphery relationship). Storm Van's Gravesande, Director-General of Essequibo-Demerara in the mid-eighteenth century, asserted that this principle should be 'a hard and fast rule, as immutable as the laws of the Medes and Persians'.[19] Whatever deviation took place from this principle was the result of either the inability of the imperial power to enforce its laws or the necessity to allow limited trade with third parties in goods which the imperial power did not want or could not supply, in order to enhance the overall profitability of the colony to the metropolis. This was the origin of the Caribbean-North American trade and the small intra-Caribbean trade which developed during the slavery period.

An important aspect was that colonies were not allowed to develop their own shipping lines or insurance firms. Even in Havana, where a large naval dockyard facility was established, it was concerned more with the repair and refitting of Spanish ships for transoceanic trade than the development of a Cuban transoceanic fleet. As it was, the monopoly exercised by Europe and the North American colonies over the maritime trade between the Caribbean and other countries meant that the profits derived from freightage and insurance went into foreign coffers. In time the Europeans and Americans developed such a stranglehold on this trade that Caribbean countries have been unable to break it.[20] As Coleman and Nixson point out: 'Since on bulky cargoes such as ores, oil and grains, ocean transport charges may account for a significant percentage of the landed price of the commodity, it is clear that the maritime nations derive substantial freight revenues from trade and that little accrues to the poorest LDCs, as in general these do not own major shipping lines.'[21]

Griffin and Khan state that the present-day concentration of international commerce among a small group of countries results in 'the restricted impact of the benefits of trade on the majority of the world's peoples'.[22] Emmanuel calls this the imperialism of trade and a form of unequal exchange, by which developed countries syphon away a substantial portion of the revenues of less developed countries.[23]

The restrictions imposed upon regional trade and manufacture helped Europe to develop its shipbuilding technology, expand its mercantile and naval facilities and enhance its oceanographic knowledge. The region made an important contribution to the development of such port cities as Liverpool, Birmingham, Bristol, London, Nantes, La Rochelle, Marseilles, Bordeaux, Amsterdam, Seville and Cadiz. The restrictions also allowed Europe to build up its refining, confectionery and other industries, and to expand its banking, insurance and brokerage services.

When, in the nineteenth century, European powers began to grant greater economic freedom to their Caribbean colonies through the so-called *laissez-faire* policy, the scientific and technological gap between the two areas was already so wide that the latter, in spite of desperate efforts, found it impossible to bridge it. Of course, for a long time European control of the international distribution and exchange network remained largely intact, ensuring that the colonies remained economically dependent on the colonial powers in trade as in most other economic areas. Even when the USA replaced the European countries as the dominant commercial and financial power in the region, the various countries became as dependent on the new imperialists as they had been on the old ones.

During the colonial era the attitude of the imperial governments towards their colonies in respect of production, trade and markets meant that during the main slavery period, Caribbean territories often found themselves selling in the cheapest market and buying in the dearest. Products essential for the smooth functioning of the plantations and the colonies were often in short supply. Most places suffered from periodic shortages of food supplies. The imperial power never bothered too much about this, provided significant profits continued to flow into its coffers from the expatriation of the colonial staples at low purchase prices. Thus the vast majority of the colonial population was kept poor and the colonies underdeveloped and dependent on the metropolitan countries.

The similarity of the commodities produced (sugar, coffee, cocoa, etc) and the strong emphasis on cash crop production reinforced the imperial fiat in keeping the colonies apart, even when, as in the Dutch mainland territories of Demerara and Essequibo, Berbice and Suriname, they shared boundaries. The result was that no adequate network of trade and communication existed within the region itself, serving the interests of the region rather than those of the metropolitan countries.[24] This is arguably the case even today.

One manifestation of this is the strong foreign competition to supply the market with goods that can be produced in the region or for which adequate substitutes can be found. For example, rice which is produced on a commercial scale in Guyana and Suriname is not only subject to severe competition internationally, but even finds it difficult to hold its own at the regional level against that imported from the USA. The competition from extra-regional sources relates not only to food production, but also to a wide range of light factory and craft goods which are produced in the region and for which a ready market is theoretically available. The list includes cheap paintings and prints, plaques, souvenirs, greetings cards, special occasion cards, book rests, book markers, pot holders, kitchen towels, clothes hangers, clothes pegs, plastic flowers and wooden toys.

Many of these items are being imported not only from the USA, but also from Japan, Taiwan and Hong Kong. In spite of the foreign exchange drain, it has proved difficult to persuade regional businesses to cease importing them. Most governments seem to lack the political will to impose bans or prohibitive tariffs, especially since the USA, the World Bank and the IMF are forcing third-world governments increasingly into the open market economy.

Efforts at strengthening regional trade are further impeded by the duplication of industries such as garment, cement and canning. This means that the market for a given product is very limited, which in turn adversely affects capital investment, the volume of production, economies of scale, product variety and research design. This has a damaging effect particularly on the economies of the least developed territories of the region, where high costs and limited volumes of production make goods uncompetitive against those of other Caribbean countries. This has led the least developed countries to request a regime in CARICOM by which certain industries would be located in their territories, to offset some of the economic effects on them of importing much more CARICOM goods than they are able to export to sister CARICOM countries. While the CARICOM agreement pays lip-service to such an arrangement, to date no practical efforts have been made to implement it.

The most important joint and single ventures, apart from those with metropolitan companies, have been carried out with Venezuela. It is therefore not surprising that the smaller territories of CARICOM have little faith in the capacity and goodwill of the larger ones to accord them the treatment which they believe they deserve in CARICOM. Even in the larger territories joint-venture initiatives have either been still-born or have failed to match up to expectations. This, for example, was the case with the proposal in the early 1980s to set up an aluminium company, utilising bauxite from Jamaica and Guyana and natural gas from Trinidad. This project seems to have no hope of materialising in the near future. The proposed cement plant joint venture between Barbados and Trinidad and Tobago in the 1980s did materialise, but it was plagued by financial and administrative problems and by misunderstanding between the governments of the two countries. Moreover, similar plants have been erected in Trinidad and Tobago and Jamaica. This duplication creates serious problems for of the viability of such enterprises, because of diseconomies of scale and limited market opportunities.

Intraregional links are also badly affected through the restriction of trade by tariff barriers and import quotas. Although the members of CARICOM have agreed in principle to the dismantling of all tariff barriers within the Treaty area, not all of them have implemented this agreement. Moreover, even among those members who have declared the implementation of the agreement, trade is often impeded by the necessity to obtain import licences for certain CARICOM-produced goods. This, in fact, has been the experience in all the CARICOM countries at one time or another, but certain countries have recently expressed their determination to end such practices. Another vexing problem has been the replacement of customs duties on CARICOM goods by consumption taxes and/or stamp duties, which have the same effect of creating hindrances to the free flow of trade among the member countries.

The situation is worse for trade which crosses or attempts to cross linguistic barriers, for instance, between the English-speaking and the Spanish-speaking zones, and the French-speaking and the Dutch-speaking zones. With the sole exception of Suriname, attempts by some non-Anglophone (and also even Anglophone) territories to join CARICOM have met with less than success. Thus Haiti, the Dominican Republic, the Netherlands Antilles, Puerto Rico and Mexico only have observer status. In 1990 applications for full membership by the Dominican Republic, the British Virgin Islands and the Turks and Caicos Islands were being considered, but up to now these countries have not been admitted.

The impact of all these restrictions has been the slow growth of trade within the region, in percentile terms. Trade within the CARICOM region was estimated in 1992 at around 10 per cent of total export trade, a figure which was reached more than ten years ago.[25] The volume of regional trade outside the CARICOM area is, if anything, less. Trade carried on outside the region with the USA, the UK, France, the Netherlands and the Council for Mutual Economic Assistance (CMEA), in the main, accounted in the 1980s for the greatest volume of trade. In the late 1980s some 87 per cent of Cuba's foreign trade was conducted with the CMEA. The USA is the principal source of imports and exports for a large number of territories, reaching levels of close to or more than 50 per cent in countries like Bermuda, the Bahamas, the Dominican Republic and Haiti.

One of the most interesting examples of regional interaction, but one which is usually omitted in discussions of intraregional economic activity, is the trade carried on by the hucksters who ply between the various territories seeking to purchase goods at the most favourable prices. The most well-known of these hucksters were the Guyanese, who in the midst of the severe downturn in their country's economy in the 1970s and 1980s went from island to island exchanging their gold and other commodities for much needed imports. They traded especially with Barbados, Curaçao, Suriname and Trinidad. We should note also the huckster trade between St Vincent and Trinidad, Grenada and Trinidad, Jamaica and Haiti, Jamaica and the Caymans, Haiti and the Dominican Republic, and Haiti and the Bahamas. These examples demonstrate that at a practical level the small man has often seized the opportunity created by the better conditions existing in sister territories, to foster intraregional trade. The volume of this trade cannot be accurately determined, even though all imports and exports are supposed to pass through customs and/or other government agencies. In practice, much of this trade operation is illicit or underground, and also often involves exchange in kind rather than in cash. Part of this underground economy involves the sale of marijuana, an activity in which the Jamaicans play the major role, but which is not entirely unknown among the Guyanese and other traders. Overall, huckstering is believed to play an imporant role in the level of domestic savings and sometimes in foreign currency earnings in these small economies.

The volume of intraregional huckstering trade appears to have decreased in the past few years, at least among the Guyanese and Jamaicans. This is due mainly to two factors: an ease in governmental restrictions on the export of foreign currency which allows the larger businessmen to import goods (principally from the USA) and wholesale them to the local hucksters; and bad treatment of the hucksters by customs and other officials, which discouraged many from continuing their trade.

One major reason for the failure to develop better trade links within the region is the underdeveloped nature of its communications network, especially shipping and air cargo services. No transportation facilities exist to service the region as a whole on a regular basis. This is true not only of cargo services but of those catering for the movement of peoples. British West Indian Airways (BWIA) is perhaps the most well-known regionally-based airline, but it services mainly the Anglophone Caribbean, with some connections in such other countries as Puerto Rico and St Maarten. The Leeward Islands Air Transport (LIAT) operates exclusively within the region, and is perhaps the airline with the most connections. It services a number of Dutch-, French-, Spanish- and English-speaking territories. Other important airlines are Empresa Consolidada Cubana de Aviacón, Compañia Dominicana de Aviacón, ALM (Antillaanse Luchtvaart Maatschappij) and Air Martinique. While it is possible to get to most of the Caribbean countries through connections with one or more of the regionally-based airlines, it is necessary sometimes to follow a roundabout route. For instance, the simplest route from the Eastern Caribbean to the Bahamas is via Miami. On the whole, communication between the Caribbean and various metropolitan countries is still much easier and sometimes much cheaper than between various Caribbean countries.

Proliferation of regional currencies

The proliferation of regional currencies since independence is another major barrier to regional trade and finance. For instance, seven different currencies exist among the Anglophone members of CARICOM, only two of which (Barbados and Belize) are on par with each other. On 25 December 1995, the local dollar values to the US dollar were; the Bahamas at $1.00, Barbados and Belize at $2.00, the OECS at $2.70, Trinidad and Tobago at $5.77, Jamaica at $36.50, and Guyana at $139.50.[26] These rates of exchange were established without consultation with other member countries. In Trinidad and Tobago, Guyana and Jamaica they were also varied from time-to-time, and government exchange regulations in the 1980s forbidding their currencies to be traded outside the issuing countries ruled out their being exchanged in other CARICOM member countries.

The desirability of a single currency within CARICOM is obvious and the possibility of creating one has been mooted. However, it would require a great deal of political will and an equal measure of economic sacrifice in the short term in order to realise it. Among the benefits perceived would be limits on individual governments' capacity to create new money arbitrarily and thus increase inflation; accelerated investment in exportable goods, tourism and international services; increased regional and extraregional trade; pooled foreign exchange reserves; and possibly a stabilisation fund to which the most heavily indebted countries would have controlled access.[27]

Judging from the experience of the EU, it will take a long time for full monetary union to develop, and it will have to be created by stages. What is required immediately is a regime which allows for the free convertibility of currencies within the region. The CARICOM governments agreed in principle in 1995 to a limited convertibility of their currencies,[28] but this awaits implementation by the individual countries. These agreements are needed for all Caribbean countries. It should be understood that Caribbean countries would be permitted to pay outstanding debts to each other in one or more Caribbean currencies, and not necessarily in hard currencies, as some have been demanding. Such minimal arrangements are critical if the region is going to make meaningful strides in the near future in the development of intraregional trade, markets and banking.

The power of the Yankee dollar is a prevailing financial reality. It is the only currency which is accepted without reservation by all strata of society and at all levels of business operations. Other hard currencies, such as those of the United Kingdom, France, the Netherlands, Germany, Canada and Japan, are variously accepted by different groups, but do not have nearly such a wide appeal. The US dollar is the legal tender in Puerto Rico, the US Virgin Islands and the Turks and Caicos Islands, and it is virtually interchangeable in business transactions in the Cayman Islands, Bermuda and the Bahamas.

In the other countries the local currencies are pegged to the US dollar at specific exchange rates, the international values of the local currencies rising or falling with that of the US dollar. These countries' financial fortunes are tied in a very direct way to the US dollar. In a few countries, such as Guyana, Trinidad and Tobago and Jamaica, the local currency is allowed to float against the hard currencies. Invariably, however, a significant *de facto* devaluation of the local currency occurs in the short and medium terms. In the French overseas departments of Martinique, Guadeloupe and French Guiana, the French currency is the legal tender and their financial fortunes are tied even more closely to those of the French franc in Europe and the wider world. What all this means is that the region suffers from financial dependency in a structural way, whether it be in relation to the French franc, the British pound or the US dollar, and this limits its capacity to be resilient and innovative in its financial and monetary policies.

Regional economic cooperation

There are other benefits which we might expect to flow from regional integration – or deeper regional cooperation – than at present. These include wider access to technology, skills, markets (regional and overseas), a greater range of industries based upon economies of scale and a greater capacity to attract and retain top-level management. A joint approach to the wider international community on matters such as tariffs, access to finance capital, tax holidays and other incentives to investors can only be of benefit to the region as a whole. Philip Mason is particularly harsh on the region for not achieving any meaningful level of economic integration: 'Caribbean societies, already impoverished, condemn themselves by their separation to further impoverishment.'[29]

To be sure, many economic institutions and economic arrangements exist in the Caribbean at both the regional and sub-regional levels. The most noteworthy of these is CARICOM, which was born in 1973 out of CARIFTA, the more limited economic arrangement forged by Guyana, Barbados and Antigua six years earlier. Today CARICOM embraces 13 English-speaking territories and the Dutch-speaking territory of Suriname. Within this institution committees and specialised agencies embrace nearly every important aspect of economic and social life, including air and sea transport, telegraphic communications, tourism, mining, agriculture, fisheries, finance, health, human rights and culture. However, even the most ardent supporters of this institution would no doubt agree that it has failed to make much headway on a number of matters that are critical to its well-being, including those mentioned above.

For example, in 1994, as a result of a study commissioned by the Caribbean Tourism Organization (CTO), a recommendation was put to the various governments that the nine airlines owned by the member states of that organisation should merge their operations. The airlines in question were BWIA, ALM, LIAT, Bahamasair, Air Suriname, Guyana Airways, Air Aruba, Air Jamaica and Cayman Airways. The recommendation called for a number of joint-venture projects, including fuel purchasing, commuter reservations, travel agency distribution, joint fleet planning and joint aircraft acquisition. It was estimated that these ventures would lead to an overall profit of US$65 million, in contrast to the overall loss of US$38 million suffered by the airlines in 1993. It was also anticipated that such an undertaking would substantially change the situation whereby 81 per cent of the region's commuter traffic was being carried by US airlines and only 15 per cent by regional ones. The CARICOM heads of government accepted the recommendations,[30] but up to the present no serious action has been taken to implement them.

Apart from CARICOM there exists regional and subregional institutions such as the Caribbean Chamber of Industry and Commerce, the Caribbean Development Bank, the Eastern Caribbean Central Bank, the Caribbean Food and Nutrition Institute, the Caribbean Labour Congress, and the Caribbean Tourism Organization. However, most of them relate exclusively to the English-speaking Caribbean or, more precisely, to some of the English-speaking Caribbean, for entities like the Cayman Islands and the Turks and Caicos Islands usually have little or nothing to do with them. The impact of the regional institutions on the regional economies is only a ripple in the water, partly because the member states do not give them the kind of support which they deserve. Nevertheless, their significance is twofold. Firstly, they demonstrate clearly the awareness of various groups and individuals of the need to create larger functional institutions to promote the economic development of the region. Secondly, they are institutions already on the ground, so to speak, and they can become agencies for greater economic and technical cooperation.

In summary, it is certain that deeper regional cooperation would have shielded the various economies from some of the worst effects of the downturn in the global economy over the last two decades. It would have reduced significantly their extraregional balance-of-payments deficits and helped them to find perhaps more meaningful, and definitely more sympathetic, solutions to their other financial problems.

Notes

1. Hoetink, 'Surinam and Curaçao', 61.
2. Ragatz, 3.
3. Lugard.
4. Pares, *A West India Fortune*; Ragatz; Williams, *Capitalism and Slavery*.
5. Griffin & Khan, 1.
6. See Williams, *Columbus to Castro*, 335-43, 444.
7. Coleman & Nixson, 5.
8. Frank, 3.
9. See the discussion in Chapter 6 on the activities of the international financial institutions.
10. Dos Santos, 79.
11. 'Embassy a Sore Point,' 5.
12. Studies dealing with the profitability of the British sugar colonies include Sheridan, ' The Wealth of Jamaica', 292-311; Carrington, 'The State of the Debate on the Role of Capitalism', 20-41. Drescher, while attacking Williams' decline thesis, strongly supports the view that the sugar colonies were very valuable to the British up to the second decade or so of the nineteenth century (see *Econocide*). See also general bibliography.
13. Ragatz, vii.
14. Ekundare, 127.
15. *South America, Central America and the Caribbean* (*1995*), 250, 265.
16. *South America, Central America and the Caribbean* (*1995*), 273, 283.
17. International Trade Statistics Yearbook 1994, I: 275, 390.
18. *Monthly Bulletin of Statistics, 50(6), 1994: 258.*
19. Cited in Harris & De Villiers, II, 455.
20. Japan has a developing but still very limited trade with the region.
21. Coleman & Nixson, 148.
22. Griffin & Khan, 12.
23. Emmanuel, *Unequal Exchange*.
24. See below for further discussion on regional communications.
25. *Time for Action*, 149.
26. *Keesing's Record*, 42 (1996), R37-51
27. For a fuller discussion of this subject see Farrell & Worrell, especially the chapters by Farrell, 12-26; Worrell, 27-50; Hilaire *et al.* 58-89; and Theodore, 110-143.
28. Samantha Scantlebury, 'Currencies to Move More Freely in the Region', *Sunday Sun*, July 9, 1995:22A.
29. Mason, introduction to Lowenthal's *West Indian Societies*, vii.
30. '$65m. To Be Made From Airlines Merger', *Daily Nation*, Sept. 28, 1995:15.

CHAPTER 6

Distorted development path II

Certainly the pattern of trade between DC and LDC countries yields a fairly clear picture of the economic relationship between them, the predominant features of which still reflect a past in which, under colonial domination, the trade of LDCs was subservient to the needs of the metropolitan countries.[1]

Coleman & Nixson

The international market

In 1988 the World Bank stated: 'An outward-oriented strategy is superior to one in which trade and industrial incentives are biased in favor of production for the domestic market over the export market.'[2] This means dismantling tariff and other barriers to production and trade. However, critics of the export-oriented and open-market approach hold that the benefits of growth in the global economy rarely trickle down to the poor countries. Moreover, such critics view such a policy as placing less developed countries in an increasingly dependent relationship with the developed countries, which may lead to large-scale interference in their economic, social and political lives and a consequent *de facto* loss of sovereignty.

While encouraging and sometimes even coercing third-world countries to liberalise their trade, the developed countries have continued to protect local industries by non-tariff barriers to trade. Japan is perhaps the most obvious example of protectionism among the Group of Seven (G7) of the most highly industrialised countries;[3] but the USA and the European countries are not without fault in this respect. A World Bank report of 1991 observed, 'Twenty of the twenty-four OECD economies are, on balance, more protectionist now than they were ten years ago.' It pointed out that the non-tariff barriers to trade erected by these countries are particularly harmful to third-world countries because they affect those items in which the latter are most competitive internationally – leather goods, textiles, clothing, footwear, travel goods and beverages, to which may be added steel, chemicals and motor vehicles.[4]

Decisions in 1995 concerning the General Agreement on Tariffs and Trade (GATT) and the creation of the World Trade Organization (WTO) give faint hope of rectifying this situation. The WTO agreements contain special provisions for developing countries and least developed countries in order to soften the impact of trade liberalisation on their fragile economies by delaying the full implementation of some of the regulations applying to developed countries. The agreements also provide for technical assistance to developing countries to allow them to enjoy the benefits of trade liberalisation.[5] Opinion is divided about the overall impact of this liberalisation on developing countries. Some writers believe that it will give them an opportunity to sell goods in which they have a comparative advantage over developed countries, and that this would be a significant benefit for small exporting economies. Others feel that they will become even more vulnerable to the developed countries, especially in respect of those industries which require large imports of raw materials and advanced technology.

It is officially estimated that the greater flow of trade resulting from the agreements of the WTO will result in an annual increase in world trade of between US$200 billion and US$300 billion over the next ten years. The main beneficiaries are expected to be Japan in a wide range of imports; the EU, especially in respect of its agricultural exports; the USA in textiles; and the former Soviet bloc countries in textiles, banking, insurance, travel and telecommunications. The EU is expected to realise an increased income of US$80.7 billion annually from 2002. The third-world countries, however, are expected to experience major negative effects, with the notable exception of China. According to the OECD's estimate, China is expected to gain US$37 billion per year, but Africa is expected to lose about US$2.6 billion annually. third-world countries will be adversely affected by the fact that tariffs on a number of their exports, such as leather, textiles and fish,[6] would remain high even in the move towards a so-called free market. No provision has been made for direct financial and other compensation to third-world countries which suffer adverse income effects from the new arrangements.[7]

The Barbadian economist, Frank Alleyne, says that the new GATT is likely to have serious effects on the region's preferential tariffs under the Lome Agreement. It will also put pressure on Caribbean exports to the US and Canadian markets, in competition with the products of other countries. Any present benefits from EPZs will be eliminated, since there will be no need to circumvent certain trade regulations by setting up such zones in developing countries.[8]

The region has been placing renewed emphasis on production for the international market. Attempts have been made to attract investment capital from overseas for private and public enterprises. The result is that since the 1970s the region has been invaded by transnational corporations (TNCs), which sometimes take over the old plantations, but mainly concentrate on manufacturing and service industries. Some nationals view them as being different from the old-style plantations in form but not in substance. They display the old plantation mentality concerning absentee ownership, the exploitation of labour and the expatriation of profits.

The TNCs, while focusing on using the region as a clearing house for international transactions, have also dug their tentacles deeply into the regional market by becoming deeply involved in the economic activities of nearly every country and every major sector. In the Caribbean their range of activities includes banking, finance, mining, advertising, construction, transportation, public utilities, communications, printing, publishing, shipping, insurance, tourism, food processing, retail outlets, real estate, agriculture, dairy farming, fisheries, marketing, management services, manufacturing, accounting and consultancy. There is hardly an area of meaningful economic activity in which TNCs are not involved, either through a parent company or a subsidiary.

Some of the international giants operating in the region are Colgate-Palmolive, Johnson & Johnson, Unilever, WR Grace, Thompson Brandt, Dunlop and Bayer in manufacturing; Nedlloyd, Booker Shipping and Sealand in shipping; General Foods, Nestlé, Procter & Gamble, Consolidated Foods, and Jacobs in coffee; Tate & Lyle, Booker McConnell and Gulf & Western in sugar; Pillsbury, Canadian Pacific (Maple Leaf) and General Mills in grain; Cable & Wireless, ITT and RCA in telecommunications; Holiday Inns, Hilton International, Club Mediterranée, Trust House Forte and Intercontinental Hotels (Grand Metropolitan) in tourism; Shell, Texaco, Mobil, Exxon, Gulf & Western, Alcan, Alcoa and Reynolds Metals in minerals; and Chase Manhattan, Royal Bank of Canada, Bank of Nova Scotia, Barclays Bank, Lloyds Bank and Canadian Imperial Bank of Commerce in banking.

The region's attraction for so many TNC giants can only mean that its assets, natural or otherwise, are thought to enhance their profitability.

Historians, economists and others have made numerous suggestions to explain it, including that a market of some 36 million people is fair-sized, the political climate of most of the countries is stable, water supplies in the urban areas are potable, an adequate telecommunications network exists between the regional capitals, the larger cities and the external metropolises, and various European languages are spoken.

Caribbean governments, have pursued a policy of industrialisation by invitation and have have intervened to ensure that the right climate is created for attracting TNCs. This policy was espoused for Puerto Rico in the 1950s by Muños Marín, and for the English-speaking Caribbean by Sir Arthur Lewis. Little financial risk is involved in most of the TNCs' operations. Governments go out of their way to ensure that the industrial climate is acceptable, including political stability through the use of state power to put down civil unrest and protect overseas personnel and property. Government erection and maintenance of industrial parks (factory shells) at minimal cost to the corporations save a good deal of money and reduce the possibility of financial loss due to social unrest or a downturn in their profits Other incentives include tax-free holidays or low taxes, the duty-free import of machinery and raw materials, the expatriation of profits and the provision of utilities at highly subsidised rates.

It has been alleged that one of the greatest incentives for setting up business in the Caribbean is the wages which can be paid to non-unionised workers, who constitute most of the working force. Wages in the Caribbean are substantially lower than in North America and Europe, although they are higher than in some Asian countries such as Taiwan and South Korea. However, the situation is partly redeemed by the proximity of the Caribbean to the USA, which reduces shipping costs of raw materials and finished goods from and to the continental mainland.

Investigations conducted by the US National Labor Committee and the US government revealed that the governments of several Caribbean and Latin American countries agreed not to allow workers in the EPZs to be unionised.[9] However, a study carried out in 1994 by Ernst & Young International, a professional services firm, polling top executive officers of 230 of the world's largest TNCs, found that market potential rather than cheap labour was the primary reason for investing in overseas markets. Potential includes a stable political climate and currency, an adequate commercial infrastructure and reasonable government regulations.[10]

The USA has offered special incentives to US corporations to invest in the Caribbean through Tariff No. 809, the Caribbean Basin Initiative (CBI) and the Enterprise for the Americas Initiative (EAI). Certain manufactured goods, for instance, such as garments and electronic components, are allowed to enter the US market duty-free, provided a certain percentage of the process of manufacture is carried out in the Caribbean. Many US firms, making use of EPZs, ship partly finished products to the region, assemble them here and re-export them to the USA duty-free, thus making handsome profits on the transactions. Other corporations, taking advantage of the special circumstances within CARICOM and other Caribbean countries, set up factories which produce specifically for the regional market. In the technical sense these goods are produced locally, but it is largely the foreign firms rather than the local ones which gain.

The concessions granted to the TNCs and the ubiquitous nature of their operations help to explain the stranglehold that they have on third-world countries in general and Caribbean countries in particular. Foreign companies, while expanding the range of goods and services available in the region, extract much more than they put into the economies. Their activities stunt the development of the local manufacturing and mercantile community because of the advantages enjoyed, such as easier access to capital, advanced technology, freightage, international markets and modern managerial techniques. They also include incentives which are often denied local businesses, such as tax holidays and factory shells. The TNCs, through their parent and sister companies and subsidiaries, are able to purchase raw materials and other essential inputs at much lower prices than can local business enterprises and are often allowed to import them duty-free into the Caribbean.

The TNCs often play crucial roles in determining the prices of raw materials from the underdeveloped countries and manufactured goods from the developed ones. Through the involvement of the large TNCS in a wide range of activities globally (wholesaling, retailing, manufacturing, freighting, banking, etc.), they are able to control prices more effectively and thus increase their profit margins. This is also facilitated through the widely practised policy of price transfers with their subsidiaries, that is, overpricing overheads (cost of imports, freightage, insurance, etc) and underpricing exports. This has the effect of artificially reducing the level of profit and the taxes they pay.

Barry *et al.* express the view that, 'If left completely uncontrolled, investment by TNCs obstructs locally owned economic development (private and public), increases the flow of imports, raises the external debt, and discourages regional economic integration.'[11] At the same time TNCs contribute little to actual capital formation in third-world countries. By expatriating their profits they reduce the potential capital resource base of the regional economies. They also utilise only a small amount of unskilled labour and their overall contribution to human resource development is minimal.

Limitations of policy of industrialisation by invitation

As important as have been the initiatives taken in the industrialisation of the region, the policy of industrialisation by invitation is widely regarded by Caribbean economists as a failure or at best only a very modest success. The most successful experiment in this sort of industrialisation was in Puerto Rico in the early period, when it led to a large inflow of capital within a short period of time and the establishment of a number of TNCs. However, the special relationship which Puerto Rico has with the USA allowed it to gain more from it than other countries have been able to do. But even there, as in other parts of the region, the policy has had only very limited success.

One big hope was that over a short period of time self-sustaining industrial development would become a reality and the regime of tax holidays would be diminished, if not completely eliminated. This has not been the case, and the experience of Puerto Rico is a striking example of the Caribbean as a whole. The foreign firms threatened to pull out if the period of tax holidays was not extended, and after an impasse the government gave in, extending the period in some cases from 10 to 30 years. Thus these firms have remained foreign enclaves instead of being integrated into the economies, speaking to the failure of the policy to create a self-sustaining programme of industrialisation.

Nearly all the machinery and technical skills utilised in production, especially for the overseas markets, remain under the control of the TNCs. For instance, the electronics industries located in the region have usually involved simply the assemblage of parts manufactured in the USA. Moreover, only rarely does a local worker assemble all the various parts of a product. The same is true of the garment industry, where semi-manufactured pieces are imported into the region and sewn together, each section often by a different worker, for re-export to the USA or elsewhere. Thus the process does not train the worker to utilise a skill outside the limited scope of the firm. When the firm closes down the worker is either thrown on the job market or is recruited by another firm doing a similar task. This lack of training is part of the process of underdevelopment of the human resources, which contributes to the persistence of poverty. The emphasis in many of the foreign industries on completing a process of manufacture already begun abroad means that the process has few spin-off effects on the wider economy.

Another important drawback of foreign-based industrialisation is the concentration on the utilisation of local labour and the almost total neglect of the use of local materials and technology. Even so, foreign firms have been low employers of labour, so that contrary to early expectations, with a few exceptions (the Dominican Republic and Haiti), the policy has not had an appreciable impact on unemployment figures.[12] The high level of unemployment has made it easy for foreign firms to underpay their workers, whom they are able to dismiss at their own whim and caprice.

Foreign-based industrialisation has also failed to achieve, or even attempt, the integration of the main economic sectors. The continued fragmentation of each territory's economy has caused Best to state that each one of them is 'hardly more than a locus of production made up of a number of fragments held tenuously together by Government controls'.[13] This is seen notably in the heavy urban concentration of industries, resulting in an exacerbation of the uneven development between town and country. Any economic links established between the two areas are coincidental, usually through the attraction of workers from the rural areas to the new urban industrial centres and the remittances sent back to family members. The new industries also tend to attract more persons to the cities than jobs available there, thus worsening unemployment there.

The economic policies pursued by the TNCs are usually determined by absentee parent companies. These policies often conflict with those of the host government, which nevertheless finds itself unwilling to interfere in the activities of the TNCs, for fear that they will relocate. But even though they try their best to retain the TNCs, with a few notable exceptions the governments have not gained much in revenue. Licensing fees are usually small, as also are corporation taxes, while (as we have said above) little or no profit tax is collected. The fact that gross revenue from the industrial activities (that is, receipts from sales of the finished products) are realised abroad and not in the Caribbean also means that foreign currency earnings are minimal.

The tourism industry

The analysis above is equally relevant to the tourism industry, perhaps more so, since all, except the mainland territories, have a suitable infrastructure. The countries boast of a fine combination of sea, sand and sun, the three ecological pillars of the industry (sex often constitutes the fourth dimension). We spend much time fostering the myth that the region is a tourist paradise, although, curiously enough, we try to outdo each other in representing our own particular island as the perfect tourist resort. The region is being increasingly sold to the international community as a place of fun and frolic in their most enchanting and alluring forms. An advertisement in a US magazine strikingly confirms this. Anguilla is described as an island which has '33 perfect white beaches'; the Bahamas has 'glittering casino resorts' on 'Paradise Island', and 'turquoise waters' which 'lap pale, creamy beaches'; Belize is 'a mecca for scuba divers'; Bonaire is simply 'unspoiled', with its 'crystal-clear waters, endless coral reefs and flocks of flamingos'; the British Virgin Islands is a place where 'rock stars and royalty seek out luxury resorts'; Curaçao is famous for its 'perfect Dutch architecture'; Dominica is 'crowned with extinct volcanoes and mountain lakes, clothed in rain forests and waterfalls, and fringed with pearl-grey beaches'; Guyana has 'the largest wooden Gothic cathedral in the world, and the biggest water lily; rare birds and animals, and superb trout fishing'; Haiti's 'hilly suburbs are a melange of art galleries, gingerbread houses, hotels and restaurants'; Jamaica is 'seductive and diverse' and in the west is 'hedonistic Negril'; Montserrat has 'silver beaches' and caters to 'rock stars'; Puerto Rico has 'spectacular beaches'; some of the Grenadine Islands are 'perfect for snorkelling or lazing on a virgin beach'; the Turks and Caicos Islands boast 'a clear aquamarine sea' and more than 200 miles of sparkling beaches, as well as 'virtually virgin coral reefs'; the US Virgin Islands have 'unblemished beaches'. These quotations are all drawn directly from the advertisement.

The advertisement portrays the Caribbean as a veritable paradise for the architect, hiker, golfer, horticulturist, treasure hunter, gourmet, shopper, ornithologist, angler, geologist, marine biologist, naturalist, watersport addict (water-skiing, snorkelling, sailboating, yachting, scuba diving, rafting), casino gambler, dancer and even the great escapist.[14] Some of the details are accurate but others are greatly exaggerated in order to attract tourists.

The writer makes no mention, direct or indirect, of sexual pleasures as part of the package which a trip to the Caribbean offers, but overt and covert sexual advertising is a normal aspect of selling the region, as we can gather from looking at the posters and brochures. In 1988 some T-shirts and buttons advertising the US Virgin Islands carried the following statement, with its oblique sexual connotations: 'I slept on a VIRGIN island.'

The existence of all-year sunshine and the other natural features of the region have made it an obviously attractive destination for people from Europe and North America, especially during the winter months, but also increasingly throughout the year. So important has this industry become to the region that it is now a multibillion dollar gross income earner. Figures released by the Caribbean Tourism Organization for 1994 indicate that just over 22 million visitors, comprising 14.04 million stay-overs and 9.76 million cruise passengers, spent about US$11.67 billion.[15]

This industry, too, is dominated by TNCs, which own many of the tourism plants in or associated with the region such as hotels, airlines, cruise ships and tour-operating businesses. TNCs are prepared to share the cost and ownership of fixed assets with government or local entrepreneurs. They still have firm control of the industry in management, marketing and transportation. In a real sense, therefore, they control its vital arteries.

The importance of this industry to the region has been the subject of much debate in recent years. Some see it as an important income-earner for the region and the lifeblood of the smaller countries such as Antigua and Barbuda, the Cayman Islands, the Turks and Caicos Islands, the Bahamas and Bermuda, which are among the most limited in their resource endowment, but which have excellent natural resources for the tourism industry. It is also argued that tourism has stimulated certain economic activities such as hotel construction and maintenance, hotel training schools, local craft industries, souvenir shops, beach-vending outlets, water sports, high-priced exotic jewellery and cosmetic boutiques, car-rental facilities, catering services, sight-seeing and other service industries. Tourists, they say, spend money in the wider society – in the stores, restaurants, supermarkets, on the beaches, among vendors by the wayside – and therefore the tourist dollar is much more widely diffused than it is in the manufacturing industry. Although there is sensitivity about the adverse effects of the industry, there is nevertheless a conviction that at this period tourism is a benefit or, at worst, a necessary evil.

The Cayman Islands offer a striking example of the financial impact of tourism on a small society. The islands have developed a thriving tourism business in the last few years. In 1994 stay-over and cruise-line visitors totalling some 940,878 persons spent approximately US$328.3 million.[16] The tourism industry, along with the offshore banking business, is said to have made the Caymans a country with one of the highest incomes per head in the world.[17]

Others argue that a good deal of foreign exchange is spent by regional governments and local businesses on creating the infrastructure for the industry, like international airports, seaports and roads, and also on software like vehicles and sports equipment. They also say that foreign exchange is spent on importing foods and beverages and on advertising in overseas markets. They allege that in general little of the money earned by the industry goes to increases national revenue. Tourists often opt for all-inclusive packages which offer them substantial discounts when they pay for their transportation, accommodation and board in their home countries, in which case little actual foreign exchange reaches the region.

Critics also suggest that much of the money that is actually spent in the region by tourists is spirited away by the hotel owners and directors, or is used to pay for services abroad, such as overseas management and promotion. For instance, it is estimated that about 70 per cent of the income derived by the Bahamas from tourism in 1990 and 1991 was gobbled up in imports and profit remissions.[18] McAfee informs us that 'an estimated 80 cents or more of every dollar earned in Antigua's tourism industry accrues not to Antiguans but to foreign companies and investors who own airlines, hotels, supply services and cruise ships'.[19] She states that although Antigua was known to have had the

'the most noticeable boom' in tourism among CARICOM countries in the 1980s, it accumulated the largest debt per head at US$3,030, and had a very high debt-service ratio. The debt in 1994 stood at about US$3,563.[20] Other critics claim that the tourism industry is not a great employer of labour,[21] introduces few skills into the region, increases the overall cost of goods and services and contributes to the degradation of the natural environment.[22]

Other critics allege that large-scale tourism breeds many social ills. Among these are imported consumer lifestyles, nudity on beaches, skimpy clothing in public places, the spread of sexually transmitted diseases and the use of illegal drugs. The perception of the region as a 'sexscape' brings with it a high risk of the spread of AIDS. There is also the drug situation. The region is being viewed increasingly as an area where drugs can be obtained easily. The selling of drugs openly on the beaches is a pressing and distressing problem for hotel managers, law enforcement officers and governments.

Other social ills associated with tourism include casino gambling, money laundering and violence directed against tourists, which has been experienced in Florida as well as the Caribbean. Of course, this sort of violence is a specific form of the generally increasing violence which manifests itself daily in these societies. The acts of violence range from larceny of items left by tourists in hotel rooms or on the beaches to armed robbery, rape and murder. This has been a growing problem in such countries as Bermuda, the Bahamas, Barbados and Jamaica and has led to bad reports in the overseas press about particular Caribbean countries, forcing the local tourism boards to advertise abroad the more positive aspects of Caribbean culture. The fact is, however, that the region as a tourism destination is being challenged by the negative impact of drugs and violence, the tourism product offered in other destinations and the opening of eastern Europe to international tourism. If we are not careful, we may be facing a situation of paradise lost.

Indeed, this is possibly already the situation for the local peoples. Formerly the beaches were regarded as the public domain and places to which locals repaired for leisure and pleasure. With the development of the tourism industry the beaches and contiguous coastlines have acquired high economic values and the social value to the locals has eroded substantially.[23] This is seen for instance, in the closing of large stretches of beaches by hotel owners, restrictions upon access of locals to certain beaches either legally or illegally, and the erection of tall buildings which obscure the seascape from the road. This has led to calls for 'windows to the sea', that is, the retention of certain spots with unrestricted sight of and access to the sea.

Larceny and physical violence against tourists on the beaches, and perhaps some social snobbery, have caused some of those with vested interests in the tourism industry to advocate more restricted access of locals to certain beaches by declaring them private property. In Barbados these calls were answered met with the response a few years ago in the popular calypso *Jack*, by Anthony 'Gabby' Carter, that the beaches were the property of all Barbadians:

> Da beach is mine
> I could bathe any time;
> Despite what he say
> I goin bathe any way.[24]

A point not to be missed is that the growing emphasis on tourism, seen in some of the smaller islands as the panacea for most of their economic ills, has reinforced foreigners' views that the region is a servant community. This is, of course, highly debatable. We like to refer to ourselves as a services-oriented community. However, it seems that some tourists expect the locals to bend backwards literally to please them – and this sometimes means more than doing the limbo, Caribbean-style.

In this context, Lowenthal notes the subtle relationship, at the level of perception, between service and backwardness:[25] 'The paradisical image . . . arouses bitter tensions because it resembles a portrait drawn by masters of slaves – a condescending rather than a complimentary likeness. Far from promoting progress, it seems to relegate the West Indies to perpetual backward- ness.' Nor did the social implications of the industry escape Naipaul: 'Every poor country accepts tourism as an unavoidable necessity,' and the Caribbean territories 'in the name of tourism, are selling themselves into a new slavery'.[26]

Although debate is focused on the positive and negative aspects of the tourism industry, there can be little doubt that it is seen as big business in the region and that it will continue to increase in importance in the foreseeable future. Even such countries as Cuba, which in the early days of the Castro regime saw the industry as a social blight on the country, Guyana, where Burnham avoided it in his efforts to create a so-called socialist republic, and Trinidad and Tobago, where Williams considered it of minor importance in his development strategy, are now pursuing it with urgency and energy. Tobago, for instance, relies heavily on tourism for its revenue. Cuba in 1994 attracted more than 800,000 visitors, more than four times those who visited a decade earlier.[27] It has recently joined the Caribbean Tourism Organization (CTO) and the Caribbean Hotel Association (CHA). It has also announced plans to lease planes to provide service for a major increase in tourist arrivals.[28]

In the past the region as a whole has eschewed taking joint initiatives to market tourism. Thus, although the CTO has existed for some years, and currently embraces some 32 countries, it was not until very recently that its members found it convenient to market the region as a single destination.[29] Even so, regional support for it is still rather lukewarm, at least if measured by its financial commitment, since it is envisaged that at least in the short term marketing the region as a single destination will have to be subsidised financially from outside the region. At the same time the fact that foreigners are prepared to invest heavily gives support to the view that they gain the greatest profits from the industry.

Degradation of the natural environment

An important feature of the growth of the manufacturing and tourism industries has been the violence being done to the natural environment. Many Caribbean countries are faced with the problem of environmental degradation. In Puerto Rico, for instance, the most industrialised country in the region, there is extensive contamination of the underground water resources and beaches.[30] Very little attention has been paid in the past to the ecology of the Caribbean landscape; indeed, little was known until recently about the importance of preserving as far as possible natural ecosystems, and of using them kindly when it becomes necessary to modify them for human survival. Earlier plantation regimes destroyed important aspects of the environment, causing macro-parasites to unleash new micro-parasites. Our knowledge of the adverse effects on human societies of the wanton destruction of the natural environment is much more advanced now. There is much talk today about eco-tourism development, but the reality is that we tend to live one day at a time and to ransom our tomorrows for the transient benefits of today. We are therefore still not paying nearly as much attention as we should to the impact of present activities on the environment and their significance for tomorrow.

In most Caribbean countries government regulations are lax on such problems as industrial waste, environmental pollution and ecological destruction. Sometimes this is deliberately so, in an effort to make a quick dollar. It is known, for instance, that our regulations concerning factory location, waste disposal and industrial pollution are much more lax than those of the USA and western Europe, and that this is an important reason why transnational corporations (TNCs) like to set up business here. This is true generally of the manufacturing industries, but especially chemicals and pharmaceuticals; it is also true of the tourism industry.

Many hotels and cruise liners dump their sewage and other disposables into the nearby sea, leading to marine pollution. The destruction of coral reefs, with the consequent damage to other forms of marine life, is also a daily by-product of tourism, as corals are mined both by locals and visitors to satisfy foreign demand for the product.[31] The oil industry has been a major pollutant both of the territorial and the marine environment. Oil refineries spew their fumes into the air, carrying with them their fall-out, which affects life both on land and sea. Marine oil spills occur frequently from offshore drilling facilities in Venezuela and Trinidad. Even worse spills occur from loading and offloading activities in these territories and also in the Netherlands Antilles, and from oil tankers plying their trade between the USA and the Middle East. Such accidents result in billions of barrels of oil being leaked into the Caribbean Sea, without much attempt to clean up the mess.

Today most Caribbean governments are much more conscious of the need to take measures to limit the impact of development projects on the environment. Some have enacted anti-pollution laws to achieve this objective. However, the will to enforce these laws is sometimes weak. The basic fear remains that too hard an anti-pollution policy might lead to the TNCs pulling out of the country and setting up in neighbouring or non-Caribbean countries with less rigid policies. The incident in Barbados when fire burned down the McBride chemical plant located in close proximity to a housing area, demonstrated the hazards of a less than strict application of laws governing the location of industries, especially in small island states.

The UN global conference in Barbados from April 25 to May 6, 1994, was entitled 'The Sustainable Development of Small Island Developing States'. The conference placed a strong emphasis on the need to achieve small-island development in an environmentally friendly way. It is left to be seen what good will come of the decisions of this conference.

One important effect of globalisation is that pollution in one country affects other countries. This is particularly true of nuclear pollution, such as the Chernobyl disaster, and major oil spills. These 'bads', as they are sometimes called, are due mainly to the activities of developed industrialised countries, but the third-world countries share the effects.

More disturbing still is the policy of industrialised countries of dumping part of the waste from their industries in the waters of third-world countries, including those of the Caribbean. Since 1989, according to the magazine *Third World Resurgence,* over 500 attempts have been made by the 24 rich and highly industrialised countries belonging to the OECD to export over 200 million tonnes of waste, much of which is hazardous. They have approached over 122 countries to accept the waste, usually for a fee. They try to convince third-world peoples that European 'bads' will do them good, by providing landfills in some instances and vitally needed foreign exchange. In 1994 Ivy Dumont, Bahamian government minister of health and environment, charged the members of the EU with making overtures to her government to accept their waste, which, as she poined out, included clinical materials from hospitals, arsenic, lead, mercury and radioactive materials from the manufacture of pharmaceutical products.[32]

In August 1995 the fears of many Guyanese environmentalists were realised when the Canadian-operated Omai Gold Mines Company had a breach in its tailings pond which caused millions of gallons of mine waste, containing cyanide, to pour into the Essequibo river. That river, some 250 miles long, with several tributaries, waters a considerable part of the country. The accident polluted the water used for drinking by thousands of the country's inhabitants and led to the death of many fish and other marine life. The general manager of the company admitted in a press statement: 'Clearly, Omai has suffered from a major industrial accident.' However, he also asserted that the incident did not amount to an environmental disaster and implied that the Guyanese authorities were over-reacting.

The industrialised countries know that many of their undertakings both at home and abroad, pose a serious threat to the global environment. Under pressure from various international conservation groups, in March 1994 the OECD countries finally agreed to ban the export of toxic waste to third-world countries. However, little immediate results were expected from this decision, since the countries also agreed to permit the export of waste for 'recycling and recovery' until 1997. One estimate is that as much as 90 per cent of all the waste exported is assigned to this category.[33] In 1992 a World Bank official is alleged to have declared that there was nothing wrong in dumping the waste of the developed countries in the underdeveloped ones. He is quoted as saying: 'The logic behind dumping a load of toxic waste in the lowest-wage country is impeccable, and we should face up to that.'[34] Polluted as this thinking may be, it informs the actions of many developed countries today. We are reminded of a former era when it was the unwanted people, the 'human waste' as far as the power-brokers in Europe were concerned, who were dumped in the region. As Ragatz says, 'The islands became . . . the dumping-ground for the riffraff of the parent country.'[35]

Although all Caribbean governments appear today to be set against the dumping of the waste of the developed countries, they seem not to have worked out any joint policy on this and other threats to the environment. The Caribbean Conservation Association (CCA) has been attempting with limited finances and personnel to increase public awareness of the ecological disaster facing the region, but most of us seem to go merrily along, blissfully unaware or uncaring about these problems. We have to be vigilant and to guard against every attempt to pollute our environment, even in the cause of our own development and still less in the cause of the development of others. Our birthright and that of our children to clean air, water, sand and land should never be exchanged for a mess of pottage.

Financial institutions

The Caribbean region remains a poor, debt-strapped and debt-trapped area. One way in which this manifested itself in the period before the nineteenth century was in the severe liquidity problems that the region faced and constant foreign borrowing.

As the systems of exploitation became more sophisticated the metropolitan powers found it convenient to establish branches of their banks within the region itself. These banks usually came with very little capital of their own, but were able to increase their financial holdings substantially through local capital deposited in them. Many of them in turn repatriated the original capital they had invested in the region, thus ensuring that come what may they would not suffer a net loss if they had to quit the region. Today by far the bulk of the capital employed by these banks for lending to local enterprises comes from indigenous Caribbean sources. Sometimes the banks even use local capital to lend to foreign businesses in the region. Sometimes also they expatriate large amounts of the capital accumulated, in the form of foreign currency, to their overseas headquarters. Such practices limit the amount of capital available to local entrepreneurs and play a critical role in divesting the region of much-needed foreign currency.

The dominance of overseas banks and other financial institutions in the lending sector of the economy has meant that foreigners have been able to play a significant role in determining the nature of the enterprises that would receive financial assistance, how these enterprises should be set up and managed, and the conditions of repayment of the loans. It has meant specifically that certain agricultural and industrial enterprises, especially in the small-sector category, are often not financed by these institutions. Thus several governments have found it necessary to establish loan facilities, such as development banks and agricultural banks, to assist small business enterprises. This in itself has achieved only a modest success because of a variety of factors, including severe restrictions on the size of loans available to such businesses.

Some governments have also set up regular commercial banks to compete for local capital with the foreign banks, for instance in Cuba, Guyana, Jamaica, Trinidad and Tobago, Puerto Rico and Barbados. However, such local banks have had little success in attracting local capital. One important reason for this is that Caribbean people who have been banking for several years with foreign banks have come to view them as more efficient and trustworthy than the local ones.

Local banks suffer from certain disabilities which hinder their regional and international operations. With few notable exceptions, such as the Republic

Bank of Trinidad and Tobago,[36] and the Jamaica Merchant Bank, Caribbean banks have not managed to establish branches which operate outside their territories of origin. Nor have the various national banks in the region been able to establish strong links with each other.

The failure of Caribbean national banks to break into the regional and international banking arena means that they have to rely upon the foreign ones, many of which have branches in the region, to carry out their foreign transactions, such as the issuing and redemption of bank drafts, travellers' cheques and foreign currency transfers. Such factors make the local banks much less attractive to locals than the foreign ones. Thus, in spite of the fact that many local banks have become technologically more sophisticated recently nationalist sentiment remains weak when it comes to the establishment of financial institutions to displace or challenge foreign ones.

The main regional banking institution in existence, the Caribbean Development Bank (CDB), is regional mainly in the sense that its funds are disbursed to the CARICOM countries. The vast majority of its funds are derived from loans and grants from metropolitan countries such as the USA, Canada, the United Kingdom and Germany. Although these countries do not directly control the purse strings of the bank, they have a strong influence on its policies. In any case, the CDB is a development bank, providing loans for specific government projects, rather than a commercial bank or general lending agency, and this fact alone imposes severe constraints upon its capacity to bail out countries that need a temporary injection of funds to mete specific balance-of-payments crises or other such contingencies.

The offshore financial sector

As Thomas has pointed out, offshore banking has been in the region, in disguised form, for several decades. It has gained importance and today it is a major part of the banking fraternity.[37] Associated with such banks are the trust, brokerage, insurance, shipping and other financial institutions, which operate in tandem with them to form the offshore financial sector of the economy. Some Caribbean economists argue that the term 'sector' is a misnomer, since these offshore activities are even less linked than the offshore manufacturing operations to the territorial or regional economies. Indeed, these financial operations are not intended to be connected with the development of the local economies. For most territories, their chief benefit is the licensing fees they pay, sometimes in hard currency, to carry on their operations The ancillary benefits include renting local business premises and employing very small numbers of local personnel, such as data processors, lawyers and accountants, and also cleaners, security guards, etc. They are therefore generally regarded as enclave industries, because with few exceptions they have hardly any links with the development of the local economies.

The Caribbean is an attractive offshore haven for the big business community, chiefly from the USA. The offshore facilities are often used to disguise the business transactions of the large corporations, to reduce tax liabilities they are required by their home governments to pay and sometimes to cover up activities such as money laundering in which some of them are allegedly involved.[38]

These transactions are mainly paper ones, so that all the paraphernalia of staff, records and technological equipment, associated with regular banks and brokerage firms, is usually absent. Indeed, often all that is maintained is a small office with a plaque indicating its existence, with one or two members of staff. In the main these businesses pay little or no tax on profits to Caribbean governments and are allowed to operate with few or no questions asked. These are the factors that have led to the burgeoning of thousands of offshore financial businesses in the region, first in Bermuda and the Bahamas, and more recently in other countries such as Anguilla, Antigua and Barbuda, the British Virgin Islands, Barbados, the Cayman Islands, the Turks and Caicos Islands, and the Netherlands Antilles. The Cayman Islands, for instance, is said to have an offshore banking sector which makes it the second largest banking centre in the world, after Switzerland. Over 130,000 companies are said to have registered in the British Virgin Islands since legislation was passed to facilitate such registration in 1984.[39]

According to Thorndike, worldwide offshore funds in bank deposits alone were estimated at the end of 1993 at US$12,000 billion, of which US$5,200 billion were estimated to be in Caribbean offshore banks.[40] How much of this money actually finds its way into the local economies is unknown, but it is believed that it remains in the metropolitan countries for lending in the eurocurrency and interbank markets. It is also believed, to contribute less than 1 per cent of the revenue of the Bahamas,[41] according to one source. On the other hand the estimated revenue to the British Virgin Islands is 35 per cent of government income.[42] Ramsaran suggests that offsore financial institutions 'have virtually no significance for domestic finance'.[43] Thus, in spite of notionally large amounts of money in the region, Caribbean countries remain largely debt-strapped, with limited foreign reserves and a severely adverse balance of payments, so that they are forced to borrow from local and overseas lending agencies to meet their financial obligations.

The International Monetary Fund (IMF)

Caribbean countries have sought funds from international lending agencies like the IMF, the World Bank and the Inter-American Development Bank (IDB) to finance programmes of structural adjustments or reforms, which in theory are designed to reduce significantly, if not completely eliminate, their balance-of-payments deficit, balance their fiscal accounts and make their exports more competitive internationally.

The IMF, in particular, is regarded by third-world countries as a bank of last resort, for its prescription for the economic healing of the nation is usually regarded as 'bad medicine'. The IMF seems to have disengaged its conscience in the search for solutions to the debt crisis facing poor countries, and are more concerned with balance-of-payment problems and stabilisation policies than with the wider economic and social effects of its prescriptions. Generally, there- fore, these countries turn to the IMF when all their other lines of credit or loans are deemed to have dried up and when their governments feel that they have no option but to seek temporary asylum in the courts of the IMF. However, they have little or no bargaining power in regard to the structural adjustments which the IMF might require them to undertake in order to secure the loan desired.

The internal detonations of IMF policies usually involve a severe regimen of financial cuts in government expenditure, an end to subsidies on a wide range of basic foods for the poor and stringent taxation. IMF demands, therefore, almost invariably mean laying off a large number of public servants; a policy of wage restraint both for the public and the private sector; a severe reduction in government welfare programmes, including unemployment, maternity and sickness benefits; cuts in expenditure on health care, education and sports; severe scaling down of infrastructural projects such as the building and repair of roads, schools and recreational facilities; the imposition of a stricter regime of direct taxation on local-income earners; and a wide range of indirect taxes on goods and services.

IMF policies often demand that the government divests itself of the ownership of, or shares in, public corporations and industries, and that it devalues the currency because the IMF usually says that its value is a cause of the uncompetitive nature of the national exports. In concert with the World Bank, which is controlled by the same group of countries that control the IMF, the IMF seeks to encourage the debtor third-world countries to open their doors to foreign investment on more liberal terms, including the sale of national assets to TNCs.

The IMF sets specific goals to be met before it will disburse the initial loan and also further loans, or future access to already negotiated loans. These goals are often very difficult to realise and it is quite common for third-world countries to fall short, so that further loans are frozen and the debtor country has to negotiate new conditionalities. The IMF rarely lends a third-world country sufficient money to allow it to climb out of the slough of economic despondency. The injection of the small amount of finance available from the IMF may result in a slight, temporary improvement in the performance of the economy, which is followed by an even deeper trough. Further injections become necessary, with basically the same effects. The result is a kind of economic spasm, which indicates that the prescription is not producing the effects desired by the debtor country.

This concept is vindicated in Jamaica, Dominica, Guyana, Grenada, Haiti, Trinidad and Tobago, the Dominican Republic, Venezuela and Brazil. In fact, economists believe that IMF loans to third-world countries generally only serve to push them further into the economic quagmire, and make them even more vulnerable to the vagaries of international capitalism, and more dependent on the injection of foreign loans for their economic survival.

Only in rare cases has a third-world country come out of the clutches of the IMF within a short period and with its economy in an improved condition. It happened to Barbados in the early 1980s, when it obtained a small loan from the IMF to bridge certain short-term gaps in its repayment schedule to foreign creditors. Barbados returned to the IMF in 1991 on a structural adjustment (austerity) programme, and so far has managed to ride the rough waves. The other Caribbean countries that have gone to the IMF, especially the Dominican Republic, Jamaica and Guyana, have found it impossible to make short-term structural adjustments and have experienced the most painful sensations in their struggles to achieve economic health.

Supporters of the IMF's policies argue that no country is forced to seek loans from it and that it is unfair to accuse it of holding developing countries to ransom. The IMF managing director, Michel Camdessus, complained that the IMF was 'the most familiar scapegoat for the difficulties of governments in dealing with problems they have created'.[44] The view is that these countries, through bad fiscal policies, have sown the wind and are now reaping the whirlwind. The critics of such policies argue that the IMF, along with the World Bank and other international financial institutions, is a creature of the developed countries, whose economic policies and *modus operandi* are designed to increase their wealth at the expense of the developing countries. Thus global trade, markets and financial institutions constitute a network which steals from the poor in order to make the rich richer. According to this view, developing countries caught in the vortex of neo-colonialism have little option but to approach the IMF and other international financial institutions to bail them out of difficult financial situations, albeit only temporarily.

Third-world countries have good reason for adopting this viewpoint. For instance, in 1993 Mr Camdessus put before the main contributors to the IMF a plan for a US$50 billion economic stimulus plan for the Caribbean, Latin America, Asia, Africa and eastern Europe. This was intended to boost their foreign reserves and allow them to buy much needed goods from other countries. However, the USA and Germany, in particular, shot down the proposal.[45]

Countries under IMF loan agreements often find that they no longer have control over their economic affairs, since in reality it is the IMF that determines the national economic priorities and goals. Under the IMF, for instance, more emphasis is placed on production for export, even though this might not be in keeping with the long-term interests of the country. Thus less attention is paid to those sectors of the economy which produce primarily for the local market, with the result that they either stagnate or decline, because of lack of governmental incentives through tax relief and a national programme of import substitution. The economies become more open, more dependent on imports for a wide range of products that could have been produced locally, and more vulnerable to the fluctuations of the international market economy. The Caribbean countries mentioned above are striking testimonies to this situation.

The Dominican Republic in the 1980s offers a striking example of the kinds of difficulties many third-world countries have faced in trying to cope with their economic and social problems under IMF conditionalities. Of course, we need to make it quite clear that the IMF was not solely responsible for the situation in which that country found itself. Poor political and economic management and the vagaries of the international market were also important contributors to the crisis.

The debt crisis was preceded by rapid industrialisation and elaborate public works programmes which served to give the impression of a buoyant economy. Many of these activities, however, including the state distribution of food, were funded from heavy external borrowing at a time when capital was readily available. The national external debt increased from US$600 million in 1973 to US$2,400 million in 1983. The decline in commodity prices in the late 1970s exposed the fragile nature of the economy. In 1982 sugar prices stood at only 5 US cents per lb, as against 76 US cents per lb in 1975. At the same time debt servicing rose from US$87 million in 1973 to US$250 million in 1982.[46]

Faced with this situation, the government decided to approach the IMF for a three-year lending facility. The IMF agreed to lend the government US$466 million over the period, but only allocated US$195.8 million for the first year; the second year's instalment was to be renegotiated on the basis of the country's economic performance in the first year. The IMF loan was not nearly enough to service even the annual debt repayments. At the same time the conditions imposed for the loan entailed devaluation of the peso to the parallel (real) market value and a stabilisation programme, which involved deep cuts in government expenditure, including reduction in Central Bank loans to the public sector and freezing public servants' salaries. The IMF, nevertheless, insisted on the payment of overdue external debts being stepped up and the removal of import restrictions. The last stipulation drove the already faltering domestic economy into competition with external producers.

The devaluation of the currency and the other conditionalities imposed by the IMF led to steep rises in the overall cost of living and in such basic commodities as milk, eggs and wheat. The government decided not to devalue the peso (that is, to maintain its parity with the US dollar) for the purchase of certain commodities such as oil and medicines, but this did not sit well with the IMF which insisted on complete devaluation before the second instalment of the loan could be paid. The stance of the IMF influenced the USA and other financial agencies not to release grants and loans until this was done. So the government reluctantly submitted, with the result that prices for imports rose sharply once again while those for exports declined. The Dominican people, bewildered by the combination of pressures upon them, began to protest, and to demand salary increases and the abrogation of the agreement with the IMF. Eventually protest turned to riot, beginning in Santo Domingo on April 23, 1984. When the riots were finally put down, with brutal efficiency by the government, the count was 112 civilians killed and at least 500 wounded. Another spate of riots in 1990 was also brutally suppressed, leaving 14 civilians dead.

Meanwhile, the government continued to impose its draconian will upon the people and to follow the IMF policies. The peso also continued to depreciate in value against the US dollar: from Ps1:$US1 in 1981, to Ps2.06:$US1.00 in 1984, and Ps12.68:$US1.00 in 1993. The economy, far from being stabilised, reached new levels of instability. The external debt escalated to US$4,200 million in 1987 and the government found itself completely unable to service it. In 1990 the US embassy estimated that the interest arrears on the debt were equivalent to 75 per cent of the country's GDP. The IMF's response was to extend a stand-by facility in 1991, amounting to the paltry sum of US$113 million; even so, it imposed further constraints in respect of government subsidies to state corporations and placed a new emphasis on a market-driven economy. In 1993 the total external debt stood at the frightening sum of US$4,633 million.

The social costs to the country of such policies were great. The significant decrease in wages in real terms affected the quality of life of all but the wealthy classes. Approximately 80 per cent of the teachers in the early 1990s were said to be earning less than the minimum wage. Educational drop-outs, no-shows and oversized classes were some of the visible effects of the emasculation of the educational system. Preventable diseases such as tuberculosis and typhoid, insanitary facilities, low-quality housing stock, bad roads, electricity outages, shortages of medicines and medical personnel and unemployment, were all in evidence in sharper relief from the 1980s. The saddest part of it was the sharp increase in the number of street children. UNICEF estimated that 60,000 children lived on the streets permanently.

The social impact of the austerity programme was also evident in the growing social and political unrest in the country, for instance, in the emergence of workers' and women's movements, and other grassroots organisations, demanding social, political and economic reform and a greater democratisation of the political system. According to Ferguson, 'The IMF riots of 1984 marked the areas where the popular movement was to be most active in the following years. The most militant organizations have grown up in slum areas of Santo Domingo such as Capotillo and La Ciénaga and in other cities such as San Pedro Macoris and Santiago.'[47]

Appeals to the IMF and other donor agencies to modify their lending policies have met with little positive response. In spite of loans, radical fiscal reforms and more open market economies, the Caribbean region's external debt more than doubled during the 1980s. Between 1980 and 1988 it grew by 125 per cent. The debt-service ratio (that is, the annual debt payment as a percentage of export earnings) continued to climb steadily and steeply[48] from 11.2 per cent to 17.2 per cent in the same period. In 1993 Barbados had to spend an estimated 12 per cent of its export revenue on servicing debts, Trinidad and Tobago 27 per cent, Jamaica 30 per cent and Guyana 70 per cent. The total CARICOM debt at that time stood at around US$11 billion.[49] Countries were forced to reschedule debts either unilaterally or by agreement with their creditors. They were also forced to borrow from private lending agencies at high interest rates to repay the debts.

The most significant effect of debt servicing is the negative transfer of resources from the third world to the developed countries. By the late 1980s the amount of capital expended in foreign debt servicing outweighed new capital imported. For instance, between 1985 and 1990 net transfers of capital from third world to developed countries amounted to roughly US$37.6 billion per year, and would have been larger had not some countries been able to reschedule their debts or simply defaulted on debt payments.[50] Between 1980 and 1988 Caribbean debt (excluding that of Cuba) rose from 31.8 to 79 per cent of the annual GNP. In 1988 Jamaica's debt represented 152.6 per cent of GNP, and Guyana's 521.5 per cent of GNP. Between 1986 and 1988 the Dominican Republic, Jamaica, Trinidad and Tobago and Guyana together transferred US$1,292 million, or approximately 3.7 per cent of their combined GNPs. By 1989 they were all making net transfers of capital,[51] although this situation has been reversed recently in Guyana (and one or two other countries).

The flow of capital from where it is most needed is a phenomenon which has dire economic consequences for third-world countries. The situation is exacerbated by the concomitant flight of skilled labour (human capital) to the developed countries, which results in an increasingly adverse net ratio between skilled and unskilled labour. In attempts to service their debts Caribbean countries have resorted to extreme measures to earn foreign exchange. In Guyana, for instance, the governments of Forbes Burnham and Desmond Hoyte resorted to exporting not simply surplus rice and sugar, but also part of the stocks needed for domestic consumption. This led to acute shortages of these staple foods, with severe repercussions on the health of the poor. In Barbados, when shortfalls occurred in sugar production, the Erskine Sandiford administration decided to meet its overseas commitments first in order to retain its quota in the US and other international markets. It attempted to satisfy local demand for sugar by importing inferior quality.

Other governments have sold state-owned lands to foreign companies at less than market values. In one of the crudest ways of earning foreign exchange, the governments of Dominica, Belize and St Kitts and Nevis adopted a policy of 'economic citizenship' by which wealthy foreigners, chiefly from Taiwan, Hong Kong and South Korea, obtained citizenship on payment of US$25,000– 40,000, on the understanding that they would introduce investments of US$100,000–150,000.[52] In 1993 the government of Dominica stated that this policy, which involved about 466 people, mainly Taiwanese, had realised US$5.8 million in investments up to 1991.[53]

Poor countries have often had to cut back on imports and increase exports in order to service their debts. Through unkind and sometimes crude economic reforms, as indicated above, involving wage reductions, currency devaluations, food quotas, exports of food needed by the local population, restrictions on imports, increased taxation, etc., third-world governments have sought to reduce demand for domestic and foreign goods, in order to cope with the exigencies of debt servicing. For instance, foreign exchange and debt servicing problems in Cuba resulted in import cuts from US$8,139 million in 1989 to US$2,236 million in 1992.[54]

The net transfer of capital also means that only small amounts of capital are available for investment in the domestic economy. This in its turn slows and reduces production, further lowering capital accumulation, in a vicious downward spiral, of both capital and production. Again Cuba provides a good example of the impact of the shortage of capital investment on domestic production. Oil production was severely reduced in 1993 and nickel production was only 25 per cent of the projected target. Energy shortages, coupled with bad weather, led to a substantial reduction in the sugar harvest in 1992-93, compared with the previous year, and an estimated revenue loss of US$450 million.[55] Of course, Cuba's problems are complicated, and some may even say that they are caused principally by the financial blockade by the USA, which has denied it access to the main capital markets. Parrilla estimated that as a result of this blockade and other acts of aggression, in 1994 alone the Cuban economy suffered damage to the tune of US$1 billion, equal to half its imports.[56]

Other spin-off effects of a shortage of investment capital include higher rates of unemployment, malnutrition and a decline in social services. At the same time, this very same circumstance tends to increase the incomes of a small local elite which makes profiteering a virtue, even at the expense of their suffering brethren. Guyana is an outstanding recent example.

A few governments have agreed to forgive the debts of the poorest third-world countries. A proposal was made in 1990 under the Enterprise for the Americas Initiative to forgive part of the Latin American and Caribbean debts to the US government, but under severe economic guidelines for the debtor countries. To date nothing concrete has emerged. Periodically, forgiveness of third-world debts is mooted in the various forums of the rich countries, such as the Group of Seven (G7) and the UN Summit for Social Development in Denmark in March 1995.[57]

Aid and special trade

The region has been the recipient of aid packages in cash and kind from various developed countries and international organisations. The most well-known of these are the Colonial Development and Welfare Fund (UK); Fonds d'Investissement et de Développment Économique et Social des Territoires d'Outre Mer (France); the Prosperity Fund (Netherlands); Caribbean Canada (CARIBCAN) and CIDA; USAID, the CBI and the Enterprise for the Americas Initiative (US); Lome I-IV (EU); the UN Development Programme; PAHO; and the World Health Organisation.

The Prosperity Fund, which was established specifically for the Dutch territories, is generally regarded as perhaps the most generous subsidy given to any of the Caribbean territories, but it is certainly rivalled by the subsidies given to the French territories which are regarded as overseas departments of the metropolitan power. Substantial aid also flows from the USA to its Caribbean territories of Puerto Rico and the Virgin Islands. Special quotas for the region's products in overseas markets, often at preferential prices, are also indirect forms of aid. The reality is that the region receives a fair amount of subsidies, though not easily quantifiable, from a wide variety of sources.

The USA's aid to the Caribbean and Latin America increased from US$238 million in 1980 to US$958 million in 1984, and to US$1.5 billion in 1990.[58] However, while aid was increasing, access to US markets was becoming more restricted. US exports to CBI countries increased from US$4.9 billion to US$8.3 billion between 1983 and 1989. During the same period US imports from these countries declined from US$8.5 billion to US$6.6 billion.[59] The figures for 1995 were US$15.7 billion for exports and US$12.8 for imports.[60] The region, therefore, continues to experience a trade deficit under the CBI. This is perhaps the most striking example of the failure of the CBI's policy to benefit the region to any substantial extent. According to the US government, one of the chief objectives of the CBI was to increase the volume of the region's exports to the USA. However, Nicholls expressed the view in 1994 that the CBI 'inherently lacks significant scope for fostering investment, employment, growth and economic development in the region'.[61]

Duty-free entry of goods into the USA under the CBI is very limited in practice, amounting to between only 7-10 per cent of the region's exports to the USA. It excludes petroleum and petroleum-derived products, textiles, shoes and other leather goods. As regards clothing, it allows for the duty-free entry into the USA of garments whose manufacture was started in the USA but is finished (mainly stitched together) in the Caribbean, usually in EPZs. This is really a concession to US garment manufacturers, who profit from the cheap, non-unionised labour in the region. Among the important provisos which could cause a country to be excluded from the provisions of the CBI are 'unfair' economic practices or 'excessive' taxes on US firms or citizens, the nationalisation of US-owned assets and trade preferences given to the products of any developed country in competition with US products.[62] It should be mentioned that the CBI was set up in 1982-83 when US sugar quotas to the region were being reduced.

Since June 30, 1996 the region has been deprived of USAID offices, which were first opened here 20 years ago. This is part of wider cutbacks of aid to the third world, initiated by the Republican-dominated Congress of Clinton's administration. What it means is that no further aid under this programme will be forthcoming to the region. Funds traditionally allocated to poor African, Asian, Pacific, Latin American and Caribbean countries are now being diverted to eastern European countries, ostensibly to facilitate their transition to market economies and stable democracies.

Taken as a whole, the aid and trade package under USAID and CBI was not very generous. Arguably, the region's economies have benefited only marginally from such concessions, and are certainly not much stronger as a result of them.[63] At the same time the USA has sought to use aid packages to prise open markets for US goods, force structural adjustment programmes on reluctant governments, press for privatisation of the economies, and further its wider economic, political and strategic goals in the region.

The same cannot be said of CARIBCAN, which the Canadian government established in 1986, specifically to assist the English-speaking Caribbean (exclusive of the US Virgin Islands). CARIBCAN allows for financial assistance by the Canadian government to the English-speaking Caribbean governments and one-way duty-free imports into Canada for a large number of their products. However, important exceptions include leather products, lubricating oils, textiles, clothing and footwear.[64]

Canadian assistance to the region is not new; it had its origins in the preferential arrangements to the sugar economies in the region at the end of the last century, when they were struggling for survival against beet sugar competition in Europe and low-cost cane sugar from other parts of the world. The Canadian government has never shown a disposition to establish a political, military or financial hegemony in the region, has never issued the equivalent of a Monroe doctrine, and has openly disavowed any intention to use CARIBCAN for any such purposes. At the same time Canadian firms operating in the region have benefited from the preferential arrangements under CARIBCAN, and the Canadian financial presence in the region is growing.

The Canadian government contributed US$90 million in aid to the region during the first five years of the agreement and US$75 million during the second five years. Operating mainly through CIDA, it has rehabilitated and enlarged airports and trained a number of professionals. It also forgave US$100 million in regional debt in 1990. At the fourth CARICOM-Canadian summit, held in Grenada in March 1996, the CARICOM leaders sought unsuccessfully to get an agreement from the Canadian prime minister, Jean Chretien, to allow preferential access to petroleum products, textiles and footwear. CARICOM leaders are worried about access to the Canadian and US markets for their products as a result of the NAFTA agreement, which involves the USA, Canada and Mexico.[65]

Overseas aid has undoubtedly been a significant source of capital for selected Caribbean countries, chiefly those in the Dutch, French and US zones. In other instances specific forms of aid – for example, through CIDA, PAHO and the Commonwealth Fund for Technical Cooperation – have assisted in the development of human capital, although it is impossible to measure this contribution accurately. However, the amount of money available for such training is very small in comparison with the region's needs. Moreover, critical areas of human development, for instance, in medicine, science and technology, have not attracted the kind of financial support desirable, without which the governments face an even tougher task to make their economies competitive internationally.

Some believe that in the long term aid to third-world countries reinforces their dependency on the developed countries. They press strongly for greater access to the markets of the developed countries, especially in respect of those goods in which the third-world countries have a comparative advantage. Arguably, the various forms of aid given to the Caribbean, while helping to train its nationals and to alleviate economic crises in the short term, have made the recipients more dependent than before on their donors. No Caribbean territory has ever managed to achieve real control over its economy. In the Netherlands Antilles, the French Overseas Departments and the US territories foreign control is stronger than elsewhere.

Conclusion

Although the standard of living in the region as a whole has risen since the end of the Second World War, the level of poverty generally is still high. Moreover, recent trends in both the regional and the global economies threaten to reduce the standards of living of some of them. Their indebtedness to the IMF and other international lending agencies is like a thick cloud on the economic horizon.

It is difficult to sustain the argument that had the Caribbean economies been more cohesive and had there been more intraregional banks and lending agencies, those countries that are in the clasp of the IMF would not have got there. The route to the IMF has been tortuous and the basic factors leading to it might well have been outside the capacity of any given country or the region as a whole to handle. Still, regional economic integration, or any appreciable level of economic cooperation, would have eased the pain and perhaps even the trauma associated with the downturn in the international economy. At the same time we must not forget that developed countries also experience negative balance-of-payments. The world's largest debtor is the USA, even with its large landmass and population, its advanced technology and its sophisticated university and research institutions. This fact is often overlooked in discussing third-world countries. We must also remember that the process by which the Caribbean became an underdeveloped and dependent economic zone has historical roots going back to the slavery period.

Not only has the Caribbean as a whole, or even any major segment or linguistic grouping, failed to make strides in respect of economic cooperation, but the region has also failed to develop significant economic ties with any of the major third-world zones in Asia, Africa and Latin America. The ACS was established in July 1994 with 25 Caribbean and Latin American countries signatories. By August 1995 some 16 governments had ratified it, thus making the ACS a functional reality. The first meeting of the new organisation was held in August 1995 and focused attention on tourism, trade and transportation. The member states have expressed a commitment to create a new shipping line and to adopt new initiatives for air transport. They have also agreed to move towards integrating their trade to meet the challenge of the projected free-trade zone of the Americas in 2005.[66] There is therefore some hope of a new, more purposeful action being taken to bridge the gap which has separated them for so long.

In the case of Asia, while Hong Kong, Taiwan and Singapore have increased their trade with the region over the two decades, Japan is the only country with which the region has developed a significant trade. Even so, the dominant aspect of that relationship is the growth of Japanese exports to Caribbean countries. The region is exporting very little to Japan, so that we cannot say that economic relations are being conducted on a basis of reciprocity. We are simply replacing Europe and America with Japan in respect of some of our imports, such as motor vehicles and electronic components. There is little technological cooperation between the region and Japan, nor do the Japanese seem interested in developing such cooperation, or in giving any economic assistance to the region.

Our failure so far to develop exchanges with other economic zones outside Europe and North America means that we are still bound by the exploitation and parasitism that have historically characterised our relationships with these zones. The unequal trading relationship existing between us and them has placed and kept us in a vulnerable position. Their ups are our downs and their downs are our lower-downs.

Notes

1. Coleman & Nixson, 139.
2. *World Bank Report*, 1988, cited in McAfee, 75.
3. The G7 consists of Japan, Germany, Italy, USA, Canada, France and the UK (Griffin & Khan, 2).
4. *Global Economic Prospects and the Developing Countries* (May 1991), 9, cited in Griffin & Khan, 16-17; Ramsaran, *Commonwealth Caribbean*, 14-16.
5. Gibbons, 26.
6. In 1995 the US government banned imports of shrimp from Trinidad and Tobago ('Shrimp Ban Will Hurt Fisherfolk', 9A).

7. 'Little in GATT for Third World', 19B.
8. 'Alleyne: GATT Threat to Lome', 18.
9. Simpson, 12A.
10. *Global 1000 Investment in Emerging Markets*, cited in 'Cheap Labour Low on Investors' List of Priorities', 1B.
11. Barry *et al.*, 25-26.
12. For discussion on the impact of EPZs on the region see Pantin, 'Export Processing Zones', 141-58; Barry *et al.* 55-74.
13. Best, 'Survival and Size', 32.
14. Gilbert Scott, 21, 60, 61. In a more recent article in the American magazine *Conde Nast Traveler* a writer, Patricia Storace, categorised Barbados as perhaps the island 'where reality and illusion flirt most unchaperoned'; and also as a 'miniature miraculously sufficient world' (Cited in Best, 'Almost Paradise', 3A).
15. *Caribbean Tourism Statistical Report 1994*, 5.
16. *Caribbean Tourism Statistical Report 1994*, 105.
17. 'Caymans Bursting at the Seams with Visitors', 16; 'Queen in Cayman Islands', 6A. The figures given in these articles for tourist arrivals and money spent differ somewhat from those given in *Caribbean Tourism Statistical Report* 1993.
18. *South America, Central America and the Caribbean (1993)*, 87.
19. McAfee, 27.
20. *Economic Survey of Latin America and the Caribbean 1994-1995*, 127.
21. Best, under the caption 'World Bank: Bajans Prefer Leisurely Life', (5A) states that the World Bank blames the high level of unemployment in Barbados to some extent on the increasing shift to a 'services-oriented economy and the failure of tourism to generate more jobs'.
22. Samir Amin, third-world economist and Africanist, believes that 'tourism brings in the main serious economic (and social) malformations' (*Neo-Colonialism*), 29.
23. See, for instance, 'Haynes Wants Law Scrapped', 18A.
24. The person referred to in the calypso was an advocate of restricted access of the beaches to locals (Anthony Carter, 'Jack'. Words and music published by Grand Music Ltd, 1982).
25. Lowenthal, *West Indian Societies*, 13.
26. Naipaul, *Middle Passage*, 191.
27. 'Castro Scolds the US', 8.
28. 'Martinique Airport Expects Triple Load', 13.
29. 'Tremendous Success', 21.
30. McAfee, 20.
31. Barry *et al.*, 84.
32. 'No Waste for the Bahamas', 13.
33. Duncan, 'Dumped on, Again and Again', 8; Best, 'Ban on Hazardous Waste Exports', 6.
34. 'A filthy assumption,' 6A.
35. Ragatz, vii. This subject will be dealt with in greater detail in Chapter 8.
36. In 1993 this bank bought the majority shares in the National Commercial Bank of Grenada ('Grenada Union Hits at PM's Divestments', 9).
37. Thomas, *Poor*, 167-72.
38. Since 1987 the British government has signed mutual legal assistance treaties with the US government which allow US federal agencies access to bank accounts if good reason exists to suspect fraud, insider trading, money laundering and the like by depositors (Thorndike, 'Making Money' 69). These treaties, however, have not prevented the extensive use of the offshore facilities in the region for illicit purposes.
39. Thorndike, 'Making Money', 70, 74.
40. Thorndike, 'Making Money', 74.
41. Ramsaran, *Commonwealth Caribbean*, 103.
42. Thorndike, 'Making Money', 70, 74.

43. Ramsaran, *Commonwealth Caribbean*, 104.
44. 'IMF to Undertake Economic Study', 10.
45. 'Aid Plan Stalled', 6.
46. The information on the economy is taken largely from Ferguson 'Pain and Protest', 566-74. Other important sources of information are *World Tables 1995*; *World Development Report 1995*; *Social Indicators of Development 1995*; *South America, Central America and the Caribbean 1995*.
47. Ferguson, 571.
48. Girvan, 'Debt Problem', 108.
49. 'Caricom/IMF Debts Agenda', 9.
50. Griffin & Khan, 31.
51. Girvan, 'Debt Problem,' 108; Girvan *et al.*, 'Debt Problem', 48.
52. Singh, 'Selling Out the Caribbean', 13C; 'St Kitts Sells 3,000 Passports', 8.
53. *Keesing's Record*, 40 (1994), R40.
54. *Keesing's Record*, 40 (1994), R39.
55. *Keesing's Record*, 40 (1994), R39.
56. Reuter's Information Service, Nov. 2, 1995.
57. 'Blueprint for Poverty Reduction', 10.
58. McAfee, 36, 38, n.5.
59. McAfee, 41-42.
60. Compiled from official statistics of the US Dept of Commerce, 1996. (Internet http:ita.doc.gov/industry/otea/usfth/cbic. e-i).
61. 'Let's Dock with NAFTA', 3A.
62. McAfee, 39; see also Thomas, *Poor,* 335-36.
63. McAfee, 38.
64. Thomas, *Poor*, 338.
65. 'Canada hand-out unlikely', 9.
66. 'Uniting for our Progress', 6A.

Race

CHAPTER 7

Types and stereotypes

Racism appears . . . not as an incidental detail, but as a consubstantial part of colonialism. It is the highest expression of the colonial system and one of the most significant features of the colonialist. Not only does it establish a fundamental discrimination between colonizer and colonized, a sine qua non of colonial life, but it also lays the foundation for the immutability of this life.[1]

Albert Memmi

Introduction

Many writers have argued that racism constitutes the fundamental element in modern colonialism and there can be no doubt that racism was used to foster antagonism between groups in colonial society, to divide and rule, and to create and sustain the myth of European superiority. According to Jean-Paul Sartre, 'Racism is ingrained in actions, institutions, and in the nature of the colonialist methods of production and exchange.'[2] Memmi argues: 'Racism sums up and symbolises the fundamental relation which unites colonialist and colonized.'[3] He states that the oppressed group is often stereotyped consciously or unconsciously as a people without even a modicum of basic sense or natural aptitude and cites as an example the view of an old physician who once told him that the 'colonized do not know how to breathe'.[4] Dickson said that Europeans in the late eighteenth century thought that 'a negro cannot lay a table even or square in a room'.[5]

Derogatory remarks like the above, when applied by one group to another over a period of time, may become stereotypes based on racial, colour or class differences, depending upon the historical and social factors at work. Over time, also, they may become so ingrained in the psyches of both groups that they persist long after the specific historical circumstances which gave rise to them have disappeared. If not addressed by both groups and dealt with intelligently, they may eventually pass into the realm of myth, and attract to themselves anecdotes which serve to illustrate and validate them, so that they come to be seen as the result of congenital rather than historical factors.

Amerindians

The Amerindians were the first of the oppressed groups in the region to be stereotyped by the Europeans. Perhaps the best example of stereotyping of them is the speech of Friar Tomas Ortiz, before the Spanish Council of the Indies in 1512, rebutting the views expressed by Friar Antonio de Montesinos and his group about the noble and gentle nature of these people. It is appropriate to quote him in some detail:

> [They] ate human flesh, and were addicted to it more than any race of men. They had no system of justice. They went about naked, and lacked all shame. They were like stupid asses, half-witted and without feeling, and thought nothing of killing themselves or others. They did not speak the truth, unless it was to their advantage. They were inconstant, did not know the meaning of counsel, were ungrateful and fond of novelty. They gloried in being drunk . . . . They were bestial in their vices. Youth showed no obedience or courtesy to age, nor children to their parents. They were incapable of learning the doctrines of the Faith, and were quite incorrigible. They were treacherous, cruel, and vindictive, enemies of religion, and never forgave a wrong. They were arrogant, thieves, liars, and of little intelligence. They kept neither faith nor order; husbands were not loyal to their wives, or wives to their husbands. They were cowardly, like the hare, dirty, like pigs; they ate lice, spiders and raw worms, wherever they found them. They lacked human art and skill . . . . The older they got the worse they were; up to the age of ten or twelve, it seemed, they had some manners and virtue, but thereafter they became like brute animals. In short, God never created a people more steeped in vice and bestiality, without the admixture of goodness or good breeding . . . .[6]

The debate on the nature of the Amerindians became crucial in the Spanish policy of exploiting the newly conquered lands and their peoples. The two basic schools of thought on their nature have been referred to as those of the 'dirty dog' and 'noble savage'. The term 'dirty dog' was actually used on a number of occasions to refer to these people and although the Spanish Crown forbade it in 1512, it remained prevalent for a long time.

Perhaps the most controversial view of their nature was that they were 'natural slaves' in the Aristotelian sense of the term. Lucas Vázquez de Ayllón expressed the view that it was better for them to be 'slave men' than 'free beasts',[7] and Juan Gines de Sepúlveda strenuously maintained that they were 'natural slaves', and that they could therefore be justly compelled by force to serve the Spanish. His opinion was based on his notion of their barbarism, evidence of which he saw, among other failings, in their lack of written records, histories or literary works, the absence of monuments and private property, especially land, and their rude institutions and customs.[8]

Fernandez de Oviedo y Valdes was one of a long line of 'witnesses' to the fact that the Amerindians were not only intellectually inferior to the Europeans, but also were incapable of rational thought. They were simply too hard-headed to learn, for their skulls were said to be four times thicker than those of the Spanish and 'so when one wages war with them and comes to hand to hand fighting, one must be very careful not to hit them on the head with the sword, because I have seen many swords broken in this fashion'.[9] Dr Chanca, who accompanied Columbus on his second expedition, commenting on the diet of the Amerindians of Hispaniola, said: 'It seems to me that their bestiality is greater than that of any beast in the world.'[10]

Beastly, hard-headed, evil-smelling, ugly, dirty dogs, these and other pejorative terms helped to create the widespread notion among the Spaniards, few of whom had ever seen an Amerindian, that these people were human beings in appearance only, or as Sepúlveda opined, 'little men in whom you will scarcely find even vestiges of humanity'. He also asserted that they were as different from the Spanish as 'monkeys from men'.[11] This statement foreshadowed the theory of the 'great chain of being' which emerged in Europe in the late eighteenth century and was given a fillip in the last years of the nineteenth century by Charles Darwin's theory of evolution. Sepúlveda's ideas about the Amerindians and Spanish were similar but without reference to pseudo-sceintific theory.

Most members of the 'dirty-dog' school argued that it was in the interest of the Amerindians to be under the jurisdiction of the Spanish, and some even saw it as an obligation on the part of the Spanish Crown to ensure that this happened, but Oviedo was of a different persuasion. He considered that they were so steeped in vices that God was soon going to wipe them off the face of the earth, in what he termed 'an enormous mercy of God'.[12] It followed, therefore, that for Oviedo the decimation of the indigenous peoples by the

Spanish was more an act of righteousness than of sin. Their time of grace had come to an end; the Spanish *conquistadores* and others were simply wielding the sword of the Lord and ensuring their quick descent into perdition.

The second school of thought, that of the 'noble savage', was represented by such notable people as Antonio de Montesinos, Bartolomé de Las Casas, Juan de Zummáraga, Ramirez de Fuenleal and Julián Garcés. These sought to show that the Amerindians were not without industries, science, monuments, highly developed institutions and other indices of civilisation, as their detractors had argued. They also tried to refute the charges made against them by Oviedo and others about their moral degeneracy. Las Casas, one of the most ardent critics of Spanish colonialism, was sure that on the whole they were the most gentle, peaceful, temperate and decent people in the world. Their chief lack was the knowledge of the true God, and even in this respect they demonstrated that when given an opportunity to convert without coercion they were willing to become Christians.

Las Casas likewise sought to refute the charge that they were 'natural slaves', on the basis that they were not 'wild men' as some supposed but a people of settled industry and developed intellect, as proven by their numerous inventions and creations. Indeed, he said: 'They are so skilled in every mechanical art that with every right they should be set ahead of all the nations of the known world on this score.'[13] However, Las Casas' most fundamental point, and the bulwark of his defence of the Amerindians, was not the demonstrated intellect of these people or their capacity to receive the Christian faith, but that they were people and that 'all the peoples of the world are men'. Time and again, he and others who stood on the side of the indigenous peoples had to affirm and reaffirm their humanity in face of those who sought to relegate them to a subhuman species.

The best example of this type of relegation was in the case of the Garifuno, or Caribs, who stoutly resisted European attempts to enslave them. The ideological basis for their enslavement was their alleged cannibalism (a kind of dog-eat-dog situation) which to their antagonists fully demonstrated that they could not be ordinary human beings. This placed them, even more than the other local peoples, outside the pale of civilisation. Columbus viewed them as being 'a people very savage and suitable for the purpose [of becoming slaves]'. His first notions of them, based on hearsay, were that anatomically they were different from ordinary human beings: some had one eye, and others had dogs' noses. He declared that he had also understood that they were cannibals who drank the blood of their victims and cut off their private parts.[14] Just as they did to the Africans later, the Spanish dubbed the Caribs (and other indigenous peoples) whom they enslaved as 'pieces' of India. They branded them like cattle and auctioned them off to the highest bidder.

Las Casas might beseech his antagonists with a tear in his eye, but he was up against a stubborn wall of hostility. His efforts and those of others did result in the Spanish government passing legislation periodically to regulate the treatment of the Amerindians by the Spanish and ameliorate their condition. However, both those who were coerced into working within the *encomienda* system and those who managed to escape it were destroyed by the cruel blows that the Spanish meted out against them and by new diseases which were introduced into their society by their conquerors. As with the other groups introduced into the region to service the labour needs of the plantation system, the tableau of the Amerindian catastrophe was etched with a high incidence of suicide. For Oviedo such suicides occurred because the Amerindians were bored and sometimes even for no reason whatsoever.[15] He saw this as yet another instance of their irrational behaviour, completely oblivious as he was, or pretended to be, of the extreme brutality of Spanish rule and treatment of the local peoples.

Africans

Influences from classical antiquity

Many of the stereotypes which the Europeans applied to the Amerindians they also applied to the Africans. Here, however, some of the stereotypes had their origins in the period before the enslavement of Africans in the new world, as far back as the Graeco-Roman period, or the period of classical antiquity. The Graeco-Romans drew distinctions between Africans living in north-east Africa and those living farther south, and also in Libya and other areas westward. They sometimes referred to the former as eastern Ethiopians and the latter as southern and western Ethiopians. They considered the eastern Ethiopians, living in the areas of modern Egypt, Sudan and Abyssinia, to be highly civilised. Diodorus, a classical writer, noted four important aspects about some of these Africans: some writers considered them to be the first men on earth; they were the most pious of men and their worship most pleasing to the gods; they were perhaps the first colonisers and civilisers of Egypt; and those living in Meroë were literate in three kinds of writing – hieratic, demotic and hieroglyphic.[16] Herodotus, another classical writer, declared that the Macrobian Ethiopians were the tallest and most handsome of men.[17] Snowden informs us that there were Africans in Greece and Italy during the classical period serving as diplomats, high government officers and commercial agents.[18]

This positive image of the eastern Ethiopians was juxtaposed against the much more negative one of the western and southern Ethiopians, about whom some of the grossest myths were believed. Among the 'human monstrosities' about which Pliny wrote were that there were some tribes without noses, others without tongues, others with a part of the mouth closed up and with a single orifice instead of nostrils; yet others who communicated by gestures since they were devoid of speech; some who were ruled over by a dog, who commanded them by his movements. One group was also said to have four legs, roving around like animals; others had dogs' heads and drank dogs' milk; still others consumed human flesh, panthers and lions.[19] Pliny became the most well-known classical writer on the subject of human monstrosities in Africa, but a host of others also had their say on the subject.[20]

Unfortunately, the more derogatory rather than the more ennobling view of Africans survived the classical period in the minds of later Western writers. They drew heavily upon the classical writers for their early knowledge of Africans and supplemented these by the writings of observers of the inhabitants of West Africa between the fifteenth and the seventeenth centuries. Occasionally, something positive was said, but by and large they viewed the Africans as a degenerate set of peoples.

Towards the end of the eighteenth century, the white Jamaican historian, Edward Long, using this literature as his basic source of information, painted one of the most extensive stereotypes of the Africans. We shall therefore use his work as an example of the views prevailing during that period.

Edward Long's racism

Long began with the common physical description of his day concerning Africans: flat noses, thick lips, wool 'like the bestial fleece' instead of hair, the large breasts of the women (which other writers likened to the udders of animals), 'their bestial or fetid smell', which seemed to be more pronounced the more barbaric they were considered to be. For Long their physical features placed them in the chain of being or line of civilisation much closer to beasts than to human beings. Physically and anatomically he deemed them to be not much different from the orang-outang, which were considered by some to be a species of 'wild men'. This was, Long declared, notably evident in the case of the 'Hottentot' (Khoisan) women, who would suffer no disgrace from having an orang-outang as a husband. He stated that this view was based upon his perusal of 'the most credible writers' on the subject, who said that the orang-outang had feelings of shame and sensibility, could be made to perform a variety of menial domestic tasks, 'conceive a passion for the Negroe women, and hence must be supposed to covet their embraces from a natural impulse of desire, such as inclines one animal towards another of the same species, or which has a conformity in the organs of generation'.[21]

If the physical traits of the Africans suggested to Long that they were a lower order of being than the Europeans, then their morals and intellectual capacities confirmed it: they possessed 'no moral sensations'; their barbarity towards their children 'debases their nature even below that of the brutes'. They were given over to sexual immorality, gluttony and drunkenness. They were:

> . . . brutish, ignorant, idle, crafty, treacherous, bloody, thievish, mistrustful, and superstitious people . . . . We find them represented by the Greek and Roman authors under the most odious and despicable character; as proud, lazy, deceitful, thievish, addicted to all kinds of lust, and ready to promote them in others, incestuous, savage, cruel, and vindictive, devourers of human flesh, and quaffers of human blood, inconstant, base, and cowardly, devoted to all sorts of superstition; and, in short, to every vice that came in their way, or within their reach.[22]

Long thought that the Africans brought to the Caribbean were marked by:

> . . . the same bestial manners, stupidity, and vices, which debase their brethren on the continent, who seem to be distinguished from the rest of mankind, not in person only, but in possessing, in abstract, every species of inherent turpitude that is to be found dispersed at large among the rest of the human creation, with scarce a single virtue to extenuate this shade of character, differing in this particular from all other men.[23]

Long considered that the African was much closer to the orang-outang than to the European in intellectual development and hardly deserved to be classified among the human species; indeed he considered some of them to be 'more brutal and savage than the wild beasts of the forest'. In short, nature had discriminated the Africans from 'any other race of mortals . . . not in *kind*, but in *species*'.[24] This subhuman view was taken a step further by other white writers. As late as 1900 Carroll was convinced that 'all scientific investigation of the subject proves the Negro to be an ape'.[25]

Long's detailed comments about the Africans omitted or barely mentioned other characteristics that helped to condition European ideas. For instance, the supposed animal-like physical features were described in an elaborate fashion by Duarte Pacheco Pereira (*c.*1506), who declared that the Wangara peoples of modern Guinea were 'monstrous folk', with faces, teeth and tails like dogs. Richard Eden (1554) wrote about a group of people in the modern Sudan who had no heads, 'having their eyes and mouth in their breasts'. Edward Topsell (1607) thought that men with low and flat noses were as libidinous as apes. One anonymous Dutchman (*c.*1600) stated that the people in lower Guinea ate dogs, cats and 'filthy stinking Elephants, and Buffold's flesh, wherein there is a thousand Maggets, and many times stinkes like carrion . . . . They are of so hot a nature, that they eat raw Dogs guts.' Other writers thought that they were liars, thieves, idolaters, sorcerers, given over to 'brutish idleness', while their 'children grow up like trees', without any instruction from them.[26]

In the mid-nineteenth century, Joseph Arthur, Comte de Gobineau, regarded as the founder of the school of Nordic racial supremacy, said that the African possessed 'an instability and capriciousness of feeling, that cannot be tied down to any single object, and which so far as he is concerned, do away with all distinctions of good and evil'.[27]

Long accused Africans of excessive immorality but did not associate this with mental retardation. However, other writers did, and their view persisted into the present century. Some alleged that bright, promising youths in Africa degenerated mentally once they reached puberty, because of their obsession with sex. Their biological clock was ticking while their intellectual one had slowed to a virtual halt.[28] According to J. D. Unwin, the ill-use of the potential of African youths through sex and through widespread polygamy as they grew older was the cause of both their mental and cultural backwardness.[29] Other theories of African mental, cultural and social retardation were related to various aspects of their physical environment. These included the heat and humidity of the tropical regions, debilitating tropical diseases, poor diets (deficiency in essential vitamins, minerals and proteins) and too long weaning periods which, it was believed, produced a dependency complex.[30]

Religion and the racial question

One theory which Long did not develop, but which became the subject of great debate from the late eighteenth century, was the biblical view of Africans and of black people generally. Long did associate blackness with inferiority, but did not go as far as to refer to it as that permanent 'blot of infection', as George Best (1578) had done. Best, drawing upon ancient Jewish Talmudic and other literature, associated blackness in the Africans with the descendants of Ham (or more specifically with Canaan, one of the sons of Ham), who was said to have disobeyed the commandment of God and copulated with his wife while in the Ark. As a result it was divinely ordained that 'all his posterite after him should bee so blacke and lothsome, that it might remaine a spectacle of disobedience to all the worlde'.[31] This curse is the origin of the frequent association in European literature of Africans with grave sexual immorality.

The divine curse on Ham and his descendants was also associated with servitude. This is based on the biblical statement that Ham saw his father lying drunk and naked in his tent, as a result of which Noah cursed him through the line of his son, Canaan, to perpetual servitude to his brethren and their descendants.[32] This part of the curse was cited frequently to justify the enslavement of Africans in the new world and elsewhere. No attention was paid to the fact that later on in the same Biblical account the sons of Ham (including Canaan) are said to have founded some of the most powerful early kingdoms and empires, including Sidon, Nineveh, Egypt (Mizraim) and Kush.[33]

Although for a long time the Europeans held that the Canaanites were black people (sons of Ham) accursed of God, they failed to make the point that Melchizedek, king of Salem (ancient Jerusalem), was a Canaanite (Amorite) king,[34] and therefore according to the Biblical record of Hamitic stock, to whom the founder of the Israelite peoples paid tribute. Melchizedek was declared in biblical literature to have been much greater than Abraham, high priest of the Most High God, with eternal attributes. He is declared to be the forerunner of Christ, who is said to be 'a priest for ever after the order of Melchisedec'.[35] Although the early European writers refused to address this point, because it would have made nonsense of their interpretation that black peoples were cursed by God to be the servants of whites, most modern white biblical scholars insist that the Canaanites were, in fact, Semites or white Hamites.[36]

The unacknowledged legacy

Europeans had little or no experience outside the context of colonialism and the new world encounter through which they could judge the Amerindians, but they had a wide range of encounters and experiences in Europe, both before and during the period of new world slavery, on which to base their judgements of Africans and their miscegenated offspring. Many of these became famous throughout Europe and their greatness has been affirmed in extant writing, painting and sculpture. It is appropriate to refer here to a few of these.

There were several noteworthy religious blacks, including over a dozen Madonnas and at least three popes: Victor I (AD189-99), Miltiades (AD311-14), and Gelasius I (AD492-96). Contemporary records depict them clearly as having 'Africoid' features, but later representations show them as European.

Many blacks became famous in the military history of Europe. The great African (Carthagenian) warrior Hannibal (*c.* 247-182BC), who became the scourge of many a Roman general, is depicted in all but one of the few extant representations (coins) as having Negroid features. Yet most European writers continue to deny him his African ancestry. In Russia there was a black man of Abyssinian origin, Abraham Petrovich Hannibal (1697-1781), whose parents claimed that they were descendants of Hannibal. He was sent from Russia to study in Paris and became one of the foremost engineers of his era and an army general. He later returned to Russia and became a powerful influence behind the throne, during the reigns of Peter the Great and his daughter. He eventually acquired the title of General-in-Chief of the Order of St Alexander Nevski. Several of his sons became famous in the military and naval life of Russia.

One of his sons married into a Russian noble family. That union produced a son, Alexander Sergevitch Pushkin (1799-1837), whose portrait shows unquestionable African ancestry. He became the leading literary figure of his time, and is regarded by some as the father of modern Russian literature. He was not the only important black literary figure of Europe. As early as the sixteenth century Juan Latino, a former slave living in Spain, had become one of the leading Latin scholars and poets in Europe. In 1565 he became professor of poetry at the University of Granada and in 1573 he wrote a book on Don Juan of Austria's battle at Lepanto, which remains an outstanding literary work. In France there was Alexandre Dumas, a 'coloured' person (1802-70) who became one of the most famous novelists of his day, and is today perhaps best remembered for two of his works: *The Three Musketeers* (1844) and *The Count of Monte Cristo* (1846).

European royalty was also infused with African blood. Among these was Alessandro dei Medici, who was made Duke of Florence in 1523 by Pope Clement VII, his alleged father. Contemporary written records and paintings depict him as having 'Africoid' (in this case 'coloured') features. He married Margaret, daughter of Charles V, emperor of Germany, Spain and Austria and ruled for five years until his assassination. He was not the only person of discernible African ancestry who graced the corridors of the European royal palaces. John VI (1767-1826) of Portugal was described by several historians of the period, including the Duchess d'Abrantes, wife of Marshall Junot, French ambassador to Portugal in the 1820s, as having 'Negro hair, thick lips, an African nose and mulatto colouring'.

Louise-Marie, who was alleged to be the daughter of Queen Maria-Theresa, wife of the celebrated seventeenth-century French king Louis XIV, was partly of African ancestry, as her portrait shows. The royal household never acknowledged her and banished her to a nunnery, but a few contemporary works link her clearly with the royal household. These include the portrait in the art gallery of the Library of St Genevieve in Paris and the now empty file (which presumably once contained documents about her maternity) in the same library under the caption 'Documents concerning the Princess Louise-Marie, daughter of Louis XIV and Maria-Theresa'. British royalty was not exempt from the infusion of African blood, although it remains a secret. A portrait of Queen Charlotte Sophia of Germany, wife of George III and grandmother of Queen Victoria, depicts her clearly as having 'Africoid' features.[37]

Without discussing the debate that has been maintained by Cheikh Anta Diop,[38] and others on the wider African contribution to European civilisation, we can conclude that blacks played outstanding roles in European life during the period of slavery and at the very time that stereotypes of Africans were crystallising.

The Europeans tried to belittle the contribution made to civilisation by Africans in many ways. They ignored their contribution or for miscegenated individuals explained it in terms of the genes from their European ancestry. Had not Dumas and Pushkin become famous their black ancestry would have been emphasised; but because of their fame it is usually their white ancestry that is emphasised.[39] For those Africans without any known or visible white ancestry the Europeans tended to claim that it was only through association with whites and their cultural heritage they had become objects of excellence. Even so, they regarded them as aberrations.

When faced with outstanding African civilisations, such as those of Egypt and Kush, they represented them as either of Semitic or 'White Hamitic' provenance. Long, who seems to have been among the few persons of his day convinced that early Egyptian civilisation was of African origin, wrote in derogatory terms about it, saying that its government was marked by 'a multitude of abuses, and essential defects'; their 'morality offended against the first rules of rectitude and probity'; they were a 'people without taste, without genius, or discernment; who had only ideas of grandeur, ill understood: knavish, crafty, soft, lazy, cowardly, and servile, superstitious in excess, and extravagantly besotted with an absurd and monstrous theology'; 'their skill in sculpture, and architecture, rose not above a flat mediocrity'.[40] It is difficult to see how any objective critic of ancient Egyptian civilisation could come to such conclusions; but then Long was not an objective critic.

The best example of bias in European attitudes towards African achievement is the civilisation of Great Zimbabwe, which reached its apogee in the fifteenth century. When the Europeans first saw the relics in the late nineteenth century, especially the acropolis and the elliptical temple, they were convinced that such impressive monuments and the civilisation which spawned them could not have been built by the linear ancestors of the 'rude' Zimbabweans. They surmised that they must have been built by foreigners, perhaps Phoenicians, Greeks, Jews, Egyptians or Arabs. Two European scientific expeditions, in 1905 and 1929, found that their unique architectural style and other evidence could lead to only one conclusion, that the monuments were of indigenous origin. European attitudes towards the Zimbabwean achievement changed immediately and dramatically. In 1931 Gertrude Caton-Thompson, a so-called expert on the subject, wrote:

> The architecture of Zimbabwe, imitative apparently of a daub prototype, strikes me as essentially the product of an infantile mind, a pre-logical mind, a mind which having discovered the way of

> making or doing a thing goes on childishly repeating the performance regardless of incongruity.[41]

The denigration of everything African served admirably the purposes of the slave traders and the imperialists. It would be used to justify their forcible seizure of the African continent. In a similar way the conquest of the Americas had been justified by the Spanish by pointing to the supposed barbarism of the inhabitants. The glories of the Aztec, Maya and Inca civilisations were played down by the conquerors and the indigenous peoples were made to look like crude savages needing the virtues of European enlightenment. East Indian and Chinese achievements, which once drew praise from European critics, also came to be viewed in an increasingly pejorative light.

East Indians

East Indians constituted the largest number of overseas labourers recruited under indentureship or contract to work on the plantations in the Caribbean. They were imported mainly into Guyana, Trinidad and Suriname, but some also went to Jamaica, St Lucia, St Vincent, Grenada, St Kitts, Martinique and Guadeloupe.

Early contacts and stereotypes

The European, and more specifically British, attitudes towards the East Indians which led to the development of stereotypes in new world plantation societies were developed over a long period of contact with them. European penetration of the subcontinent started in the early decades of the seventeenth century, with gradual conquest and the establishment of a colonial hegemony over the local people. By the second decade of the nineteenth century Britain had acquired the lion's share of territory, by using her naval supremacy during the Napoleonic wars virtually to wipe out the last rival European (mainly French) presence there. At the end of the war the French retained only three small possessions on the subcontinent.[42]

British attitudes were formulated against this background of relegating to a colonial status a once proud and independent people whom they gradually grew to despise and stereotype. The stereotyping of the Indians was therefore not a function of new world indentureship, but of the circumstances of the colonial relationship. No doubt, also, old stereotypes were reinforced and new ones developed.

It is important to note that, like with the Chinese, the Europeans showed some respect and even reverence for the Indian past, at the outset of regular contact. This was based on the notion of Sanskrit as the foundation of all

Indo-European languages and on the view that Indian civilisation was of Aryan provenance. Indian society was regarded for some time by the Conservatives in British society as a model of civilisation, human order, social stability, equity, gentility and non-violence. Writers such as Edmund Burke, William Robertson, Sir William Jones and James Cumming were among the representatives of this school of thought.

Burke praised the caste system as the basis of the social order, in which each group (or caste) knew its place and role in society – rulers, craftsmen, peasants, etc. He admired the Indians for their laws and traditions, built up over centuries. He was one of the few British political thinkers to admit to the terror and despotism that British rule had unleashed upon the subcontinent.

Indian art, literature and cultural heritage came in for high praise from Sir William Jones, who spent many years investigating, translating and bringing to the attention of the West the depth of Indian cultural and literary achievements in science, law, history and philosophy. He founded the Royal Asiatic Society in Bengal in 1784 to advance the study of Indian culture among the British and other Europeans in that country. Jones and other Conservatives saw deficiencies in Indian society but were firmly convinced that on the whole their achievements were noteworthy. Sir Thomas Munro, who later became governor of Madras, said in the House of Commons in 1813 that the British stood to benefit from cultural exchanges with India.[43]

This attitude persisted for some time longer in the British Romantic movement, which was taken up with the natural environment and stories of valour and romance. The idyllic Indian environment of lofty hills, exotic plants and animals was matched by fables of Indian streams which washed sands of gold and precious stones, sultans on peacock thrones, rich and elegant costumes, and elaborate ceremonies. As Bearce put it, 'For many Britons, India represented very little except these romantic scenes.'[44] Some Romantics, of course, criticised Indian life and customs, especially religion. However, their criticisms were much more restrained than those of the Utilitarians. On the whole the Conservative and Romantic schools viewed India in positive terms, an attitude which persisted among some elements in British society up to the time of the Indian Uprising (or 'Indian Mutiny') in 1857.

However, a more pronounced trend from the early nineteenth century was the development of an increasingly critical attitude towards contemporary (and to some extent past) Indian civilisation. Their institutions and social systems were seen by the Evangelicals and Utilitarians as barbaric. Hinduism as a whole and such practices as caste, sacred cows, suttee, thuggee and infanticide came in for some of the strongest criticism. India was perceived as a society afflicted by despotism, mendacity, venality, prostitution, perfidy and many other sins. The Evangelicals were particularly critical of their religions, and the Utilitarians critised the perceived lack of rationality and individualism. The 'Mutiny' served to confirm these schools of criticism in their attitudes. Indians were now perceived as being quick to violence and lacking in any real regard for human life. As with other subjugated peoples, social Darwinism was soon to give pseudo-scientific credibility to the view that Indians were lower in the scale of evolution than Europeans.[45]

Attacks on Indian religion were made by several writers. Charles Grant (in the late eighteenth century) had painted a picture of the Indians as a people engulfed in a whirlpool of superstition and social corruption. According to Stokes, Grant's depiction conjured up images of a 'veritable Sodom and Gomorrah'.[46] William Wilberforce also attacked the religion. For him, the Hindu gods were 'absolute monsters of lust, injustice, wickedness and cruelty. In short, their religious system is one of great abomination.'[47] Bishop Heber felt: 'They have, unhappily, many of the vices arising from slavery, from an unsettled state of society, and immoral and erroneous systems of religion.'[48] The Utilitarian thinker, James Mill, was convinced that the 'barbaric state' of their society was due to political and religious tyranny, 'by a system of priestcraft, built upon the most enormous and tormenting superstition ... of the human race'.[49]

British writers attacked Indian laws, institutions, arts, personal manners and attitudes to work and sex. In the words of Honoria Lawrence (1837), to live among the Indians was to live 'among the seven deadly sins'.[50] James Mill wrote that 'the love of repose reigns in India', and that there was a dictum: 'It is more happy to be seated than to walk; it is more happy to sleep than to be awake; but the happiest of all is death.' For him, the 'phlegmatic indolence' of 'this listless tribe' pervaded the society: 'Few pains, to the mind of the Hindu, are equal to that of bodily exertion.'[51] Thomas Macaulay went further: 'The Bengalee ... would see his country overrun, his house laid in ashes, his children murdered or dishonoured, without having the spirit to strike one blow.' [52]

Some European writers thought that Indians were much too preoccupied with sex. James Mill regarded their sexuality as the normal pattern in all 'rude' societies: 'In the barbarian, the passion of sex is brute impulse.'[53] Hutchins expressed the view that to the Victorians the Hindu religion was 'a systematic encouragement of lust; the Indian conception of women in Indian society seemed the epitome of barbarity', and that Indians were depicted as sensuous and delighted by immorality in art.[54]

Honoria Lawrence found 'nothing attractive' in the Indian's character; Macaulay thought that the physique of the men was 'feeble even to effeminacy' and 'deceit' was as natural to them as horns are to a buffalo.[55] Bolt tells us that especially after the 'Mutiny' the Indians were perceived by the British soldiers in the country as 'fiends' and 'brutes'.[56]

The notion of moral regression accompanying the advancement of age was also applied to the Indians. It was not an unfamiliar script: it had also been written of the Amerindians and the Africans. According to Dubois, 'As they get older, incontinence and all its attendant vices increase at the same time.'[57]

The general picture drawn above needs to be modified by the observation that India was made up of many communities and British attitudes were not uniform. In fact, the key to British rule in India was the manipulation of communities, facilitated by the creation of suitable stereotypes. Sometimes, for instance, the peasant was regarded as diligent, the salt of the earth, whereas the newly educated elite were seen as mimic men, infuriatingly ingratiating and utterly untrustworthy. At other times, the educated elite were seen as the hope of the future, while the peasant was said to be hopelessly backward. British attitudes to Muslims and Hindus were not always the same, nor were the stereotypes of the respectable castes the same as those of the lower ones. Christine Bolt informs us that the Aryans of the north were often regarded as measuring up to the European standards of beauty, being dubbed by a British administrator, Sir George Campbell, as often 'magnificently handsome', with English-type features and 'a gratifying inclination to revere a pale skin'.[58]

Among British officials opinions varied from genuine sympathy to boorish paternalism. Administrators did not always share the same ideas as the planters, and the business elite in the towns of Bombay, Calcutta and Madras did not always have the perspective of the military, who had their own highly developed sense of which groups in India were worthwhile.[59]

Recruitment and indentureship

The first Indians arrived in the region in 1838. They were recruited specifically to replace the Africans on the plantations, many of whom were distancing themselves physically from their old workplaces and their former masters. Several historians now think that the flight of the Africans from the estates was not nearly as massive as had been supposed. Some have argued that in Suriname, Guyana and Trinidad the movement of the Africans from the estates was exacerbated by the introduction of indentured labourers and the consequent reduction of the wages of the freedmen. The introduction of contract labourers in large numbers helped in the expansion of the sugar industry in Guyana and Trinidad, and in Suriname it assisted in effecting a smoother transition, from the point of view of the plantocracy, from slave labour to completely free labour.

Indentured labour was legally supposed to be a special arrangement whereby free labourers contracted themselves to work for a stipulated time for another individual, for stipulated wages and allowances. For the Indian labourers in the Caribbean the usual period of contract was five years, although they could enter into further contracts, or circumstances might lead to the involuntary extension of a given contract. In spite of its supposed free nature, the system functioned as a form of captive labour, and has been classified by several writers as tantamount to a new form of slavery.

Alleged docility and laziness

What the planters wanted most of all was a docile labour force. There is little historical basis for the view that the East Indians were a docile people, if what is meant by docility is that they were malleable to planter control. Still, this view seemed to have been shared by a large number of planters. One reason for this may have been that they did not stage resistance, marronage and revolt on a scale comparable with the Africans. Haraksingh, who rejects the view that Indians were on the whole docile, has attempted to account for this seemimg docility by pointing to the fact that the conditions under which they were recruited, transported and accommodated on the plantations, and the legal framework within which the system operated, kept the labourers in their place. Among these were penal sanctions for failure to work, extension of periods of indentureship for time in prison or time away from work, monetary fines for supposed delinquency, severe diseases, transfers of perceived trouble-makers to other plantations, and the anxiety of people who had already worked for some years that they would be punished by the involuntary extension of their contracts if they should resort to acts of overt resistance.[60] He might have mentioned also that it was extremely difficult for the Indians to desert in large numbers and establish maroon communities as the Africans had done. The much larger number of free persons in the colonies after slavery and their occupation of the rural areas must have made such a venture much more hazardous than it had been for the slaves. Haraksingh (and others) have shown that relations between the Indians and the plantocracy were punctuated by strikes and riots as well as other forms of resistance.[61]

The plantocracy justified their treatment of the Indian labourers by stereotypes depicting them as another species of 'low-life' beings. In 1868, Hunter wrote of two groups of Bengali that they were patient labourers, living very close to nature, capable of surviving on a penny a day, and contented to eat roots when nothing better was to be obtained. They were among the out-casts of Hindu society, but at the same time they 'furnish the sinews by which English enterprise is carried on in Eastern Bengal'.[62]

When the recruitment system was beginning to be organised, Gillanders, Arbuthnot & Co, the prospective agents of John Gladstone, a planter in Guyana, set the stage by declaring that the Dhangars, from whom he apparently intended to recruit, 'have no religion, no education, and in their present state no wants beyond eating, drinking and sleeping: and to procure which they are willing to labour'. The agent also injected the opinion similar to the odious statement made of the Amerindians by Oviedo and of the Africans by Long: '[T]hey are always spoken of as more akin to the monkey than the man.'[63] By portraying the potential recruits as a kind of subhuman species with only the most elemental of desires, the recruiting agents were reinforcing the planter's view of the cheapness of Indian labour and, by extension, Indian life. At the same time they were careful to say that the labourers would work to satisfy their wants.

Planters developed an idea of these labourers as an idle and lazy lot. This may have been a reflex action that they had developed about the labouring class as a whole as being lazy and idle by nature. Few bothered to examine the kinds of persons often recruited, the circumstances in which they lived and worked, and the impact this had upon their physical and mental capacity to work hard. Many of those recruited were not agricultural labourers. They included priests, weavers, scribes, lime-burners, cowherds, washermen, messengers, domestics, barbers, shoemakers, hawkers, soldiers and policemen.[64] Many did not come out as voluntary labourers or were tricked into believing that they would be assigned light, non-agricultural work. Even so, most of them were prepared to work, given the proper incentives.

That the supposed laziness of the Indians was a function of the plantation system, and more particularly planter perception of them, is obvious from the fact that those who stayed after their contracts expired became successful among the Caribbean peasantry from the late nineteenth century. They were largely responsible for the development of the rice industry in Guyana, Suriname and, on a smaller scale, Trinidad. They also cultivated crops such as coconut, cocoa, sugar, vegetables and ground provisions, and became involved in the dairy industry.

The use of the term 'coolie'

Although the recruits represented a wide variety of occupations, they were all lumped together under the term *kuli* or *coolie.* The origin of the word is obscure, but by the time the indentureship system came into being its use was already widespread in Asia, where it had acquired a variety of meanings. In Fiji it had acquired the derogatory meaning 'dog', perhaps in much the same way that the Arab/Swahili word *kafir* ('unbeliever') acquired a similar meaning when applied to blacks in South Africa.[65] The more common usages of the term *kuli* were as a wage labourer, a load bearer, a dock worker or, as Tinker put it, 'the lowest level of the industrial labour market'.[66] In Chinese the word was composed of two characters: *k'u* ('bitter') and *li* ('strength').[67] The word emphasises the harsh, bitter and sometimes backbreaking nature of the task of the labourer.

During the early indentureship period the term was used in its normal sense to designate both Indian and Chinese labourers. However, in European usage it came increasingly to designate more a 'racial' or ethnic group than an occupational one. Thus in the Caribbean all Indians, regardless of occupation, came to be designated 'coolies'. Contract labourers were often referred to as 'coolie labourers'. Pejorative as was the term in itself, it acquired greater stigma when associated with the status of slavery, by the designation of those under indentureship as 'coolie slaves'. The Indians (and Chinese) came to resent the term, and up to today it is one of the most derogatory terms one can use when referring to an Indian.[68] It is no longer applied to the Chinese in the English-speaking Caribbean, although scholars, unaware or insensitive of its present-day connotation, sometimes use it to refer to the Asian contract labourers.[69]

Other stereotypes of East Indians

Another stereotype applied to East Indians in the Caribbean plantation colonies was that they had a natural tendency to wander and to be vagrants. The two activities were closely associated in the European mind, for planters expected the Indians to be on the estates or in jail at all times. In the early post-emancipation period African freedmen who could not give a satisfactory reason to the police for their presence in a given place were often deemed to be vagrants. The intention was to restrict mobility and keep them as near as possible to their places of work. In the case of Indians, vagrancy was often treated as much more than a misdemeanour, becoming a criminal offence punishable by imprisonment, the withholding of wages or the extension of the period of indentureship. There was a tendency to criminalise the Indians in order to extend their contracts or to achieve more control over them. Many planters believed that most of those who came to the colonies were the 'criminal types'. As Tinker points out, '[T]he Indians were almost always stigmatized as the dregs of their country: lowborn, even criminal.'[70]

The most striking evidence to which the planters could point of their criminal mentality was the high incidence of wife murder among them. This phenomenon was noticed in all the Caribbean territories with large Indian populations, and also in Fiji to which many of them were sent. Only rarely did Europeans recognise that the situation was connected with the small number of Indian women brought to the region, and the fact that Indian men, much more than Chinese, were reluctant to marry local women. Thus four or five men would live in the same compound with one woman and share her bed, or a man would encourage the wife of another to form an amorous relationship with him; and European plantation hands sometimes did the same thing. Such situations bred jealousy, resentment and even homicide. But they also reinforced planter images of the Indian women as promiscuous and even prostitutes.[71]

The phenomenon illustrates the oppressors' perceptions of the oppressed groups. Wife murders were taken completely out of their historical context by the European planters and treated as the result of the natural disposition of the Indians. Memmi, dealing with stereotypes, notes: 'The colonialist removes the factor from history, time and therefore possible evolution. What is actually a sociological point becomes labeled as being biological or, preferably, metaphysical. It is attached to the colonized's basic nature.'[72]

Indian men were also said to be short-tempered and liable to let fly the blade (cutlass or machete) to settle disputes. Even Tinker, who on the whole demonstrates much sensitivity to the problems which the indentured labourers faced, falls into the trap of believing that they possessed remarkably little restraint. In his own words: 'If an argument occurred, it was almost automatic to raise the blade to settle the issue.' He suggests that not only was the cutlass which they used for cutting the canes the visible symbol of their oppression and degradation, but in a way it was also the symbol of their efforts to liberate themselves.[73]

Indians might strike a blow for freedom by killing or attempting to kill their oppressors; they might also do so by committing suicide. This was the ultimate stroke which would set them free from the trammels of bondage. We do not know what influence their ideas about reincarnation had on the incidence of suicide, but it may have had some bearing. The incidence of suicide was said to be disturbingly high in some of the plantation territories.

The evidence shows that Indians took to consuming alcohol. Rum shops were set up on some plantations by the owners, who thus made money out of the misery of the Indians.[74] Only a few Europeans at the time were perceptive enough to see a relationship between alcohol and the abject conditions of Indian life. Alcohol was as much an anaesthetic as an elixir; the same could be said about ganja and opium. These substances taken in large quantities could only have had a deleterious effect on the health of the Indians.

When the Indians displayed more positive responses to their situation, they were the subject of unhealthy criticism. Some attempted to save something from the little that they earned, in the hope of improving their lot later on. The responses of many Europeans, Africans and other groups to this ranged from regarding them as being thrifty to a fault, to considering them to be penny-pinchers.

The Chinese

Indians were not the only Asian contract labourers brought to the Caribbean. Chinese also came in small numbers to territories such as Martinique, Guadeloupe, French Guiana, Suriname, Trinidad and Guyana, and in large numbers to Cuba. In fact, Cuba was second only to Peru in terms of the number of Chinese that were recruited to labour on the plantations. Again, virulent stereotypes developed in the Caribbean. This is the more interesting because for a long time after the Europeans first established regular contacts with the Chinese they viewed Chinese civilisation as being in many ways more advanced than theirs.

Early and later perceptions of the Chinese

The voyages and writings of the Venetian Marco Polo in the thirteenth century during the period of Kublai Khan were instrumental in opening the eyes of the Europeans to Chinese civilisation. In the following centuries the writings of other European visitors, including Catholic missionaries, resounded in praise of the attainments under the Mongol, Ming and Manchu (Ch'ing) dynasties. The Chinese were praised for their system of government, calligraphy, language, architecture, paintings, porcelain, garments and, not least, the Great Wall.

Gradually, however, cracks in this edifice of praise began to appear and to become much more frequent from the eighteenth century as European civilisation became more militant and began to push against the stubborn Chinese wall of defiance. The Chinese were chastised by Europeans as a people lacking in notable scientific and technological achievements, gamblers, the greatest cheats upon earth, unpunctual, living in filth and speaking filth when contradicted or put to shame, 'not strict observers of truth', incapable and even unconcerned about understanding logic, possessing an inordinate belief in their superiority to all other peoples, infantile, obstinate and feeble-brained, and with an inconceivable greediness for gain. Curiosity and criticism blended in comments about their long fingernails, their pigtails, their habit of smoking opium, their eating of rats.[75] Fairbank commented early in the present century that the Chinese did 'everything' in the opposite way from the Europeans: 'The men wear gowns and the women trousers. They read from down to up and right to left. The soup comes last. Mourners wear white and brides red. The last name comes first. The compass points south. Left is the seat of honor, and so on.'[76] It was a short step from translating difference into backwardness.

Almost inevitably, amidst such criticisms, derogatory remarks about the subjects' physical features appear. So it was with the Chinese. In the sixteenth century Gaspar da Cruz mentioned that they had small eyes and flat noses. No doubt others made similar remarks. In the late nineteenth century James Woodforde described them as 'uncommonly ugly'. It was usual by that time to depict them with slanting eyes, high cheekbones, the men with an unsightly pigtail, and a generally clumsy appearance. The men were often shown to have a small physique, thin whiskers and effeminate manners.[77]

Von Herder, in a more elaborate caricature, implied that their physical features limited their capacity for greatness as a people:

> This north-eastern mungal nation could no more change its natural form by artificial regulations, even though enduring for thousands of years, than a man can change his nature, that is, the innate character of his race and complexion . . . . Chinese they were, and will remain: a people endowed by nature with small eyes, a short nose, a flat forehead, little beard, large ears, and a protuberant belly: what their organization could produce, it has produced; nothing else could be required of it.[78]

The criticisms of the Chinese never descended to the depths of those of the Amerindians and Africans. But, appearing at a time when Europe was looking for cheap labour outside the continent of Africa, they were opportunistic. This is not to suggest that Europeans would not have engaged Chinese labour had the dominant seventeenth-century image of China remained unimpaired in the nineteenth. Capitalists looking for cheap labour sought it in every quarter of the globe, including Ireland, Madeira, England, Germany, Spain, Egypt, Abyssinia, Polynesia and Yucatán. The French even adopted the expedient of sending some 70,000 convicts between 1852 and 1939 to a penal settlement just off the coast of French Guiana.[79] Many of these were recruited as a servile labour force for governmental and other undertakings on the mainland. Convict labour was also used on Cuban plantations in the second half of the nineteenth century.[80]

The Europeans could find a pretext for their recruitment of Chinese labour, not only on the basis of need in the colonies and surplus in China, but also on the basis that the immigrants would have a chance to be civilised by the Europeans. Raymond Dawson notes that the 'old residents of China perceived the coolies as animals'.[81] We do not know how long people thought this in China, but we know that for centuries they had been used as beasts of burden, conveying the notables in palanquins and performing other jobs of a servile nature. Thus a suitable labour force was available to the Europeans when they wanted to recruit Chinese 'coolies'. The Chinese had a reputation for being industrious,[82] which made them theoretically of great value to the planters in the Caribbean. But they were reluctant to migrate in large numbers and often had to be dragged from their country, just like the Africans and the Indians. Some also displayed a marked reluctance to work under servile or semi-servile conditions, which caused the planters to regard them as lazy.

Recruitment and indentureship

An estimated 125,000 Chinese are believed to have gone to Cuba as indentured labourers between 1840 and 1874, and an overall total of some 300,000 up to the start of the Second World War. A significant number in time returned to China. This was a period, of course, of Chinese migration to other places besides Latin America and the Caribbean, such as California and South Africa. Some Chinese came out as entirely voluntary migrants (especially in the period after 1880), but the vast majority of them before that time arrived in the Caribbean as indentured labourers.

From the European standpoint, the Chinese were simply another group of labourers needed for the plantations and were to be made as pliable as possible to serve those needs, but specific conditions in the various colonies had some effect on their treatment. In the British and French colonies they worked alongside Indian contract labourers and free Africans. In Suriname they worked with Indian and Javanese contract labourers and for a short time with African slaves. In Cuba they worked for a long time largely alongside slaves rather than other contract labourers and were by far the largest number of contract labourers there.

New World stereotypes of the Chinese

As with other labourers in the region, the Chinese, notably in Cuba, experienced the violation of their contracts and their persons by the planter class (and others). Nor did they, any more than the other oppressed groups, accept their lot with equanimity. From the outset they expressed their discontent by a variety of forms of resistance, ranging from work stoppages, to revolt, homicide and suicide.[83] The Europeans developed a wide variety of stereotypes of them, which often replicated those commonly applied to other labouring groups. Thus, contrary to the perceptions of them by the Europeans in China, they were often thought to be lazy, too weak and psychologically unsuited for hard plantation work.[84] They were also widely regarded as thieves, liars, cruel and incorrigible. They were thought to be particularly prone to revolt, a perception strengthened by anti-European acts and anti-Christian riots unleashed by the Chinese masses against the foreigners in China. For this reason the Cuban plantocracy was opposed to the time-expired labourers remaining in the country.

The Chinese were also regarded as naturally suicidal. Their code of honour, which made it imperative to commit suicide in certain situations of disgrace or failure, was interpreted in plantation society as offering a way out of desperate and seemingly hopeless bondage.

One noteworthy aspect of race relations in the region was the alarming incidence of suicide among all the major groups brought under the coercive labour regimes of the Europeans. Few Europeans seem to have appreciated that the violence and degradation to which the Chinese and other groups were subjected were making them desperate.

Most of the attitudes towards the Chinese developed during the period before 1870, when the Chinese were introduced almost exclusively as indentured labourers. This system of labour came to an end in 1879 as a result of the report of the Ch'ên Lanpin Commission sent out by the Chinese government in 1874 to inquire into the treatment of its nationals in Cuba. The commission's report was highly critical of the operation of the system and exposed numerous brutalities meted out to the immigrants.[85] Backed by the British government, the Chinese government decided to terminate the migration of its people as contract labourers. As a result of an agreement with the Spanish government, the Chinese government placed consular officials in Cuba to look after the interests of its nationals.

From around 1870 a number of Chinese businessmen began to visit the island and to invest there. Some Chinese who disliked the racial discrimination in the USA found the situation in Cuba somewhat more tolerable and became voluntary immigrants. They were joined by their compatriots from Mexico and Spain.[86] It appears that from around 1870 the situation became more tolerable for the Chinese, and especially for voluntary migrants and time-expired labourers. Some became wealthy business persons in the following years, and were involved in banking, commerce, wholesale and retail businesses, restaurants, grocery stores, and so on. Chinese schools, places of worship and recreational centres were opened in Havana and other towns. Gradually the Europeans came to view some Chinese in a different light. In fact, they came to draw a distinction between 'cultured' and 'uncultured' Chinese, those adopting European culture being regarded as the most civilised of all. Still, the 'yellow peril' remained a persistent problem in Cuban society. As late as 1939 a law was passed reaffirming an earlier one prohibiting the migration into the island of any but Chinese government officials and their families, businessmen and tourists. This law was repealed in 1942.[87]

The Chinese experience in Cuba was similar in many respects to that of the Indians in Guyana, Trinidad and Suriname. The Chinese in other Caribbean territories did not play nearly as significant a role in the plantation life of those colonies because the planters preferred Indian labourers. The reasons for this are not clear, for no firm evidence exists that the Indians were better agricultural workers than the Chinese, and the Cuban experience would certainly refute this contention. It may be that the British territories opted for Indian labour because of the British government's reluctance to allow recruitment from China and also because the British held a captive market in India. In any event, the Chinese were not well liked by the British planters as agricultural hands, not surprising when one notes the preference different colonies had for different African ethnic groups during the slavery period.

A comparison of statements made by Europeans about the various subject peoples shows their similarity. Intellectually, they were said to be stupid, of little intelligence, half-witted and lacking artistic and scientific skills; also morally degenerate, unjust, lacking shame, devoid of human affection, cowardly, dirty, thieves, liars and idolators.

Memmi has noted in his analysis of colonialism that the coloniser's stereotyping of the colonised as lazy is a basic strategy to justify his exploitation and oppression, and that the laziness is often declared to be monumental: 'The colonized doesn't let grass grow under his feet, but a tree, and what a tree! A eucalyptus, an American centenarian oak! A tree? No, a forest.'[88] This stereotype serves two functions. Firstly, it explains the colonised's persistent poverty and supposed lack of progress and scientific achievement. Secondly, it justifies the coercive methods employed to get him to work. Bryan Edwards, the Jamaican planter-historian, justified this coercion with the sophistry: 'Men in savage life have no incentive to emulation: persuasion is lost on such men, and compulsion, to a certain degree, is humanity and charity.'[89] Thus the oppressor claims to use coercive labour as a means of humanising and civilising the oppressed.

The Europeans

The Europeans perceived the other groups as the drudges of the world and themselves as the natural rulers, the philosopher-kings. Through their system of brainwashing they managed to get the oppressed to see life through their own distorted prism. But it is clear that many among the subordinate groups developed their own images of the Europeans, some of which were similar to those which the latter held of them. One of the dominant images was that the Europeans were lazy. The following extract, written by a European in Guyana in the mid-nineteenth century, seems clearly to have been derived from creole reminiscences of the rich planter:

> Aroused at early morn by his attendants, he sipped his cup of coffee . . . . Having held parley, or rather 'levée' with his assistants or overseers, he sallied forth on horseback, followed by a running footboy or page,

> armed with the pouch of tobacco or cigars . . . . His equestrian tour was round the plantation . . . . After a careful inspection, and having given necessary orders for the day, he leisurely returned to an elaborate breakfast . . . where fish, hams, sausages, pepperpot, cheese, formed the staple articles . . . . After this solid repast came the hour of contemplation and repose, ushered in by the fumes of the fragrant tobacco . . . . The morning 'siesta' over, the time was spent in visiting or receiving neighbours, looking over the buildings and machinery, writing or other light employment, not forgetting a stimulating lunch- eon and occasional draughts of sangaree, punch, or brandy-and-water. As evening approached, preparations were made for the great object of the day, dinner, which consisted of soups, fish, fowl, and viands of all kinds, to which a vigorous appetite did justice. Punch, beer, wine, were again handed round . . . . The night was marked by copious libations and smoking, until at length, overpowered with fatigue, repletion, and happiness, the lordly planter sank into the arms of repose, to dream of insurrections and earthquakes.[90]

It is interesting to observe that the major racial groups have all been perceived by others as being lazy. The laziness of the rich European is difficult to explain simply in terms of reverse stereotyping or racism. Possibly the view was the logical outcome of oppressed people's perception that their oppressors derived profits from their labour, and the fact that many plantation owners were absentee landlords would only have served to enhance this view of them.

The lifestyles of the rich and famous in Caribbean slave society spoke to their affluence and has been commented on by many writers.[91] The spendthrift mentality and the love of ease have been projected over the years as being among the more enduring memories of the planter class. Thus Bulhan, as late as 1985, wrote about the planter as 'idle and unproductive', and 'comfortable in mere consumption', with 'little motivation to change himself or his ways'. Above all, 'mastery' over people was perceived by him to be 'the supreme value', the *summum bonum*.[92]

There were, of course, many small farmers who directly superintended their estates and worked hard to earn a living. Even so, these usually had at least a few slaves in their employ, the profits of whose labour they appropriated to themselves. They were part of the system of exploitation of the labour class and were seen by the latter as being such. Even when this group of farmers were not actually seen as lazy, they must still have been regarded as oppressors.

The oppressed groups also considered the Europeans to be exceptionally cruel. The decimation of the Amerindians through warfare with more advanced weaponry, the use of bloodhounds and the cutting off of their heads for sport must have seemed to the local people as havoc rather than heroism. Many Peruvians in the sixteenth century questioned whether Europeans were human beings because of their extreme cruelty and inhumanity.[93] The experiences of Africans and Asians on the Middle Passage gave them an early taste of such cruelty, and daily life on the plantations and in the mines reinforced their view of European cruelty, brutality and utter callousness. The punishments meted out to the African slaves, including hanging them on meat hooks, burning them on slow fires, killing or maiming them for often frivolous reasons, separating them from their families by sale, and a number of similar acts, reinforced their view of European brutality. Chinese, East Indians and Javanese also suffered brutal treatment, although not usually in as extreme a form as during slavery (with perhaps the exception of those in Cuba).

The Chinese in Cuba intensely resented the Europeans as 'an incomparably barbarous group'.[94] Three petitioners to the Ch'ên Lanpin Commission which investigated the treatment of the indentured labourers in Cuba in 1874 declared that 'the administrator and overseers are as wolves or tigers' who chastised them 'until the blood drips to the ground'. Another spoke about the 'exceptional cruelty' of the administrator. Yet another deposed: 'I myself witnessed the death of an old man, whom the administrator had directed to move a heavy implement. He was unable to do so and was at once struck dead.'[95] These accusations and incidents were not isolated, as the commission detailed in its report.

Not only were the Europeans considered to be cruel, they were also considered to be unjust. For a long time in the region's history the other groups did not have even the façade of the law to protect them from unjust punishments. Incidents have been recorded of injustices meted out to the lower classes, who had no recourse to the law. Even when later on they were protected by law from some of the worst aspects of planter brutality, they still generally found it impossible to get the courts to give them a fair hearing.[96]

The Europeans were also considered to be avaricious because they wanted what the other groups had for little or nothing. Even Columbus accused his followers of this vice. They were deemed lascivious because of their lust not only for their own women, but for the women of the Amerindian, African, East Indian, Chinese and other groups. This has been explained in terms of European ideas of seigneurial rights, a concept, however, of which other groups could have known little and cared less. Rape of women of the labouring classes by European men was a common feature of plantation life. Stedman recorded an instance of a European in Suriname who stripped naked, tied up and flogged a young girl with over 200 lashes because she refused to yield to his sexual desires.[97] Thistlewood, a planter in Jamaica, had sexual relations with many of his slaves at his pleasure.[98]

Other stereotypes of the Europeans were that they were liars and cheats. The notion of white cannibalism also gained some currency in Africa and Asia, for these people could not understand why they wanted to transport such large numbers of persons overseas. The former Fante slave, Ottobah Cugoano, related how frightening was the thought that he would end up in the bellies of the Europeans.[99] To some orientals the whites were like vultures busy at their prey. Jerome Ch'en states that in the early sixteenth century the efforts of the Portuguese, Fernao Peres Andrade, to obtain boys to work for him were interpreted by the Chinese as 'kidnapping tender flesh for food'. He also said that the Russians were looked upon as evil beings, 'who also survived on human flesh and blood'.[100] Helly informs us that in the nineteenth century the Cantonese were opposed to the recruitment of their compatriots because they believed that they were being taken to Cuba to be eaten.[101] Thomas said that another view was that the Europeans killed them to extract an ointment from their bodies, or boiled them down to make soap. East Indians likewise feared that they would be used as raw material for the manufacture of oil.[102]

There were other images of white men. At first the Amerindians believed that they were gods of cosmic dimension. Appearing as they did in 'sea monsters', strange clothes, weapons that flashed lightning and belched thunder, and with other strange creatures such as the horse and rider (which some Amerindians mistook at first for a single being), they 'stared, and saw, and did not understand'.[103] What could they make of these strange ghost-like beings who seemed not like the inhabitants of the earth but yet were on it? They could not fit them into a meaningful Amerindian cosmology except under the title of 'gods'. The newcomers seemed to fulfil prophecies, widespread both on the mainland and in the islands, about the imminent return of white ancestor gods. But gradually the Amerindians began to regard them more as devils than gods.[104] The Amerindian chief, Hatuey, who was about to be burnt at the stake by the Spanish, wanted nothing more to do with them in this life or in the beyond. To him their heaven would be his hell.

The assimilation of Europeans to devils seems also to have existed in at least some parts of Africa and Asia. In 1661 a king of one of the states on the Gold Coast is said to have referred to a Dane as being 'too white, like a devil'.[105] The thirteenth-century Venetian traveller, Marco Polo, had this to say of the Dravidians of Southern India: '[I]n very truth these people portray and depict their gods and their idols black and their devils white as snow. For they say that God and all the saints are black and the devils are all white. That is why they portray them as I have described. And similarly they make the images of their idols all black.'[106] It was therefore a short step mentally to associate white men with devils, just as some whites associated blacks with devils.[107] This was perhaps not a literal assimilation, but rather the perception of whites as agents of spiritual wickedness. This is certainly the impression conveyed in the account of an experience which the Italian slaver, Theophilus Conneau, recorded when he visited an African interior village to obtain slaves:

> As I took my usual walk every morning I found the children ran with great fright at my appearance. Since the seizure of the night before, all under the yoke of captivity on seeing me, thought their time had come, and I am certain that the poor part of the population looked on me as their Satan. Once or twice I detected women pick up a handful of earth and throw it toward me, exclaiming a short sentence. This was done to drive the evil spirit from them.[108]

The Chinese also viewed the Europeans as repulsive, ghost-like creatures and even devils. Frank Dikötter writes: 'The Westerner was often negated by being perceived as a devil, a ghost, an evil and unreal goblin hovering on the border of humanity. Many texts of the first half of the nineteenth century referred to the English as 'foreign devils' (*yangguizi*), 'devil slaves' (*guinu*), and 'barbarian devils' (*fangui*).'[109]

Chinese writers also referred to the Europeans as 'barbarians', 'island barbarians', 'blue-eyed barbarian slaves' and 'red-haired barbarians'.[110] Hollanders in Canton were stereotyped not only with the last description, but also seen as a people with 'sunken eyes, long nose, red hair, red eyebrows, red beard, and their feet when bare measuring some 14 inches long . . . unusually big'. Concerning the Europeans generally, another writer said that the Europeans' 'shins and chest are covered with hair, their green eyes suffer when they look in the distance'. They were said to be 'ugly', 'physically hideous and socially repulsive', and as 'cold and dull as the ashes of frogs'. They were also referred to contemptuously as 'foreign dogs' and 'goats'; a stubborn and rapacious people, so greedy for gain that they were driven to seek it thousands of miles away from their homeland.[111]

Their manner of speech also came in for critical comment. According to one Chinese writer, '[T]he sounds of their speech are similar to birds.'[112] This comment is particularly interesting, since in the nineteenth and twentieth centuries Europeans made many derogatory remarks about the language of the Chinese.[113]

Chinese ideas about the Europeans began to change noticeably from around the second half of the nineteenth century when the foreigners began to impose their will on them by force. They began to perceive the Europeans as cunning and intelligent, with a strong and advanced civilisation worthy of imitation.

East Indians in the subcontinent, and no doubt also in the Caribbean, looked down upon the Europeans because they ate the flesh of the cow, an act which Abbé Dubois informs us the Hindu considered 'a much more heinous offense than eating human flesh'.[114] The Muslims despised them as being 'eaters of pork and drinkers of wine'.[115] Hindus considered them to be ritually polluted because they not only utilised *pariahs* as domestic servants, but also often had sexual relations with them.[116] Indians looked down upon the European women who went about in 'bare-shouldered evening fashions'.[117] European architecture, Indians thought, was 'graceless', especially their bungalows; but worse still was their greed: 'always counting their – or worse, other people's – money.' They were likewise contemptuous of what they did not understand. They were boorish, arrogant, scandalously lax and repulsive in their habits. They were notorious for their infidelity.[118]

Africans who had gone through an extensive process of western acculturation often viewed white persons as the epitome of beauty. But among those not so acculturated, Europeans were disliked for their 'aquiline nose, scant lips and cat-like eyes' which 'afflict[ed]' the Africans.[119] The whiteness of the European skin, to those who had not seen a white person before, 'suggested the unsightly discolouration of a person who had been dead long in the water'.[120] The general features, colour, manners and smell of the whites were also repugnant to Africans. Their smell was said to be rancid and disagreeable.[121]

The stereotypes developed of the major groups in Caribbean society were wide-ranging and much more negative than positive. We have attempted to show that, with the exception of the Amerindians, these stereotypes began to emerge before the encounter of the different groups in the Caribbean. The Caribbean situation, however, helped to reinforce and expand them as the various groups strove to carve out their niche in society. Although stereotypes also developed of the Europeans, they did not suffer from discrimination in the same way as other groups because of their political, economic and social dominance.

Notes

1. Memmi, 75.
2. Memmi, xxiv.
3. Memmi, 70.
4. Memmi, 67.
5. Dickson, 82.
6. Cited in Williams, *Documents*, I, 108-09.
7. Hanke, *All Mankind is One*, 10.
8. Hanke, *Aristotle and American Indians*, 47.
9. Cited in Hanke, *All Mankind is One*, 41-42.
10. Cited in Elliott, 42.
11. Cited in Hanke, *Aristotle and American Indians*, 47, 50; Williams, *Documents*, I, 110.

12. Cited in Hanke, *All Mankind is One*, 44-45.
13. Cited in Hanke, *All Mankind is One*, 74; see also 82.
14. Cited in Williams, *Documents*, I, 48, 54.
15. Hanke, *All Mankind is One*, 44.
16. *Diodorus,* Bk III, Vol.II, 89-95.
17. *Herodotus*, Bk III, Vol.I, 206.
18. Snowden, 108, 116, 186-87.
19. Pliny, Bk VI, Vol.II, 477-87.
20. For a more detailed study of this subject see Thompson, 'Race and Colour Prejudices', 29-59.
21. Long, II, 364-65.
22. Long, II, 352-54.
23. Long, II, 354.
24. Long, II, 371, 373, 375.
25. C. Carroll, *The Negro a Beast or in the Image of God?* (1900), 87, cited in Burns, *Colour Prejudice*, 22. For a more detailed study of the history of European racist thought see Poliakov.
26. See Thompson, 'Race and Colour Prejudices', 43-49.
27. Cited in Miller & Dolan, 237-38.
28. Burns, *Colour Prejudice*, 103-05. Leakey's views are cited in Burns, *ibid.;* Sir Harry Johnson, *British Central Africa* (1897), 408, cited in Burns, *Colour Prejudice*, 125-26.
29. J. D. Unwin, *Sex and Culture* (1934), 382, cited in Burns, *Colour Prejudice*, 133.
30. See Burns, *Colour Prejudice*, 127-36.
31. George Best, *Discourse*, in Walvin, 36-37.
32. *Holy Bible*, Gen. 9:20-26.
33. *Holy Bible*, Gen. 10:6-20.
34. Salem was an Amorite kingdom in the days of Joshua, the Israelite leader (*Holy Bible*, Joshua 10:5). The Amorites are said by the writer of the Genesis record to have been a Canaanite group of peoples (*Holy Bible*, Gen. 10:15-16; see also Joshua 12:1-2, 7-10).
35. *Holy Bible*, Hebrews 5:6; 7:11-10 (KJV); see also Gen. 14:18-20.
36. For instance, in T. Alton Bryant's edition of *The New Compact Bible Dictionary*, 100) we are told: 'The Canaanites were part of a large migration of Semites (Phoenicians, Amorites, Canaanites) from NE Arabia in the third millennium BC. The word *Semitic* is purely a linguistic term, first used by A. L. Schloezer in 1781 to identify a family of closely-related languages, the most significant of which are Babylonian-Assyrian, Canaanite, Aramaic, Arabic, and Ethiopic. Marvin H. Hope reminds us that the term should not be used in an ethnic sense, 'since the peoples who spoke and still speak these languages are of diverse genetic make-up and admixtures' (*Anchor Bible,* Vol.15, xlviii; see also *Shorter Oxford English Dictionary*, 3rd ed., II, 1937). For one of the most detailed studies on blackness in English religious thought see Washington.
37. Scoble, 'African Popes', 96-107; Van Sertima, 'African Presence', 137-42; Scoble, 'The Black in Western Europe', 190-202; Scoble, 'African Women', 205-12; Holte, 264-70. We have only selected examples where there is clear contemporary documentary evidence (written records, sculpting, paintings, etc) in the works mentioned above to support our conclusions.
38. Cheikh A. Diop, *African Origin of Civilisation.*
39. See, for instance, Burns, *Colour Prejudice*, 80-81.
40. Long, II, 355-56.
41. Caton-Thompson, 103.
42. Bearce, 16-19.
43. Bearce, 20-21, 32.
44. Bearce, 114.
45. Bearce; Stokes, *The English Utilitarians*; Bolt, 126-47.
46. Stokes, 31.

47. Cited in Stokes, 31.
48. Heber, III, 333.
49. James Mill, *History of British India*, 1820 ed., II, 166-67, cited in Stokes, 54.
50. Cited in Edwards & Merivale, 104.
51. Mill, *British India*, 1840 ed., I, 478, cited in Hutchins, 64.
52. Thomas Macaulay, 'Warren Hastings', in *Essays and Poems*, Boston, nd, II, 567, cited in Hutchins, 55.
53. Mill, *British India*, 1840 ed., 445-46, cited in Hutchins, 65.
54. Hutchins, 55, 56.
55. Edwards & Merivale, 104; Macaulay, 'Warren Hastings', cited in Hutchins, 54-55.
56. Bolt, 141.
57. Dubois, 308. As mentioned above, Tomas Ortiz declared that the older the Amerindians became 'the worse they were' (Cited in Williams, *Documents*, I, 108-09). A Dutchman wrote around 1600 of the Africans that the older the children grew, the more savage they became (cited in Purchas, VI, 261, 268).
58. Bolt, 137.
59. I owe a debt of gratitude to Dr Kusha Haraksingh, Senior Lecturer in History at the University of the West Indies, St Augustine, Trinidad, for sharing many of his insights on this subject with me.
60. Haraksingh, 'Control and Resistance', 63-68, 75.
61 Haraksingh, 'Indian Leadership', 17-38; Ramnarine, 119-44; Rodney, *Guyanese Working People*, 153-54.
62. W. W. Hunter, *The Annals of Rural Bengal*, 226-27, cited in Tinker, 48-49.
63. Tinker, 63. This is what Naipaul said years later about Indians and Africans in Trinidad: 'Like monkeys pleading for evolution, each claiming to be whiter than the other, Indians and Negroes appeal to the unacknowledged white audience to see how much they despise one another' (*Middle Passage*, 80).
64. Tinker, 51-52.
65. It was not uncommon to find notices at the entrance of whites-only clubs and recreational centres such as 'Dogs and kafirs not allowed'.
66. Tinker, 43.
67. Tinker, 41.
68. Basdeo Mangru defines *coolie* as 'a term of opprobrium currently in use to describe East Indian' (*Benevolent Neutrality*, 251).
69. See Scott, *Slave Emancipation*, 32, 100; Tinker, 191, 192.
70. Tinker, 221.
71. On the subject of the recruitment of East Indian women and European perception of them as prostitutes see Basdeo Mangru, 'Sex-Ratio Disparity', 211-30.
72. Memmi, 71.
73. Tinker, 226.
74. See Samaroo, 'Two Abolitions', 35.
75. Dawson, 152, 197, 198, 204, 215; Ch'en, 43-46.
76. Dawson, 215.
77. Ch'en, 43, 44.
78. Cited in Dawson, 182, 201.
79. Claypole & Robottom, 61.
80. Scott, *Slave Emancipation*, 102-03; Fraginals, 'Plantations in the Caribbean', 19.
81. Dawson, 152.
82. Ch'en, *China and the West*, 47.
83. *Cuban Commission Report*, 99-109.
84. Look Lai, in his study of the Chinese in British Guiana and Trinidad, came to the conclusion that planters' sentiments did not tilt drastically to the view that the Chinese were lazy. Many of them were deemed to be good workers, especially in British Guiana (90-101).

85. See *Cuban Commission Report.*
86. Helly, 240-44.
87. Corbitt, *Chinese in Cuba,* i-ii.
88. Memmi, 80.
89. Edwards, *History, Civil and Commercial,* II, 41.
90. Dalton, I, 49-50.
91. See, for instance, Dunn; Ragatz.
92. Bulhan, 104.
93. Hanke, *Aristotle and American Indians,* 26.
94. Scott, *Slave Emancipation,* 33.
95. *Cuban Commission Report,* 49, 57.
96. *Cuban Commission Report,* 53-55, 60-62, 91-92; [Jenkins], *The Coolie;* Beaumont; Des Voeux.
97. Stedman, 177-78.
98. Hall, *In Miserable Slavery,* 50, 185, 221, 283, 302.
99. Cited in Pope-Hennessy, 32.
100. Ch'en, 59.
101. Helly, 95.
102. Thomas, *Cuba,* 188; Tinker, 120-21.
103. Squire, 42.
104. Walker, 63-67. The view that gods often appeared in the likeness of men was widespread in early European and Asiatic societies. The writer of the New Testament book of *Acts* noted that Paul and Barnabas were once mistaken for the Greek gods Apollo and Jupiter, and that the local peoples could scarcely be restrained from offering gifts and sacrifices to them (*Holy Bible,* Acts 14:11-18).
105. Cited in Hanke, *All Mankind is One,* 11; see also Washington, 18, on the issue of 'white devils'.
106. *The Travels of Marco Polo* (trans. R. Latham; Middlesex: Penguin Books, 1982), 276, cited in Rashidi, 'Africans in Early Asian Civilisations', 40.
107. According to Philip Mason, 'In the fourth century AD, one of the desert ascetics from Alexandria records his temptation by the devil who appeared to him in the form of a Negro; St Teresa of Avila on successfully resisting temptation saw a small Negro boy chattering with rage at his frustration; James I and IV of England and Scotland in his *Demonologie* tells us that witches' covens habitually met under the presidency of a black man, who was the Devil in person; in the eighth century, Bede argued that the Ethiopian baptized by Philip (as recounted in the Acts of the Apostles) must have turned white on his conversion' (*Patterns of Dominance,* 31). Washington also mentions that Francis Bacon wrote about the spirit of fornication appearing as 'a little foul ugly Aethiop' (100).
108. Conneau, 142.
109. Dikötter, 422; see also Ch'en, 59.
110. Dikötter, 422.
111. Cited in Ch'en, 59-60; Dikötter, 422.
112. Dikötter, 422.
113. Dawson, 194-95.
114. Dubois, 305.
115. Hardy, 61.
116. Dubois, 305.
117. Hardy, 61.
118. Hardy, 61.
119. S. W. Molema, *The Bantu Past and Present* (1920), 310, cited in Burns, *Colour Prejudice,* 111. Malinowski, writing about the Melanesians said: 'Europeans, the natives frankly say, are not good-looking. The straight hair . . . the nose, 'sharp like an axe blade', the thin lips, the big eyes 'like water puddles', the white skin with spots on it like those of an albino – all

these the natives say (and no doubt feel) are ugly.' B. Malinowski, *The Sexual Life of Savages in North-Western Melanesia* (1932), 258, cited in Burns, *Colour Prejudice*, 113.

120. W. D. Weatherford & C. S. Johnson, *Race Relations. Adjustment of Whites and Negroes in the United States* (1934), 543-44, cited in Burns, *Colour Prejudice*, 111.

121. Burns, *Colour Prejudice*, 111.

CHAPTER 8

The dynamics of race and colour

'Look, a Negro!' It was an external stimulus that flicked over me as I passed by. I made a tight smile.

'Look, a Negro!' It was true. It amused me.

'Look, a Negro!' The circle was drawing a bit tighter. I made no secret of my amusement.

'Mama, see the Negro! I'm frightened!' Frightened! Frightened! Now they were beginning to be afraid of me. I made up my mind to laugh myself to tears, but laughter had become impossible.[1]

Frantz Fanon

Race and working-class conflicts

From early days colonial policy aimed to create and exploit divisions among the ethnic groups, especially among the working people. Bringing together various racial groups in competitive economic relationships was in itself a potential source of division and conflict. But at the same time, had the working groups been able to form durable alliances they could have been a powerful bargaining force against the planters. The latter, however, made sure that such alliances never emerged, at least not before the period of trade union organisation in the present century.

Contract labourers

Records show clearly that one great reason for the import of contract labour was that it allowed the planter class to depress wages. This was explicitly stated in a report of a Select Committee of the British House of Commons in 1842, set up to inquire into the possibility of importing Indian labour into Guyana: '[O]ne obvious and most desirable mode of endeavouring to compensate for this diminished supply of labour, is to promote immigration of a fresh labouring population, to such an extent as to create competition for employment.'[2] What Haraksingh says about competition between time-expired Indian labourers and contract labourers is equally true of the relationship between Africans and contract workers: 'The presence of a group of workers who were legally bound to work undermined the bargaining power of free workers and reduced the pressure which a strike could exert on the planters.'[3]

The wages and other expenses that the plantocracy were required by law to provide for contract labourers generally fell far below the expense of hiring other forms of labour. In Cuba in the 1860s, Chinese contract labourers were paid 4 pesos per month, plus the usual plantation allowances, at a time when the cost of hired slaves was 15-20 pesos and of free persons 20-30 pesos (and sometimes as much as 40 pesos). In Guyana wages in the early 1840s were between 1s 4d and 2s per day. In Trinidad it was between 1s 8d and 2s 1d per day. With the influx of a large number of indentured labourers wages declined appreciably. Between the 1870s and the end of Indian immigration in 1917 the legal minimum wage was established at 1s 1/2d per day for task work (based on an estimated amount of work an able-bodied adult male could perform). In practice, however, actual wages for indentured workers fell even below the minimum, especially since planters often increased the size of the task. In 1895-96 a significant number of these workers were said to be earning less than 6d per day.[4] Worse still, many of the indentured labourers were rarely or never paid wages. Several of the Chinese in Cuba complained that they had not received wages for several years.[5]

The Chinese, Indians and other contract labourers were, of course, unaware of the market value of their labour at the time of their recruitment, and in any case, they were often involuntary recruits brought to the colonies. It is not unusual for migrant labourers to accept wages and other conditions of employment which the locally resident labour force would be reluctant to accept. This is true today of migrant labour to Europe, Canada, the USA, the Dominican Republic and the Bahamas. In many cases the labourers are illegal aliens in the territories and therefore can be more easily exploited than other categories of labour. In a sense they become a captive labour force, like the Indians, Chinese, Javanese and other contract labourers.

Contract labourers were not free to negotiate their conditions of work during the period that they were under contract, nor were they able to change employers without their masters' permission. But sometimes their masters deployed them to any of his plantations or other workplaces, contracted out their labour to other persons, and even assigned them to other masters for all or part of their period of indenture, without seeking their consent. These restrictions on their rights, together with the fact that they could be punished by their employer for what he considered to be their delinquency, and that they were prevented from leaving the plantations without his written permission, meant in effect that they were reduced to labour conditions reminiscent of slavery.

In Guyana, Trinidad and the French Antilles the accommodation was that formerly occupied by the slaves. In Cuba and Suriname they shared the same food, clothing, medicine, lodging and hours of work with the slaves. Forty Chinese in Cuba deposed that they were 'forced to remain slaves in perpetuity'. Another deposed: 'I am treated exactly like a negro slave.' Many of them said that they were treated worse than slaves, and others declared that they were treated as dogs, horses and oxen.[6] Brereton states that a common taunt of Indian contract workers from Africans was: 'Slave, where is your free paper?' She says that to Africans indentureship and slavery were the same thing.[7]

Like the slaves, contract labourers in all the territories where they were introduced in substantial numbers committed suicide, ran away, revolted, were hunted down, brutalised and kept in jail until redeemed by their masters. In such circumstances it was difficult for other labourers and the wider society to regard them as anything but slaves. The fact that they were paid wages was of little significance, for it was not uncommon for certain categories of slaves to be given stipends, especially those who were allowed by their masters to work on their own. The Ch'ên Lanpin Commission submitted:

> The distinction between a hired labourer and the slave can only exist when the former accepts, of his own free will, the conditions tendered, and performs in a like manner the work assigned to him, but the lawless method in which the Chinese were – in the majority of cases – introduced into Cuba, the contempt there evinced for them, the disregard of contracts, the indifference as to the tasks enforced and the unrestrained infliction of wrong, constitute a treatment which is that of 'a slave, not of a man who has consented to be bound by a contract.'[8]

The contract labourers were held in contempt not only because they were viewed as new categories of slaves, but also because they were often assigned jobs which special slaves or free persons would otherwise be employed to perform. Gradually Indians began to replace Africans on the plantations as artisans and boilermen, which were regarded as among the most prestigious jobs. In Cuba an increasing number of factory and skilled jobs were performed by the Chinese, instead of the Africans. Other longer established groups felt that the competition militated against their economic interests. The situation was exacerbated by the fact that payment for the import of contract labourers was often supplemented from government funds. In the case of Guyana, one-third of such money came from the taxes imposed on the colony as a whole. Africans were outraged that these funds should be used to introduce workers who would compete with them for jobs. Rodney argues of contract labour on the Guyanese plantations: 'Objectively, the free African wage earners were engaged in a level of struggle which was higher than that of other laborers on the estates. Free workers were fighting against the backward-looking tendency of landed capital to extract surplus through legal coercion reminiscent of feudalism.'[10]

Rodney indicates another problem in Guyana, Trinidad and Suriname. In the early post-emancipation period the plantocracy attempted to arrest the development of the African peasantry by preventing them from occupying the land. They passed legislation to prevent the sale of estate land in small lots, and asked exorbitant prices for certain plots. Sometimes the freed people simply occupied crown or abandoned estate lands. In the late nineteenth century the government granted cash and/or tracts of land in place of return passages to the Indians in an attempt to keep them in Guyana and Trinidad. Sometimes the government even moved African 'squatters' off land in order to accommodate the Indians.[11] Although the Indians were not at fault for what happened, African antagonism often turned against them, for they were regarded as joining with the planter class to deprive the Africans of their rights.

Indians and Chinese in turn complained that Africans were on the side of the plantocracy in oppressing them. It was not uncommon, especially in the early days of indentureship, for Africans to be employed as policemen or overseers on the plantations, thus exercising authority over the indentured labourers, who intensely resented it. Africans were also used sometimes to put down Indian and Chinese riots or revolts. Contract labourers complained of wrongs done them by Africans, either on their own or instigated by Europeans.

The charges of abuses are documented much more extensively in the case of the Chinese in Cuba, because of the Ch'ên Lanpin Commission which investigated the operation of the system of indenture there in 1874. The Chinese complained that the African slaves, many of whom were Cuban-born, were usually treated better than themselves and often joined with the European personnel on the plantations to deny them their rights as free persons, to dispossess them of their property and even to mete out violence against them. They also complained of the black overseers as possessing 'tiger's claws', as being more cruel than 'tigers or wolves', 'as terrible as the thunder', 'savage', and 'evil-minded'. The overseers, they deposed, treated them like animals, kicked them, threw bricks at them and incited dogs to tear them to pieces. They viewed the black overseers as an integral part of the system of brutality which forced them to commit suicide in such large numbers.[12]

Cultural and racial differences sharpened the conflict arising from the competition for the more prestigious jobs on the plantations. Language barriers also impeded their free communication with each other. Social customs acted as a barrier to mutual interaction. The ex-Cuban slave, Esteban Montejo, complained that the Chinese 'kept apart' from the Africans,[13] but the Chinese might well, with equal justification, have made the same comment about the Africans. The evidence suggests that the Chinese and Indians accepted many of the stereotypes which the Europeans had developed of the African – that he was lazy, a liar, a thief, improvident and given over to the pursuit of sensuous pleasures. Within China itself racist ideas about Africans were very evident in the nineteenth century. In 1861 Xu Jiyu wrote of Africa that 'It is scorching, miasmatic, and pestilential. Its climate and its people are the worst of the four continents.' Other writers compared the continent with the chaotic state of the primeval universe.[14] These views were similar to those expressed by Europeans and may reflect Chinese assimilation of Western views about the Africans. The extent to which these ideas informed the attitudes of the Chinese in the Caribbean is unknown.

The various ethnic groups in the Caribbean used the derogatory terms which were commonly used by the Europeans to designate them,[15] such as 'nigger', 'coolie', 'chink' and 'chinaman', and this generated a great deal of animosity. Bulhan points out:

> The oppressed depend on and share the paranoia and false beliefs of their oppressors . . . . [T]hey project on themselves the negative attributes cast on them and those emanating from their condition. This further compounds their experience of depression, disorganisation, and an inferiority complex. It also reinforces and 'validates' the false beliefs and narcissism of the dominant group. The oppressed therefore become victims of others and of themselves.[16]

Europeans stopped short of pitting the different ethnic groups against each other in head-on conflict, conscious that this was likely to lead to race riots, to the detriment of the planters' interests. However, they fostered a certain degree of rivalry and animosity, in the hope that these would keep the various groups apart and make it easier to exploit them. Although there were several instances of animosity and petty conflict between the Chinese and Indian contract labourers on the one hand and the Africans on the other, there were apparently no incidents of large-scale communal violence among them during the period of indentureship. This suggests that there was sufficient spatial and economic distance between them to reduce competition or prevent it from coming to the boil. It may also reflect a certain consciousness among them that they were all victims of European exploitation. They, especially the contract labourers who worked alongside slaves, must have been aware of their similar material and social conditions when compared with the ruling classes.

'Time-expired' immigrants

Many of the time-expired contract labourers left the plantations and sought work elsewhere. Some, especially the Chinese, drifted into the urban areas. But many Indians and Javanese in particular, were granted, bought or simply occupied land and enlarged the numbers of the peasantry. The Indians and Javanese planted chiefly rice, coconut and vegetables; they also became involved in cocoa and sugar-cane cultivation, and in dairy farming. Later they became engaged in a wide range of wholesale and retail businesses and in manufacturing. The Chinese became involved to a small extent in rice and vegetable farming. In Guyana they entered the timber and gold-mining industries. They were, however, much more well-known for their occupations as wholesalers and retailers, restaurant and rum-shop owners, and grocers.

As they drifted into the towns the Chinese, like all other groups at the time, came to have their own residential quarters, and it was quite common to find a Chinatown in urban communities. In time, however, these quarters lost their exclusive, and even their distinctive, Chinese character. As Lowenthal stated in 1972, by that time the populations of most so-called Chinese communities consisted of less than 40 per cent Chinese. He also made the point that the Chinese did not practise endogamy and so became considerably miscegenated.[17] In Jamaica, for instance, they formed durable unions with African women, with whom they often had children. Their main cultural retentions today are in the areas of cooking, pictures and paintings, and clothing. But they have become largely assimilated to the dominant creole culture.

The Indians' settlement areas and the occupations which they pursued from the late nineteenth century until about the time of the First World War were in the main outside the spatial and occupational zones of the Africans. In Suriname, both they and the Javanese occupied different geographical areas, which reinforced their ethnicity. Since that period Indians have vied with Africans and other groups in the urban areas for positions in all walks of life. They have also been able to maintain a much more distinctive cultural identity than other ethnic groups in those societies in which their numbers are large. Conflict has been most evident and most serious in the political arena, but this is in itself only a reflection of a broader but less overt arena of competition, especially between Africans and Indians.

Rodney sees racial conflict as being a complicating factor in an essentially class situation on the Guyanese plantations in the late nineteenth century.[18] He argues that academics (and others) tend to view race relations in terms of conflict, a view which has dominated the historiography of African-Indian relations. He stresses that until the political events of the 1960s the two groups were never locked in large-scale conflict and that there were areas of interaction in the social sphere from the late nineteenth century.[19] John La Guerre, however, stressed the seemingly inevitable interplay of race and politics in Guyana and Trinidad in 1985: '[I]n Trinidad and Guyana with substantial Indian populations race and politics were bound to go together.' In Suriname, Hira argues that in the economic and social realms class is predominant, although politically ethnic factors prevail.[20]

Africans, in particular, have resented the economic advancement of other, more recently arrived, groups in the region, such as the Chinese, Syrians and Portuguese, who emphasise that it was hard work, dedication and sacrifice that have accounted for their advancement. Africans believe that these groups were given much better opportunities by the colonial governments: greater patronage, access to loans, etc. They repudiate the argument that Africans failed to make equivalent progress through a combination of laziness, lost opportunities, lack of business acumen and a spendthrift mentality.

Antagonistic race relations have led to strident verbal criticisms and even to riots, such as the anti-Portuguese riots in Guyana in 1848, 1856 and 1905; anti-Chinese riots in Jamaica in 1965, and riots caused by decisions made by Chinese umpires in cricket matches between the Anglophone Caribbean and the UK in the region in 1953-54, 1959-60 and 1968; race riots in Cuba in 1912, Martinique in 1958 and 1961, and Guyana in 1963-64. However, these groups are now much more socially integrated within the Caribbean community and much of the hostility has evaporated.

There are both centrifugal and centripetal forces operating in those countries with large or high-profile ethnic minorities. There is always the danger that a particular event may act as a catalyst or incitement to race riots, like when there was a split in the dominant party in Guyana along allegedly racist lines. However, recent events in the region have spread more than a ray of hope that the spectre of embittered race relations will not reveal itself here. The present governments in Guyana and Trinidad and Tobago comprise persons from various racial groups, in significant numbers from the two dominant ones, and elected on multiracial ballots. Since 1992 Suriname has also shown a strong attempt to establish governments that reflect the multi-racial nature of its society.

Colour prejudice and discrimination

Racial prejudice and discrimination often have as their bedfellows colour prejudice and discrimination. Gordon Lewis rightly asserts: 'The characteristic trilogy of the Caribbean social drama has been family, religion and color'.[21] So close historically was the relationship between race and colour that it was common to substitute a colour classification for a racial one. Thus Europeans are often referred to as whites, Africans as blacks, Amerindians as reds and Chinese as yellows. Some groups, such as Indians, Javanese, and Syrians, were not differentiated by colour-specific attributes, but these usually fell somewhere between the two extremes – black and white

Miscegenation

There was another group: the miscegenated offspring of unions between the various groups identified above. These added another dimension to race relations in the region and the confusion between race and colour is best exemplified here. They were often referred to as the coloured race. During the period of slavery marriages between blacks and whites were forbidden either by law or custom in most colonies. White men, however, commonly developed concubinal relations with black women or coerced them into sexual unions. The practice went adrift from its intellectual moorings, which held that blacks were inferior humans, and perhaps not humans at all.

This practice passed without censure in white society, but it was altogether a different matter when a black man developed intimate relations with a white woman. Governor de Goyer of Suriname (1707-15) spoke for the whole community of white men and the vast majority of white women when he described such unions as 'unnatural whoredom and adultery'. He decreed that such women should be flogged and banished from the colony for life, and the men were to be put to death.[22] This different punishment underscores the point that blacks and whites were not regarded as equal, and the ultimate sanction was applied only to the black party that had violated the law. This law throws into sharp relief the ethos of a society immersed in racial prejudice and discrimination.

The children of mixed unions did not fit into any of the specific racial or colour categories mentioned. They were included under the amorphous category designated coloureds, but they were also often classified in a wide range of sub-categories. By the eighteenth century Caribbean society had become intensely colour-conscious, with a long gradation of colour categories from black to white. Douglas Hall gives the following gradations for Jamaica: *tawny* (offspring of black and mulatto), *mulatto* (offspring of black and white), *quadroon* (offspring of mulatto and white), *mustee* (offspring of quadroon and white), *mustifino* (offspring of mustee and white), *quintroon* (offspring of mustifino and white) and *octroon* (offspring of quintroon and white).[23] In Curaçao the discriminating terms included *sambo, grief, mestiche, castiche* and *poestiche*. Usually, a person four or five gradations removed from his or her black ancestry would be regarded as white. This was a literal (but not deliberate) application of the biblical curse of visiting the iniquity of the fathers on the children to the third and fourth generations.[24]

There were also colour variations produced by crossing other racial groups. These included persons of mixed African and Indian descent, known variously as *dougla* (in Guyana and Trinidad), *rial* (Jamaica), *chappé-coolie* (Martinique and Guadeloupe); mixed Amerindian and African descent, known as *zambaligo* in Spanish territories; and mixed Amerindian and European descent, known as *mestizo*, also in Spanish territories.

Colour and social mobility

During slavery Caribbean society became stratified along lines of colour, roughly with the whites at the top, the coloureds in the middle and the blacks at the bottom. Broadly speaking, the degree of access to political and economic power and the accompanying social prestige was related to the colour of one's skin; but skin colour in itself did not guarantee material or social success in a society full of contradictions.

There were poor whites in various colonies, the largest numerically being resident in Cuba, Puerto Rico, Santo Domingo and St Domingue. There were smaller numbers in St Kitts, St Thomas, Barbados, the French Antilles and Suriname. At the beginning of the sixteenth century Columbus declared the vast majority of the whites in Hispaniola to be 'vagabonds' and 'a dissolute people . . . full of vices and wickedness'. Storm Van's Gravesande referred to those in Essequibo in the mid-eighteenth century as having 'only the shape or figure of human beings – *vix nomine digni*'.[25] According to Josiah Child:

> Virginia and Barbados were first peopled by a sort of loose, vagrant People, vicious and destitute of means to live at home (being either unfit for labour, or such as could find none to employ themselves about, or had misbehaved themselves by Whoring, Thieving, or other Debauchery, that none would set them to work) which Merchants and Masters of Ships by their Agents . . . gathered up about the streets of London and other places, cloathed and transported to be employed upon Plantations.[26]

Sometimes the poor whites worked alongside slaves, as in Puerto Rico and Cuba in the nineteenth century. Many of those in the Dutch colonies were illiterate, mercenary soldiers, recruited from European countries. European writers and administrators spoke in pejorative terms about the poor whites, referring to them as 'riff-raff', 'trash', 'garbage', 'scum', 'refuse', etc.[27]

Although many of the poor whites worked hard to make a living, the chief aim of others was to make a killing by the shortest route possible. Many refused to do manual work, and Columbus wrote that they had to be compelled to work. They often behaved like a new nobility, requiring the Amerindians to bear them on their shoulders, requisitioning large quantities of food and forcing the local inhabitants to perform dances for their amusement.[28] One early nineteenth-century writer was highly critical of the poor whites in Barbados. He accused them of being lazy, idle and diseased, and declared that some of them were walking the streets begging alms.[29] The rich whites despised them as economic and social failures, and a disgrace to white society. They sought to separate themselves as far as possible from the poor whites, which might mean even disclaiming that they were indeed white. A description of the physical appearance of those in Barbados in the early nineteenth century depicted them as anything but a 'true white'. Rather they were more a sort of 'white nigger' or 'red nigger': 'Their hue and complexion are not as might be expected; their colour resembles more that of the Albino than that of the Englishman when exposed a good deal to the sun in a tropical climate; it is commonly sickly white or light red.'[30]

Similarly, the Portuguese introduced into Guyana, and in smaller numbers into Trinidad, Suriname, the French Antilles and other territories as poor white labourers, were despised by both rich whites and Africans as 'white niggers'. They are often described in the records of that period as dark-skinned rather than truly white. As Lowenthal says, 'In the eyes of the colonial elite, the Portuguese were scarcely even 'white' in appearance.'[31] The feeling has persisted into modern times that poor whites are a disgrace to white society in the Caribbean. Poverty is supposed to be the experience of other groups, but not whites. Poor whites are therefore a degenerate breed. It is no doubt with this attitude in mind that Daniel Guérin castigates the poor whites in Martinique as being 'degenerate and asleep on their feet'.[32]

Poor whites often resembled blacks in their occupations, dress, speech patterns and general lifestyle. In 1950 Patrick Leigh Fermor wrote of those in Iles des Saintes: 'The remarkable thing about them is that they have turned themselves into Negroes in all but colour .... They have long ago forgotten the French language, and speak nothing but the Afro-Gaulish patois of the Negroes.'[33]

Although many poor whites were not in the mainstream of Caribbean society and displayed a closer affinity, socially and culturally, to Africans, they were proud that their whiteness conferred on them freedom from slavery. Bryan Edwards declared that the whites in Jamaica displayed a 'conscious equality throughout all ranks and conditions. The poorest White person seems to consider himself nearly on a level with the richest, and, emboldened by this idea, approaches his employer with extended hand'.[34] Similarly, a visitor to Barbados in the nineteenth century said that the poor whites 'are as proud as Lucifer himself, and in virtue of their freckled ditch-water faces consider themselves on a level with every gentleman in the Island'.[35]

It is alleged that this category of whites showed the greatest hostility towards the blacks and coloureds, who often rivalled them for economic and sometimes social positions (although ironically it was the existence of these groups that helped to bolster the poor whites' claims to social elevation). They perceived the high browns and light coloureds as the greatest threats, for some social passing was often allowed to these groups. As Mauricio Solaún and Sidney Kronus note, '[I]t is not the volume of biological miscegenation *per se* that mainly distinguishes the infused racial system, rather it is the cultural ethos toward the miscegenated.'[36] In the Caribbean, Knight observes: 'The prevailing ambiguities and inherent contradictions of the plantation structure continually undermined rigidity and permitted vagueness, overlap, and social 'passing' on a limited scale along the peripheral penumbra of the two free castes as well as between the coloreds and the slaves.'[37]

The lack of rigidity allowed some members of the coloured population to obtain wealth through the ownership of plantations and slaves, and the inheritance of property willed to them by their parents. The economic position of the wealthy free coloureds became a source of envy to the white plantocracy in Jamaica, and in the latter half of the eighteenth century laws were passed by the legislature severely limiting the value of property that they could inherit. In Cuba during the nineteenth century they were allowed to own slaves and amass some wealth, but strenuous efforts were made to prevent them from becoming members of the plantocracy. In St Domingue they acquired more wealth than their counterparts elsewhere, but they chafed under the yoke of social discrimination from which many of the economically less fortunate whites were exempt. The struggle to assert their rights became one of the significant factors which precipitated the revolution there in the last decade of the eighteenth century.

As a group the coloureds sought to distance themselves as far as possible from the blacks, whom they regarded as belonging to the slave class. They therefore stressed their white rather than their black racial origins. As Bowser shows, they 'became very sensitive to racial classification, and were offended when referred to by a term for darkness greater than that which they claimed'.[38] Born in the Caribbean colonies, they were more thoroughly socialised than any other community in the creole culture. They, nevertheless, sought to imitate white cultural variants in language, religion, dress and social pastimes.

In spite of their efforts to insinuate themselves into white society, as a group they never managed to do so in any Caribbean colony. As Handler has pointed out in Barbados they remained an 'unappropriated people' throughout the slavery period.[39] The vast majority of them, though legally free from slavery, were still generally regarded by the whites as belonging more properly to the slave class. Thus, like the slaves, laws were passed against them restricting their physical, economic, political and social mobility. Even where the law was silent, custom often prevented them from rising appreciably above the slave category. Coloureds in the French Antilles suffered restrictions on the clothes they could wear and the place in the church in which they could sit.

Coloureds were also restricted in most colonial jurisdictions in respect of access to capital and the amount of property they could own. They paid head taxes in the French and Dutch colonies; they were legally prevented from holding commissions in the colonial armies, or from exercising authority over whites; they were barred from giving evidence against whites. They were likewise victims of many of the stereotypes associated with blacks: lazy, drunken, degenerate, depraved, useless, vicious, uncivilised.[40] The legal restrictions against those in the British Caribbean were removed on the eve of slave emancipation, but beyond the law, the social discrimination against them continued for a long time.

A few, however, succeeded in becoming assimilated. Hoetink informs us that in Brazil in the early nineteenth century when coloureds were admitted to the priesthood or the magistracy their personal papers recorded them as 'white'.[41] In Curaçao those with a great degree of 'whiteness', material prosperity and a certain level of education were classified as *mesties* and given the status of burghers, although in practice they often suffered ostracism by the leading whites.[42]

Rich coloureds sometimes married into poor white families, and on some occasions even into respectable white families who had lost their wealth but still maintained social respectability. However, colonial law and practice did not always look kindly on such unions. In 1703 in Martinique two brothers lost their noble status because they had married coloured women. In 1731 in St Domingue, whites who married coloureds were threatened with exclusion from government posts. But such marriages continued. Therefore, in 1768 a law was passed forbidding them, and it was made applicable to all the French colonies in the early nineteenth century. The law did not last very long and was repealed in 1827.[43] In Cuba in the early nineteenth century, marriages between whites and coloureds had to receive the consent of the appropriate civil official, but such requests were usually approved. However, such marriages were not very common, since the whites obviously did not wish to risk social ostracism. When the marriage was allowed, the coloured party often achieved a new status, that of being white.[44]

Since the end of the slavery period the coloureds and other groups have had greater access to political and economic power. In fact, in most Caribbean colonies formal control of political power now rests in the hands of the coloured and black groups who constitute the majority of the population. Of course, today the groups formerly referred to as coloured are now regarded as part of the black population. However, some individuals still insist on being called coloured or brown.

The changing ideological position of the coloureds is best exemplified in the case of Haiti. Before the revolution in the late eighteenth century most coloureds gravitated ideologically towards Europe. After the revolution, which resulted in the expulsion of the Europeans and the resurgence of a strong African consciousness, the coloureds began to identify strongly with the African *race*. However, the sharp colour divide remained in the society and even intensified with the competition for political and economic power between blacks and coloureds. Lundhal notes: 'Race and colour have played very different roles in the history of [post-independence] Haiti. The idea of race served to unify the nation, at least up to the 1960s . . . . Color, on the other hand, has frequently served to divide the nation.'[45]

Most scholars assert that, although the modern political landscape of the Caribbean reveals a dominant black and coloured hierarchy, social stratification still broadly reflects, although less rigidly, the racial and colour classification of the slavery and early post-emancipation periods, and specifically that the commanding heights of the region's economy are still mostly in the hands of white local and expatriate groups. It is still easier for whites than for other groups to secure loans. Expatriate Europeans, unlike other expatriates, are still largely treated as untouchables by the law enforcement agencies. In very few Caribbean societies are whites found doing menial jobs, and even in such circumstances it is rare to find them working alongside blacks. 'Race' is still very important in Caribbean societies, although this is often officially denied, particularly in Cuba, Puerto Rico and Martinique. It is also true of Brazil. Its importance is evident from the large body of literature still being produced on the subject.

Blackness

At the ideological level the region still reflects much of its slave past. This is exemplified in the pervasiveness of race and colour consciousness throughout all ranks of society, and in the response to the notion of 'blackness'. Lundhal commented in 1983 that no national of the Dominican Republic is considered black: 'The people are either white, light Indian, dark Indian, *mestizo* or *moreno*, but never black.' He also asserted that, although the majority of them were blacks and mulattos, they usually rejected their African heritage.[46]

Lewis, felt that little 'genuine racial democracy' existed in Puerto Rico in 1963 'in any complete way'. He spoke about 'the torture of an ambivalent racial identity' which often confronted the coloured Puerto Rican. The 'mulatto', according to him, by denying his black ancestry and clinging to his white one, displayed 'a virulent sense of racial shame' in regard to his black paternity, and paid a high 'emotional price . . . for living in a multi-racial society [that has] not yet come to satisfactory terms with its color question'. 'The real bar in Puerto Rico comes from the existence of an elaborate and subtle system of informal social pressures and prohibitions based upon an ambivalent attitude to color.'[47] In 1956 Guérin found widespread racial prejudice among the whites in all the Caribbean islands with which he was acquainted and described the social snobbery of the rich whites (especially the plantocracy) in Barbados as 'grotesque'.[48]

In the slavery period whiteness became associated with brain and blackness with brawn. Thus the blacker an individual was the more physically robust and even animalistic he was thought to be. He was also considered to be more capable than others of withstanding the heat of the tropical sun, and therefore more useful to the plantations.[49]

In time the myth of black inferiority was stretched to the point where some whites believed that most blacks were all brawn and no brain. The view developed that blackness was the outward symbol of an inner inferiority. Miscegenation 'improved' not only the complexion of blacks by whitening it, but also their intellectual capacity. E. F. L. Wood, UK Under-Secretary of States for the Colonies, declared in 1922 that in the Caribbean there was a large mixed population, coloured in appearance but possessing 'a large infusion of European blood . . . . 'Those of mixed race throw up not a few individuals of somewhat exceptional capacity and intelligence.'[50]

Blackness is sometimes seen as the albatross around an individual's neck. George Lamming, the Barbadian author, writes in his book, *In the Castle of my Skin*, 'They often said of the village teacher how very very bright he was, but he was so black.' That was the rub: he was very bright, but he could not attain his full potential as an academic because he was 'so black'.[51]

'Blackness' has acquired wide ideological, colour and racial connotations in Caribbean societies. The word 'nigger' (a derivative of the word *negro*, meaning black) has evocative and even provocative overtones. This term was sometimes used by other groups against blacks, and was even occasionally used by blacks against each other.[52] As Moton points out, 'even when the term is used in badgering among themselves it is intended to convey, good-naturedly, a certain contemptuous disregard for the other's estimate of himself'.[53] Solaún and Kronus say that in Latin America 'the term *negro*. . . is employed (with its variations) to express endearment by whites to other whites and as an affectionate nickname'.[54] Lewis says much the same thing about Puerto Rico,[55] although, as noted above, he does admit that racial prejudice exists there.

A more descriptive term used to describe someone of African descent is *niggerman*. It conjures up a number of pejorative images: blackness, roguery and brawn rather than brain. In some Caribbean territories the term niggeritis or nig'ritis is still used, most often by black people themselves. It means literally 'negro inflammation' (laziness), and is obviously a relic from the slave days.

Sometimes the term 'nigger' was used in a wider sense to refer to persons who, while not specifically black in colour, were considered to be socially or ideologically assimilated to the black groups. Thus the term 'red nigger' was sometimes applied to miscegenated individuals of different shades of colour. The Portuguese, who were said to be somewhat darker than the average European, and who in the early days of their residence in Guyana were on the same socio-economic level as the blacks, were sometimes dubbed 'white niggers' by the blacks.[56] In the USA whites who sided with black civil rights leaders were sometimes referred to as 'nigger-lovers', 'white niggers' and simply 'niggers'. In both of the last two examples cited the term 'nigger' was used to define a social or an ideological category rather than a colour or a racial one. Similarly, the term 'nigger locusts' was used by a newspaper writer in the Dominican Republic in 1912 of immigrant workers from various other Caribbean territories.[57] This ascription of notional colour is best exemplified in Haiti after the revolution, when the new constitution designated all Haitians as 'black'.[58]

The widespread association of the term 'black' (and its derivatives) with inferiority has caused some groups to reject it. The Indians not only stoutly refused to join the Black Power Movement in Guyana, Trinidad (and elsewhere), but some of them saw it as a threat to their well-being. The response is hardly surprising, since the term 'black'[59] was (and is) associated in their consciousness with much more than skin colour: it incorporated the whole body of African-Caribbean socio-culture.

Many Africans think that since most Indians in the Caribbean are also dark-skinned, the term 'black' should apply equally to both of them. Some Indians are, in fact, darker than some Africans. Indeed, scholars have shown that many of the inhabitants of southern India closely resemble Africans. Marco Polo said about the Dravidians: 'I assure you that the darkest man is here the most highly esteemed and considered better than the others who are not so dark.'[59] Risley, wrote in 1891 about the Oraons (who were said to be Dravidians and either identical with the Dhangars or closely related to them and also the Paharias): 'The colour of most Oraons is the darkest brown, approaching to black; their hair being jet black, coarse, and rather inclined to be frizzy. Projecting jaws and teeth, thick lips, low narrow foreheads, broad flat noses, are the features which strike a careful observer as characteristic of the tribe.'[60] Many writers, including Marco Polo in the thirteenth century, Godfrey Higgins in the nineteenth, and Runuko Rashidi and Wayne Chandler in the twentieth, have mentioned that some Indian gods are black, including the Buddha, Krishna and Memnon.[61] Rashidi and Chandler (amongst others) believe that the Dasas and Dasyus (called by Rashidi 'Africoid Dravidians' and Chandler 'Ethiopian Negritos') built the Indus Valley civilisation, represented by the achievements at Mohenjo Daro and Harappa, around 3,000 BC, and that they were later driven southwards by an invading ('white') Aryan horde.[62]

In the nineteenth century Europeans commented upon the blackness of the southern Indians, often in pejorative terms. In 1858 the authors of an anthology of Indian information wrote that 'the European is white, the Hindoo black'. Tim Kelly in G. A. Henty's *With Clive in India* (1884) believed that Indians were 'black heathens'. Sometimes Indians were also referred to as 'niggers'; and, sarcastically, as 'sable friends' and 'gallant black sons of Mars'. A group of British officers in the 1840s refused to greet an Indian rajah and his courtiers, dismissing them as 'beastly niggers'. Indian languages were also occasionally referred to as 'damned black lingo'.[63] According to Hutchins, the view gained currency in Europe in the nineteenth century that 'Indians were morally blackened *because* they were dark in colour'. Bolt, informs us that Queen Victoria 'was most insistent that Indians should not be called black men'.[64]

Most Indians who came to the Caribbean were dark-skinned people. In spite of this, they sought to repudiate the association of 'black' with themselves, because they connected the term almost exclusively with Africans and the outcasts of Indian society. Shahani was candid when he wrote that 'an Indian does not wish to be confounded with a Negro'.[66] Ramchand notes that the highest degree of darkness for an Indian in the Caribbean comes in the taunt, 'Look at you, you just like a nigger.'[67] Indians of Madrasi origin resident in the

French Antilles, Guyana, or Trinidad were regarded as social outcasts. A Trinidadian female is reported to have declared scornfully, 'Madrassi and Nigger is de same ting.'[68] Such remarks are becoming much more rare, but it would be naïve to assume that the attitudes and prejudices which gave rise to them have been totally eliminated. Although Indians in the Caribbean are reluctant to be identified as black, Samuel Selvon, a person of Indian descent, makes it clear that they are perceived in Europe as being black: 'to the English, as long as you were not white you were black, and it did not matter if you came from Calcutta or Port-of-Spain'.[69] Ramchand makes the same point more laconically: to Europeans 'all West Indians are black'.[70]

Blackness came to be widely regarded as the nadir of almost all things ugly, but whiteness was perceived as the summit of almost all things beautiful. Images of blackness and whiteness existed in Europe before slavery started in the new world, but they were translated and reinforced by the peculiar circumstances of slavery. They came to be adopted as standards by which individuals, groups, events and issues should be judged. Thus it would have been considered redundant to refer to a beautiful white woman as 'white and beautiful'. One simply referred to a white woman as being 'beautiful' without reference to colour. However, occasionally a black woman might be regarded as being 'black but beautiful'. The inference was that she was supposed to be ugly.[71] Similarly, holiness, chastity, good fortune, uprightness were depicted in images of white, and their opposites were depicted in images of black. God and the angels were white; Satan and demons were black. White was (and still is) the most appropriate colour for weddings, black for funerals. A bad day is a black day, an underground market is a black market, an errant member of the family is a black sheep, one's nemesis is a *bête noire*, and so on.

The European aesthetic was and is expressed not only by reference to colour but also to various facets of European life. Thus 'good hair' is straight, European-type hair; a 'good nose' is a long rather than a flat nose. European languages and speech patterns are exalted while all others are debased. To be civilised is to conform to the dominant European values in respect of dress, speech, eating habits, religion, etc.

Various people have tried to approximate to the European ideal and have assessed an individual's intrinsic worth by reference to his or her approximation to the racial characteristics of the Europeans. Africans are furthest removed from the European type. They are usually described as having black skins, flat noses, thick lips, large genitalia, kinky hair, steatopygia and large breasts (women). Of course many Africans do not conform to this image, which is more ascriptive than real.

The Syrians most closely reflect the European type and as a group they are economically and socially less powerful than the whites. In fact, many can pass as whites. Even less powerful are the Chinese, who by their colour and the texture of hair (but not their facial features) are close to the European type than the Africans. They climbed the economic and social ladder fairly rapidly in the present century, in spite of periodic racial discrimination. Since, however, the social structure of the region is much less rigid that before, Africans and Indians have been able to climb the ladder, although in percentile terms those who have amaged to do so are much fewer than other ethnic groups.

The attempts to conform to the European aesthetic perpetuate inferiority and dependency complexes, sometimes producing a kind of neurosis, an obsession with European values, which is a kind of spiritual necrosis. Naipaul speaks of those in Caribbean society who are 'made neurotic by their incomplete whiteness'.[72] Morris stated in the 1960s that the Caribbean was 'a hot-bed of racial neurosis',[73] and arguably that condition has not changed appreciably. Bastien asserts that slavery and colonialism taught the black man to despise himself; Guérin says much the same thing, that slavery has turned him into a 'Negrophobe'.[74] But let us hear Fanon speaking from the 'blackness' of self, as he grapples with the problem of social rejection in Europe because of the colour of his skin:

> I was responsible . . . for my body, for my race, for my ancestors. I subjected myseelf to an objective examination. I discovered my blackness, my ethnic characteristics; and I was battered down by tom-toms, cannibalism, intellectual deficiency, fetichism, racial defects, slave-ships, and above ancestors. I subjected myself to an objective examination, I all else, above all: "Sho' good eatin".[75]

It is this feeling of rejection, this spirit of unworthiness, that cripples colonial peoples in their attempts to stand on their own feet. They believe that they need the crutches of the coloniser, or erstwhile coloniser, in order to walk, and they are often taught to believe that they cannot walk on their own. Indeed, Memmi mentions that a white professor once claimed that the colonial peoples 'don't know how to walk, they make tiny little steps which don't get them ahead'.[76] This last remark perhaps had both a literal and a metaphorical application. It certainly conjures up images of the 'backwardness', 'invalidity' and 'infancy' of the colonised, who require the assistance of the coloniser.

People who are tied to the apron strings of the so-called mother country are unwilling, or perhaps unable, to strike out on their own, to assume their own independence of thought and action. Sometimes this phenomenon manifests itself at the group level, where large sections of the former colonial population are still mentally enslaved to the traditions and values of their erstwhile colonial masters. Sometimes we hear the view being articulated in former colonial jurisdictions that it is only white persons who can run governments or businesses efficiently. Many of our politicians, businessmen and others use the scarce foreign exchange in the region to send their children to be educated in European and North American universities, even when equivalent programmes are offered at universities in the region. They show by this that they have little or no confidence in the academic capabilities of the local institutions. People in the Caribbean are quick to imitate the fashions of Europe and North America, no matter how incongruous these may be in the local Caribbean context. We in the region still have a tendency to exalt all things European and denigrate all things Caribbean.

Racial pluralism and Caribbean identity

Naipaul says of Trinidadian identity: '[T]here was no community. We were of various races, religions, sets and cliques . . . it was only our Britishness, our belonging to the British Empire, which gave us any identity.'[77] For Naipaul Trinidad was a society without form, or at best with an anarchy of form. While not giving whole-hearted support to him, it is necessary to recognise that ethnicity has so far been more a divisive rather than an integrative force in Trinidad as in other countries of the region.

The migration of groups into the region resulted in the introduction of various culture segments from the sending societies. Some people see these as culture fragments, rather than whole or integrated cultures, because only small portions of them were transmitted to the region. This is true even of the Europeans, who were allowed greater scope for transplanting and implanting their culture. As Naipaul points out, 'The white community was never an upper class in the sense that it possessed a superior speech or taste or attainments; it was envied only for its money and its access to pleasure.'[78] Mason refers to them as 'a debased backwater from the mainstream of European culture',[79] a statement emphasising that in the vast majority of cases it was the poor, ordinary, illiterate folk from Europe (and elsewhere) who migrated to the region and who were therefore not the representatives of the most sophisticated aspects of their home cultures.

The Europeans have, of course, wielded an influence in the cultural sphere (and in other spheres) quite out of proportion to their demographic size. Their position as the master class gave their cultural expressions a validity and authenticity which led the subordinate groups to seek to imitate them. It also allowed them to use their influence and authority to attempt to suppress the cultures of the other groups of which they did not approve. This was perhaps most evident in the ways in which they attempted to destroy the African culture of the slaves. African religions, for example, were officially proscribed because they were deemed to be ungodly and subversive of the authority structure on the plantations. The Europeans also tried periodically to ban the use of African musical instruments, particularly the drum, which was considered a means of communicating revolutionary ideas among the slaves. African songs were regarded as monotonous, and their dances lewd and immoral. Similar observations may be made about the attempts at cultural deracination of the other oppressed groups, although (with the possible exception of the Amerindians of the islands) not in as absolute a way as in the case of the African.

The Europeans also realised the social and psychological importance of reshaping the material environment which they encountered on their arrival. They claimed to have discovered the islands, indigenous peoples, fauna and flora and they gave all of them, as far as possible, European names or names which they considered appropriate. Then they set about recreating just about every aspect of the social environment in their own image. The European-ordered landscapes replaced the indigenous ones; European buildings towered over indigenous ones; European monuments displaced indigenous ones. The Europeans, of course, recognised the importance of monuments – statues, cenotaphs, mausoleums, etc. – and other visible images for establishing and reinforcing cultural values and traditions. All over the colonial world they erected monuments to their great statesmen and their great colonial conquerors. Their deeds had to be carved in stone and enshrined in myth and legend. These were more than monuments to culture; they were monuments to remind the 'natives' of the greatness of their rulers and the 'privilege' that was theirs to be ruled by such persons. They were also monuments to greed and covetousness.

But so thorough has been the brain-washing in several instances that it is considered anathema among the once colonised peoples to remove these images of colonialism. The leaders of the newly independent countries, and those of the upper classes who are nostalgic about the 'good old colonial days', and frequently burst forth into paeons of praise for their erstwhile rulers, experience psychological trauma at the thought of doing away with these monuments. The colonial heroes have in many instances become national heroes in the post-independence period. Yet we should be reminded how quickly the Russian people got rid of Lenin's statue once the Communists had been overthrown.

It is equally noteworthy in the Caribbean that few local heroes have so far emerged, at least few who receive general acclaim. With the exception of Haiti, none of the great resistance leaders during the period of slavery has been genuinely accepted as a national hero, in spite of official recognition in a few countries. The situation is worse in countries with more than one large ethnic group. This is another of the sad legacies of colonialism. Bulhan reminds us that cultural domination was 'but the intellectual and emotional counterpart of economic enslavement' under colonialism.[80]

The fact that the Europeans have had such a tremendous cultural impact on the region has led some to believe, quite wrongly, that very little has been retained of the cultures of the other ethnic groups. Although many of the cultural practices of the other groups fell casualty to the dynamics of the colonial situation, some did survive in attenuated and reinterpreted forms. Studies have shown that many African retentions can be found throughout the region, and indeed throughout the Americas, though not always in as overt a form as those of the European. A study by the Guyanese linguist, Richard Allsopp, demonstrates that the thought and speech patterns of Afro-Caribbean peoples are more affected by their African background than by European influence, so that even when they are using a European-derived language (such as English or French) their idioms, etc., are often informed by this African influence. Allsopp, in fact, concludes that this influence has given a remarkable, underlying unity to all the Caribbean dialects and creole languages.[81]

Intra-regional contact and migration have led to a certain degree of cultural enrichment and fusion. Oral and audio communications media, while still underdeveloped regionally, have added to the understanding, appreciation and adoption of each other's cultural expressions. The Jamaican contribution in this respect has been arguably the most obvious and the most significant, especially in respect of music and song, Bob Marley being the most well-known apostle. But the greatest Jamaican contribution has been in religion: the birth and spread of Rastafarianism. No Caribbean territory today is without a Rastafarian presence, and this presence is significant throughout the English-speaking Caribbean. Although carnival owes its original impulses to Africa and to the slaves who came from there, few would argue against the statement that it has reached its highest level of expression in the Caribbean in Trinidad (and on the mainland, in Brazil) and has radiated its influence from there to other parts of the Caribbean. It was also in Trinidad that the *kaiso* (calypso) and the steel-band (also derived from earlier African forms) reached their most sophisticated levels and inspired those in other Caribbean lands.

While many aspects of African-derived cultural elements have spread throughout the region, the same cannot be said about Indian- or Asian-derived elements. This is partly because, as we have noted above, Indians were introduced in large numbers only into Guyana and Trinidad; other places such as Jamaica, Martinique, Guadeloupe and Suriname had fewer; and St Vincent and others even fewer, so that the Indian presence in most of the Caribbean was numerically quite insignificant. Nor have the Indians in most of the Caribbean islands maintained themselves as a separate ethnic or cultural segment; they have largely integrated themselves into the mainstream African population, for instance, in St Vincent, St Lucia, Dominica and Martinique. Recent inward and intra-regional migration of Indians to countries such as Barbados has resulted in the emergence of Indian cultural elements there, but these so far have not appreciably affected the mainstream cultures and have certainly not assumed national significance.

Thus Hindu cultural expressions such as Diwali (Divali) and Pagwah are celebrated or observed on a large scale in Suriname, Trinidad and Guyana, and to a much lesser extent in Barbados, Jamaica and elsewhere. The same may be said about Muslim religious and cultural expressions, such as the fast during the month of Ramadan and the Eid el Fitr. These Hindu and Muslim festivals have gained increasing respect among non-adherents in territories in which they are observed, and some of their holy days have even become national holidays. The forms in which the festivals are being celebrated have been modified over time in their Caribbean context and have taken on a Caribbean flavour, for instance, in the Diwali Queen contests in Guyana, but they have not drawn a large non-Indian group of participants. Of course, Indian cultural elements have only been introduced recently. Bisnauth has said that until the 1930s Indian culture went through a period of 'encystment' which helped to keep it as a distinct cultural element in Guyanese society, before going through a kind of renaissance afterwards.[82] The same is perhaps broadly true of Suriname and Trinidad.

The pull of the 'homeland'

Craton has written about the influence of the original sending society on the peoples of the region: 'If one is pessimistic about integration and identification . . . one is bound to observe that a prevailing characteristic of West Indian peoples is the will to get away, chasing the rainbows of an idyllic original homeland, or a promised better future land.'[83] This is true of all groups with the notable exception of the Amerindians, who are in a much more fundamental sense than the others children of the land, because of their much longer identification with the region. All the other groups have maintained varying degrees of contact with their ancestral homelands, the two with the strongest ties being arguably the Europeans and the Indians.

The Europeans maintain both strong emotional and physical bonds with their homeland, and return frequently for business, for vacation and to visit family members. Many Europeans have emigrated permanently from the region, especially during three periods. The first was the early development of the sugar industry in the English and the French Caribbean when African slaves were being introduced in large numbers to replace European indentured servants as labour hands. The second took place immediately after the abolition of slavery in the various islands, both for economic and social reasons. The third occurred with the advent of independence, forcibly in Haiti, the Dominican Republic and Cuba, and peaceably in the other colonies. This has been the experience in all third-world countries where the whites were a significant element in the population before independence.

Many Africans of the diaspora have maintained a nostalgia for their ancestral homeland and during the slavery period some of them even killed themselves in hope of returning there. There has, however, been no large-scale physical remigration there. Indeed, the largest remigrations have been involuntary ones, forced on African maroons and slaves by the colonial regimes. In the present century the Jamaican, Marcus Garvey, had in mind a large-scale scheme of repatriation of blacks from the Caribbean, America and elsewhere to Liberia, Ethiopia and other African countries, but this came to naught due to the machinations of the UK and US governments. Nevertheless, blacks have always remigrated in small numbers to Africa, Edward Wilmot Blyden being perhaps the most well-known of those from the Caribbean. Caribbean blacks have also played a prominent part in the Pan-African Movement and have maintained a high level of black consciousness.

Martin, the most prolific writer on Marcus Garvey, has asserted: 'Throughout the Caribbean we find that the most revolutionary Black groups . . . have always had a Pan-African orientation.'[84] Over the last 20 or 30 years the Caribbean cultural identification with Africa has expressed itself in the wearing of African robes, the assuming of African names and the adoption of African coiffure. Some critics see this as being largely cosmetic, and a few even argue that it is somewhat anachronistic, since many Africans on the continent are adopting European names, hairstyles and modes of dress.

Indians in the Caribbean have maintained close contact with their homeland. About a third, according to some authorities, remigrated after their terms of indentureship had expired. Those who remained have retained contact, although very few of them visit. They import food, clothing, religious materials, books, musical equipment, etc., as well as films; in Guyana one or two cinemas show almost exclusively Indian films, often in Indian languages. Events in India are monitored closely by the Indians in Guyana, Trinidad and Suriname. In general, the Indians seem to have much closer daily connections with their ancestral homeland than the Africans. This may be because to a large extent their migration into the Caribbean has been more recent. It was not until 1917 that the system of indentured Indian migration came to an end in the British Caribbean.

Other groups, such as the Javanese, Chinese and Syrians have likewise maintained contact with their homelands. They retain contact with their extended families at home, although this is truer of the Syrians (who are perhaps the latest arrivals in the region) than of the Javanese and Chinese. They also import clothing and other domestic items. However, apart from cooking, their cultural retentions are in low profile, mainly because of their small numbers.

The task facing the Caribbean is to create an integrated culture out of the diversity of cultural elements introduced into the region. This is not to suggest that cultural diversity should be done away with; rather it is to suggest that the region needs to reflect a much greater degree of cultural unity within its diversity. Those elements which tend towards cultural unity need to be stronger than those which tend towards diversity. Suriname and Guyana have a larger number of ethnicities and a greater measure of cultural diversity than most other countries within the region, and perhaps those countries more than any others highlight the problems associated with ethnicity and cultural integration. Perhaps also out of their rich ethnic and cultural diversity will emerge that unique blend of ethnic and cultural characteristics most expressive of the region's identity.

Notes

1. Fanon, *Black Skin*, 111-12.
2. Cited in Williams, *Columbus to Castro*, 345.
3. Haraksingh, 'Control and Resistance,' 72.
4. Dookhan, *Post-Emancipation History*, 55.
5. *Cuban Commission Report*, 51-52, 56-57, 64-65.
6. *Cuban Commission Report*, 49-50, 88-89. See also Scott, *Slave Emancipation*, 30, 32-33.
7. Brereton, 'Experience of Indentureship,' 29.
8. *Cuban Commission Report*, 88-89.
9. Rodney, *Guyanese Working People*, 174-75.
10. Rodney, *Guyanese Working People*, 175.
11. Rodney, *Guyanese Working People*, 182-84.
12. *Cuban Commission Report*, 49-50, 66.
13. Montejo, 24.
14. Dikötter, 423.
15. Rodney, *Guyanese Working People*, 180-81.
16. Bulhan, 152.
17. Lowenthal, *West Indian Societies*, 204.
18. Rodney, *Guyanese Working People*, 179, 188-89.
19. La Guerre, xix.
20. Hira, 202-03.
21. Lewis, *Puerto Rico*, 280.
22. Cited in Goslinga, 359.
23. Hall, 'Jamaica,' 196.
24. *Holy Bible*, Exodus 20:5. The original biblical context, of course, did not have any thing to do with the race/colour situation, but rather with idolatry and forsaking of devotion solely to Yahweh.

25. Williams, *Documents*, I, 36; Thompson, *Colonialism*, 181.
26. Cited in Knight, *Genesis*, 120.
27. See Goslinga, 231; Thompson, *Colonialism*, 74, 84; Handler, 73.
28. Williams, *Documents*, I, 99.
29. Cited in Hoyos, *From Amerindians*, 96-98.
30. Cited in Hoyos, *From Amerindians*, 97. See below for further discussion on the concepts of 'white nigger' and 'red nigger'.
31. Lowenthal, *West Indian Societies*, 201.
32. Guérin, 69.
33. Leigh Fermor, 31.
34. Edwards, II, 7-8.
35. Cited in Hoyos, *From Amerindians*, 97.
36. Solaún & Kronus, 7.
37. Knight, *Genesis*, 94.
38. Browser, 55.
39. Handler.
40. Elisabeth, 165; Knight, 'Cuba', in Cohen & Greene, eds, 290-92.
41. Hoetink, *Caribbean Race Relations*, 32.
42. Hoetink, 'Surinam and Curaçao', 70, 72.
43. Elisabeth, 143, 155, 161-63; Hall, 'St Domingue', 190.
44. Helly, 276-80.
45. Lundhal, 56; see also Lewis, *Main Currents*, 257-64.
46. Lundhal, 133.
47. Lewis, *Puerto Rico*, 283-85.
48. Guérin, 70.
49. Herskovits, 93.
50. Wood, 6.
51. Lamming, 127.
52. About 17 years ago a fairly well-educated black person was recounting to me an incident with one of his colleagues, which came to the boil when he (the narrator) called the other person a nigger.
53. R. P. Moton, *What the Negro Thinks* (1929) 186, cited in Burns, *Colour Prejudice*, 65.
54. Solaún & Kronus, 22-23. For further information on its usage, see Pierson, 139.
55. Lewis, *Puerto Rico*, 282.
56. Lowenthal, *West Indian Societies*, 201.
57. Bryan, 'The Question of Labor', 244.
58. Lewis, *Main Currents*, 254.
59. *The Travels of Marco Polo* (1982), 276, cited by Rashidi, 'Africans', 40.
60. H. Risley, *Tribes and Castes of Bengal* (1891), II, 139, cited in *Encyclopædia of Religion and Ethics*, XI, 502; see also Tinker, 47.
61. See Rashidi, 'Africans,' 30, 40; Chandler, 95-104.
62. Rashidi, 'Africans', 40-42; Chandler, 82-84.
63. Hutchins, 59, 68; Bolt, 141; Bearce, 258-59, 274.
64. Hutchins, 69.
65. Bolt, 137.
66. Ranjee Shahani, *Indian Pilgrimage* (1939), 173, cited in Burns, *Colour Prejudice*, 34.
67. Ramchand, 28.
68. Lowenthal, *West Indian Societies*, 150, 152.
69. Selvon, 'Three Into One Can't Go', 18.
70. Ramchand, 28.
71. This myth existed, of course, purely at the ideological level, for John Stedman made it clear that white men in the colonies often chose black and coloured women instead of white women because of their beauty and charm (18-19).

72. Naipaul, *Middle Passage*, 197.
73. Morris, 8.
74. Bastien, 47, 49; Guérin, 72.
75. Fanon, *Black Skin*, 112.
76. Memmi, 67. Eric Williams states that Europeans refused to introduce the plough during slavery on the grounds 'that the inability of the Negro to see straight rendered the use of the plough impossible' (*History of Trinidad and Tobago*, 109).
77. Naipaul, *Middle Passage*, 43.
78. Naipaul, *Middle Passage*, 57.
79. Foreword to Lowenthal, *West Indian Societies*, ix.
80. Bulhan, 189.
81. Allsopp, 160.
82. Bisnauth, 502; see also Mangru, 'Sex-Ratio Disparity', 216.
83. Craton, 'Recipe for Perfect Calalu', 4.
84. Martin, 72.

Conclusion

CHAPTER 9

Targets for revolution

I come from the nigger yard of yesterday
leaping from the oppressors' hate
and the scorn of myself;
from the agony of the dark hut in the shadow
and the hurt of things;
from the long days of cruelty and the long nights of pain
down to the wide streets of to-morrow, of the next day
leaping I come, who cannot see will hear.
....
I come from the nigger yard of yesterday
leaping from the oppressors' hate
and the scorn of myself.
I come to the world with scars upon my soul
wounds on my body, fury in my hands . . . .[1]

Martin Carter

This excerpt from one of the poems of Martin Carter, the Guyanese poet, strikingly depicts the unfulfilled expectations of the ex-slave, and by implication his posterity, over a century after the abolition of slavery. His hopes and expectations of a brighter tomorrow following abolition were great; he was going to etch his name in the annals of history so that those 'who cannot see will hear'. But his post-abolition experience made him realise that 'the Act which abolished slavery did not emancipate the slaves'.[2] He had simply moved on, from one 'nigger yard' to another. In the 'nigger yard' of slavery he had crept on 'an aching floor'; in the 'nigger yard' of abolition he was 'born again stubborn and fierce/screaming in a slum', and once again living 'on the aching floor'. The scars upon his soul, the wounds upon his body evidenced the inward and outward cries of his agonies and pains. He now takes his fury in his hands.

Carter's ex-slave is a symbol of the oppressed Caribbean man of all races (but especially of the African) who has experienced grinding poverty and powerlessness. In a desperate effort to empower himself he has often taken his fury in his hands and may well do so again. The revolts in the region during the 1930s and the frequent upheavals both before and since speak eloquently to this point. Indeed, observers believe that the present-day situation in some Caribbean territories replicates that of the 1930s.

What is happening in Haiti, in particular, cries out for redress. Successive governments unheeding and unfeeling for the sufferings of the masses have given them less than a fair opportunity of achieving the dignity and progress for which their ancestors fought so bravely. Many people feel they are like ghosts walking through the cemetery of buried hopes. An excerpt from 'The Poem of the Righteous Sufferer' comes to mind:

> Open was my grave, ready my shroud,
> While I was not yet dead, the weeping was finished.[3]

For many Haitians the future is like gazing into an empty horizon, and it is arguably so with the peoples in other Caribbean countries.

We have dealt in detail above with the historical factors which have led to the present situation. Colonialism has cast too long and too sinister a shadow over us. Still, Peacocke reminds us that while 'history cannot be undone . . . one does not have to be kept in servitude by it all the time'.[4] We are not and should not see ourselves as the playthings either of circumstances or of an insouciant and sometimes seemingly malevolent world. We must lift ourselves up from the degradations of the past as we attempt to shape a more positive future for ourselves and our descendants.

This means, first and foremost, that we must develop a new sense of pride in ourselves and in our capacity to effect or at least to influence positive change in our society in our lifetimes. This, in itself, involves a new beginning, a kind of revolutionary consciousness. We must demonstrate that we are willing to be part of society in a meaningful and constructive way, and that we are no longer content to be exploited by internal or external agencies.

The divide which often separates the politicians from the masses must be removed. Neville Duncan issues a clarion call for action on this score: 'It is time the electorate takes a personal and lasting interest in regional and international affairs and seeks to control our leaders, if not choose better ones.'[5] The way forwards is not for the masses to opt out of the political arena, as many have done recently, through becoming disenchanted with the process or progress of democracy. Our politicians must also develop a new commit- ment to the people, rather than fighting over the spoils of electoral victory. For:

> [W]hile the pythons of sickness
> Swallow the children
> And the buffalos of poverty
> Knock the people down
> And ignorance stands there
> Like an elephant,
> The war leaders
> Are tightly locked in bloody feuds,
> Eating each other's *liver* . . . .[6]

This struggle of the politicians to achieve political ascendancy is an ill wind that does the masses no good. Politicians must become more interested in promoting the well-being of the people they serve. There are some politicians like this, but sadly they are too few. There is also need for much more regional cooperation among our political leaders. They must stop sniping at each other in public. A political federation is an obvious desirability, but the strength of anti-federal sentiment in the region at this time makes such a development seem a distant reality.

At the economic level it is necessary to repair the image we are acquiring of being the 'Vanity Fair' of the modern world. Francisco Céspedes evokes a loud echo from many Caribbean people when he asserts: 'To most people, the Caribbean consists primarily, if not exclusively, of the islands of the Caribbean and the ports on the mainland touched by winter cruises.'[7] There is a real danger that at least some of the countries will end up being a rendezvous for gamblers, money- launderers, drug-dealers, prostitutes, and the like. The real question is whether the Caribbean must forever exist for the profit and pleasure of the citizens of the developed world: yesterday, primarily sugar, tobacco and other raw materials; today, sun, sex and obsequious service.

Our dependency on external markets and other external agencies for our development must be reduced and we must strengthen our local and regional resources. There is, of course, a significant body of opinion which asserts that in an increasingly interdependent world any hope of achieving economic independence or even autonomy is a chimera. Others say that, in fact, the region is likely to be even more dependent than before on external agencies and forces to stimulate economic growth. They also point out that our high external debt hangs like an albatross around our necks.

These arguments are weighty; but at the same time we have to guard against a situation in which we come to believe that there is little that we ourselves can do to influence the course and pattern of our development and the quality of life we enjoy. Revolutionary internal measures involving more equitable income distribution, more efficient use of our natural and human resources, agrarian (including land) reform, greater emphasis on rural (including peasant) development, more careful monitoring of our imports and our use of foreign exchange and higher levels of accountability by public officials could go far towards reinvigorating our economies.

A more determined move towards regional integration must also be high on our agenda. It is more important and more sensible to focus attention on developing CARICOM into a single market than to concentrate on wider institutional integration, such as in the ACS, NAFTA and AFTA. We must also develop a regional approach not only in respect of Lome, but also NAFTA, the WTO, the IMF and other international institutions and programmes. This concentric approach is more rational than the one we are pursuing at present.

The need for more regional banks, greater currency convertibility and ultimately a regional currency is obvious, and the authorities must move urgently to deal with these issues. The various countries in the region must jointly tackle the problem of food insecurity more aggressively. We simply cannot afford to be so heavily dependent on external sources for our food needs.

In Chapter 4 we placed great emphasis on the role of education in economic development, and particularly on the need to develop our scientific and technological base. However, we must also stress education's role in equipping our people to make greater use of their freedom. Indeed, for some, it might well be the avenue towards the achievement of any freedom. We must be careful, however, to ensure that in place of a pedagogy that oppresses we employ one that liberates.

The most challenging task in this respect is to divest our people of the colonial mentality, which is the most deep-rooted aspect of colonialism. One way of doing so is to develop an internal or Caribbean perspective on the history of the region. We can no longer afford to see such imperialists as Christopher Columbus, Francis Drake, François Le Clerc, Ponce de León, Cornelis Van Sommelsdijk, Horatio Nelson and the like as our heroes. We have to replace them by those who fought for our freedom and dignity, and we must not be equivocal about or apologetic for our action. Our real heroes must be seen as people like Toussaint L'Ouverture, Nanny Sharpe, José Martí and Marcus Garvey.

We must also place greater emphasis than we have done so far on the history and culture of the region in an integrated way. We should not be content simply to teach the history of a set of territories linked by a common European language; rather we need to teach the history of the region as a whole. This integrated approach should help to strengthen our awareness that, broadly speaking, we share a common history of exploitation and deprivation.

Traditionally, we have paid little attention to our cultural history. This constitutes one of the most undeveloped research areas of our historical past. Greater emphasis should be placed both on the research and pedagogical aspects of this important area of Caribbean life. Much has been done through Carifesta to raise our level of consciousness about our cultural heritage, especially in music, song, dance, storytelling, and the graphic and plastic arts. But the work has only just begun. Financial constraints have diminished the scope of Carifesta. Although we understand the reasons for this decision, we feel that much more needs to be done in the cultural field, which is arguably the most dynamic and potentially unifying force in Caribbean life.

On the issue of race and ethnicity, we know, of course, that the region has advanced appreciably from the days of slavery when the solid divide was overt and was institutionalised by laws and regulations. We also know that many scholars argue that the dominant factor in social stratification today is class rather than race and ethnicity. At the same time, in countries such as Guyana, Trinidad and Tobago and Suriname, race still plays a prominent role in all the major aspects of daily life, and is especially prominent during election time. In the Dominican Republic, Puerto Rico and even Cuba, where there are large light-coloured populations, one of their greatest concerns remains that they might be considered as being darker than they really are. In Barbados many whites are afraid to discuss the race issue, believing that this may open a new can of worms, which would lead to verbal and physical attacks against their businesses and their persons. These examples indicate that racial sensitivity is still very high in the region.

Unfortunately, the world has still not devised a formula to deal with this problem intelligently and to get rid of racism once and for all. The process of ethnic cleansing in Bosnia-Herzegovina and the racial sentiments expressed by blacks and whites in the USA following the O. J. Simpson trial tell us that racism is alive and well also in the metropolitan countries. Nevertheless, as Caribbean people we have to make a new determination to expunge the word 'racism' and all its synonyms from our vocabulary when dealing with each other, and indeed with all other groups. This is much more easily said that done. But the first steps must be a mental and verbal commitment to developing a new order in which race and ethnicity are seen as an enriching rather than a divisive factor in our culture.

It should be clear that we believe that the time has come, indeed is long overdue, for revolutionary action. Revolutionary change always demands sacrifice. Caribbean peoples are not averse to sacrifice; indeed, their history has been one largely of sacrifice, with much too little returns. Those who hold the reins of power can prevent revolutionary violence by seeking to effect meaningful changes in Caribbean life. Duncan makes a frightening observation and issues an indirect warning when he points out: '[I]n Caribbean political history, violence has led to all the significant changes. It should be possible to develop institutions of change that can deal with problems of transformation of these societies before change is wrought by calamitous violence.'[8]

For Césaire, the islands, 'scars of waters . . . evidence of wounds . . . crumbs' remain 'unformed'. For him, these islands have yet to be formed into something beautiful and wholesome: 'Your completion, my challenge.'[9] It is basically with these same sentiments in mind and the realisation that Caribbean peoples are demanding change that the West Indian Commission Report of 1992 warned that it was 'time for action'. Caribbean peoples everywhere are crying out in their political, economic and social wasteland, 'Hurry Up Please, It's Time'.[10]

Notes

1. Carter, 7-9.
2. This quotation is extrapolated from Mathieson's statement about the apprenticeship system in the British Caribbean, 243.
3. Cited by Marvin Hope in *Anchor Bible. Job*, lxiii.
4. Peacocke, 7.
5. Duncan, 'Order or Disorder?' 8A.
6. Bitek, Okot p', 196.
7. Céspedes, 51.
8. Duncan, 'Political Violence', 74; see also Duncan, 'Barbados', 88.
9. Césaire, *Return*, 119.
10. Eliot, 'The Wasteland', 68, 69.

Bibliography

Newspapers

'$65m. To Be Made From Airlines Merger', *Daily Nation*, Sept. 28, 1995:15.
'A filthy assumption', reproduced from *The Miami Herald*, International Edition, Feb. 15, 1992, in *Daily Nation*, Feb. 19, 1992:6A.
'Aid Plan Stalled', *Daily Nation*, May 3, 1993:6.
'Alleyne: GATT Threat to Lome, *Daily Nation*, Oct. 18, 1994:18.
Best, Tony. 'Almost Paradise. Travel Writer Sees Barbados as "sum of all desires", *Sunday Sun*, Jan. 8, 1995:3A.
———. 'Ban on Hazardous Waste Exports', *Daily Nation*, Mar. 29, 1994:6.
———. 'World Bank: Bajans Prefer Leisurely Life', *Sunday Sun*, Nov. 24, 1991:5A.
'Blueprint for Poverty Reduction', *Daily Nation*, Mar. 14, 1995:10.
'Call for War on Poverty in the Region', *Daily Nation*, Apr. 5, 1994:12.
'Canada Hand-out Unlikely', *Daily Nation*, Mar. 5, 1996:9.
'CARICOM Calls for New Order', *The Barbados Advocate*, Mar. 15, 1994:10.
'Caricom/IMF Debts Agenda', *Weekend Nation*, Mar. 11, 1994:9.
'Caricom Response Vital', *Daily Nation*, March 25, 1993:6.
'Castro Scolds the US', *Sun on Saturday*, Aug. 19, 1995:8.
'Castro's Confident', *Sun on Saturday*, Feb. 3, 1993:8.
'Caymans Bursting at the Seams with Visitors', *Daily Nation*, Jan. 27, 1994:16.
'Cheap Labour Low on Investors' List of Priorities', *Daily Nation*, Nov. 21, 1994:1B.
'Chirac Wins French Polls', *Daily Nation*, May 8, 1995: 10A.
'Cuba Gets "Gift" of Expired Medicine', *Daily Nation*, Aug. 9, 1995:16C.
'Deadly Diseases Returning to Region', *Daily Nation*, Apr. 13, 1994:12A.
Duncan, Neville. 'A Tendency to Dependency?' *Weekend Nation*, Dec. 2, 1994:8A.
———. 'Dumped on, Again and Again', *Weekend Nation*, Jan. 6, 1995:8.
———. 'Order or Disorder in 1994?', *Weekend Nation*, Dec. 30, 1994:8A.
'Embassy a Sore Point. US Speaker Rules out Reprisals Though', *Weekend Nation*, Jan. 20, 1994:5.

'Forum for Consultation: ACS to Promote Regional Interest in International Economic and Trade Fora', *Weekend Nation*, Jul. 29, 1994:19B.

Gibbons, Kathy Ann. 'What GATT Means', *Sunday Advocate*, Aug. 6, 1995:26.

'Grenada Backtracks on Political Union', *The Barbados Advocate*, Feb. 25, 1994:10.

'Grenada Union Hits at PM's Divestments', *Daily Nation*, May 3, 1993:9.

'Haynes Wants Law Scrapped', *Daily Nation*, Mar. 15, 1995:18A.

'IMF to Undertake Economic Study', *The Barbados Advocate*, Mar. 15, 1994:10.

Jimenez, Manuel. 'The Columbus Jinx', *Sunday Sun* ('Sun SHINE' section), Oct. 18, 1992:2.

'Leaking Sub "No Danger" to Bermuda', *Weekend Nation*, Jan. 11, 1994:15A.

'Let's Dock with NAFTA', *Daily Nation*, Jan. 26, 1994:3A.

'Little in GATT for Third World', *Weekend Nation*, Dec. 17, 1993:19B.

McDonald, Ian. 'Quincentenary', *Daily Nation*, Oct. 20, 1992:6.

'Manley Hails Ramphal and ACS. Turning Point in W. I. History', *Weekend Nation*, July 29, 1994:15A.

'Martinique Airport Expects Triple Load', *Daily Nation*, Feb. 17, 1994:13.

'Maynard: Count Bahamas Out', *Daily Nation*, Jul. 7, 1992:8.

Niles, Bertram & Hayden Boyce. 'Trinidad Vies for ACS, Jagan Tired of "Talk", *Daily Nation*, Jul. 5, 1994:13.

'No Waste for the Bahamas', *Sunday Advocate*, Apr. 3, 1994:13.

'Omai Shut Down', *The Barbados Saturday Advocate*', Aug. 26, 1995:10.

Peacocke, Nora. 'Caricom in Danger of Missing Boat', *Daily Nation*, Feb. 11, 1993:7.

'Queen in Cayman Islands', *Sunday Sun*, Feb. 27, 1994:6A.

'Quincentenary', *Daily Nation*, Oct. 20, 1992:6.

Scantlebury, Samantha. 'Currencies to Move More Freely in the Region', *Sunday Sun*, Jul. 9, 1995:22A.

'Shrimp Ban Will Hurt Fisherfolk', *Daily Nation*, May 24, 1995:9A.

Simpson, Trevor. 'CANA's Story About CDS', *Sunday Sun*, Feb. 20, 1994:12A.

Singh, Rickey. 'Contrasting Views on Regional Unity', *Daily Nation*, Jul. 5, 1994:14.

———. 'Key to Caricom Success Given', *Weekend Nation*, Jun. 26, 1992:15.

———. 'Selling Out the Caribbean. Citizenship Passports and Property Going Cheaply', *Sunday Sun*, Mar. 22, 1992:13C.

Springer ,Basil. 'People – Most Precious Resource', *The Barbados Advocate*, Mar.15, 1994:8.

'St. Kitts Sells 3,000 Passports', *Daily Nation*, Feb. 15, 1992:8.

'Study Says '936' Loan Programme Improving', *Daily Nation*, Oct. 6, 1994:22.

'Tremendous Success. CTO's Image Campaign Gets Positive Response', *The Barbados Saturday Advocate*, Feb. 26, 1994:21.

'UN: Poverty, a Leading Killer', *Daily Nation*, May 2, 1995:10.

'Uniting for our Progress', *Daily Nation*, Aug. 17, 1995:6A.

Wickham, John. 'The West Indies – Myth or Reality?' *Daily Nation*, Aug. 26, 1992:6A.

Books and Periodicals

Achéen René & Francis Rifaux. 'The French West Indies: a Socio-Historical interpretation', in Craig, ed. *Contemporary Caribbean*, I, 191-212.

Adamson, Alan. *Sugar Without Slaves: The Political Economy of British Guiana, 1838-1904.* New Haven: Yale Univ. Press, 1972.

Agorsah, E. Kofi, ed. *Maroon Heritage. Archaeological, Ethnographic and Historical*

Perspectives. Kingston: Canoe Press, 1994.
Ajayi J. F. Ade & Michael Crowder, eds. *History of West Africa*, Vol. 2. London: Longman, 1974.
Allen, H. R. *Buccaneer: Admiral Sir Henry Morgan*. London: Arthur Baker, 1976.
Allen, Michael. 'Struggle and Synthesis: Toward Theory for the Dutch Caribbean Experience', in Sedoc-Dahlberg, ed. *The Dutch Caribbean*, 269-87.
———. 'The Dutch Caribbean and Transitions in United States-Caribbean Relations', in Sedoc-Dahlberg, ed. *The Dutch Caribbean*, 151-71.
Allsopp, Richard. 'African Linguistic Survivals in the Caribbean', in Cobley & Thompson, eds. *The African-Caribbean Connection*, 144-61.
Aluko, Olajide. 'Politics of Decolonisation in British West Africa, 1945-1960', in Ajayi & Crowder, eds. *History of West Africa*, II, 622-63.
Americas Watch. *Haiti: Terror and the 1987 Elections*. New York: Americas Watch, 1987.
Ameringer, Charles. *The Democratic Left in Exile: The Anti-Dictatorial Struggle in the Caribbean 1945-1959*. Miami: Univ. of Miami Press, 1974.
Amin, Samir. *Neo-Colonialism in West Africa*. Trans. by Francis McDonagh. New York: Monthly Review Press, 1973.
Ammar, Nellie. 'They Came From the Middle East', *Jamaica Journal*, 4(1), 1970:2-6.
Anchor Bible, Vol. 15: Job. Trans. & notes by Marvin Hope. New York: Doubleday, 1965.
Andrade, Jacob. *A Record of the Jews in Jamaica from the English Conquest to the Present Time*. Kingston: Jamaica Times, 1941.
Andrews, Kenneth. *Trade, Plunder and Settlement: Maritime Enterprise and the Genesis of the British Empire 1480-1630*. New York: Cambridge Univ. Press, 1984.
Ankum-Houwink, J. 'Chinese Contract Migrants in Surinam Between 1853 and 1870', *Boletín Estudios Latinoamericanos y del Caribe*, 17, 1974:42-68.
Asante, Mofefi and Kariamu. 'Great Zimbabwe: an Ancient African City-State', in Van Sertima, ed. *Blacks in Science*, 84-91.
Attema, Ypie. *St Eustatius: A Short History of the Island and Its Monuments*. Trans. by Peter Daniels. Zutphen, Netherlands: De Walburg Pers, 1976.
Aufhauser, R. K. 'The Profitability of Slavery in the British Caribbean', *Journal of Interdisciplinary History*, 5(1), 1974:45-67.
Augier, F. *et al. The Making of the West Indies*. Essex: Longman, 1960.
Azicri, Max. *Cuba: Politics, Economics and Society*. London: Frances Pinter, 1988.
Bacchus, M. K. *Utilization, Misuse, and Development of Human Resources in the Early West Indian Colonies*. Waterloo: Wilfrid Laurier Univ. Press, 1990.
Badejo, Fabian. 'Sint Maarten: The Dutch Half in Future Perspective', in Sedoc-Dahlberg, ed. *The Dutch Caribbean*, 119-150.
Baptiste, Fitzroy. *War, Cooperation and Conflict. The European Possessions in the Caribbean, 1939-1945*. New York: Greenwood Press, 1988.
Barker, David & Duncan McGregor, ed. *Environment and Development in the Caribbean. Geographical Perspectives*. Kingston, Jamaica: The Press, Univ. of the West Indies, 1995.
Barraclough, Solon & Peter Marchetti. 'Agrarian Transformation and Food Security in the Caribbean', in Gorostiaga & Irvin, eds. *Towards an Alternative for Central America and the Caribbean*, 154-193.
Barry, Norman. *An Introduction to Modern Political Theory*. 2nd ed. London: Macmillan, 1989.
Barry, Tom, Beth Wood & Deb Preusch. *The Other Side of Paradise: Foreign Control in the Caribbean*. New York: Grove Press, 1984.
Bastide, Roger. *The African Religions of Brazil. Towards a Sociology of the*

Interpenetration of Civilizations. Orig. pub. 1960. Trans. by Helen Sebba. Baltimore: The Johns Hopkins Univ. Press, 1978.

Bastien, Elliot. 'The Weary Road to Whiteness and the Hasty Retreat into Nationalism', in Tajfel & Dawson, eds. *Disappointed Guests*, 38-54.

Bauer, P. T. *Dissent on Development*. London: Wiedenfeld & Nicolson, 1976.

———. *Equality, the Third World and Economic Delusion*. London: Wiedenfeld & Nicolson, 1981.

Bearce, George D. *British Attitudes Towards India 1784-1858*. Orig. pub. 1961. Reprint, Westport, Connecticut: Greenwood Press Publishers, 1982.

Beard, J. *Toussaint L'Ouverture: Biography and Autobiography*. Orig. pub. 1863. Reprint, New York: Books for Libraries Press, 1971.

Beaucage, Pierre. 'The Economic Anthropology of the Black Caribs of Honduras'. Ph.D. dissertation, Univ. of London, 1970.

Beaumont, Joseph. *The New Slavery; An Account of the Indian and Chinese Immigrants in British Guiana*. London, 1871.

Beckford, George. *Persistent Poverty. Underdevelopment in Plantation Economies of the Third World*. New York: Oxford Univ. Press, 1972.

Beckles, Hilary. *Black Rebellion in Barbados: The Struggle Against Slavery, 1627-1838*. Bridgetown: Antilles Publications, 1984.

———. *Natural Rebels. A Social History of Enslaved Black Women in Barbados*. London: Zed Books, 1989.

———. *White Servitude and Black Slavery in Barbados, 1627-1715*. Knoxville: Univ. of Tennessee Press, 1989.

———, & Verene Shepherd, eds. *Caribbean Freedom: Society and Economy from Emancipation to the Present*. Kingston, Jamaica: Ian Randle Publishers, & London: James Currey Publishers, 1993.

———, & Verene Shepherd, eds. *Caribbean Slave Society and Economy*. Kingston: Ian Randle Publishers, & London: James Currey Publishers, 1991.

Bell, Ian. *The Dominican Republic*. Boulder, Colorado: Westview Press, 1981.

Bellegarde-Smith, Patrick. *Haiti: Breached Citadel*. Boulder, Colorado: Westview Press, 1989.

Bengelsdorf, Carollee. 'Cuba: Unchanging Change – The Boundaries of Democracy', in Edie, ed., *Democracy in the Caribbean*, 181-197.

Bennett, Herman L. 'The Challenge of the Post-Colonial State. A Case Study of the February Revolution', in Knight & Palmer, eds. *The Modern Caribbean*, 129-46.

Bernstein, Henry, ed. *Underdevelopment and Development*. Middlesex: Penguin Books, 1973.

Best, Lloyd. 'Outlines of a Model of Pure Plantation Economy', *Social and Economic Studies*, 17(3), 1968:283-326.

———. 'Survival and Size', in Girvan & Jefferson, eds. *Readings in the Political Economy of the Caribbean*, 29-34.

Betancourt, Cardozo de. 'Notes on the Spanish and Portuguese Jews in the United States, Canada, and the Dutch and British West Indies During the Seventeenth and Eighteenth Centuries', *Publications of the American Jewish Historical Society*. New York: The Society, No. 29, 1925, 7-38.

Bethell, Leslie, ed. *Cambridge History of Latin America*. Cambridge: Cambridge Univ. Press, 1984.

Biervliet, Wim. 'Surinamers in the Netherlands', in Craig, ed. *Contemporary Caribbean*, I, 75-100.

Bilby, Kenneth. 'Maroon Culture as a Distinct Variant of Jamaican Culture', in Agorsah, ed. *Maroon Heritage*, 72-85.

Bishop, Maurice. *In Nobody's Backyard: Maurice Bishop's Speeches 1977-1983. A Memorial Volume*. Chris Searle, ed. London: Zed Books, 1984.

Bisnauth, Dale. 'The East Indian Immigrant Society in British Guiana, 1891-1930'. Ph.D. dissertation, Univ. of the West Indies, Mona, 1977.

Bitek, Okot p'. *Song of Lawino*. Nairobi: East Africa Publishing House, 1966.

Bitterli, Urs. *Cultures in Conflict. Encounters Between European and Non-European Cultures 1492-1800*. California: Stanford Univ. Press, 1982.

Black, Jan. 'Democracy and Disillusionment in the Dominican Republic', in Payne & Sutton, eds. *Modern Caribbean Politics*, 54-72.

———. *The Dominican Republic: Politics and Development in an Unsovereign State*. Boston: Allen & Unwin, 1986.

Boland, O. Nigel. *On the March. Labour Rebellions in the British Caribbean, 1934-39*. Kingston, Jamaica: Ian Randle Publishers, 1995.

———. 'Systems of Domination After Slavery: The Control of Land and Labour in the British West Indies After 1838', in Beckles & Shepherd, eds. *Caribbean Freedom*, 107-23.

Bolt, Christine. 'Race and the Victorians', in Eldridge, ed. *British Imperialism*, 126-47.

Bou, Ismael Rodríguez. 'Illiteracy, Freedom, and Justice in the Caribbean', in Wilgus, ed., *The Caribbean: Contemporary Education, 3-19.*

Bourne, Compton. *Caribbean Development to the Year 2000*. London: Commonwealth Secretariat, 1989.

Boxer, Charles. *The Dutch Seaborne Empire 1600-1800*. London: Hutchinson, 1965.

Boyce, Rupert. *Health Progress and Administration in the West Indies*. London: John Murray, 1910.

Brana-Shute, Gary. 'Love Among the Ruins: the United States and Suriname', in Sedoc-Dahlberg, ed. *The Dutch Caribbean*, 191-202.

Brana-Shute, Rosemary. *A Bibliography of Caribbean Migration and Caribbean Immigrant Communities*. Gainesville, Florida: Univ. of Florida Libraries in cooperation with the Center for Latin American Studies, Univ. of Florida, 1983.

Brereton, Bridget. 'The Experience of Indentureship: 1845-1917', in La Guerre, ed. *Calcutta to Caroni*, 21-31.

———. *Race Relations in Colonial Trinidad, 1870-1900*. Cambridge, 1979.

Bridenbaugh, Carl & Roberta Bridenbaugh. *No Peace Beyond the Line: the English in the Caribbean, 1624-1690*. London: Oxford Univ. Press, 1972.

Browser, Frederick. 'Colonial Spanish America', in Cohen & Greene, eds. *Neither Slave Nor Free*, 19-58.

Bruijne, A. de. 'The Lebanese in Suriname', *Boletín de estudios latinoamericanos y del Caribe*, 26, 1979:15-37.

———. 'De Libanezen van Suriname – een Detail Studie', *Een Sociaal-Geografisch Spectrum. Opstellen Aangeboden aan Prof. Dr A.C. de Vooys 1949-1974*. Utrecht, 1974.

Bryan, Patrick. 'The Question of Labor in the Sugar Industry of the Dominican Republic', in Fraginals *et al.* ed, *Between Slavery and Free Labor*, 235-51.

Bryant, Alton T. *The New Compact Bible Dictionary*. Minneapolis: Billy Graham Evangelistic Assn, 1967.

Bulhan, Hussein. *Frantz Fanon and the Psychology of Oppression*. New York: Plenum Press, 1985.

Burac, Maurice. 'Current Problems Facing the Peasantry in the North-East of Martinique', in Craig, ed. *Contemporary Caribbean*, I, 383-403.

Burn, W. L. *Emancipation and Apprenticeship in the British West Indies*. London: Johnathan Cape, 1937.

Burns, Alan. *Colour Prejudice, with Particular Reference to the Relationship Between Whites and Negroes*. London: George Allen & Unwin, 1948.

———. *History of the British West Indies*. London: George Allen & Unwin, 1954.

———. *In Defence of Colonies. British Colonial Territories in International Affairs*. London: George Allen & Unwin, 1957.

Calder, Bruce. *The Impact of Intervention: The Dominican Republic During the US Occupation of 1916-1924*. Austin: Univ. of Texas Press, 1984.

Campbell, Mavis. *The Dynamics of Change in a Slave Society: A Socio-Political History of the Free Coloreds of Jamaica, 1800-1865*. Rutherford, New Jersey: Fairleigh Dickinson Univ. Press, 1976.

———. *The Maroons of Jamaica 1655-1796. A History of Resistance, Collaboration and Betrayal*. Trenton, New Jersey: Africa World Press, 1990.

Carew, Jan. *Fulcrums of Change*. Trenton, New Jersey: Africa World Press, 1988.

Caribbean Community in the 1980s. Report by a Group of Caribbean Experts. Georgetown, Guyana: The Caribbean Community Secretariat, n.d.

Caribbean Development Bank. 'Adjustment Problems in CARICOM States', in Lalta & Freckleton, eds, *Caribbean Economic Development*, 35-46.

Caribbean Tourism Statistical Report 1993. Barbados: Caribbean Tourism Organisation, 1994.

Caribbean Tourism Statistical Report 1994. Barbados: Caribbean Tourism Organisation,

Carr, Raymond. *Puerto Rico: A Colonial Experiment*. New York: Vintage Books, 1984.

Carrington, Selwyn. 'The State of the Debate on the Role of Capitalism in the Ending of the Slave System', *Journal of Caribbean History*, 22(1 & 2), 1988:20-41.

Carrión, Arturo M. ed. *Puerto Rico: A Political and Cultural History*. New York: Norton & Co, 1983.

Carter, Martin. 'I Come From the Nigger Yard', in *The African-Guyanese Achievement*, No. 1. Georgetown: The Free Press, 1993, 7-9.

Casimir, Jean. 'Two Classes and two Cultures in Contemporary Haiti', in Craig, ed. *Contemporary Caribbean*, II, 181-210.

Castaner, Juan & Angel Calderón Cruz. 'Puerto Rico's Trade Linkages with the Rest of the Caribbean', *Caribbean Affairs*, 2(4), 1989:123-140.

Caton-Thompson, Gertrude. *The Zimbabwe Culture. Ruins and Reactions*. Orig. pub. 1931. Reprint, London: Frank Cass, 1971.

Césaire, Aimé. *Discourse on Colonialism*. Orig. pub. 1955. Trans. by Joan Pinkham. New York: Monthly Review Press, 1972.

———. *Return to my Native Land*. Orig. pub. in 1956. Trans. & reprinted; Val-d'Oise, France: Editions Présence Africaine, 1968.

Céspedes, Francisco. 'Public Elementary Education in the Caribbean', in Wilgus, ed. *Contemporary Education*, 51-64.

Chandler, Wayne. 'The Jewel in the Lotus: The Ethiopian Presence in the Indus Valley Civilization', in Van Sertima, ed. *African Presence in Early Asia*, 95-104.

Ch'en, Jerome. *China and the West. Society and Culture, 1815-1937*. London: Hutchinson & Co, 1979.

Chernick, S. *The Commonwealth Caribbean: The Integration Experience*. Baltimore: The Johns Hopkins Univ. Press, 1978.

Christopher Columbus Encyclopedia. Vol. I. Silvio A. Bedini, ed. USA: Macmillan Publishers, 1992.

Clarke, Colin, ed. *Society and Politics in the Caribbean*. Oxford: Macmillan, in association with St Antony's College, 1991.

———. 'Sovereignty, Dependency and Social Change in the Caribbean', *South America, Central America and the Caribbean 1993, 33-38.*

Claypole, William & John Robottom. *Caribbean Story Book Two: The Inheritors*. San Juan, Trinidad: Longman Caribbean, 1981.

Clementi, Cecil. *The Chinese in British Guiana*. Georgetown: Argosy Co, 1915.

Cobley, Alan. ed. *Crossroads of Empire. The Europe-Caribbean Connection 1492-1992*. Bridgetown, Barbados: Dept of History, UWI, & National Cultural Foundation, 1994.

———, & Alvin Thompson, eds. *The African-Caribbean Connection: Historical and Cultural Perspectives*. Bridgetown, Barbados: Dept of History, Univ. of the West Indies, 1990.

Cohen, David & Jack Greene, eds. *Neither Slave nor Free. The Freedman of African Descent in the Slave Societies of the New World*. Baltimore: The Johns Hopkins Univ. Press, 1972.

Coleman, David & Frederick Nixson. *Economics of Change in Less Developed Countries*. 2nd ed. Oxford: Philip Allan Publishers, 1986.

Conneau, Theophilus. *A Slaver's Log Book or 20 Years' Residence in Africa*. Orig. pub. 1854. New ed., London: Prentice Hall International Inc., 1976.

Conniff, Michael. *Black Labor on a White Canal: Panama,1904-1981*. Pittsburgh: Pittsburgh Univ. Press, 1985.

Conzemius, Edward. 'Ethnographical Notes on the Black Carib', *American Anthropologist* (new series), 30(2), 1928:183-205.

Cook, Sherburne, F. & Woodrow Borah. 'The Aboriginal Population of Hispaniola', in Cook & Borah, eds. *Essays in Population History. Mexico and the Caribbean*. I, 376-410.

———. *Essays in Population History: Mexico and the Caribbean*. Berkeley: Univ. of California Press, 1971.

Corbitt, Duvon. *A Study of the Chinese in Cuba, 1847-1947*. Kentucky: Ashbury College, 1971.

———. 'Immigration in Cuba', *Hispanic American Historical Review*, 22, 1942:280-308.

Corten, André. 'The Migration of Haitian Workers to the Sugar Factories of the Dominican Republic', in Craig, ed. *Contemporary Caribbean*, I, 349-66.

Costas, Aida R. C. 'The Organization of an Institutional and Social Life', in Carrión, ed. *Puerto Rico*, 25-40.

Coupland, Reginald. *East Africa and Its Invaders. From Earliest Times to the Death of Seyyid Said in 1856*. Orig. pub. 1938. Reprint, London: Oxford Univ. Press, 1956.

———. *The British Anti-Slavery Movement*. London: T. Butterworth, 1933.

Craig, Susan. 'Background to the 1970 Confrontation in Trinidad and Tobago', in Craig, ed. *Contemporary Caribbean*, II, 385-423.

-----, ed. *Contemporary Caribbean. A Sociological Reader*. 2 vols. published by editor. Port-of-Spain: By Editor, 1981.

Craton, Michael. 'A Recipe for the Perfect Calalu: Island and Regional Identities in the British West Indies'. Goveia Memorial Lecture, Univ. of the West Indies, Cave Hill Campus, 1991.

———. 'Continuity Not Change: The Incidence of Unrest Among Ex-Slaves in the British West Indies, 1838-1876', in Beckles & Shepherd, eds. *Caribbean Freedom*, 192-206.

———. *Testing the Chains. Resistance to Slavery in the British West Indies*. Ithaca: Cornell Univ. Press, 1982.

Croes, Robertico & Lucita Moenir Alam. 'Decolonization of Aruba Within the Netherlands Antilles', in Sedoc-Dahlberg, ed. *The Dutch Caribbean*, 81-102.

Crosby, Alfred. *The Columbian Exchange: Biological and Cultural Consequences of 1492*. Westport: Greenwood Publishing Co, 1972.

Crowder, Michael. 'The Second World War: Prelude to Decolonisation in Africa', in Crowder, ed. *Cambridge History of Africa*, VIII, 8-47.

——, ed. *Cambridge History of Africa.* Cambridge: Cambridge Univ. Press, Vol. VIII, 1984.

——, & D. Cruise O'Brien. 'French West Africa, 1945-1960', in Ajayi & Crowder, eds. *History of West Africa,* II, 664-99.

Cuban Commission Report: A Hidden History of the Chinese in Cuba. Report of the Ch'ên Lanpin Commission, 1874. Orig. pub. in English in 1876. Reprinted with intro. by Denise Helly. Baltimore: The Johns Hopkins Univ. Press, 1993.

Dabydeen, David & Brinsley Samaroo, eds. *India in the Caribbean.* London: Hansib Publishing, 1987.

Dalton, Henry. *The History of British Guiana.* London: Longman, 1855.

Davis, Ralph. *The Rise of the Atlantic Economies.* London: George Wiedenfeld & Nicolson, 1973.

Dawson, Raymond. *The Chinese Chameleon: An Analysis of European Conceptions of Chinese Civilization.* London: Oxford Univ. Press, 1967.

De Gobineau, Arthur. 'Races', in Miller & Dolan, eds. *Race Awareness,* 237-242.

De Groot, Sylvia. *Djuka Society and Social Change. History of an Attempt to Develop a Bush Negro Community in Surinam 1917-1926.* Assen: Van Gorcum, 1969.

——. 'The Boni Maroon War 1765-1793, Surinam and French Guiana', *Boletín de Estudios Latinoamericanos y del Caribe,* 18, 1975:30-48.

De Kadt, Emmanuel. *Patterns of Foreign Influence in the Caribbean.* London: Oxford Univ. Press; published for the Royal Institute of International Affairs, 1972.

De La Riva, Francisco Pérez. 'Cuban Palenques', in Price, ed. *Maroon Societies,* 49-59.

De Saint-Méry, M. L. E. Moreau. 'The Border Maroons of Saint-Domingue: Le Maniel', in Price, ed. *Maroon Societies,* 135-42.

De Waal Malefijt, Annemarie. *The Javanese of Surinam: Segment of a Plural Society.* Assen: Van Gorcum, 1963.

Debbasch, Yvan. 'Le Maniel: Further Notes', in Price, ed. *Maroon Societies,* 143-48.

Debien, Gabriel. 'Le Marronage aux Antilles Françaises aux XVIIIe siècle', *Caribbean Studies,* 6(3), 1966:3-44.

——. *Les Esclaves aux Antilles Françaises XVIIe-XVIIIe siècle.* Basseterre: Société d'Histoire de la Guadeloupe, 1974.

——. 'Marronage in the French Caribbean', in Price, ed. *Maroon Societies,* 107-134.

Delince, Kern. *Armée et Politique en Haiti.* Paris: L'Harmattan, 1979.

Demas, William. *Essays in Caribbean Integration and Development.* Kingston, Jamaica: Institute of Social and Economic Research, 1976.

——. *The Economics of Development in Small Countries with Special Reference to the Caribbean.* Published for the Centre for Developing Area Studies; Montreal: McGill Univ. Press, 1965.

Denevan, William, ed. *The Native Populations of the Americas in 1492.* Madison: Univ. of Wisconsin Press, 1976.

Deosarran, Ramesh. 'The "Caribbean Man": A Study of the Psychology of Perception and the Media', in Dabydeen & Samaroo, eds. *India in the Caribbean,* 81-117.

Des Voeux, George W. *Experiences of a Demerara Magistrate, 1863-1869.* Georgetown: Daily Chronicle, 1948.

Dew, Edward. *The Difficult Flowering of Surinam: Ethnicity and Politics in a Plural Society.* The Hague: Martinus Nijhoff, 1978.

Dickason, Olive. *The Myth of the Savage and the Beginnings of French Colonization in the Americas.* Alberta: Univ. of Alberta Press, 1984.

Dickson, William. *Letters on Slavery.* Orig. pub. 1789. Reprint, Westport, Connecticut: Negro Univ. Press, 1970.

Dikötter, Frank. 'Group Definition and the Idea of "Race" in Modern China (1793-1949)', *Ethnic and Racial Studies* 13(3), 1990:420-432.

Diodorus of Sicily. Trans. by C. H. Oldfather. London: Heinemann, 1953.

Diop, Cheikh A. *The African Origin of Civilization, Myth or Reality?* Westport: Lawrence Hill & Co, 1974.

Dirks, Robert. *The Black Saturnalia. Conflict and its Ritual Expression on British West Indian Slave Plantations*. Gainesville: Univ. of Florida Press, 1987.

Dominguez, Jorge. *To Make a World Safe for Revolution: Cuba's Foreign Policy*. Cambridge: Harvard Univ. Press, 1989.

_____. ' The Caribbean Question: Why Has Liberal Democracy (Surprisingly) Flourished?' in Dominguez *et al.*, eds. *Democracy in the Caribbean*, 1-28.

_____, *et al.*, eds. *Democracy in the Caribbean. Political, Economic and Social Perspectives*. Baltimore: The John Hopkins Univ. Press, 1993.

Dookhan, Isaac. *A History of the Virgin Islands of the United States*. Epping, Essex: Caribbean Univ. Press, in association with Bowker Publishing Co, for College of the Virgin Islands, 1974.

———. *A Post-Emancipation History of the West Indies*. London: Collins, 1975.

Dore y Cabral, Carlos. 'The Eastern Situation and Agrarian Reform in the Dominican Republic', in Craig, ed. *Contemporary Caribbean*, I, 367-82.

Dos Santos, T. 'The Crisis of Development Theory and the Problem of Dependence in Latin America', in Bernstein, ed. *Underdevelopment and Development*, 57-80.

Drescher, Seymour. *Econocide: British Slavery in the Era of Abolition*. Pittsburgh: Pittsburgh Univ. Press, 1977.

Dubois, Abbé J. A. *Hindu Manners, Customs and Ceremonies*. Trans. Henry K. Beauchamp. London, 1959.

Duncan, Neville. 'Barbados: Democracy at the Crossroads', in Edie, ed. *Democracy in the Caribbean*, 75-91.

_____. 'Political Violence in the Caribbean', in Griffith, ed. *Strategy and Security in the Caribbean*, 55-75.

_____. 'The Future of Regional Security in the Caribbean', in Dominguez *et al.*, eds. *Democracy in the Caribbean*, 238-54.

Dunn, Richard. *Sugar and Slaves. The Rise of the Planter Class in the English West Indies 1624-1713*. New York: W.W. Norton & Co, 1972.

Dutton, R. *et al. Caribbean Landscapes*. London: Collins Educational, 1983.

Economic Survey of Latin America and the Caribbean 1994-1995. Santiago, Chile: United Nations, 1996.

Edie, Carlene J. ed. *Democracy in the Caribbean. Myths and Realities*. Westport, Connecticut: Praeger, 1994.

Edwards, Albert. 'Maroon Warfare: the Jamaica Model', in Agorsah, ed. *Maroon Heritage*, 149-162.

Edwards, Bryan. *The History, Civil and Commercial, of the British Colonies in the West Indies*. 5th ed. Orig. pub. 1793-1801. Reprint, New York: AMS Press, 1966.

Edwards, Sir Herbert & Herman Merivale. *Life of Sir Henry Lawrence*. New York: Macmillan, 1873.

Eisner, Gisela. *Jamaica 1830-1930; a Study in Economic Growth*. Manchester: Manchester Univ. Press, 1961.

Ekundare, R. Olufemi. *An Economic History of Nigeria 1860-1960*. London: Methuen & Co, 1973.

Eldridge, C. ed. *British Imperialism in the Nineteenth Century*. London: Macmillan, 1984.

Elisabeth, Léo. 'The French Antilles', in Cohen & Greene, eds. *Neither Slave Nor Free*, 134-71.

Eliot, Thomas S. 'The Wasteland', in *Collected Poems, 1909-1962*. London: Faber & Faber,1963.

Elliott, John H. *The Old World and the New 1492-1650*. New York: Cambridge Univ. Press, 1992.

Eltis, David. *Economic Growth and the Ending of the Transatlantic Slave Trade*. New York: Oxford Univ. Press, 1987.

Emmanuel, Arghiri. *Unequal Exchange. A Study of the Imperialism of Trade*. Trans. by Brian Pearce. New York: Monthly Review Press, 1972.

Emmanuel, Isaac & Susan Emmanuel. *History of the Jews of the Netherlands Antilles*, 2 Vols Cincinnati: American Jewish Archives, 1970.

Emmanuel, Patrick, Farley Brathwaite & Eudine Barriteau. *Political Change and Public Opinion in Grenada 1979-1984*. Institute of Social & Economic Studies, Univ. of the West Indies, Cave Hill, Occasional Paper 19, 1986.

Encyclopædia of Religion and Ethics. Vol. XI, 1974.

Erisman, H. Michael. *Cuba's International Relations: The Anatomy of a Nationalistic Foreign Policy*. Boulder, Colorado: Westview Press, 1985.

———. 'The Odyssey of Revolution in Cuba', in Payne & Sutton, eds. *Modern Caribbean Politics*, 212-37.

Esquemelin (Exquemelin), Alexander. *The History of the Buccaneers*. Orig. pub. 1678. Reprint, London: George Rutledge & Sons, 1893.

Europa World Year Book 1991. London: Europa Publications, 1991.

The Europa World Year Book 1995. London: Europa Publications, 1995.

Fage, John D. *A History of West Africa. An Introductory Survey*. London: Cambridge Univ. Press, 1969.

Fanon, Frantz. *Black Skin White Masks*. Orig. pub. 1952. Trans. by Charles Lam Markmann. New York: Grove Press, 1967.

———. *The Wretched of the Earth*. Orig. pub. 1961. Trans. by C. Farrington. Middlesex: Penguin Books, 1967.

Farley, Rawle. 'The Rise of a Peasantry in British Guiana', *Social and Economic Studies*, 2(4), 1953:87-103.

Farrell, Terrence. 'Monetary Union: A Guide for the Perplexed', in Farrell & Worrell, eds. *Caribbean Monetary Integration*, 12-26.

_____, & Delisle Worrell, eds. *Caribbean Monetary Integration*. Port-of-Spain, Trinidad: Caribbean Information Systems & Services, 1994.

Farrell, Trevor. 'Some Notes Towards a Strategy for Economic Transformation', in Lalta & Freckleton, eds. *Caribbean Economic Development*, 330-42.

———. 'The Caribbean State and its Role in Economic Management', in Lalta & Freckleton, eds. *Caribbean Economic Development*, 200-14.

Ferguson, James. 'Pain and Protest: The 1984 Anti-IMF Revolt in the Dominican Republic', in Beckles & Shepherd, eds. *Caribbean Freedom*, 566-74.

———. 'The Duvalier Dictatorship and its Legacy of Crisis in Haiti', in Payne & Sutton, eds. *Modern Caribbean Politics*, 73-97.

Fieldhouse, D. K. *Economics and Empire 1830-1914*. London: Weidenfeld & Nicolson, 1976.

———. *The Colonial Empires. A Comparative Survey from the Eighteenth Century*. 2nd ed. London: Macmillan, 1982.

Finch, Charles. 'The African Background of Medical Science', in Van Sertima, ed. *Blacks in Science: Ancient and Modern*, 140-56.

Fitzgerald, Frank. 'The Direction of Cuban Socialism: a Critique of the Sovietization Thesis', in Craig, ed. *Contemporary Caribbean*, II, 243-74.

Foner, Philip S. *A History of Cuba and Its Relations with the United States*. 2 Vols. New York: International Publishers, 1962-1963.

———. *The Spanish-Cuban-American War and the Birth of American Imperialism 1895-1902*. 2 vols. New York: Monthly Review Press, 1972.

Forde, A. N., ed. *Talk of the Tamarinds. A Anthology of Poetry for Secondary Schools*. London: Edward Arnold Publishers, 1971.

Forde, C. & P. M. Kaberry, eds. *West African Kingdoms in the Nineteenth Century*. London: Oxford Univ. Press, 1967.

Fouchard, Jean. *Les Marrons de la Liberté*. Paris: Éditions de l'École, 1972.

Fraginals, Manuel. 'Plantations in the Caribbean: Cuba, Puerto Rico and the Dominican Republic in the Late Nineteenth Century', in Fraginals *et al.* eds. *Between Slavery and Free Labor*, 3-21.

———, Frank Pons & Stanley Engerman, eds. *Between Slavery and Free Labor. The Spanish Speaking Caribbean in the Nineteenth Century*. Baltimore: The Johns Hopkins Univ. Press, 1985.

France, Lesley & Brian Wheeler. 'Sustainable Tourism in the Caribbean', in Barker & McGregor, eds. *Environment and Development in the Caribbean*, 59-69.

Francis, Al. 'Structural Change in the World Bauxite Alumina/Aluminum Industry with Particular Reference to the Caribbean Bauxite Industry', in Lalta & Freckleton, eds. *Caribbean Economic Development*, 227-44.

Franco, José. 'Maroons and Slave Rebellions in the Spanish Territories', in Price, ed. *Maroon Societies*, 35-48.

Frank, André G. *Lumpenbourgeoisie: Lumpendevelopment: Dependence, Class and Politics in Latin America*. New York: Monthly Review Press, 1972.

Fraser, Peter. 'The Fictive Peasantry: Caribbean Rural Groups in the Nineteenth Century', in Craig, ed. *Contemporary Caribbean*, I, 319-48.

Freckleton, Marie. 'Jamaica's Balance of Payments Performance 1975-1988', in Lalta & Freckleton, eds. *Caribbean Economic Development*, 120-29.

Freire, Paulo. *Pedagogy of the Oppressed*. Trans. by Myra Bergman Ramos. Middlesex: Penguin Books, 1972.

Frostin, Charles. *Les Revoltes Blanches à Saint-Domingue aux XVIIe et XVIIIe siècle: Haiti avant 1789*. Paris, 1975.

Frucht, Richard, ed. *Black Society in the New World*. New York: Random House, 1971.

García-Passalacqua, Juan Manuel. 'The Role of the Puerto Rican People in the Caribbean', in Dominguez *et al.* eds. *Democracy in the Caribbean*, 173-88.

Gastman, Albert. *The Politics of Suriname and the Netherlands Antilles*. Rio Piedras: Univ. of Puerto Rico, 1968.

Gautier-Mayoral, Carmen. 'Puerto Rico: Problems of Democracy and Decolonization in the Late Twentieth Century', in Edie, ed. *Democracy in the Caribbean*, 163-79.

Geggus, David. *Slavery, War and Revolution: The British Occupation of Saint-Domingue 1793-1798*. Oxford: Clarendon Press, 1982.

———. 'The Haitian Revolution', in Beckles & Shepherd, eds. *Caribbean Slave Society and Economy*, 402-18.

Giacalone, Rita. 'Venezuela's Relations with Curaçao and Aruba: Historical Linkages and Geopolitical Interests', in Sedoc-Dahlberg, ed. *The Dutch Caribbean*, 219-40.

Gibson, Charles. *Spain in America*. New York: Harper & Row, 1966.

Gill, Henry. 'The Association of Caribbean States: Prospects for a "Quantum Leap", *The North-South Agenda*. Paper No. 11, North-South Center, Univ. of Miami, Jan. 1995.

Ginzberg, Eli. *Human Resources: The Wealth of a Nation*. New York: Simon & Schuster, 1958.

Giraud, Michel. 'Political Subordination and Society in the French Antilles', in Clarke, ed. *Society and Politics in the Caribbean*, 233-44.

Girault, Christian. 'Society and Politics in Haiti: the Divorce Between the State and the Nation', in Clarke, ed. *State and Politics in the Caribbean*, 185-206.

Girvan, Norman. 'The Debt Problem of the Caribbean and Central America: an Overview', in Lalta & Freckleton, eds. *Caribbean Economic Development*, 105-19.

———. 'The Development of Dependency Economics in the Caribbean and Latin America', *Social and Economic Studies*, 22(1), 1973:1-33.

———, *et al.* 'The Debt Problem of Small Peripheral Economies: Case Studies from the Caribbean and Central America', *Caribbean Studies*, 24(1-2), 1991:45-115.

———, & Owen Jefferson, eds. *Readings in the Political Economy of the Caribbean*. Kingston: New World Group, 1971.

Gleijeses, P. *The Dominican Crisis. The 1965 Constitutionalist Revolt and American Intervention*. Trans. by L. Lipson. Baltimore: The John Hopkins Univ. Press, 1978.

Gorostiaga, Xabier. 'Towards Alternative Policies in the Region', in Irvin & Gorostiaga, eds. *Towards an Alternative for Central America and the Caribbean*, 13-37.

———, & George Irvin. *Towards an Alternative for Central America and the Caribbean*. London: George Allen & Unwin, 1985.

Goslinga, Cornelis. *The Dutch in the Caribbean and the Guianas 1680-1791*. Assen: Van Gorcum, 1985.

Goveia, Elsa. *The West Indian Slave Laws of the 18th Century*. Barbados: Caribbean Univ. Press, 1970.

Gowricharn, Ruben. 'The State in Primary Export Societies: the Case of Suriname', in Craig, ed. *Contemporary Caribbean*, I, 283-309.

Green, William. *British Slave Emancipation: The Sugar Colonies and the Great Experiment, 1830-1865*. Oxford: Clarendon Press, 1976.

Greenburg, D. 'U. S. Destroyers for British Bases. Fifty Old Ships go to War', *United States Naval Institute Proceedings*, 88(11), 1962:70-83.

Griffith, Glyne. *Deconstruction Imperialism and the West Indian Novel*. Kingston, Jamaica: The Press, Univ. of the West Indies, 1996.

Griffith, Ivelaw, ed. *Strategy and Security in the Caribbean*. New York: Praeger, 1991.

———. *The Quest for Security in the Caribbean. Problems and Promises in Subordinate States*. New York: M. E. Sharpe, 1993.

Griffin, Keith. *Land Concentration and Rural Poverty*. New York: Macmillan, 1976.

———, & Azizur Rahman Khan. *Globalization and the Developing World: An Essay on the International Dimensions of Development in the Post-World War Era*. Geneva: UNRISD, 1992.

Guérin, Daniel. *The West Indies and Their Future*. Orig. pub. 1956. Trans. by Austryn Wainhouse. London: Dobson Books, 1961.

Gullick, C. J. *Exiled from St. Vincent. The Development of Black Carib Culture in Central America up to 1945*. Malta: Progress Press, 1976.

Hall, Douglas. *In Miserable Slavery. Thomas Thistlewood in Jamaica 1750-86*. London: Macmillan, 1989.

———. 'Jamaica', in Cohen & Greene, eds. *Neither Slave nor Free*, 193-213.

Hall, Gwendolyn Midlo. *Social Control in Slave Plantation Societies: A Comparison of St. Domingue and Cuba*. Baltimore: The Johns Hopkins Univ. Press, 1971.

Hall, Neville. 'Slave Laws of the Danish Virgin Islands in the Later Eighteenth Century', *Annals of the New York Academy of Sciences*, 292 (1977):174-86.

———. *Slave Society in the Danish West Indies: St. Thomas, St. John and St. Croix*. B. Higman, ed. Kingston, Jamaica: Univ. of the West Indies Press, 1992.

Hamilton, Bruce. *Barbados and the Confederation Question 1871-1885*. London: Crown Agents for Oversea Govts & Administrations, on behalf of the Govt of Barbados, 1956.

Handler, Jerome. *The Unappropriated People. Freedmen in the Slave Society of Barbados*. Baltimore: The Johns Hopkins Univ. Press, 1974.

Hanke, Lewis. *All Mankind is One. A Study of the Disputation Between Bartolomé de Las Casas and Juan Ginés de Sepúlveda in 1550*. Illinois: Northern Illinois Univ. Press, 1974.

———. *Aristotle and the American Indians. A Study in Race Prejudice in the Modern World*. Chicago: Henry Regnery Co, 1959.

———. *The Spanish Struggle for Justice in the Conquest of America*. Orig. pub. 1949.; Reprint, Boston: Little, Brown & Co, 1965.

Haraksingh, Kusha. 'Control and Resistance Among Indian Workers: A Study of Labour on the Sugar Plantations of Trinidad 1875-1917, in Dabydeen & Samaroo, eds. *India in the Caribbean*, 61-77.

———. 'Indian Leadership in the Indenture Period', *Caribbean Issues* 2(3), 1976:17-38.

Hardy, P. *The Muslims of British India*. London: Cambridge Univ. Press, 1972.

Harewood, Jack. 'Unemployment and Underemployment in the Commonwealth Caribbean', in Craig, ed. *Contemporary Caribbean*, I, 143-66.

Haring, Clarence. *The Buccaneers in the West Indies in the XVII Century*. Orig. pub. 1910. Reprint, Hamden, Connecticut: Archon Books, 1966.

Harker, Trevor. 'A Brief Overview of Economic Performance in the Eighties', in Lalta & Freckleton, eds. *Caribbean Economic Development*, 17-34.

———. 'Development Planning: Reflections and Reconsiderations', in Lalta & Freckleton, eds. *Caribbean Economic Development*, 353-70.

Harris, C. A. & J. A. J. de Villiers. *Storm van's Gravesande: the Rise of British Guiana*. Orig. pub. 1911. Nendeln, Liechtenstein: Kraus, 1967.

Hart, Richard. *Slaves Who Abolished Slavery*. Vol. I. *Blacks in Bondage*. Univ. of the West Indies, Jamaica: Institute of Social & Economic Research, 1980.

Hartlyn, Jonathan. 'The Dominican Republic: Contemporary Problems and Challenges', in Dominguez *et al.* eds. *Democracy in the Caribbean*, 150-172.

Heber, Reginald. *Narrative of a Journey Through the Upper Provinces of India*. London: John Murray, 1829.

Heemstra, J. 'De Indonesiërs in Suriname', *Indonesie*, 6, 1952-53:429-38.

Hegel, Georg W. F. *The Philosophy of History*. Orig. pub. 1837. Trans. by J. Sibree. New York: Dover Publications, 1956.

Heine, Jorge. *A Revolution Aborted: The Lessons of Grenada*. Pittsburgh: Univ. of Pittsburgh Press, 1991.

– – – – –, & Juan M. Garcia-Passalacqua. 'Political Economy and Foreign Policy in Puerto Rico', in Payne & Sutton, eds. *Modern Caribbean Politics*, 198-211.

Helly, Denise. *Idéologie et Ethnicité. Les Chinois Macao à Cuba*. Montreal: Les Presses de L'Université de Montreal, 1979.

Helms, M. W. 'The Indians of the Caribbean and the Circum-Caribbean at the end of the Fifteenth Century', in Bethell, ed. *Cambridge History of Latin America*, I, 37-57.

Henige, David. 'The Contact Population of Hispaniola: History as Higher Mathematics', *Hispanic American Historical Review*, 58(2), 1978:217-37.

Henry, Paget & Carl Stone. *The Newer Caribbean: Decolonization, Democracy, and Development*. Philadelphia: Institute for the Study of Human Issues, 1983.

Herodotus. Trans. & ed. by J. Enoch Powell. Oxford: Clarendon Press, 1949.

Herskovits, Melville. *The New World Negro*. Bloomington: Indiana Univ. Press, 1966.

Heuman, Gad. *The Killing Time: The Morant Bay Rebellion in Jamaica*. Knoxville: Univ. of Tennessee Press, 1994.

Higman, Barry. 'The Chinese in Trinidad, 1806-1838', *Caribbean Studies*, 12(3), 1972:21-44.

———. *Slave Populations of the British Caribbean 1807-1834*. Baltimore: The Johns Hopkins Univ. Press, 1984.

———, ed. *Trade, Government and Society in Caribbean History 1700-1920*. Kingston, Jamaica: Heinemann Educational Books, 1983.

Hilaire, Alvin *et al*. 'Options for Money Integration in the Caribbean', in Farrell & Worrell, eds. *Caribbean Monetary Integration*, 58-89.

Hilfman, P. A. 'Notes on the History of the Jews in Suriname', *Publications of the American Jewish Historical Society*, 18, 1909:179-207.

Hintzen, Percy. *The Cost of Regime Survival: Racial Mobilization, Elite Domination, and Control of the State in Guyana and Trinidad*. New York: Cambridge Univ. Press, 1989.

Hira, Sandew. 'The Evolution of the Social, Economic and Political Position of the East Indians in Surinam, 1873-1980', in Dabydeen & Samaroo, eds. *India in the Caribbean*, 189-209.

Hoetink, Harry. *Caribbean Race Relations. A Study of Two Variants*. Orig. pub. 1962. Abridged and trans. by Eva M. Hooykaas. London: Oxford Univ. Press, for Institute of Race Relations, 1971.

———. 'Surinam and Curaçao', in Cohen & Green, eds. *Neither Slave nor Free*, 59-83.

———. *The Dominican People, 1850-1900. Notes for an Historical Sociology*. Trans. by Stephen K. Ault. Baltimore: The Johns Hopkins Univ. Press, 1982.

———. 'The Dutch Caribbean and Its Metropolis', in De Kadt, ed. *Patterns of Foreign Influence*, 103-20.

———. 'The Future of the Netherlands Antilles', in Sedoc-Dahlberg, ed. *The Dutch Caribbean*, 241-52.

Holte, C. L. 'The Black Presence in Pre-Revolutionary Russia', in Van Sertima, ed. *African Presence in Early Europe*, 264-70.

Hook, Sidney. 'Violence', *Encyclopedia of the Social Sciences*. 1963 ed. New York: Macmillan, IX.

Hope, Kempe. *Guyana: Politics and Development in an Emergent Socialist State*. New York: Mosaic Press, 1985.

Horowitz, Michael, ed. *Peoples and Cultures of the Caribbean. An Anthropological Reader*. New York: The National History Press, 1971.

Huber, Evelyne. 'The Future of Democracy in the Caribbean', in Dominguez *et al*. eds. *Democracy in the Caribbean*, 74-98.

Hutchins, Francis. *The Illusion and the Permanence. British Imperialism in India*. New Jersey: Princeton Univ. Press, 1967.

Hutton, J. E. *A History of Moravian Missions*. London: Moravian Publication Office, 1922.

International Financial Statistics. Vol.60, No. 11. Washington: IMF Statistical Dept, 1995.

International Trade Statistics Yearbook 1994. New York: United Nations, 1995.

Ismael, Joseph. 'De positie van de Indonesiër in het niewe Suriname', *Indonesie*, 4, 1950-51:177-93.

James, C. L. R. 'Birth of a Nation', in Craig, ed. *Contemporary Caribbean*, I, 3-35.

———. 'From Toussaint L'Ouverture to Fidel Castro', in Frucht, ed. *Black Society in the New World*, 324-44.

———. *The Black Jacobins*. 2nd ed. New York: Vintage Books, 1963.

Jeffrey, Henry & Colin Baber. *Guyana: Politics, Economics and Society: Beyond the Burnham Era*. Boulder, Colorado: L. Rienner Publishers, 1986.

[Jenkins, Edward]. *The Coolie: His Rights and Wrongs*. London: Strahan & Co, 1871.

Joseph, Cedric. 'The Strategic Importance of the British West Indies, 1882-1932, *Journal of Caribbean History*, 7, 1973:23-67.

Karabel, Jerome & A. H. Halsey, 'Educational Research: A Review and Interpretation', in Karabel & Halsey, eds. *Power and Ideology in Education*, 1-85.

———, ed. *Power and Ideology in Education*. New York: Oxford Univ. Press, 1977.

Karch, Cecilia. 'The Growth of the Corporate Economy in Barbados: Class/Race Factors, 1890-1977', in Craig, ed. *Contemporary Caribbean*, I, 213-42.

Keesing's Record of World Events, 40, 42. London: Longman, 1994, 1996.

Klein, Herbert. *African Slavery in Latin America and the Caribbean*. New York: Oxford Univ. Press, 1986.

Klomp, Ank. 'Bonaire Within the Dutch Antilles', in Sedoc-Dahlberg, ed. *The Dutch Caribbean*, 103-17.

Knight, Franklin. 'Cuba. Politics, Economy and Society, 1898-1985', in Knight & Palmer, eds. *The Modern Caribbean*, 169-84.

_____. 'Cuba', in Cohen & Greene, eds. *Neither Slave nor Free*, 278-308.

———. *Slave Society in Cuba During the Nineteenth Century*. Madison: Univ. of Wisconsin Press, 1970.

———. *The Caribbean. The Genesis of a Fragmented Nationalism*. 2nd ed. New York: Oxford University Press, 1990.

———. 'The Societies of the Caribbean Since Independence', in Dominguez *et al.* eds. *Democracy in the Caribbean*, 29-41.

———, & Colin Palmer, eds. *The Modern Caribbean*. Chapel Hill: Univ. of North Carolina Press, 1989.

Knoll, Arthur & Lewis Gann, eds. *Germans in the Tropics: Essays in German Colonial History*. New York: Greenwood Press, 1987.

Koot, Wim. 'Socio-Economic Development and Emigration in the Netherlands Antilles', in Craig, ed. *Contemporary Caribbean*, I, 129-42.

Kopytoff, Barbara. 'The Maroons of Jamaica: An Ethnohistorical Study of Incomplete Polities, 1655-1905'. Ph.D. dissertation, Univ. of Pennsylvania, 1973.

Kryzanek, Michael & Howard J. Wiarda. *The Politics of External Influence in the Dominican Republic*. New York: Praeger, 1988.

LaCerte, Robert. 'The Evolution of Land and Labour in the Haitian Revolution', in Beckles & Shepherd, eds. *Caribbean Freedom*, 42-47.

La Guerre, John, ed. *Calcutta to Caroni. The East Indians of Trinidad*. 2nd ed. Trinidad: Univ. of the West Indies, 1985.

Lalta, Stanley & Marie Freckleton, eds. *Caribbean Economic Development: the First Generation*. Kingston, Jamaica: Ian Randle Publishers, 1993.

Lamming, George. *In the Castle of My Skin*. London: Longman, 1953; Drumbeat, 1979.

Lampart, Camille. 'The Struggle for Sustainable Development', in Lalta & Freckleton, eds. *Caribbean Economic Development*, 371-79.

Lamur, Humphrey. 'Slave Mortality in Suriname in the Nineteenth Century: the Role of Internal factors'. Paper presented at Conference of the Association of Caribbean Historians, April 14-18, 1981.

Langenberg, William. 'Destroyers for Naval Bases: Highlights of an Unprecedented Trade', *Naval War College Review*, 22(9), 1970:80-92.

Langley, Leslie. *The United States and the Caribbean in the Twentieth Century*. Georgia: Univ. of Georgia Press, 1980.

Lappe, F. M. & J. Collins, with C. Fowler. *Food First. Beyond the Myth of Scarcity*. Revised and updated ed. New York: Ballantine Books, 1984.

Lasserre, Guy & Albert Mabileau. 'The French Antilles and Their Status as Overseas Departments', in De Kadt, ed. *Patterns of Foreign Influence in the Caribbean*, 82-102.

Law, Robin. *The Oyo Empire c.1600-c.1836. A West African Imperialism in the Era of the*

Atlantic Slave Trade. Oxford: Clarendon Press, 1977.

Leigh Fermor, Patrick. *The Traveller's Tree. A Journey Through the Caribbean Islands*. London: J. Murray, 1950.

Lemoine, Maurice. *Bitter Sugar*. Orig. pub. 1981. Trans. by Andrea Johnston. Chicago: Zed Books, 1985.

Lewis, W. Arthur. 'The Industrialisation of the British West Indies', *Caribbean Economic Review*, 2(1), 1965:1-61.

———. *The Agony of the Eight*. Bridgetown, Barbados: Advocate Commercial Printery, 1965.

Lewis, Gordon K. *Main Currents in Caribbean Thought. The Historical Evolution of Caribbean Society in Its Ideological Aspects, 1492-1900*. Baltimore: The Johns Hopkins Univ. Press, 1983.

———. *The Growth of the Modern West Indies*. London: MacGibbon & Kee, 1968.

———. *Puerto Rico. Freedom and Power in the Caribbean*. New York: Monthly Review Press, 1963.

Lewis, Vaughan. 'The Eastern Caribbean States: Fledgling Sovereignties in the Global Environment', in Dominguez *et al.* eds. *Democracy in the Caribbean*, 99-121.

Lind, Andrew. 'Adjustment Patterns among the Jamaican Chinese', *Social and Economic Studies*, 17(2), 1958:144-64.

Lobdell, Richard. 'Patterns of Investment and Sources of Credit in the British West Indian Sugar Industry, 1838-1897', in Beckles & Shepherd, eds. *Caribbean Freedom*, 319-29.

Lockhart, James & Stuart Schwartz. *Early Latin America: A History of Colonial Spanish America and Brazil*. New York: Cambridge Univ. Press, 1983.

Loker, Zvi. 'Jews in the Grand'Anse Colony of Saint Domingue', *American Jewish Archives*, 34, 1982:89-97.

Long, Edward. *The History of Jamaica*. Orig. pub. 1774; Reprint, London: Frank Cass, 1970.

Look Lai, Walton. *Indentured Labor, Caribbean Sugar. Chinese and Indian Migrants to the British West Indies, 1838-1918*. London: The Johns Hopkins Univ. Press, 1993.

Louis, William. *Imperialism at Bay 1941-45*. Oxford: Clarendon Press, 1977.

Lowenthal, Abraham. *The Dominican Intervention*. Cambridge: Harvard University Press, 1972.

Lowenthal, David, ed. *The West Indies Federation. Perspectives on a New Nation*. New York: Columbia Univ. Press, for the American Geographical Society & Carelton Univ., 1961.

———. *West Indian Societies*. London: Oxford Univ. Press, 1972.

Lugard, Sir Frederick. *The Dual Mandate in British Tropical Africa*. 5th ed. Orig. pub. 1922. London: Frank Cass, 1965.

Lundahl, Mats. *The Haitian Economy. Man, Land and Markets*. New York: St Martin's Press, 1983.

Macaulay, Thomas B. 'Speech on the Government of India', (1823), in G. M. Young, ed. *Macaulay: Prose and Poetry*. Cambridge: Cambridge Univ. Press, 1970.

Maingot, Anthony. 'The Offshore Caribbean', in Payne & Sutton, eds. *Modern Caribbean Politics*, 259-91.

Malthus, Thomas R. *An Essay on the Principle of Population*. Orig. pub.1798. Reprint, London: J. M. Dent & Sons, 1960.

Mandle, Jay. 'British Caribbean Economic History. An Interpretation', in Knight & Palmer, eds. *The Modern Caribbean*, 229-58.

Mangru, Basdeo. *Benevolent Neutrality. Indian Government Policy and Labour Migration to British Guiana 1854-1884*. London: Hansib Publishing, 1987.

———. *Indenture and Abolition. Sacrifice and Survival on the Guyanese Sugar Plantations*. Toronto: TSAR, 1993.

———. 'The Sex-Ratio Disparity and its Consequences under the Indenture in British Guiana', in Dabydeen & Samaroo, eds. *India in the Caribbean*, 211-30.

Manley, Michael. *Jamaica: Struggle in the Periphery*. London: Third World Media, 1982.

Mannoni, Dominique O. *Prospero and Caliban. The Psychology of Colonization*. New York: Praeger, 1962.

Márquez, Roberto. 'Nationalism, Nation and Ideology. Trends in the Emergence of a Caribbean Literature', in Knight & Palmer, eds. *The Modern Caribbean*, 293-340.

Marshall, Dawn. 'Haitian Migration to the Bahamas', in Craig, ed. *Contemporary Caribbean*, II, 101-28.

Marshall, Woodville. 'Peasant Development in the British West Indies since 1838', in Beckles & Shepherd, eds. *Caribbean Freedom*, 100-06.

Martin, Tony. 'The Caribbean and Pan-Africanism', in Cobley & Thompson, eds. *African-Caribbean Connection*, 69-91.

Martin, Gaston. *Histoire de L'Esclavage dans les Colonies Françaises*. Brionne: Gérard Monfort, 1948.

Marx, Jenifer. *Pirates and Privateers of the Caribbean*. Malabar, Florida: Kreiger Publishing Co, 1992.

Mason, Philip. *Patterns of Dominance*. London: Oxford Univ. Press, 1971.

Mathieson, William. *British Slavery and Its Abolition 1823-1838*. London: Longmans, Green & Co, 1926.

May, Rollo. *Power and Innocence. A Search for the Sources of Violence*. New York: W. W. Norton & Co, 1972.

McAfee, Kathy. *Storm Signals. Structural Adjustment and Development Alternatives in the Caribbean*. London: Zed Books, 1991.

McBain, Helen. 'Foreign Capital Flows and Caribbean Economic Development', in Lalta & Freckleton, eds. *Caribbean Economic Development*, 130-40.

Meel, Peter. 'The March of Militarization in Suriname', in Payne & Sutton, eds. *Modern Caribbean Politics*, 125-46.

Meikle, Louis. *Confederation of the British West Indies Versus Annexation to the United States of America. A Political Discourse on the West Indies*. London: Sampson Low, Marston, 1912.

Memmi, Albert. *The Colonizer and the Colonized*. Orig. pub. 1957. Trans. by Howard Greenfield. New York: Orion Press, 1965.

Merrill, Gordon. 'The Role of the Sephardic Jews in the British Caribbean Area During the Seventeenth Century', *Caribbean Studies*, 4(3), 1964:32-49.

Mesa-Lago, Carmelo. *Cuba in the 1970s: Pragmatism and Institutionalization*. Albuquerque: Univ. of New Mexico Press, 1974.

Miles, William F. S. *Elections and Ethnicity in French Martinique. A Paradox in Paradise*. New York: Praeger Publishers, 1986.

Mill, John Stuart. *On Liberty*. Orig. pub. 1859. Reprint, Harmondsworth: Penguin, 1982.

Miller, Ruth & Paul Dolan, eds. *Race Awareness. The Nightmare and the Vision*. New York: Cambridge Univ. Press, 1971.

Millett, Richard & W. Marvin Will, eds. *The Restless Caribbean: Changing Patterns of International Relations*. New York: Praeger, 1979.

Milton, John. *The Poetical Works of John Milton*. Vol. II. Helen Darbishire, ed. Oxford: Clarendon Press, 1955.

Mintz, Sidney. 'Labour and Sugar in Puerto Rico and Jamaica, 1800-1850', *Comparative Studies in Society and History*, 1(3), 1959:273-83.

———. 'The Caribbean as a Socio-Cultural Area', in Horowitz, ed. *Peoples and Cultures of the Caribbean*, 17-46.

———. 'The Origins of Reconstituted Peasantries', in Beckles & Shepherd, eds. *Caribbean Freedom*, 94-98.

———, ed. *Papers in Caribbean Anthropology*. Yale Univ. Press Publications in Anthropology, No. 57. Orig. pub. 1960. Reprint, New Haven: Human Relations Area Files Press, 1970.

———, & Douglas Hall. 'The Origins of the Jamaican Internal Marketing Systems', in Mintz, ed. *Papers in Caribbean Anthropology*, 3-26.

Moen, Adrian. 'Curaçao 1969: Crisis and Change', in Craig, ed. *Contemporary Caribbean*, II, 337-63.

Montejo, Esteban. *The Autobiography of a Runaway Slave*. Orig. pub. 1966. Trans. by The Bodley Head. Middlesex: Penguin Books Ltd, in association with The Bodley Head, 1970.

Mordecai, John. *The West Indies: The Federal Negotiations*. London: George Allen & Unwin, 1968.

Moreno, José. 'The Dominican Republic Revolution Revisited', in Craig, ed. *Contemporary Caribbean*, II, 311-36.

Morgenthau, R. & L. Behrman. 'French-speaking Tropical Africa', in Crowder, ed. *Cambridge History of Africa*, VIII, 611-74.

Morris, Mervyn. 'Feeling, Affection, Respect', in Tajfel & Dawson, eds. *Disappointed Guests*, 5-26.

Murch, Arvin. *Black Frenchmen. The Political Integration of the French Antilles*. Cambridge, Mass.: Schenkman Publishing Co, 1972.

Naipaul, Vidiadhar. *The Middle Passage: Impressions of Five Societies – British, French and Dutch – in the West Indies and South America*. London: André Deutsch, 1974.

———. *The Mimic Men*. London: André Deutsch, 1967.

Nettleford, Rex. 'The Caribbean: Crossroads of Americas', in Cobley, ed. *Crossroads of Empire*, 1-14.

Nicholls, David. *From Dessalines to Duvalier – Race, Colour and National Independence*. Cambridge: Cambridge Univ. Press, 1979.

———. *Haiti in Caribbean Context. Ethnicity, Economy and Revolt*. New York: St Martin's Press, 1985.

———. 'No hawkers and pedlars: Levantines in the Caribbean', *Ethnic and Racial Studies*, 4, 1981: 415-31.

Ott, Thomas. *The Haitian Revolution, 1789-1804*. Knoxville: Univ. of Tennessee Press, 1973.

Oxall, Ivar. *Black Intellectuals Come to Power*. Cambridge, Mass.: Schenkman, 1968.

Oxford Dictionary of Quotations. 4th ed. Oxford: Oxford Univ. Press, 1922.

Palmer, Colin. 'Identity, Race and Black Power', in Knight & Palmer, eds. *The Modern Caribbean*, 111-28.

Pantin, Dennis. 'The Political Economy of Natural Resource Rentier States: the Case of Oil and Natural Gas-Rich Trinidad and Tobago', in Lalta & Freckleton, eds. *Caribbean Economic Development*, 248-61.

———. 'The Role of Export Processing Zones in Caribbean Economic Development', in Lalta & Freckleton, eds. *Caribbean Economic Development*, 141-58.

Paquin, Lyonel. *The Haitians: Class and Color Politics*. New York: Multi-Type, 1983.

Pares, Richard. *A West India Fortune*. London: Longmans Green, 1956.

———. *War and Trade in the West Indies, 1739-1763*. Oxford: Clarendon Press, 1936.

Pastor, Robert. *Whirlpool. U. S. Foreign Policy Toward Latin America and the Caribbean*. Princeton: Princeton Univ. Press, 1992.

Patterson, H. Orlando. *An Absence of Ruins*. London: Hutchinson, 1967.

———. 'Slavery and Slave Revolts: a Sociohistorical Analysis of the First Maroon War, 1663-1740', in Price, ed. *Maroon Societies*, 246-92.

———. *Slavery and Social Death. A Comparative Study*. Cambridge, Mass.: Harvard Univ. Press, 1982.

———. 'Social Aspects of the Sugar Industry', in Girvan & Jefferson, eds. *Readings*, 64-66.

———. *The Children of Sisyphus*. London: New Authors, 1964.

Paturau, Maurice, J. *By-Products of the Cane Sugar Industry: An Introduction to Their Industrial Utilization*. 2nd ed. New York: Elsevier Scientific Publishing Co, Amsterdam, 1982.

Payne, Anthony. 'Liberal Economics Versus Electoral Politics in Jamaica', in Payne & Sutton, eds. *Modern Caribbean Politics*, 28-53.

———. 'Westminster Adapted: The Political Order of the Commonwealth Caribbean', in Dominguez *et al.* eds. *Democracy in the Caribbean*, 57-73.

———, & Paul Sutton. *Dependency Under Challenge: The Political Economy of the Commonwealth Caribbean*. Manchester: Manchester Univ. Press, 1984.

———, & Paul Sutton. 'Introduction: the Contours of Modern Caribbean Politics', in Payne & Sutton, eds. *Modern Caribbean Politics*, 1-27.

———, & Paul Sutton, eds. *Modern Caribbean Politics*. Kingston, Jamaica: Ian Randle Publishers, 1993.

Pérez, Louis, A. Jr. *Cuba Between Empires 1878-1902*. Pittsburgh: Univ. of Pittsburgh Press, 1983.

———. *Cuba Under the Platt Amendment, 1902-1934*. Pittsburgh: Pittsburgh Univ. Press, 1986.

———. *Lords of the Mountain: Social Banditry and Peasant Protest in Cuba, 1878-1918*. Pittsburgh: Pittsburgh Univ. Press, 1989.

Persaud, Wilbernc. 'Europe 1992 and the Caribbean: Crisis Challenge and Opportunity', in Lalta & Freckleton, eds. *Caribbean Economic Development*, 189-99.

Philalethes, Demoticus. 'Hunting the Maroons with Dogs in Cuba', in Price, ed. *Maroon Societies*, 60-63.

Pierson, Donald. *Negroes in Brazil. A Study of Race Contact at Bahia*. Chicago: Chicago Univ. Press, 1942.

Plamenatz, John. *On Alien Rule and Self-Government*. New York: Longmans, Green & Co, 1960.

Pliny, *Natural History*. Trans. by H. Rackham; London: Heinemann, 1947.

Plummer, Brenda. *Haiti and the Great Powers, 1902-1915*. Baton Rouge: Louisiana State Univ. Press, 1988.

———. *Haiti and the United States: the Psychological Moment*. London: Univ. of Chicago Press, 1992.

———. 'Race, Nationality and Trade in the Caribbean: The Syrians in Haiti 1903-1934', *International History Review*, 3, 1981:517-39.

Poliakov, Léon. *The Aryan Myth. A History of Racist and Nationalist Ideas in Europe*. Orig. pub. 1971. Trans. by Edmund Howard. London: Sussex Univ. Press, in association with Heinemann, 1974.

Poon, Auliana. 'Caribbean Tourism and the World Economy', in Lalta & Freckleton, eds. *Caribbean Economic Development*, 262-79.

Pope-Hennessy, John. *Sins of the Fathers. A Study of the Atlantic Slave Traders 1441-1807*. London: Weidenfeld & Nicolson, 1967.

Post, Ken. Strike the iron: A Colony at War: Jamaica 1939-1945. 2 vols. New York: Humanities Press, Hague, 1981.

Poujol, Alexandre. *La Question des Syriens en Haïti*. Paris: Imprimerie A. Pedone, 1905.

Premdas, Ralph. 'Elections and Campaigns in a Racially Bifurcated State', *Journal of Interamerican Studies and World Affairs*, 14(3), 1972: 271-96.

———. 'Guyana: Ethnic Politics and the Erosion of Human Rights and Democratic Governance', in Edie, ed. *Democracy in the Caribbean*, 43-58.

———. 'Race, Politics and Succession in Trinidad and Guyana', in Payne & Sutton, eds. *Modern Caribbean Politics*, 98-124.

Price, Richard. *Maroon Societies: Rebel Slave Communities in the Americas*. 2nd ed. Baltimore: The Johns Hopkins University Press, 1979.

———. *To Slay the Hydra. Dutch Colonial Perspectives on the Saramaka Wars*. Michigan: Ann Arbor, 1983.

Purchas, S. ed. *Purchas: His Pilgrims*. Glasgow, 1905 ed.

Quick, Stephen. 'The International Economy and the Caribbean: The 1990s and Beyond', in Dominguez *et al*., eds. *Democracy in the Caribbean*, 212-28.

Ragatz, Lowell. *The Fall of the Planter Class in the British Caribbean, 1763-1833*. Orig. pub. 1926. Reprint, New York: Octagon Books, 1977.

Ramchand, Kenneth. 'The Colour Problem at the University: A West Indian's Changing Attitudes', in Tajfel & Dawson, eds. *Disappointed Guests*, 27-37.

Ramnarine, Tyran. 'Over a Hundred Years of East Indian Disturbances on the Sugar Estates of Guyana 1869-1978: An Historical Overview', in Dabydeen & Samaroo, eds. *India in the Caribbean*, 119-41.

Ramsaran, Ramesh. 'Domestic Policy, the External Environment, and the Economic Crisis in the Caribbean', in Payne & Sutton, eds. *Modern Caribbean Politics*, 238-58.

———. *The Commonwealth Caribbean in the World Economy*. Warwick Univ. Caribbean Studies; London: Macmillan, 1989.

———. *United States Investment in Latin America and the Caribbean*. London: Hodder & Stoughton, 1985.

Rashidi, Rukono. 'Africans in Early Asian Civilizations: A Historical Review', in Rashidi, ed. *African Presence in Early Asia*, 15-52.

———, ed. *African Presence in Early Asia*. New Brunswick: Transaction Books, 1985.

Renard, Rosamunde. 'Labour Relations in Post-Slavery Martinique and Guadeloupe 1848-1870', in Beckles & Shepherd, eds. *Caribbean Freedom*, 80-92.

Richardson, Bonham C. 'Caribbean Migrations, 1838-1985', in Knight & Palmer, eds. *The Modern Caribbean*, 203-28.

_____. *The Caribbean in the Wider World, 1492-1992. A Regional Geography*. Cambridge: Cambridge Univ. Press, 1992.

Riviere, Bill. 'Contemporary Class Structure in Dominica', in Craig, ed. *Contemporary Caribbean*, I, 265-82.

Roberts, George. 'A Life Table for a West Indian Slave Population', *Population Studies*, 5, 1951-52:238-43.

Robinson, Carey. 'Maroons and Rebels (a Dilemma)', in Agorsah, ed. *Maroon Heritage*, 86-93.

Rodney, Walter. *A History of the Guyanese Working People, 1881-1905*. Baltimore: The Johns Hopkins University Press, 1981.

———. *How Europe Underdeveloped Africa*. London: Bogle L'Ouverture Publications, 1972.

———. *Walter Rodney Speaks. The Making of an African Intellectual*. (Based upon interviews with him and published posthumously.) New Jersey: Africa World Press, 1990.

Rogozinski, Jan. *A Brief History of the Caribbean. From the Arawak and the Carib to the Present*. New York: Facts on File, 1992.

Rotberg, Robert & Christopher Clague. *Haiti: The Politics of Squalor*. Boston: Houghton-Mifflin, 1971.

Salmon, Charles S. *The Caribbean Confederation. A Plan for the Union of the Fifteen British West Indian Colonies*. London: Cassell, 1888.

Samaroo, Brinsley. 'Two Abolitions: African Slavery and East Indian Indentureship', in Dabydeen & Samaroo, eds. *India in the Caribbean*, 25-41.

Samuel, Wendell. 'Caribbean Economic Integration', in Lalta & Freckleton, eds. *Caribbean Economic Development*, 159-73.

Sauer, Carl. *The Early Spanish Main*. Berkeley: Univ. of California Press, 1966.

Scarano, Francisco A. 'Labor and Society in the Nineteenth Century', in Knight & Palmer, eds. *The Modern Caribbean*, 51-84.

Schmidt, Hans. *The United States Occupation of Haiti, 1915-1934*. New Brunswick: Rutgers Univ. Press, 1971.

Schultz, Theodore. 'Investment in Human Capital', in Karabel & Halsey, eds. *Power and Ideology*, 313-24.

Scoble, E. 'African Popes', in Van Sertima, ed. *African Presence in Early Europe*, 96-107.

———. 'African Women in Early Europe', in Van Sertima, ed. *African Presence in Early Europe*, 205-12.

———. 'The Black in Western Europe', in Van Sertima, ed. *African Presence in Early Europe*, 190-202.

Scott, Gilbert L. 'Caribbean Alternatives to European Travel', *Class*, May 1991:8, 21, 60, 61.

Scott, Rebecca. *Slave Emancipation in Cuba. The Transition to Free Labor 1860-1899*. Princeton: Princeton Univ. Press, 1985.

Sedoc-Dahlberg, Betty. 'Struggle for Democracy in Suriname', in Sedoc-Dahlberg, ed. *The Dutch Caribbean*, 173-89.

———. 'Suriname: 1975-1989. Domestic and Foreign Policies Under Military and Civilian Rule', in Sedoc-Dahlberg, ed. *The Dutch Caribbean*, 17-33.

———, ed. *The Dutch Caribbean. Prospects for Democracy*. New York: Gordon & Breach, 1990.

Selvon, Samuel. 'Three Into One Can't Go – East Indian, Trinidadian, Westindian', in Dabydeen & Samaroo, eds. *India in the Caribbean*, 13-24.

———. *An Island is a World*. London: Wingate, 1955.

Senghor, Léopold. *Anthologie de la Nouvelle Poésie Nègre et Malgache en Langue Française*. 2nd ed. Orig. pub. 1948. Paris: Presses Universitaires de France, 1972.

Seymour, A. J. 'Tomorrow Belongs to the People', in Seymour, *Selected Poems*. Georgetown: British Guiana Lithographic Co, 1965.

Sheridan, Richard. *Doctors and Slaves. A Medical and Demographic History of Slavery in the British West Indies 1680-1834*. Cambridge: Cambridge Univ. Press, 1985.

———. 'The Wealth of Jamaica in the Eighteenth Century', *Economic History Review*, 2nd ser., 18(2), 1965:292-311.

———. 'The Wealth of Jamaica in the Eighteenth Century: A Rejoinder', *Economic History Review*, 21(1), 1968:46-61.

Sherlock, P. M. *West Indian Nations. A New History*. London: Macmillan, 1973.

Shorter Oxford English Dictionary. 3rd ed. Oxford: Clarendon Press, 1978.

Silvestrini, Blanca. 'Contemporary Puerto Rico. A Society of Contrasts', in Knight & Palmer, eds. *The Modern Caribbean*, 147-67.

Singh, Kelvin. *The Bloodstained Tombs – The Muharram Massacre in Trinidad 1884*. London: Macmillan Caribbean, 1988.

Slater, Jerome. *Intervention and Negotiation. The United States and the Dominican Republic*. New York: Harper & Row, 1970.

Smith, C. Alphonso. 'Battle of the Caribbean', *United States Naval Institute Proceedings*, 80(9), 1954:976-82.

———. 'Martinique in World War II', *United States Naval Institute Proceedings*, 81(2), 1955:169-74.

Smith, Courteny. 'The Grenadian Revolution in Retrospect', in Payne & Sutton, eds. *Modern Caribbean Politics*, 176-97.

Smith, M. G. *Culture, Race and Class in the Commonwealth Caribbean*. Kingston, Jamaica: Department of Extra-Mural Studies,1984.

———. *The Plural Society in the British West Indies*. Orig. pub. 1965. Reprint, Kingston, Jamaica: Sangsters Book Store, in association with Univ. of California Press, Berkeley, 1974.

Smith, Robert, ed. *Background to Revolution. The Development of Modern Cuba*. Orig. pub. 1966. Revised ed., New York: Robert E. Kreiger Publishing Co, 1979.

Snowden, Frank. *Blacks in Antiquity. Ethiopians in the Graeco-Roman Experience*. Cambridge, Mass.: Harvard Univ. Press, 1971.

Solaún, Mauricio & Sidney Kronus. *Discrimination Without Violence. Miscegenation and Racial Conflict in Latin America*. New York: John Wiley & Sons, 1973.

Solow, Barbara L. 'Caribbean Slavery and British Growth: The Eric Williams Hypothesis', *Journal of Development Economics*, 17(1-2), 1985:99-115.

Soomer, June. 'An Assessment of the Factors Affecting the Structure and Functioning of the British West Indies Federal Civil Service, 1947-1962'. Ph.D. dissertation, Univ. of the West Indies, Cave Hill, Barbados, 1993.

South America, Central America and the Caribbean 1993. 4th ed. London: Europa Publications, 1992.

South America, Central America and the Caribbean 1995. 5th ed. London: Europa Publications, 1994.

Spinner, Thomas, Jr. *A Political and Social History of Guyana 1945-1983*. Boulder: Westview Press, 1984.

Springer, Hugh. *Reflections on the Failure of the First West Indian Federation*. Occasional Papers in International Affairs, No. 4, Cambridge: Harvard Center for International Affairs, 1962.

Spurdle, Frederick. *Early West Indian Government in Barbados, Jamaica and the Leeward Islands, 1650-1783*. Published by the author. New Zealand, *c*. 1963.

Squire, Sir John. 'There was an Indian', in Forde, ed. *Talk of the Tamarinds*, 42.

St Cyr, Eric. 'The Theory of Caribbean-Type Economy', in Lalta & Freckleton, eds. *Caribbean Economic Development*, 8-16.

St Pierre, Maurice. 'The 1962-64 Disturbances in Guyana', in Craig, ed. *Contemporary Caribbean*, II, 281-310.

Statistical Yearbook for Latin America and the Caribbean. 1994 ed. Chile: UN, Economic Commission for Latin America and the Caribbean.

Stedman, John G. *Narrative of a Five Years' Expedition Against the Revolted Negroes of Surinam*. Orig. pub. 1796. Reprint, Amherst, Mass.: Univ. of Massachusetts Press, 1972.

Steward, Julian & Louis Faron. *Native Peoples of South America*. New York, 1959.

———, ed. *Handbook of South American Indians, IV. The Circum-Caribbean Tribes*. Washington, DC: US Govt. Printing Office, 1948.

Stoecker, Helmuth. 'The Position of Africans in German Colonies', in Knoll & Gann, eds. *Germans in the Tropics*, 119-29.

———, & Peter Sebald. 'Enemies of the Colonial Idea', in Knoll & Gann, eds. *Germans in the Tropics, 59-72.*

Stokes, Eric. *The English Utilitarians and India*. Orig. pub. 1959. Reprint, Glasgow:

Oxford Univ. Press, 1963.
Stokes, William. 'National and Local Violence in Cuban Politics', in Smith, ed. *Background to Revolution*, 142-148.
Suret-Canale, Jean. *French Colonialism in Tropical Africa 1900-1945*. New York: Pica Press, 1971.
Sutton, Paul. 'Black Power in Trinidad and Tobago: the Crisis of 1970', *Journal of Commonwealth and Comparative Politics*, 21(2), 1983:116-31.
———. 'U. S. Intervention, Regional Security, and Militarization in the Caribbean', in Payne & Sutton, eds. *Modern Caribbean Politics*, 277-93.
Szulc, Tad. *Fidel: A Critical Portrait*. New York: Avon, 1986.
Taiwan Statistical Data Bank 1995. Council for Economic Planning & Development, Republic of China. June 1995.
Tajfel, Henri & John Dawson, eds. *Disappointed Guests: Essays by African, Asian and West Indian Students*. London: Oxford Univ. Press, for Institute of Race Relations, 1965.
Taylor, Douglas. *The Black Carib of British Honduras*. New York: Wenner-Gren Foundation for Anthropological Research; Viking Fund Publications in Anthropology, No. 17, 1951.
———. 'The Island Caribs of Dominica', *American Anthropologist* (new series), 39 (2, pt. 1), 1935:265-72.
Taylor, Frank. 'From Hellshire to Healthshire: The Genesis of the Tourist Industry in Jamaica', in Higman, ed. *Trade, Government and Society*, 139-54.
Theodore, Karl. 'Fiscal Issues in Caribbean Monetary Integration', in Farrell & Worrell, eds. *Caribbean Monetary Integration*, 110-43.
Thomas, Clive Y. 'Agriculture in the Commonwealth Caribbean: a General Survey', in Lalta & Freckleton, eds. *Caribbean Economic Development*, 215-26.
———. 'Alternative Development Models for the Caribbean', in Lalta & Freckleton, eds. *Caribbean Economic Development*, 314-29.
———. *Plantations, Peasants and State*. Los Angeles: Univ. of California, Center for Afro-American Studies, 1984.
———. *The Poor and the Powerless. Economic Policy and Change in the Caribbean*. New York: Monthly Review Press, 1988.
Thomas, Hugh. *Cuba or the Pursuit of Freedom*. London: Eyre Spottiswood, 1971.
Thomas, Robert. 'The Sugar Colonies of the Old Empire: Profit or Loss for Great Britain?' *Economic History Review*, 21(1), 1968:30-45.
Thompson, Alvin O. *Colonialism and Underdevelopment in Guyana 1580-1803*. Bridgetown, Barbados: Carib Research & Publications, 1987.
———. 'Historical Writing on Migration into the Commonwealth Caribbean: A Bibliographical Review of the Period *c.*1838-*c.*1938', *Immigrants and Minorities*, 5(2), 1986:145-66.
———. 'Race and Colour Prejudices and the Origin of the Trans-Atlantic Slave Trade', *Caribbean Studies*, 16(3-4), Oct. 1976 – Jan. 1977:29-59.
Thorndike, Tony. 'Making Money in the Sun', *BWee Caribbean Beat*, Autumn 1995: 69-74.
———. 'Revolution, Democracy, and Regional Integration in the Eastern Caribbean', in Payne & Sutton, eds. *Modern Caribbean Politics*, 147-75.
———. 'Suriname and the Military', in Sedoc-Dahlberg, ed. *The Dutch Caribbean*, 35-62.
Thurow, Lester. 'Education and Economic Equality', in Karabel and Halsey, eds. *Power and Ideology*, 325-35.
Tinker, Hugh. *A New System of Slavery. The Export of Indian Labour Overseas 1838-1920*. London: Oxford Univ. Press, 1974.

Trevor-Roper, Hugh. 'The Rise of Christian Europe', *The Listener*, 70, 1963.

Trouillot, Michel-Rolph. *Peasant and Capital: Dominica in the World Economy*. Baltimore: The Johns Hopkins Univ. Press, 1988.

Troup, Freida. *South Africa: An Historical Introduction*. Middlesex: Penguin Books, 1975.

Turner, Mary. 'Chinese Contract Labour in Cuba 1847-1874', in Beckles & Shepherd, eds. *Caribbean Freedom*, 132-40.

Valdes, Nelson. 'Ideological Roots of the Cuban Revolutionary Movement', in Craig, ed. *Contemporary Caribbean*, II, 211-42.

Van Lier, R. A. J. *Frontier Society. A Social Analysis of the History of Surinam*. 2nd ed. Orig. pub. 1949. The Hague: Martinus Nijhoff, 1971.

Van Sertima, Ivan, ed. *Blacks in Science, Ancient and Modern*. New Brunswick: Transaction Books, 1983.

———. 'The African Presence in Early Europe: The Definitional Problem', in Van Sertima, ed. *African Presence in Early Europe*, 137-42.

———. 'The Lost Sciences of Africa: an Overview', in Van Sertima, ed. *Blacks in Science*, 1-26.

Van Wengen, G. D. *De Javanen in de Surinaamse Samenleving*. Amsterdam: Sticusa, n.d.

Vergne, Teresita Martínez. 'Politics and Society in the Spanish Caribbean During the Nineteenth Century', in Knight & Palmer, eds. *The Modern Caribbean*, 185-202.

Verton, Peter. 'The Dutch Decolonization: Independence for the Netherlands Antilles?' in Sedoc-Dahlberg, ed. *The Dutch Caribbean*, 203-17.

———. 'Politics and Government in Curaçao', in Sedoc-Dahlberg, ed. *The Dutch Caribbean*, 63-80.

Walker, D. R. J. *Columbus and the Golden World of the Arawaks*. Kingston, Jamaica: Ian Randle Publishers, 1990.

Wallace, Elisabeth. *The British Caribbean. From the Decline of Colonialism to the end of Federation*. Toronto: Univ. of Toronto Press, 1977.

Walvin, James. *The Black Presence: A Documentary History of the Negro in England, 1555-1860*. London: Orbach & Chambers, 1971.

Ward, J. R. 'The Profitability of Sugar Planting in the British West Indies, 1650-1834', *Economic History Review*, 31(2), 1978: 197-213.

Washington, Joseph R. *Anti-Blackness in English Religion 1500-1800*. New York: Mellen Press, *c*.1984.

Watson, Hilbourne, 'Transnational Banks and Financial Crisis in the Caribbean', in Gorostiaga & Irvin, eds. *Towards an Alternative for Central America and the Caribbean*, 126-53.

Watts, David. *The West Indies. Patterns of Development, Culture and Environmental Change Since 1492*. Cambridge: Cambridge Univ. Press, 1990.

Waugh, Alec. *A Family of Islands. A History of the West Indies from 1492 to 1898*. London: Wiedenfeld & Nicolson, 1964.

Weisskoff, Richard. *Factories and Foodstamps: The Puerto Rican Model of Development*. Baltimore: The Johns Hopkins Univ. Press, 1985.

Welles, Sumner. *Naboth's Vineyard: The Dominican Republic, 1844-1924*. New York: Payson & Clarke, 1928.

West Indian Commission. *Time for Action* (postscript by Shridath Ramphal). 2nd ed. Orig. pub. 1992., Kingston, Jamaica: The Press, Univ. of the West Indies, 1993.

Wiarda, Howard. *The Dominican Republic. Nation in Transition*. London: Pall Mall Press, 1969.

———, & Mark Falcoff, eds. *The Communist Challenge in the Caribbean and Central America*. Washington, DC: American Enterprise Institute, 1987.

Wilgus, Alva C. ed. *The Caribbean: Contemporary Education*. Gainesville: Univ. of Florida Press, 1960.

Williams, Eric. *Capitalism and Slavery*. Orig. pub. 1944. Reprint, London: André Deutsch, 1964.

———. *Documents of West Indian History, Vol. I, 1492-1655*. Port-of-Spain: PNM Publishing Co, 1963.

———. *From Columbus to Castro. The History of the Caribbean 1492-1969*. London: André Deutsch, 1970.

———. *History of the People of Trinidad and Tobago*. London: André Deutsch, 1963.

Williams, J. J. *Hebrewisms of West Africa. From Nile to Niger with the Jews*. Orig pub. 1930. Reprint, New York: Biblio & Tannen, 1967.

Wood, E. F. L. *Report by the Honourable E. F. L. Wood on his Visit to the West Indies and British Guiana*. London: HMSO, Harrison & Sons, 1922.

World Bank. *Social Indicators of Development, 1995, 1996*. Baltimore: The Johns Hopkins Univ. Press, 1995 & 1996.

World Bank. 'The Caribbean: Exports Preferences and Performance', in Lalta & Freckleton, eds. *Caribbean Economic Development*, 78-104.

World Tables 1995. Baltimore: The Johns Hopkins Univ. Press, 1995.

Worrell, Delisle. 'A Common Currency for the Caribbean', in Farrell & Worrell, eds. *Caribbean Monetary Integration*, 27-50.

_____. 'The Economies of the English-Speaking Caribbean Since 1960', in Dominguez *et al.* eds. *Democracy in the Caribbean*, 189-211.

Wrong, Humphrey Hume. *Government of the West Indies*. Oxford: Clarendon Press, 1923.

Wyndham, Hugh. *The Atlantic and Emancipation*. London: Oxford Univ. Press, 1937.

Young, Alma. 'Decolonization in the Dutch Caribbean: Lessons from the Commonwealth Caribbean', in Sedoc-Dahlberg, ed. *The Dutch Caribbean*, 253-67.

Young, G. M., ed. *Macaulay: Prose and Poetry*. Cambridge: Harvard Univ. Press, 1970.

Index